THE LETTERS OF
Mark Twain and Joseph Hopkins Twichell

THE LETTERS OF
Mark Twain and Joseph Hopkins Twichell

Edited by Harold K. Bush, Steve Courtney, and Peter Messent

Supplementary text by Peter Messent

The University of Georgia

ATHENS

Publication of this work was made possible, in part, by a generous gift from the University of Georgia Press Friends Fund and Asylum Hill Congregational Church of Hartford, Connecticut.

We thank the University of California Press for permission to reproduce the following material:

Mark Twain's Letters, vol. 2: *1867–1868*, copyright 1990 by the Mark Twain Foundation, and published by the University of California Press. ISBN 0520036697. (Twain-Twichell letters).
Mark Twain's Letters, vol. 3: *1869*, copyright 1992 by the Mark Twain Foundation, and published by the University of California Press. ISBN 0520036700. (Twain-Twichell letters).
Mark Twain's Letters, vol. 4: *1870–1871*, copyright 1995 by the Mark Twain Foundation, and published by the University of California Press. ISBN 0520203607. (Twain-Twichell letters).
Mark Twain's Letters, vol. 5: *1872–1873*, copyright 1997 by the Mark Twain Foundation, and published by the University of California Press. ISBN 0520208226. (Twain-Twichell letters).
Mark Twain's Letters, vol. 6: *1874–1875*, copyright 2002 by the Mark Twain Foundation, and published by the University of California Press. ISBN 0520237778. (Twain-Twichell letters).
Mark Twain's Letters: 1876–1880, copyright 2007 by the Mark Twain Foundation, and published by the California Digital Library, University of California Press.
Unpublished manuscripts and works in the Bancroft Library of the University of California, by Mark Twain, copyright 2001 by the Mark Twain Foundation, and published by the Bancroft Library (Twain-Twichell letters from 1876 to 1910).

Athens, Georgia 30602
www.ugapress.org

Designed by Erin Kirk New
Set in 10/13 ITC New Baskerville by Graphic Composition, Inc., Bogart, Georgia
Printed and bound by Thomson-Shore
The paper in this book meets the guidelines for permanence and durability of the Committee on Production Guidelines for Book Longevity of the Council on Library Resources.

Most University of Georgia Press titles are available from popular e-book vendors.

Printed in the United States of America

17 18 19 20 21 C 5 4 3 2 1

Library of Congress Cataloging-in-Publication Data

Names: Twain, Mark, 1835–1910, author. | Twichell, Joseph Hopkins, 1838–1918, author. | Bush, Harold K. (Harold Karl), 1956– editor. | Courtney, Steve, 1948– editor. | Messent, Peter B., editor.
Title: The letters of Mark Twain and Joseph Hopkins Twichell / edited by Harold K. Bush, Steve Courtney, and Peter Messent.
Description: Athens : The University of Georgia, 2017. | Includes index.
Identifiers: LCCN 2016039451 | ISBN 9780820350752 (hard bound : alk. paper) | ISBN 9780820350745 (e-book)
Subjects: LCSH: Twain, Mark, 1835–1910—Correspondence. | Twain, Mark, 1835–1910—Friends and associates. | Twichell, Joseph Hopkins, 1838–1918—Correspondence. | Authors, American—19th century—Correspondence. | Clergy—Connecticut—Correspondence. | Military chaplains—United States—Correspondence.
Classification: LCC PS1331 .A487 2017 | DDC 818/.409 [B] —dc23
LC record available at https://lccn.loc.gov/2016039451

To all our colleagues in the Mark Twain community
and to Mark Twain enthusiasts everywhere

Contents

Acknowledgments

First and foremost, we express our most grateful thanks to Robert H. Hirst, general editor of the Mark Twain Papers & Project, for the huge amount of help he gave us as we prepared this book and for the expertise and enthusiasm he brought to this task. Without him this volume could not have been published. We know just how busy he is and the fact that he prepared and sent letter transcripts and scans to us in such good time and with such good grace is deeply appreciated. Our work cannot possibly live up to the high editorial standards consistently delivered by Bob (as everyone knows him) and his team and we only hope that they do not judge our efforts too harshly! We also wish to express our thanks to Vic Fischer, one of the Project editors, who also was tireless in checking material for us and answering our numerous queries. Our grateful thanks, too, to Benjamin Griffin, Harriet Elinor Smith, Melissa Martin, and Leslie Myrick—all from the Project—for the swift and willing assistance they offered in our research. Thanks, too, to the Beinecke Rare Book & Manuscript Library at Yale, and their helpful librarians, for access to the Twichell papers. We also thank research assistants Collin Stansberry and Keith Wilhite (now professor of English at Siena College) for their assistance on the project. And we thank Jon Davies, Ed Vesneske Jr., and Walter Biggins for their invaluable help as they worked with us to prepare this manuscript for publication.

Thanks are also due to two members of the Twichell family, poet Chase Twichell and Kathie Michie, for their encouragement and support as we undertook this project. We thank, too, the Asylum Hill Congregational Church, via the good offices of the Reverend Matt Laney, its senior minister, and the College of Arts and Sciences at Saint Louis University in Missouri, for their generous help with permissions fees for this book. In Asylum Hill's case, Twichell would have appreciated the ongoing historical connection. We thank Susan Barlow, Andrea Learned, and Carol Cheney from the Manchester Historical Society, Tracy Brindle and Mallory Howard from the Mark Twain House & Museum, and Kevin Mac Donnell, K. Patrick Ober, and the Mark Twain community more generally for information and material given as we researched this book. Any errors made are ours alone.

At some points in Peter Messent's introductions to the sections in this book, he reuses or refashions material from his previous work, *Mark Twain and Male Friendship* (2009). He thanks Oxford University Press for their permission in this respect.

THE LETTERS OF
Mark Twain and Joseph Hopkins Twichell

Introduction

THE LONG, DEEP FRIENDSHIP of Mark Twain—Samuel L. Clemens—and Rev. Joseph Hopkins Twichell, Congregationalist minister of Hartford, Connecticut, rarely fails to surprise, given the general reputation Twain has of being antireligious. But an examination of the growth, development, and shared interests composing that friendship make it quickly clear that, as in most things about him, Mark Twain defies such easy categorization or judgment.

Twichell appears in Twain's writings most prominently in his travel book *A Tramp Abroad* as the narrator's companion and "agent," called "Harris." Novelist Russell Banks has called Harris "Butch Cassidy to Twain's Sundance, Sancho to his Quixote, Tonto to his Lone Ranger, Hardy to his Laurel."[1] But Harris's lack of color and background is simply a way for Twain to get his comic effects and belies the man, Twichell himself, and his importance to the author's life and work.

Twichell, though amiable and a lover of a quiet life, had been involved in a good amount of violent conflict in his early manhood. He was born in a small Connecticut mill town, played ball on the village green, attended a private academy, and then went on to Yale—where in his junior year he took part in a town-gown riot in which a local fireman was killed. This led to his suspension from the college. After returning to graduate, he entered seminary study in a tumultuous New York City on the eve of the Civil War and, when war broke out, joined a regiment formed by the politician and reprobate Daniel Sickles, to serve as chaplain to rowdy men from the New York slums.

In 1865, having "breathed [in Twain's words] the smoke of a hundred battles," Twichell was called to the pastorate of a new suburban church being built on the western fringe of Hartford, Connecticut, the wealthy and thriving state capital.[2] He married (Julia) Harmony Cushman, a deeply religious young woman and daughter of David Cushman, an abolitionist and experimental farmer from West Exeter, New York, in the same year. Three years later, in 1868, he encountered the distinctive presence of Twain, then known as "the Wild Humorist of the Western Slope," in a Hartford parlor.

Samuel Langhorne Clemens (or Mark Twain, as—in line with Twichell's own use—he is called in this book) had arrived in that parlor by a circuitous route. Born in rural Missouri, he had left school early and become an itinerant printer, traveling to New York, Philadelphia, and Washington as a teenager. In 1859 he obtained a Mississippi River pilot's license, seeming to guarantee him a lifelong profession—a guarantee, however, smashed by the Civil War, which both made the lower Mississippi a site of conflict and ended civilian trade on it. After a brief stint in a quasi-Confederate unit, he traveled west with his brother, who had been appointed secretary of the Nevada Territory by President Lincoln. In Nevada and California he fell into the trade of journalism, writing dozens of humorous "sketches" and finally the one that won him national fame, now known as "The Celebrated Jumping Frog of Calaveras County."

Working for the *Alta California* of San Francisco, in 1867 he lobbied for an assignment to accompany a group of travelers through the Mediterranean to the Holy Land to write a series of letters reporting on that trip. His portraits of European and Middle Eastern scenes and characters, of innocent Americans and sophisticated Europeans, and the fun he made of them, had wide appeal and were republished nationwide. When he returned, Elisha Bliss of the American Publishing Company in Hartford, Connecticut, negotiated to turn his reports into a book and ultimately published Twain's bestseller *The Innocents Abroad, or The New Pilgrims' Progress* in 1869. It was during a visit to his publisher prior to that publication that the parlor meeting took place.

What then happened is the story of this book. From the moment of that first encounter, a rapport was established. When Twain went to dinner at the Twichell home, he wrote to his future wife that he had "got up to go at 9.30 PM, & never sat down again—but [Twichell] said he was bound to have his talk out—& *I* was willing—& so I only left at 11."[3] This conversation continued, in various forms, for forty-two years; in both men's houses, on Hartford streets, on Bermuda roads, and on Alpine trails. There was one break in the friendship (see 22 July 1883—Letter 84—and what followed) but the by-then old friends reconciled: a behavioral rarity in Twain's case.

The dialogue between these two men—one an inimitable American literary figure, the other a man of deep perception who himself possessed both narrative skill and wit—has been much discussed by Twain biographers. But it has never been presented in this way before: as a record of their surviving correspondence; of the various turns of their decades-long backs-and-forths; of what Twichell described in his journals as the "long full feast of talk" with his friend, whom he would always call "Mark."[4]

Theirs was a rich exchange. Indeed, quotations from letters to Twichell turn up regularly in collections of Twain's wit. "When a man is a pessimist before 48 he knows too much; if he is an optimist after it, he knows too little" (Letter 243) is one; "Oh, this infernal Human Race! I wish I had it in the Ark again—with an auger" (Letter 294) another. At times the two men joyously share experiences just too good not to share; at other times they dispute and disagree with some passion, only to offer heartfelt love to their respective families at the close; at moments, particularly during the great tragedies of Twain's life, Twichell offers consolation, a consolation gratefully accepted and appreciated.

The editors of this collection include two literary critics and one historian. It is our privilege to present the dialogue between these two extraordinary voices, a dialogue that has—as an entire record—remained hidden for more than a century.

Harold K. Bush
Steve Courtney
Peter Messent

1. Russell Banks, "Introduction" to *A Tramp Abroad* (New York: Oxford University Press, 1996), xxxiii.

2. Manuscript of *The Innocents Adrift*, 107B-14, Mark Twain Papers, Bancroft Library, University of California, Berkeley.

3. Harriet Elinor Smith and Richard Bucci, eds., *Mark Twain's Letters*, vol. 2: *1867–1868* (Berkeley: University of California Press, 1990), 267.

4. Entry for 2 October 1875, Twichell Journal, Beinecke Rare Book & Manuscript Library, Yale University.

A Note on the Text and the Apparatus Used

THIS BOOK CONTAINS the complete texts of all known correspondence between Samuel L. Clemens (Mark Twain) and Joseph Hopkins Twichell. On the few occasions Olivia Clemens (whom we call Livy, following Twain and Twichell's own usage) adds a note to Twain's letters, we include it. Also included are all newspaper clippings and similar items pasted into the letters. In the case of additional material enclosed within (but not pasted in) the letters, we normally paraphrase and/or give selected highlights. Where once-enclosed materials are now missing, we footnote that fact when their presence is judged crucial to the meaning of the letter. When either man uses paper with a printed letterhead, we use a different font to signal it. We look to be as rigorous as possible while taking into account the book's length and readability.

The texts have been transcribed from the letters originally sent, where these were available. Where this is not the case, or where (in Twain's case) an amanuensis has been used, that information is given following the initial details concerning the date and location of each letter. A good number of Twain's letters are only available as transcripts of the originals made by Albert Bigelow Paine, Twain's biographer and editor of the two-volume *Mark Twain's Letters* of 1917. On occasions, Paine made more than one copy of a letter, with some variation between them. Where a Paine copy is involved, again that information is given beneath the letter title. In such cases the version of the letter used—for these transcripts are sometimes problematic—is the one determined by the editors of the Mark Twain Papers & Project at the Bancroft Library, University of California, Berkeley (henceforth the Mark Twain Papers). Indeed, the text of all Twain letters we use relies on the authorized versions established and supplied by this body. Accurate versions of the letters up to 1875 are available in, and taken from, the six volumes of *Mark Twain's Letters* prepared by editors working at the Mark Twain Papers and published by the University of California Press. The texts of letters from 1876 to 1879 are taken from the database of Twain's correspondence curated by the Mark Twain Papers. The letters from 1880 onwards—the only ones to this point not available in authorized form—have been supplied to us by

Robert H. Hirst, the general editor of the Mark Twain Papers. We set the majority of the addresses given in the letters on the right-hand side of the page to provide regularity. Some long letterheads are omitted when judged of scant importance.

The texts of Twain's letters which we give here are based on the above-noted material from the Mark Twain Papers but do not exactly reproduce it. The form used by the Project is exemplary, with full details of all deletions and insertions, transcriptions of all enclosed materials, and with the fullest of editorial apparatus deployed. We look for a simpler version of the letters where insertions and deletions are noted (usually in a footnote) but only when seen to be of some importance. We recognize the subjectivity involved here. Where, occasionally, deletions are considered of major importance they appear embedded within the text in square brackets.

In the case of the Twichell letters, almost all are transcribed from the original handwritten text. We thank both the Mark Twain Papers and the Beinecke Rare Book & Manuscript Library at Yale University for their help in giving access to his side of the correspondence. In Twichell's case we generally silently drop the majority of deletions and insertions within the letters without comment. Our justification for this difference in treatment lies (partly at least) in the spirit of intentionality, playfulness, and reflexivity in Twain's letters, where lightly made deletions in particular become part of what we might call his epistolary armory and where insertions sometimes carry notable weight and significance.

Where there is an obvious error in either side of the correspondence that we judge has been made entirely accidentally, we silently correct it. Thus, on occasion, for example, Twain fails to close a bracket, while Twichell inserts a full stop rather than a comma midsentence, following it by the use of a lowercase letter. Occasionally both authors repeat words at the end and beginning of line breaks. We regularize the texts accordingly. In terms of punctuation marks not fully legible or not present in the text such as Mrs or Mr (without the period, as in "Mrs.," etc.) or a possessive without an apostrophe, we leave as is. In the latter case, however—when this is not a repeated particularity of its author—we use "[*sic*]" after the words in question. Where full stops or quotation marks are clearly missing, and where their use would be normally clearly expected and their placement is obvious, we silently correct. Both men are, now and then, eccentric in their spelling—see, for instance, Twain's "dam," "nickle," and "befals," and Twichell's recurrent "havn't." Where this is the case, we leave the words unaltered. For other incorrect spellings, where individual eccentricity is clearly not the case, we use "[*sic*]." But we do silently correct one particular recurrent spelling error in Twichell's letters, a sometimes incorrect use of an *i* before *e* in combinations following the letter *c*.

Square brackets are used to enclose editorial information, descriptions, additions, words, or characters omitted by the writer and now interpolated by the editors, and text modified by description, such as "[In margin: 'OVER']." Where Twain and Twichell (occasionally) themselves make use of square brackets we use square brackets in bold—as "**[ ]**."

As noted, some of Twain's letters to Twichell, and especially those written later in Twain's life, were published in the two-volume edition of *Mark Twain's Letters* edited by Albert Bigelow Paine in 1917. Paine, though, in line with the editorial conventions of his day, silently edited out sections of these letters, sometimes lengthy ones. He also edited out phrases which, one assumes, he saw as revealing Twain's more indelicate, ribald, or intemperate side (the last as often as not in a political context). Two such examples follow. In Twain's letter of 27 September 1896, he speaks to Twichell of Susy's death. In Paine's edition of the letters, we find him telling Joe how he brought "the peace and comfort of your beloved presence, first to that poor child, and again to the broken heart of her poor desolate mother." What Twain in fact wrote, after that first comma, was "first to the broken mind of that poor frantic child." Again, on 23 and 24 January 1901, Paine has Twain writing: "I'm going to stick close to my desk for a month, now, hoping to write a small book." He omits what Twain then went on to say, for the full version runs: "I'm going to stick close to my desk for a month, now, hoping to write a small book, full of playful & good-natured contempt for the lousy McKinley. Oh, think of that nickle-plated patriot, Joe Hawley!" Such omissions are significant. This is the first time the full range of these letters has been published in their original true version.

We should note, too, that it is quite possible that Twain did not send quite every letter he wrote to Twichell to him. For in the 17 April 1909 letter to William Dean Howells, mentioned in the introduction to part 5 of this book, Twain writes of his scheme of writing letters to friends and then not sending them. The fact that such letters—and there were very few of them—were addressed to Twichell and written as if he were to receive them justifies their inclusion. There are also a few letters which appear as part of Twain's autobiographical dictations. In the case of the letter of 17 April 1908, again this may not actually have been sent to Twichell.

It is clear that there are a good number of letters that have gone missing over the years, so the correspondence sometimes lacks the continuity one might expect and hope for. Our reader needs to be alert to the resulting jumps in time and location. It is still possible, however, that further letters might surface to fill some of these gaps. A number of the letters by both men (and especially by Twichell) are not fully dated. For the most part, editors at the Mark Twain Project have attributed dates to those letters, working both from internal and contextual evidence. In a very small number of cases, with the Twichell correspondence only, we have altered such attributed dating in the light of later knowledge, if we have firm evidence to do so. Where the Mark Twain Papers have not, until now, attributed dates and we do, we footnote information leading to our decision. In some cases, the detective work of Bob Hirst has helped us greatly in this process. With a very few letters, or partial letters, the full dating remains tentative or unknown: these appear at the very end of the correspondence. Whatever our care here, and that of the Mark Twain Papers, it is possible that some letters are still misdated. Future scholarship may correct any such mistake.

In the case of footnoting, there are some references to people, places, and events that we have not been able to identify. Where this is the case, we offer a note of the "person unknown" variety when that seems necessary.

PART 1

1868–1871

First Meeting (Hartford);
the Twain–Olivia Langdon Courtship and Marriage;
the Buffalo Residence

MARK TWAIN AND JOE TWICHELL, as he was generally known by his parishioners and his friends, first met in Hartford, Connecticut, in October 1868. Three years earlier, Twichell, just married and then only twenty-seven years old, had—in what was an unexpectedly adventurous move on behalf of the church—been appointed as minister of the brand-new Asylum Hill Congregational Church in a wealthy part of the town. Twain, thirty-two when they met, was in Hartford to work with Elisha Bliss on the printer's copy and illustrations for his first travel narrative, *The Innocents Abroad*, the book that would effectively launch his career as a successful author.[1] The two men met at an evening reception held by a member of the Asylum Hill Church. The popular story runs that Twain indiscreetly referred to Asylum Hill as the "Church of the Holy Speculators" in the hearing of Twichell, that the two men were then introduced, and as Albert Bigelow Paine, Twain's biographer, put it, "so, in this casual fashion, [Twain] met the man who was presently to become his closest personal friend and counselor, and would remain so for more than forty years."[2]

Even if Paine's comment about the friendship is pretty much true, there may not have been an instant rapport between the two men. Twain was, at this time, and following his departure from California in late 1866, still looking to make the full transfer from his past western and bohemian world to this respectable eastern social world. He could, accordingly, at this stage of his career, gain more from Twichell than Twichell could from him. Indeed, there is, on Twichell's part, evidence of a certain initial coolness, even condescension, in his later accounts of the friendship's start. So, in his 22 April 1910 obituary notice for Twain, his recall of their first meeting is lukewarm: "I cannot say that at that period we were wholly sympathetic in either thought or feeling. . . . He was eminently a man 'with the bark on.'" Despite this, Twichell recalls being taken by "the brightness of [Twain's] mind, the incomparable charm of his talk, and his rare companionableness," quickly discovering that behind these there lay a "big, warm and tender heart." The relationship did then quickly blossom and "soon grew into a friendship which continued unbroken ever after, and went on strengthening with the flight of years."[3]

Indeed, this blossoming seems to have been quicker than Twichell's later recollections might suggest. The speed with which, on Twain's part, the relationship developed is evident in a letter he wrote to wife-to-be, Livy (Olivia Langdon), on 18 October 1868: "Set a white stone—for I have made a friend. It is the Rev. J. H. Twichell. I have only known him a week, & yet I believe I think almost as much of him as I do of Charlie [Livy's brother]. I could hardly find words strong enough to tell how much I *do* think of that man. (And his wife, too.)"[4] By early December, the warmth of Twichell's own regard for his new friend is clear. Twain took obvious pleasure in visits to the Twichell household—he was first invited there for dinner and what was clearly an enjoyable evening together on 14 October 1868. Sometime in the next week or so, he was invited to meet a group of Twichell's fellow Hartford ministers, probably including Edwin Pond Parker, Nathaniel Burton, and Henry Clay Trumbull, at Twichell's house, a meeting that clearly, for Twain certainly, went well.[5]

More crucially, this was the period when Twain was courting Livy, the refined and delicate daughter of wealthy Elmira coal and timber merchant Jervis Langdon. Twain had apparently seen Livy's picture on an ivory miniature carried by her brother, Charles, on the *Quaker City* trip: the pleasure cruise to Europe and the Holy Land recounted in *The Innocents Abroad.* He then met her in person at the end of 1867 and had gradually brought her round to accepting his attentions by the autumn of the following year. Twain knew that, in terms of current social status, he was aiming above himself in this match and that his somewhat dissolute background did not square up to her family's notions of moral and religious propriety. Accordingly, he saw Twichell as just the man to act as a spiritual mentor in the scheme of moral reform to which he then committed himself. The letters between the two men reflect this mentoring relationship, with Twain very much in the role of a serious man looking for self-improvement, seeking, in the words of Harriet Smith and Richard Bucci: "to rise to [Olivia's] level—to reform his rough habits, overcome his religious skepticism, and adopt a more conventional, self-consciously Christian way of life."[6] Twain is better known for his later reputation as a religious skeptic, but at this point in his life he was entirely serious about the program of spiritual betterment he adopted. Twichell played a vital role as religious advisor and confidante in the period leading up to his marriage. Indeed, with his previous experience as a young Civil War chaplain in a regiment of (mainly) rough Irish-Catholic New Yorkers, and with his tendency to value individual strength of character over the finer details of theology, he was the ideal man to assist sympathetically with this task.[7]

The letters Twain wrote to Livy in this period record both his reliance on Joe and his own stumbling moves toward a more religious state of heart and mind. In a letter written on 9 and 10 December 1868, he recounts a three-hour late-night talk with Twichell when:

> We had . . . held a long & earnest conversation upon the subject of religion. I told him, Livy, what was the truth—that although I had been praying more or less since about the middle of September, & here latterly day by day & earnestly, I feared I had not made as much progress as I ought to have done—& that *now* I began clearly to comprehend that one *must* seek Jesus for himself alone, & uninfluenced by selfish motives. . . . And Livy, that most excellent friend told me *clearly & concisely* HOW to seek the better life. . . . And at last, in the midst of the solemn night, he prayed fervently for my conversion, & that your love & mine might grow until it was made *perfect* love by the approving spirit of God—& that hand in hand & with hearts throbbing in unison we might compass that only worthy journey of life whose latest steps ushered the wayfarer into the home of eternal peace. But when he dropped his voice to a gentler tone, & prayed so touchingly & tenderly for *you*, Livy, . . . I felt as if the light from the Better Land shot its rays above the dark horizon of my mind & gilded its barren wastes with its glory.[8]

The letters between the two men start in a somewhat sporadic manner, as we might expect, given their day-to-day contact during Twain's early Hartford residence. It is when Twain is away in Elmira pursuing his romantic suit that the conversation starts to develop. When that suit was successful and he and Livy married in Elmira on 2 February 1879, Twichell assisted the local pastor, Thomas K. Beecher, in conducting the ceremony.[9] Twichell and his wife, Harmony, visited Twain and Livy five days later at their new house in Buffalo, New York. The house was a gift from Livy's father, who had also loaned Twain the money to buy a one-third interest in the *Buffalo Express*. (Twain was looking to establish himself as a journalist and newspaper owner and had turned to the *Express* after his expressions of interest in buying into Hartford's *Courant* had been turned down.) The growing closeness between the two families is evident in the joint Adirondacks vacation they planned in August 1870. Twain and Livy, though, were forced to pull out, most immediately due to Jervis Langdon's serious illness, followed by his death from stomach cancer on 6 August. Livy was also pregnant at this time. Langdon Clemens was born on 7 November; a sickly child, he would die just nineteen months later on 2 June 1872.

Twain and Livy's time in Buffalo did not work out well, and after a series of "catastrophes and near catastrophes," including the death from typhoid fever of Emma Nye, a friend of Livy, while she was visiting them, the couple decided to leave the city after just over a year there.[10] Twain had earlier indicated his desire to live in Hartford—and to become a member of Twichell's congregation. A letter to Livy of 15 February 1869 reads, "I told [Twichell] we meant to live a useful, unostentatious & earnest religious life, & that I should unite with the church as soon as I was settled; & that both of us, on these accounts, would prefer the quiet, moral atmosphere of Hartford. . . . I wanted him to understand that what we want is a *home*."[11] In late September 1871, this family move to Hartford finally took place.

1. Elisha Bliss, who published *The Innocents Abroad* and Twain's other early books (up to *A Tramp Abroad*, 1880) ran the American Publishing Company in Hartford.

2. Albert Bigelow Paine, *Mark Twain: A Biography* (New York: Harper, 1912), 1:371. The "Holy Speculators" comment referred to the fact that Hartford was a very wealthy city, with the church membership of Asylum Hill composed of many of its richest citizens.

3. The obituary was published in the *Hartford Courant* (henceforth abbreviated, where appropriate, to the *Courant*).

4. Harriet Elinor Smith and Richard Bucci, eds., *Mark Twain's Letters*, vol. 2: *1867–1868* (Berkeley: University of California Press, 1990), 267. The letter continues, to say how welcome the Twichells have made Twain in their home and to praise Twichell's religious fervor: "[H]ow beautiful his strong love for his subject made his words seem. When religion, coming from your lips & his, shall be distasteful to me, I shall be a lost man indeed." The speed of the developing friendship is seen in the two men's joint visit to the local almshouse that same day ("I . . . helped him preach & sing to the inmates") and their plans for a drive to the country the next day, with supper and an evening together ("to last till midnight") to follow (267–68).

5. See Steve Courtney, *Joseph Hopkins Twichell* (Athens: University of Georgia Press, 2008), 127. See Courtney, too, for more on the way Twichell took responsibility for Twain's "Hartford education" at both ends of the social spectrum (128–29).

6. *Mark Twain's Letters*, 2:xxiv.

7. For more on Twichell's past military life and his religious beliefs, see Harold K. Bush Jr., *Mark Twain and the Spiritual Crisis of His Age* (Tuscaloosa: University of Alabama Press, 2007); Courtney, *Joseph Hopkins Twichell*; Peter Messent and Steve Courtney, eds., *The Civil War Letters of Joseph Hopkins Twichell: A Chaplain's Story* (Athens: University of Georgia Press, 2006); and Peter Messent, *Mark Twain and Male Friendship: The Twichell, Howells, and Rogers Friendships* (New York: Oxford University Press, 2009).

8. *Mark Twain's Letters*, 2:318–19.

9. Thomas K. Beecher, brother of Henry Ward Beecher, was minister of the Elmira Independent Congregational Church (Park Church), which the Langdons attended.

10. Victor Fischer and Michael B. Frank, eds., *Mark Twain's Letters*, vol. 4: *1870–1871* (Berkeley: University of California Press, 1995), xxviii.

11. Victor Fischer and Michael B. Frank, eds., *Mark Twain's Letters*, vol. 3: *1869* (Berkeley: University of California Press, 1995), 103.

1. Twain to the Twichells

18 November 1868. Cleveland, Ohio

Cleveland, Nov. 18.

Dear T.'s—[1]

Congratulate me, my often remembered friends—for lo, the child is born![2] It was most flatteringly received—1200 applausive & appreciative people present. I have dropped a note to the S. & K., Yale College, inclosing the paragraphs.[3] I speak in Pittsburgh tomorrow & Elmira 23d. Love to you both. Good-bye. Yrs

Always—

Mark.

1. Twain initially wrote "Dear J T." then changed it.

2. He alludes to his lecture performance of "The American Vandal Abroad."

3. The Scroll and Key Society, a Yale College secret society. Twain had been made an honorary member earlier that month under Twichell's sponsorship. The "paragraphs" may well have been newspaper reviews of the Cleveland lecture. (Many of the notes to the Twain letters in the first parts of this book are based on information in the University of California Press edition of Twain's *Letters*. We gratefully acknowledge our reliance on the superb editorial work to be found there.)

2. Twain to Twichell

28 November 1868. New York, New York

DANIEL SLOTE.

SLOTE, WOODMAN & CO.,
BLANK BOOK MANUFACTURERS,
NOS. 119 & 121 WILLIAM STREET,

WEBSTER WOODMAN.
WM. A. MAUTERSTOCK.
FRANK BOWMAN.
P.O. BOX 21. NEW YORK, Nov. 28 1868

Private.

My Dear J. H.

Sound the loud timbrel!—& let yourself out to your most prodigious capacity,—for I have fought the good fight & lo! I have won![1] Refused three times—warned to *quit*, once—accepted at last!—& beloved!—Great Caesar's ghost, if there were a church in town with a steeple high enough to make it an object, I would go out & jump over it. And I persecuted her parents for 48 hours & at last they couldn't stand the siege any longer & so they made a *conditional* surrender:—which is to say, if *she* makes up her mind thoroughly & eternally, & I prove that I have done nothing criminal or particularly shameful in the past, & establish a good character in the future & *settle down,* I may take the sun out of their domestic firmament, the angel out of their fireside heaven. [Thunders of applause.] She felt the first symptoms last Sunday—my lecture, Monday night, brought the disease to the surface—Tuesday & Tuesday night she avoided me & would not do more than be simply polite to me because her parents said *NO* absolutely (almost,)—Wednesday night they capitulated & marched out with their side-arms—Wednesday night—she said over & over & over again that she loved me but was sorry she did & hoped it would yet pass away—Thursday I was telling her what *splendid, magnificent* fellows you & your wife were, & when my enthusiasm got the best of me & the tears sprang to my eyes, she just jumped up & said she was *glad & proud* she loved me!—& Friday night I left (to save her sacred name from the tongues of the gossips)—& the last thing she said was: "Write *immediately* & just as often as you can!" Hurra! [Hurricanes of applause.] There's the history of it.[2]

Oh, no—there isn't any persistence about *me*—certainly not. But I am so happy I want to scalp somebody.

My fervent love to you both. Write me, now—address 121 William street.

I walk in the clouds again. I bow my reverent head—thy blessing!

Mark.

1. Twain's exultant, even jubilant, letter marks the success of his wooing of Livy. The tone of the letter speaks of the already warm intimacy of the two men's relationship. "Sound the loud timbrel" are the opening words of a hymn by Thomas Moore (1779–1852): "Sound the loud timbrel o'er Egypt's dark sea! / Jehovah has triumph'd—His people are free!"

2. The "NO" is underlined and italicized in the original. Twain first wrote "a *splendid, magnificent* fellow" before changing it to take in Harmony too.

3. Twichell to Twain

[Letter no longer extant and exact date unknown, but written between 30 November and 3 December 1868. Twain quoted "an extract or two" of it in his letter to Livy of 4 December 1868, reproduced here. After the quote, Twain adds, "It is just like him—the gorgeous, whole-souled fellow! What splendid nights we had together!—& how gently & how tenderly he taught the religion that is all in all to him. And shall be to me, likewise, I hope & pray."][1]

Receive my benediction, Mark—my very choicest! I breathe it toward you—that particular doxologic & hallelujah formula thereof which I use on occasions which but for the sake of propriety I should celebrate by a smiting of my thigh, a grand *pas seul*, & three cheers with a tiger! A style of Te Deum which somehow I never *could* manage to execute successfully in the pulpit.[2] Bless you, my son!—yea, Bless you, my children both! . . . I do congratulate you, dear friend, with all the power of congratulation that is in me, (I speak for my wife, of course, when I say "I," as I always do when writing to any of our common loves) & I congratulate *her*. If I could do anything to help you in the matter, I would, joyfully. Command me if you have any use for me. I don't know anything about your past; but it does seem to me that a fellow, whom I have found so thoroughly lovable for a whole fortnight of quite free intercourse can't have become incapable of a character worthy any man's or woman's respect. I don't care very much about your past, but I do care very much about your future. I hope & expect, that it will be a nobly lived, happy, pure & useful future, ending with the dear life eternal which our Savior gives us for repentance & faith. Now is the best time you will ever see for giving your heart to God. Your heart, with this new, sacred love in it is a more precious thing to offer God than it was without it. You never have been able to bring so worthy a gift to Him as now. And while you are in the mood of gratitude, as I know you are, & all full of tender feelings, begin with gentle diligence to pray for & seek that peace in believing in Jesus Christ & knowing Him that is so sweet as to sweeten even the most joyful earthly joys. Be assured, my friend, I have not forgotten you in my secret hours with God, & I shall not.[3]

1. *Mark Twain's Letters*, 2:305–6.

2. A "*pas seul*" is a solo dance in ballet. A "tiger" was "a student shout at a regatta victory [Twichell had rowed in the Harvard-Yale regatta when at Yale], a shrieked T-I-I-I-I followed by a roared GER!" (Courtney, *Joseph Hopkins Twichell*, 129). The "Te Deum" is a Latin hymn traditionally used to celebrate times of public rejoicing.

3. Twichell starts off here, as he writes back so jovially, by gently satirizing the ministerial language expected of his calling. He then substitutes for it a more colloquial tone, his eastern response to Twain's joyful westernism ("scalp somebody"). Such a move between "propriety" and something more spontaneous and unrestrained is typical of Twichell. As the letter proceeds, though, his deep concern for Twain's spiritual betterment becomes obvious.

4. Twain to Twichell

12 December 1868. Norwich, New York

Norwich, N.Y., Dec. 12.

Dear Twichell—

Hip—hip—Hurrah! She just goes on "accepting the situation" in the most innocent, easy-going way in the world. She writes as if the whole thing were perfectly understood, & would no doubt be unpleasantly astonished if she only knew I had been regarding it differently & had been ass enough to worry about a cousin whom she merely gives the passing mention accorded to the humblest guests.[1] *She* don't know anything about beating the devil around the bush—she has never been used to it. She simply calls things by their right names & goes straight at the appalling subject of matrimony with the most amazing effrontery. I am in honor bound to regard her grave, philosophical dissertations as *love letters,* because they probe the very marrow of that passion, but there isn't a bit of romance in them, no poetical repining, no endearments, no adjectives, no flowers of speech, no nonsense, no bosh. Nothing but solid chunks of wisdom, my boy—love letters gotten up on the square, flat-footed, cast-iron, inexorable plan of the most approved commercial correspondence, & signed with stately & exasperating decorum. "Lovingly, LIVY L. LANGDON"—*in full,* by the Ghost of Caesar! They are more precious to me than whole reams of affectionate superlatives would be, coming from any other woman, but they *are* the darlingest funniest *love* letters that ever were written, I do suppose. She gets her stateliness of epistolary composition from her native dignity, & she gets that from her mother, who was born for a countess.

Hip—hip—Hurrah! I have badgered them & persecuted them until they have yielded, & I am to stop there for one day & night, on Dec. 17!

I am full of gratitude to God this day, & my prayers will be sincere. Now write me a letter which I can read to her, & let it reach Elmira a day or so before I get there—enclose it in an envelop [*sic*] directed to "*Chas. J. Langdon, Elmira, N.Y.*"[2] Good-bye. My love to you *all.*

Yrs always—

Mark.

[In margin] P.S. She knows you & Mrs. T. know all about it—she likes that.

1. He refers here to Livy's cousin, Captain Edward L. Marsh ("a handsome young bachelor"), who had been staying with the Langdons in the November to December period. See *Mark Twain's Letters,* 2:292, 332.

2. Smith and Bucci refer to a "cautious procedure" here, probably used by Twain to avoid public knowledge of his visits to the Langdons. *Mark Twain's Letters*, 2:332.

5. Twain to Twichell

1 January 1869. Cleveland, Ohio

Cleveland, New Year's.

Dear J. H.

While they get the carriage ready (for I am with my dear old Quaker City adopted mother,)—for we are going out to pay New Year's calls, I will snatch a moment to say I have just received yours.[1] And along with it a handful of dainty letters from that wonderful miracle of humanity, little Miss Livy. She has a most engaging commercial reliability & promptness allied to her stately commercial style of correspondence. I can always depend on an 8-page letter, every day. Never any whining in it, or any nonsense, but wisdom till you can't rest. Never any foolishness—but whenever she *does* miss fire & drop *herself* into her epistle accidentally, it is perfectly gorgeous. She thinks about me all the time, & informs me of it with Miltonic ponderosity of diction. She loves me, & conveys the fact with the awful dignity of an Ambassador construing an article of international law. But in her **sermons** she excels.[2] They are full of a simple trust & confidence, & touched with a natural pathos, that would win a savage. Ours is a funny correspondence, & a mighty satisfactory one, altogether. My letters are an ocean of love in a storm—hers an ocean of love in the majestic repose of a great calm. But the waters are the same—just the same, my boy.

And I have delightful Christmas letters, this morning, from her mother & father—full of love & trust. Lo! the world is very beautiful—very beautiful—& *there is a God.* I seem to be shaking off the drowsiness of centuries & looking about me half bewildered at the light just bursting above the horizon of an unfamiliar world.

The carriage waits! Good-bye—love to you both—God send you a happy New Year that shall continue happy until the year is old again—& forevermore.

Yrs always
Mark

1. Twain's "adopted mother," as he so called her, was Mary Fairbanks, close friend and mentor from the *Quaker City* trip.

2. Twain uses a wavy underscore for "sermons." Such underscore in manuscript submitted to a printer meant boldface or similar, certainly by 1900 and perhaps before: thus the boldface here.

6. Twain to the Twichells

23 January 1869. Cleveland, Ohio

Cleveland, Jan. 23, 1869.

Dear J. H. & Tribe—

Hurrah!—because you *do* rise to the dignity of a Tribe, now, since this last accident.[1] I am *glad* to hear it—don't see why I should be glad, but I *am*—I should actually be appalled if *I* were to have a baby. But I know *you* are glad, & so I go it blind. That you are glad, is enough for me—count me in. I am *mighty* glad, Twichell. I am, indeed. It must be awful—I mean it must be splendid—but then the whole subject is a little confusing & bewildering to me, & I don't really know whether this ecstasy of mine is gratitude or consternation—because—well, *you* know how it is with us fellows who have never had any experience—we *mean* well, but then we are so dreadfully off soundings in *these* waters. But I *am* glad, if I bust. And I'll stick to it & take the chances.

I'll scratch out a suggestive sentence or two & send your letter to Livy—maybe she can raise a hurrah, & have sense enough to know what she means by it—

[Five lines (about 25 words) are torn away here, seemingly a remark about Livy's naiveté concerning the reproductive process.][2]

She must learn to rejoice when we rejoice, whether she knows what she is rejoicing about or not; because we can't have any member of the family hanging fire & interrupting the grand salute merely because they *don't know.* By *George,* I'm mighty glad. I wish there'd been six or seven. Wouldn't we have had a time, though? You hear *me.*

Elmira? Why it just goes on like clock-work. Every other day, without fail, & sometimes *every* day, comes one of those darling 8-page commercial miracles; & I bless the girl, & bow my grateful head before the throne of God & let the unspoken thanks *flow* out that never human speech could fetter into words.

If you could only see her picture! It came last night. She sat six times for a ferrotype—taking 3 weeks to it—& every picture was a slander, & I gently said so—very gently—& at last she tried a porcelain-type—& when I opened the little velvet case last night, lo! a messenger-angel out of upper Heaven was roosting there![3] I give you my word of honor that it is a very marvel of beauty—the expression is sweet, & patient, & *so* far-away & dreamy. What respect, what reverent honor it compels! *Any* man's unconscious impulse would be to take his hat off in its presence. And if he had not the impulse, I would give it him.

I have lectured about 30 times, so far, & from the way the invitations keep coming in, I believe I could stay in the West & never miss a night during the entire season. But I *must* close with the West Feb. 13 & go forward to fill eastern engagements. I *repeated* here, last night & cleared for the Orphan Asylum 807^{00}, over & above everything. That is as far as heard from—it *may* reach $1,000.[4]

Shall be in Hartford about March—& then make a flying trip to California. I swept Nasby's dung hill (Toledo,) like a Besom of Destruction—don't know what a Besom of Destruction is, but it is a noble sort of expression.[5] Came off with flying colors. Print the notices for me.[6] Love to all four of you.

Yrs, always,
Mark

1. The letter follows the 9 January birth of Joe and Harmony's second child, Julia. They had had their first child, Edward, in August 1867. Twain was in Cleveland on a lecture tour.

2. The first five words, partially torn, appear to be "though I don't know—I'll."

3. Deletion of "mel" before "ferrotype"—Twain was evidently going to write "melainotype," an early name for ferrotype. Deletion of "presto!" before "when I opened."

4. The lecture was in aid of the Cleveland Protestant Orphan Asylum.

5. Petroleum V. Nasby (David Ross Locke) was a fellow humorist, based in Toledo, Ohio. "Besom of destruction" is from Isaiah 14:23.

6. Reviews of Twain's lectures which he wished reprinted in Hartford. This apparently never happened.

7. Twain to the Twichells

14 February 1869. Ravenna, Ohio

GILLETTE HOUSE,
RAVENNA, OHIO, St. Valentine's 1869

Dear J. H & Tribe—

I greet you all with the great accession of love that naturally comes to one on the feast-day of St Valentine. And you can just rise up & blow your horn, too, & blow it *loud*—because the subscriber is *engaged to be married*!—hip, hip, hip ——[*now*, ALL together!] On bended knees, in the presence of God only, we devoted our lives to each other & to the service of God.[1] And let this writing be a witness of it, to you.

And so, as soon as I am permanently settled in life, we shall be married. [I don't sigh, & groan & howl so much, now, as I used to—no, I feel serene, & arrogant, & stuck-up—& I feel such pity for the world & everybody in it but just us two.] I have suddenly grown to be prodigiously important to the world's welfare, somehow—though it didn't use to seem to me that my existence was such a very extraordinary matter.

I do wish you knew Miss Livy. She already knows & loves you both—loves you *all*, I should have said—on my account.[2]

I have received & answered Gen. Hawley's letter.[3] He suggests that I make my California trip first, & then Warner will be home & we can talk business.[4] I think the General would rather *employ* me than sell me an interest—but that won't *begin* to answer, you know. I can buy into plenty of paying newspapers, but my future wife wants me to be surrounded by a good moral & religious atmosphere (for I shall unite with the church as soon as I am located,) & so she likes the idea of living in Hartford. We could make more money elsewhere, but neither of us are much fired with a mania for money-getting. That is a matter of second-rate, even third-rate importance with us.

I shall reach Hartford during the last week of this month, & remain *several* weeks. I shall spend Saturday & Sunday, Feb. 20th & 21st, in Elmira.

Good-bye & God-bless you.

Always yrs

Mark.

1. This is his formal engagement to Livy.

2. Livy, who had by now heard a great deal of Twain's new friend, made her first visit to the Twichell household in June 1869. (She and her family were in Hartford for the wedding of Alice Hooker, daughter of feminist and reformer Isabella Beecher Hooker, a friend of Livy's mother).

3. Joseph Hawley, a man of many parts and a past governor of Connecticut, was editor-in-chief of the *Hartford Courant.* Twain was looking to invest in the paper as a shareholder, but the plan came to nothing. See Letter 8, note 3.

4. Charles Dudley Warner, associate editor of the *Courant,* then on a lengthy tour of Europe. Warner was also a founding member of the Nook Farm community, a travel writer, sketch writer, and critic. He is best known now for *The Gilded Age* (1873), which he co-wrote with Twain.

8. Twain to Twichell

28 December 1869. New York, New York

New York, Dec. 28

Dear J. H.—

I hasten to enclose to you my R R ticket from New Haven to New York, before I forget to recollect it. You see, when I found, last night, that there was a *boat* at 11 P.M., & that a man would have to get up as early as day before yesterday to catsh [*sic*] any train that would leave before noon, I of course sent down & engaged a stateroom—& as I haven't any earthly use for this R R ticket, my soul swells with a boundless generosity, & I send it to you.[1] If it shall be the means of making one small year of your sad earthly pilgrimage seem happier, & brighter, & bullyer, it is all I ask. Pax Vobiscum! (I don't know what Pax Vobiscum means, but it is the correct thing to say in the way of a benediction, I believe.) Good-bye. Great love to the wife & the boys.[2]

Yrs always

Mark. ["Sam" deleted before "Mark."]

I wrote Livy about your coming Feb. 1—& to be ready for the woods the first of August—& what Mrs. Hooker said to us—& everything.[3]—Hello, I didn't see that blank page on the other side.[4]

1. There were a number of coastal steamers running between New Haven and New York City.

2. An error—the Twichells then had one boy (Edward) and one girl (Julia).

3. See Twain's letter to Livy of 27 December. In it Twain reports that Isabella Beecher Hooker had told him how keen Joseph Hawley and Charles Dudley Warner now were to have him take an ownership in the *Courant*. Twain says, "It afforded me a malicious satisfaction to hear all this & contrast it with the insultingly contemptuous indifference with which the very same matter was treated last June, (by *every one of them.*)" *Mark Twain's Letters*, 3:440.

4. The postscript was crammed into the left margin rather than written on the blank page available.

9. Twain to the Twichells

12 November 1870. Buffalo, New York

Buffalo, Nov. 12.[1]

Dear Uncle & Aunt

I came into the world on the 7th inst., and consequently am about 5 days old, now.[2] I have had wretched health ever since I made my appearance. First one thing & then another has kept me under the weather. One hour it would be wind—next, indigestion—next, colic—& as a general thing I have been chilly & uncomfortable.

I am not corpulent, nor am I robust in any way. At birth I only weighed 4½ pounds with my clothes on—& the clothes were the chief feature of the weight, too, I am obliged to confess. But I am doing finely, all things considered. I was at a standstill for 3 days & a half, but during the last 24 hours I have gained nearly an ounce, avo[i]rdupois.

They all say I look very old & venerable—& I am aware, myself, that I never smile. Life seems a serious thing, what I have seen of it—& as my observation teaches me that it is made up mainly of hiccups, unnecessary washings, & wind in the bowels. But no doubt you, who are old, have long since grown accustomed & reconciled to what seems to me such a disagreeable novelty.

My father said, this morning, when my face was in repose & thoughtful, that I looked precisely as young Edward Twichell of Hartford used to look some 12 months ago.—chin, mouth, forehead, expression—everything.[3]

My little mother is very bright & cheery, & I guess she is pretty happy, but I don't know what about. She laughs a great deal, notwithstanding she is sick abed. And she eats a great deal, though she says that is because the nurse desires it. And when she has had all the nurse desires her to have, she asks for more. She is getting along very well indeed.

My aunt Susie Crane has been here some ten days or two weeks, but goes home today & Granny Fairbanks of Cleveland arrives to take her place.[4]

I was not due here on this planet until about the first week in December, but my mother took a hurried drive to the depot one day & the consequence was that it was all the doctors & nurses could do to keep me from looking in on the family that night. But by faithful exertions they got me staved off two weeks, & by jings I missed the earthquake.[5]

But we appear to be all right now, uncle, & some day we'll come & see you & my young cousins.[6]

Very lovingly,

Langdon Clemens.

P.S. Father said I had better write, because you would be more interested in me, just now than in the rest of the family.[7]

1. The monogram or initial *C* is printed or embossed in bold within a circle at the head of this letter on personalized stationary. This appears on a number of other early letters.

2. Twain writes in the voice of his newborn son, Langdon, born on 7 November 1870. In

the lengthy period prior to this letter, which included Twain and Livy's wedding on 2 February, there were a number of occasions when it seems Twain wrote to Twichell (and, no doubt, vice versa). See, for instance, *Mark Twain's Letters,* 4:139, 167. However, none of these letters is extant.

3. Edward, the Twichells' eldest child, was born on 10 August 1867.

4. Susan Crane, Livy's adopted sister. On Jervis Langdon's death, she became the owner of Quarry Farm, Elmira, the vacation home of the Langdon family.

5. There was an earthquake, with significant tremors in Buffalo, on 20 October 1870.

6. Edward, Julia, and Susan (born 15 October 1870). The Twichells would go on to have a further six children.

7. Twichell would label the letter "(Langdon *natus*)."

10. Twain to Twichell

19 December 1870. Buffalo, New York

Buf. 19th

Dear J. H.—

All is well with us, I believe—though for some days the baby was quite ill. We consider him nearly restored to health now, however. Ask my brother about us—you will find him at Bliss's publishing office where [he] is gone to edit Bliss's new paper—left here last Monday.[1] Make his & his wife's acquaintance. Take Mrs. T. to see them as soon as they are fixed.

Livy *is* up, & the prince keeps her busy & anxious these latter days & nights, but I am a bachelor up stairs & don't have to jump up & get the soothing-syrup—though I would as soon do it as not, I assure you. [Livy will be certain to read this letter.]

Tell Harmony (Mrs. T.) that I *do* hold the baby, & do it pretty handily, too, although with occasional apprehensions that his loose head will fall off. I don't have to quiet him—he hardly ever utters a cry. He is always thinking about something. He is a patient, good little baby.

Smoke?[2] I *always* smoke from 3 till 5 on Sunday afternoons—& in New York the other day I smoked a week, day & night. But when Livy is well I smoke only those 2 hours on Sunday. I'm "boss" of the habit, now, & shall never let it boss me any more. Originally, I quit solely on Livy's account (not that I believed there was the faintest *reason* in the matter, but just as I would deprive myself of sugar in my coffee if she wished it, or quit wearing socks if she thought them immoral), & I stick to it yet on Livy's account, & shall always continue to do so, without a pang.[3] But somehow it seems a pity that *you* quit, for Mrs. T. didn't mind it if I remember rightly. Ah, it is turning one's back upon a kindly Providence to spurn away from us the good creature he sent to make the breath of life a *luxury* as well as a necessity, *enjoyable* as well as useful, to go & quit smoking when there ain't any sufficient excuse for it. Why my old boy, when they used to tell me I would shorten my life ten years by smoking, they little knew the devotee they were wasting their puerile words upon—they little knew how trivial & valueless I would regard a decade that had no smoking in it! But I won't persuade you, Twichell—I won't until I see you again—but *then* we'll smoke for a week together & then shut off again.[4]

I would have gone to Hartford from New York last Saturday but I got *so* homesick I couldn't. But maybe I'll come soon. [Can you keep a secret? Among other reasons, I would have had to stay at Bliss's—wouldn't let me go to the hotel—why didn't you offer me bread & board? I'm expecting to run over there in a couple of weeks or more.][5]

No, Sir, *catch* me in the metropolis again, to get homesick.

I didn't know Warner had a book out.[6]

We send oceans & continents of love—I have worked myself down, to-day.

Yrs always
Mark.

1. See Twain's 5 November 1870 letter to his brother, Orion Clemens (*Mark Twain's Letters*, 4:219–22). For Orion's response to Twichell and his wife—who had accordingly called on him—see ibid., 299. In a letter to Mollie, Orion's wife, in early January 1871, Twain describes Twichell in a colloquial but clearly fond and commendatory way as "a bully boy with a glass eye" (298).

2. Twichell—in a missing letter—has clearly asked him, presumably in the context of the new baby, about his smoking.

3. See Twain's 13 January 1870 letter to Livy, *Mark Twain's Letters*, 4:21–23.

4. Deletion of "Ha!" before "But I won't."

5. Twain has circled this bracketed material for emphasis.

6. Twichell, in a missing letter, had evidently told Twain about Charles Dudley Warner's (first and very successful) book of humorous nature essays, *My Summer in a Garden*. And see Letter 11.

11. Twain to Twichell

3 January 1871. Buffalo, New York

Buf., 3d.

Dear J H—

I tell you it is magnificent!——rich, delicious, fascinating, brim full of meat—the humor transcends anything I have seen in print or heard from a stage this many a day—& every page glitters like a cluster-pin with many-sided gems of fancy—Warner's book I mean—it is splendid. But I haven't dressed yet—the barber is waiting to shave me, Livy & the rest of the family are clamoring for breakfast & it does seem that a body can't sit down in his shirt-tail to drop a friendly line to a friend without all the elements "going for" him.[1]

All well here. Hope same to you & yrs. Happy N. Y.r & all that.

Gd bye—

Ys

Mark

1. Livy's mother, Olivia Lewis Langdon, was staying with them.

12. Twichell to Twain

8 May 1871. Hartford, Connecticut

Hartford, Conn.
May 8th 1871

Mark! Mark! dear friend of days gone by, whose delights we tasted in those happy though distant times when thou didst lodge with us and sit smoking at our fireside, where art thou? And again our hearts ask, where art thou? And in this cry please understand the soft accents of Mrs. T. mingling with my baritone. But, dear old fellow, truly and seriously what in the world has become of you? You are become little more than a memory and a shade here i.e. you would have, had we not loved you too well to allow you to suffer from your own neglect. We have passed many an evening hour talking of you, and lately wondering how it was going with you and Livy and the little boy. To be sure we have heard about you once in a while through your brother, but what is that, I should like to know, for people like us who are, so to speak, i.e. as we feel, members of you.

Well, probably you have not enough to do getting moved and watching over those two sweet children (for Livy seems as a young girl to me) both of whom need so much of your care. Therefore don't think I complain. No doubt if either of us has fallen behind the requirements of friendship in the case, it is I.

What set me off writing this morning was hearing so much said about you at our Monday Evening Club last night. The topic was "American Humor," and Hon. Hammond Trumbull (brother of the Rev.) in the course of his remarks said that he had lately met Josh Billings in Boston, who, in a conversation, declared his conviction that you were by all odds the brightest light of humour in the land, and incomparably superior to all rivals on the platform, which I thought very handsome of him and a thing you ought to hear.[1] Several other of the gentlemen had a word today about you when their time came, and hearing you talked of awakened my conscience so that I went home determined that I would drop you a line right off. We have been sorry to know that Livy's strength was returning so slowly, and have tried to imagine your common affliction therein that we might sympathize with it. Dear Mark, your great, kind heart must be much burdened, and it must take a deal [of] patience in both of you to bear your trials. Our best love to Livy and the baby. We are all in our usual health. To-day the whole crowd set out for New Jersey to see the old folks.[2] I go as far as New York with them. Pray let us hear from you soon.

Yours as ever,

J.H.T.

1. J. Hammond Trumbull was a bibliographer, historian, and philologist and co-founder of the Monday Evening Club in Hartford, whose members, including Twichell and Twain, met fortnightly for discussion on papers presented by members. For more on the Monday Evening Club and the type of papers delivered, see Bush, *Mark Twain and the Spiritual Crisis of his Age*, 114–19. Trumbull would write the chapter epigraphs (in a wide variety of languages) for Twain and Warner's novel, *The Gilded Age* (1873). Josh Billings was the nom de plume of Henry Wheeler Shaw, a popular humorist of the time.

2. Harmony Twichell's family, the Cushmans, lived in Orange, New Jersey.

PART 2
1871–1891

Twain's Hartford Years

Twain and Livy's life in Buffalo, with the deaths and illnesses attending it from mid-1870 onward into 1871, was particularly fraught. Meanwhile, partly as result of this but also due to problems in his professional life, Twain himself had become deeply unhappy with life there. In consequence, he and Livy left the city in April 1871 to go back to Elmira. Planning then to set up home in Hartford, Twain moved to the city in August to work on the proofs of *Roughing It.* Livy, now pregnant with their second child, and Langdon followed him down in early October, Twain having leased a large house ("while I build") on the corner of Forest and Hawthorne Streets.[1] "Hartford," he wrote to an unidentified correspondent on 20 November 1871, "is now my home."[2]

The twenty-year period when Twain and his family lived in Hartford was probably the happiest in his life. Twichell and his own ever-growing family lived close by and the two men became near-constant companions, at least when they were both in town. Twain's earlier attempt at religious reform had, however, clearly run out of steam before his married life had advanced very far, although he continued in many of the social aspects of Christianity. Livy, in turn, was affected by this, as is clear from her letter to her husband (away lecturing) of 2 and 3 December 1871, where she writes:

> Mother and I went to church this morning. . . . It is so long since I have been to church that I was mellowed by the very atmosphere I think, Mr Twichells [*sic*] prayer touched me and made me cry, he prayed particularly for those who had fallen away and were longing to come back to God—Youth I am ashamed to go back, because I have fallen away so many times. . . . Mr Twichell is such a good earnest man and gave us a good sermon, I think we shall enjoy our church there very much. . . . Mrs Warner was speaking this P.M. of lukewarmness toward God. . . . I told her if I felt toward God as I did toward my husband I should never be in the least troubled—I did not tell her how almost perfectly cold I am toward God—[3]

What is noticeable here is how, to a degree, Livy separates off her churchgoing from any sense of deep doctrinal commitment. We should remember here the deep changes in the nature of religious belief at this time and the erosion of the cultural influence of the Protestant and other churches in an increasingly secular age. Kenneth Andrews's description of Hartford's liberal Congregationalism in his important book *Nook Farm: Mark Twain's Hartford Circle* gives a crucial insight into the effects of such a change. Speaking of Twichell and two other local ministers, he says,

> They were instinctively adapted to the new post-War atmosphere. . . . Their status derived almost entirely from the strength of their personal hold on their fellows. . . . Their churches became institutions for community good works and centers of information and appropriate recreation. . . . The individual's right to determine his own relationship to God would not be contested . . . so long as personal morality, necessary for a secure society, was not threatened and public morality was not undermined.[4]

Twain, too, attended Twichell's church at Hartford, indeed played a relatively conspicuous part in its affairs in terms of financial support, fund-raising activities, educational and welfare activities, and the like.[5] But it is clear that in matters of formal belief he was something of a heretic. Again, Andrews's summary seems as accurate as we can know: "He had rejected Christianity, . . . ruled out all theology, and the supernatural that it attempted to interpret, but he was not contemptuous of Christianity as a basis for an equitable society and not at all at odds with his community's regard for personal and public morality."[6]

No doubt, then, it was exactly the liberal nature of religious practice in Hartford and the relaxed attitude to expressions of theological dissent that made Twichell's Asylum Hill Church so comfortable to Twain, and to Livy. And Twichell, though he did worry about his friend's spiritual welfare, by and large let sleeping theological dogs lie.[7] The basis for the two men's friendship, after all, lay in their personal compatibility. Meeting another clergyman, the Reverend James P. Foster of Syracuse, in December 1871, Twain refers to him to Livy as "a noble, splendid fellow—a Twichell." He then continues, with words that also apply to his Hartford friend: "He tells yarns, smokes occasionally, has weaknesses & lovable vices, just like a good, genuine human being, instead of a half-restored theological corpse, like *some* preachers. Sails right into the meat & marrow of a thing with a whole-hearted cordiality."[8] Twain's easy fit with Twichell, the latter's personality and religious liberalism, and the fact that, accordingly, Twain could take their relationship as parishioner and minister very much for granted are suggested in the fact that, certainly as late as 1898, he was still absolutely happy to refer to Joe as "my pastor."[9]

Twain's religious beliefs and consequent relationship with Twichell have been matters of critical commentary. Until Kenneth Andrews's *Nook Farm* book, it was generally held that Twain completely lost any religious commitment after the early period of his marriage. Twain's biographer Albert Bigelow Paine was largely responsible for this understanding, suggesting the parting of Twain and Twichell's religious ways in his report of a conversation between them during their 1878 trip to Europe. Paine quotes Twain as follows: "Joe, . . . I'm going to make a confession. I don't believe in your religion at all. I've been living a lie right straight along whenever I pretended to. For a moment, sometimes, I have been almost a believer, but it immediately drifts away from me again. I don't believe one word of your Bible was inspired by God." Paine continues, "So the personal side of religious discussion closed between them, and was never afterward reopened."[10] Joe, however, wrote a letter to Harmony during that same trip which is invaluable for any consideration of his relationship with Twain.

In the light of this letter, it becomes difficult (as most critics now concur) to take Paine's account as the crystal truth.[11] For Twichell's letter to Harmony carries no such sense of rupture—at least, at that particular stage of their expedition.[12] It does, though, suggest that both men were fully aware of Twain's failings on the spiritual and moral front. But this is a significant letter in more than one respect, as it contains some of Twichell's most considered judgments on his friend's character:

> Mark and I had a good talk after dinner this evening on religion. A good talk, I say: he got to speaking of himself in a way that gave me a chance to declare gospel truth to him. "Romola" [George Eliot's 1863 novel] started it. Mark observed that he had been seeing himself as in a looking glass in the skilful uncovering of the working of motives which characterizes the book. And presently he said "There's nothing that makes me hate myself so, and feel so mean as to have Livy praise me and express a good opinion of me, when I know all the while that I am a humbug, and no such person as she takes me to be." He said this very heartily and I sympathized with him, dear, and told him that I knew just how it was, having experienced the same humiliation from a like cause myself. And so we got onto the subject of character and the state of the heart, and the application of Christ's gospel to the wants of a sinful man.
>
> People don't know Mark's best side. I am more persuaded of it than ever. . . . Would that the grace might touch him with power and lead him

> into larger views of things spiritual than he has ever yet seen!! He is exceedingly considerate toward me in regard of everything, or most things, where he apprehends that my religious feelings are concerned [Twichell then gives an example regarding Twain's cancellation of plans to travel on a Sunday]. . . . And when we kneel down together at night to pray, it always seems to bring the spirit of gentleness upon him, and he is very likely to be affectionate after it. After all, coarse as he is in streaks, he is a genuinely loveable fellow. As to the whiskey, most of the time he doesn't take any, and drinks no more wine and beer than I should, if I indulged, as I feel I might without sin. Anybody here would call him temperate.[13] Really I am enjoying him exceedingly and take delight in being with him.[14]

Twichell's much later remark to his son, following Harmony's death, suggests that the pattern of his relationship with Twain, at least when they were away together, changed little over the years: "When he and I have been off together and sleeping in the same room, Uncle Mark always knelt with me in the evening when I prayed for the families and in the morning repeated the Lord's prayer for me. When it was time for our prayer he would say, 'Come on Joe.'"[15] The extended story Twichell's journals tell is also rather different than the one Paine would suggest, with repeated references to the regular part Twain played in church activities and the financial support he and Livy gave to the church during the period in which they lived in Hartford. The reference in the letter to Twain's less attractive side ("coarse as he is in streaks") is, at the same time, a reminder that there were matters on which Twichell was never quite on the same wavelength as his friend.

Twichell's relationship with Twain during these Hartford years took a number of different forms. When both men were in Hartford there were occasional short notes to each other but, naturally, little else in the way of written correspondence, as they were in more-or-less daily contact. Twichell was often present at the dinners Twain organized for visiting celebrities and the local community. The two men also shared membership in the Monday Evening Club. Twain and Twichell shared, too, their liking for walking, and especially for the regular eight-mile walk (approximately) they would take to Bartlett's Tower, or Talcott Tower, as they called it, on Talcott Mountain.[16] There were in addition a number of joint ventures on which the two men worked together, Twain supporting Twichell's work on behalf of both the Chinese educational mission in Hartford and the Hartford City Mission run by "Father" David Hawley.[17]

Twain, though, was also away for lengthy periods, sometimes lecturing, sometimes travelling to collect material for his books. Both men, too, were away from Hartford for part or all of the summers: the Twichells on their annual Adirondacks holiday; Twain with his family in Elmira. At such times, the stimulus for letter writing increased.

During this period, Twain also came to rely on Joe as a (usually comic) source for literary material. So, in November 1874, early in Twain's Hartford life, he and Twichell set out to walk from Hartford to Boston, engaging in mock competition with one of the great walkers of their time, Edward Weston. Twain made comic capital of the walk and the somewhat farcical way in which it developed, both in newspaper publicity at the time and in his later reworking of one particular incident (featuring Twichell) as the "profane hostler" story—one version of which was published posthumously in *Mark Twain in Eruption* (1940).[18] Later, in May 1877, Twichell would travel with Twain to Bermuda and feature as "the Reverend" in "Some Rambling Notes of an Idle Excursion" (1882), Twain's account of the trip.

Twichell appears in an often thin fictional disguise elsewhere in Twain's writing but nowhere more importantly than in *A Tramp Abroad* (1880), the latter's second European travel book. Twain paid for Twichell to join him in Germany and Switzerland, walking in the Black Forest and touring the Rhine valley and the Alps in August and September of 1878, and used him when he wrote his book as the basis for Mr. Harris, "the narrator's foil, fool, goad, guide, and all-purpose straight man."[19] Hearing Twain tell the tales of his earlier piloting history, Twichell would also prompt him to write them up for the *Atlantic Monthly* as "Old Times on the Mississippi" (1875).

There was one significant falling out during this period, one of the very few we know of in the course of the friendship. This was on Twain's rather than Twichell's part. On 20 July 1883, Twain had written to Twichell from Elmira explaining the history game he had just thought up for his children's entertainment and education (see Letter 83). This part of the letter was published, at Twichell's instigation, in the *Hartford Courant* of 24 July. By giving details of Twain's game to the papers—for the piece in the *Courant* was widely copied—in what Justin Kaplan calls a moment of "boyish indiscretion," Twichell unwittingly instigated what was probably the most serious fissure in their whole friendship.[20] Twain had been swept up in his enthusiasm for the new game and had immediately determined to investigate its commercial possibilities. Twichell, to his mind, kiboshed this plan when he made its details public knowledge.

Twain was just furious, though he would, nonetheless, proceed with the game's development.

The extent of Twain's anger can be measured by the comment he wrote at the top of Twichell's 22 July 1883 letter (Letter 84), which he then sent on to his brother Orion and his wife, Mollie, and his mother, Jane: "I send this to beg that at least *you* folks will avoid this damned fool's example. I shall never thoroughly like him again. S.L.C."[21] He also wrote to Howells, saying how "appalled" he was "to get a note from [Joe] saying he was going to print part of my letter, & was going to do it before I could get a chance to forbid it." Twain continues, "I telegraphed him, but was of course too late. He not only made me feel ridiculous, but he broke up & ruined a fine large plan of mine.[22] So I wrote him a letter which was pretty much all English—& he hasn't replied yet, after all these weeks. But he didn't print any of it."[23] This was the fiercest criticism of Twichell he would ever make. The "all English" letter Twain wrote to Joe is now missing.[24] But it is clear that whatever he said, though having some effect on Twichell, did not entirely discommode him. Aware of Twain's anger, he looked to rebuild bridges while nonetheless very much downplaying the seriousness of his actions, insisting indeed that he had done nothing particularly wrong (see 8 September 1883, Letter 86).

The tension between the two men was eventually resolved as Twain evidently (and unusually, for he was especially good at bearing grudges) decided to put the incident behind him. He wrote to Edward H. House on 1 October 1883 about Twichell's response following the original incident:

> He was silent during 3 weeks, & that angered me further, for I thought he ought to apologize. A few more days elapse, & now he writes me a chipper letter from the mountains chaffing, at my concern, & saying he is still calmly convinced that he did the right thing. We shall remain friends, but I shan't answer his letter just the same. When I trust him again, it will be my fault. So you see that when over-friendly muggins chooses to destroy you with a kind turn, he can do it, whether you be 300 miles away or 10,000.[25]

As time passed the friendship gradually returned to normal. It would, however, apparently be over a year before Twain wrote to Twichell again and the correspondence between the two men would be sparse for some time. (This may, though, have been a product of other circumstances or simply reflect correspondence now lost.)

One sign of the renewed closeness of the Twichell-Twain friendship lies in the ease with which Twain could make himself at home in the

Twichell household. In early October 1888, just back from Elmira, he asked Twichell if he could work on the book he was then writing (*A Connecticut Yankee*) in the latter's house. (Possibly Livy was not yet back and he wanted company around him.) Despite the building work then going on, he made good progress. As he wrote to his brother-in-law, Theodore Crane, on 5 October:

> I am here in Twichell's house, at work, with the noise of the children & an army of carpenters to help. Of course they don't help, but neither do they hinder. It's like a boiler-factory, for racket, and in nailing a wooden ceiling onto the room under me the hammering tickles my feet amazingly sometimes, and jars my table a good deal; but I never am conscious of the racket at all. . . . I began here Monday morning, and have done eighty pages since.[26]

By and large the content of the letters in this period is relatively limited. There is little about religion, save reference to the Henry Ward Beecher trial of 1875—a high-profile case concerning the accusation made against the enormously popular reformist minister of adultery with Elizabeth Tilton, one of his parishioners. There is little, too, about politics—though the assassination attempt and later consequent death of President James Garfield and the death of General Ulysses S. Grant do stimulate comment. The trips the two men took together, in particular the *Tramp Abroad* one, recur as subject matter, and Twichell relatively frequently suggests materials in which Twain might take a literary interest. Both men, when away from Hartford, report on their ongoing family lives and on the places and incidents they encounter. There are other, more "domestic" letters, including thank-yous from Twichell for the financial assistance Twain and Livy would—throughout the friendship—give their relatively impoverished friends. This was the period also when both families were having their children—the Twichells the more frequently!—and there are periodic references to each other's changing family circumstances.

Such themes recur in later letters, too, but the importance of the Hartford period in the lives of both families and the firming up of both men's careers and positions in the world make this a highly significant time. This phase of the Twichell-Twain friendship, however, came to an end in 1891 when Twain and Livy closed the Nook Farm house they had had built for them in 1873–74, early in their residency in the town, and went to Europe. Though this was meant as a temporary remove, the series of reverses that followed—first the 1894 bankruptcy of Charles L. Webster & Co., Twain's publishing firm, and then, crucially, the 1896 death of daughter Susy in the Hartford home while she was living apart from the family—effectively closed off this period of Twain's life.

1. Victor Fischer and Michael B. Frank, eds., *Mark Twain's Letters*, vol. 4: *1870–1871* (Berkeley: University of California Press, 1995), 455. Letter to lecture agent James Redpath.

2. Ibid., 495.

3. Ibid., 510. "Youth" was Livy's pet name for her husband. See, too, Livy's letter of 7 Jan 1872, when she writes to her husband of a church visit and how, when she realized it was a communion service, "my heart sank because I do feel so unfit to go to the table of communion, yet cannot bear to go away from it." She also praises Twichell here: "I do love Joseph Twichell, he is a good man—a Godly man—I love to hear him preach and pray." Lin Salamo and Harriet Elinor Smith, eds., *Mark Twain's Letters*, vol. 5: *1872–1873* (Berkeley: University of California Press, 1997), 17.

4. Kenneth R. Andrews, *Nook Farm: Mark Twain's Hartford Circle* (Cambridge, Mass.: Harvard University Press, 1950), 49, 69.

5. See Andrews, *Nook Farm.* See also Harold K. Bush Jr., *Mark Twain and the Spiritual Crisis of His Age* (Tuscaloosa: University of Alabama Press, 2007), esp. 83–160; and Peter Messent, *Mark Twain and Male Friendship: The Twichell, Howells, and Rogers Friendships* (New York: Oxford University Press, 2009), 63–81.

6. Andrews, *Nook Farm*, 70.

7. For Twichell's private anxieties about Twain in this regard, see Messent, *Mark Twain and Male Friendship*, 74.

8. *Mark Twain's Letters*, 4:506.

9. See Messent, *Mark Twain and Male Friendship*, 200n56.

10. Albert Bigelow Paine, *Mark Twain: A Biography* (New York: Harper, 1912), 2:631–32.

11. See, for instance, Andrews, *Nook Farm*, 72, and Steve Courtney, *Joseph Hopkins Twichell* (Athens: University of Georgia Press, 2008), 199. Courtney does, however, add, "But it is wrong to dismiss Paine's story entirely. [Twain] was thinking about the issues of life, death, and eternity in 1878, and could well have had arguments about religion with Twichell. . . . [He] was growing increasingly impatient with the hypocrisy of conventional religion."

12. The letter is undated but, from internal evidence, was written on Sunday, 11 August 1878. See also *Mark Twain and the Spiritual Crisis of His Age*, 7–9, where Harold K. Bush Jr. argues that Twain would remain sympathetic to many Christian values throughout most of his life.

13. In Twain's *Tramp Abroad* notebook, he wrote, "I keep a clergyman to remonstrate against my drinking—it gives zest & increase of appetite." See Frederick Anderson, Lin Salamo, and Bernard L. Stein, eds., *Mark Twain's Notebooks & Journals*, vol. 2 (Berkeley: University of California Press, 1975), 166.

14. Twichell Correspondence, Beinecke Rare Book & Manuscript Library, Yale University (henceforth Beinecke).

15. David C. Twichell, "Memoranda on His Mother's Death, 1910," Mark Twain Papers, Bancroft Library, University of California, Berkeley (hereafter Mark Twain Papers). This might refer only to the years up to the *Tramp Abroad* trip, but the grammar of the sentence suggests something more regular and extended.

16. Twain judged it ten miles, and spoke of it as a regular Saturday custom. See Benjamin Griffin and Harriet Elinor Smith, eds., *Autobiography of Mark Twain*, vol. 2 (Berkeley: University of California Press, 2013), 156, 536.

17. See, for instance, Bush, *Mark Twain and the Spiritual Crisis of his Age*, 126–35; Courtney, *Joseph Hopkins Twichell*, 112, 145–48, 204–7; and Messent, *Mark Twain and Male Friendship*, 71. See also *Mark Twain's Letters*, 5:287–90. Hawley's honorary title, "Father," was given

to him by those living on Hartford's East Side waterfront to whom he brought clothing, provisions, and prayers.

18. Bernard DeVoto, ed., *Mark Twain in Eruption: Hitherto Unpublished Pages about Men and Events* (New York: Harper, 1940). For more on this, see Messent, *Mark Twain and Male Friendship*, 47–50.

19. Russell Banks, "Introduction" to *A Tramp Abroad* (New York: Oxford University Press, 1996), xxxii.

20. See Justin Kaplan's description of the incident in *Mr. Clemens and Mark Twain: A Biography* (London: Jonathan Cape, 1967), 252–53.

21. Twain's mother lived in Keokuk, Iowa, with Orion and his wife.

22. Twain crossed out the words, "—a several thousand dollar plan."

23. Letter of 22 August 1883, in Henry Nash Smith and William M. Gibson, *Mark Twain–Howells Letters: The Correspondence of Samuel L. Clemens and William D. Howells, 1872–1910*, vol. 1 (Cambridge, Mass.: Belknap Press, 1960), 438–39. William Dean Howells, recognized by contemporaries as America's most important literary figure in the late nineteenth century, would become one of Twain's closest friends. The two men first met in 1869.

24. "All English" presumably means a blunt and unelaborated spelling-out of his annoyance. Twichell biographer Steve Courtney comments, "I've never found [the letter]—I think it went into Twichell's New England anti-unpleasantness shredder" (private correspondence).

25. Mark Twain Papers. One is reminded here of the maxim in *Pudd'nhead Wilson*: "An enemy can partly ruin a man, but it takes a good-natured injudicious friend to complete the thing and make it perfect." Edward H. House was a journalist on the *New York Tribune* when Twain first met him in 1867. He spent a decade from 1870 onward in Japan where he taught English and founded the English-language newspaper, the *Tokyo Times*.

26. Mark Twain Papers.

13. Twain to Twichell

19–22 March 1872. Elmira, New York

Born, in Elmira, N.Y., at 4.25 A.M., March 19, 1872, to the wife of Saml. L. Clemens, of Hartford, Conn., a daughter. Mother & child doing exceedingly well.

In witness whereof, &c.,

Sam[l]. L. Clemens.

Wrote Buffalo about Lawson.[1]

1. Salamo and Smith say that this letter was "probably directed to the Twichells" on the birth of eldest daughter Susy, as yet unnamed. The appended word ("Susie"), referring to the content of the letter, they write, "appears to be in the hand of Harmony Twichell." Susie / Susy is spelt variously by the two families: we use the latter spelling throughout. *Courant* journalist George Lawson would soon flee Hartford to avoid a bigamy charge, with a wife and two children having been discovered in Buffalo. Salamo and Smith assume Twichell had asked Twain to make enquiries in Buffalo about Lawson. See *Mark Twain's Letters*, 5:62–64.

14. Twichell to Twain

2 April 1872. Hartford, Connecticut

Hartford. April 2nd 1872

Dear Mark,

We were so taken aback by the sudden news of the nativity at Elmira that really we could not find breath for a speedy remark on the subject. And since we put off speech in the first moment, later silence has not signified. You deprived us of a luxury we had much reckoned on by your confounded precipitation. We had supposed that we should have ample scope to wait and wonder, and surmise and hope and expect, but lo, you cut us off from even a single hour of sweet uneasiness for you by your desperate earliness. The little maid ought to be called "Festina"—the hasty or hastening one. Well, God grant she may keep well ahead of all the world's worst troubles as long as she lives.

We greet and salute and bless her. And to her dear mother we send our best love. Now that we have had Livy among us, we find her absence irksome, and want her back. Indeed, about the first thing we thought of when your bulletin announced the birth was that now you would return sooner than you had been proposing. Is it so?

By the way Mark, you are not going to be in New York in the next few days, are you? For, you see, I am going down Saturday to stay till the following Wednesday—and going alone. So that we could get at least one regular old classic and attic night together in case we were there together. Again, our love to Livy.

Yours as ever

J. H. Twichell

Regards to *T.K.B.*[1]

P.S. A telegram just received upsets my plan of going to New York as within described. I shall not be there till Tuesday.[2]

1. Thomas K. Beecher.

2. Twain and Twichell may have met up in New York on Twain's 11 or 12 April (onward) visit. See *Mark Twain's Letters*, 5:75.

15. Twain to Twichell

20–22 December 1872. Hartford, Connecticut

P.S. Enclosed
is the money }

To-day, PM.

Dear Twichell—

I wrote a note to Dr Bushnell & abused you like a pickpocket—Oh I did give it to you![1]

Now you go straight off & get that book & take it to him and try to make your peace & get yourself forgiven. And tell him we Clemenses thank him just as sincerely & as cordially as we can for letting us down so gently & so kindly. And you must say that although mother has returned to Elmira, *we* are still here & shall be very glad indeed to try to make the new acquaintanceship as pleasant as if it bore the generous flavor of age.

Now you go & make *another* lot of blunders, you splendid old muggins!

Come around, you & Harmony, & I will read to you my (bogus) *protest of the Publishers against the proposed foreign copyright.*[2]

Yrs Ever

Mark.

Good news—Susie Crane is here! Come & see her—help us worship her. [Cross-written:]
Return the Doctor's letter to me.

1. Note now missing. Horace Bushnell was Twichell's mentor and minister of North Church of Christ, Hartford. Twain enclosed a letter from Bushnell with this letter (see *Mark Twain's Letters*, 5:256). It seems Twichell had somehow disrupted Twain's intention to get the gift of a book to Bushnell and Twain was now sending the money to Twichell to go and buy it. Approximate dating of letter according to Salamo and Smith.

2. The matter of international copyright and the protection of authors' rights was one that concerned Twain throughout his career. For more detail on this "(bogus) protest," see *Mark Twain's Letters*, 5:257.

16. Twain to Twichell

29 June 1873. London, England

London, June 29.

Dear Old Joe—

I consider myself *wholly* at liberty to decline to pay Chew anything, & at the same time strongly tempted to sue him into the bargain for coming so near ruining me.[1] If he hadn't happened to send me that thing in print, I would have used the story (like an innocent fool) & would straightway have been hounded to death as a plagiarist. It would have absolutely destroyed me. I cannot conceive of a man being such a hopeless ass (after serving as a legislative reporter, too,) as to imagine that I or any other literary man in his senses would consent to chew over old stuff that had already been in print. If that man weren't an infant in swaddling clothes, his only reply to our petition would have been "It has been in print." It makes me as mad as the very Old Harry every time I think of Mr. Chew & the frightfully narrow escape I have had at his hands. Con*found* Mr. Chew, with all my heart! I'm willing he should have ten dollars for his trouble of warming over his cold victuals—*cheer*fully willing to [pay] that—but no more. If I had had him near when his letter came, I would have got out my tomahawk & gone for him. He didn't tell the story half as well as you did, anyhow. I wish to goodness you were here this moment—nobody in our parlor but Livy & me,—& a very good view of London to the fore.[2] We have a luxuriously ample suite of apartments in Langham Hotel, 3d floor, our bedroom looking straight up Portland Place & our parlor having a noble array of great windows looking out upon both streets (Portland Place & the crook that joins it on to Regent street.)

9 P.M. Full twilight—
rich sunset tints lingering in the
west.[3]

I am not going to write anything—rather tell it when I get back. I love you & Harmony, & that is all the fresh news I've got, anyway. And I mean to *keep* that fresh, all the time.

Lovingly
Mark.

Am luxuriating in glorious old Pepys' Diary & smoking.

[Livy has added a note below the letter: "Indeed it is *fresh all the time, and we grow warm, and genial, and enthusiastic when we speak of Joseph or Harmony— Bless your dear old hearts we love you*

Livy—]

1. Evidently a Mr. Chew had told Twichell a story with publication potential. Twichell had suggested that Twain write the story up, sharing its profits with Chew. The project was aborted on Twain finding out that the story had already appeared in the newspapers. We see something of the way here (for this was not an isolated example) that Twichell tended to look for projects that might stimulate Twain's literary interest.

2. Twain and Livy were visiting England, a follow-up to Twain's very successful 1872 trip there. Twain was there in part to expedite British publication of *The Gilded Age.*

3. From "9 P.M." to "the west" is an insertion.

17. Twain to Twichell

5 January 1874. London, England

London, Jan. 5 1874.[1]

My Dear Old Joe:

I knew you would be likely to graduate into an ass if I came away; & so you have—if you have stopped smoking. However, I have a strong faith that it is not too late, yet, & that the judiciously managed influence of a bad example will fetch you back again.

I wish you *had* written me some news—Livy tells me precious little. She mainly writes to hurry me home & to tell me how much she respects me: but she's generally pretty slow on news. I had a letter from her along with yours, today, but she didn't tell me the book is out.[2] However, it's all right. I hope to be home 20 days from today, & then I'll see *her,* & that will make up for a whole year's dearth of news. I am right down grateful that she is looking strong & "lovelier than ever." I only wish I could see her look her level best, once—I think it would be a vision.

I have just spent a good part of this day browsing through the Royal Academy Exhibition of Landseer's paintings.[3] They fill four or five great salons, & must number a good many hundreds. This is the only opportunity ever to see them, because the finest of them belong to the queen & she keeps them in her private apartments. Ah, they're wonderfully beautiful! There are such rich moonlights & dusks in "The Challenge" & "The Combat;" & in that long flight of birds across a lake in the subdued flush of sunset (or sunrise—for no man can ever tell tother [*sic*] from which in a picture, except it has the filmy morning mist breathing itself up from the water). And there is such a grave analytical profundity in the faces of "The Connoisseurs;" & such pathos in the picture of the fawn suckling its dead mother, on a snowy waste, with only the blood in the footprints to hint that she is not asleep. And the way he makes animals absolute flesh & blood—insomuch that if the room were darkened ever so little & a motionless living animal placed beside a painted one, no man could tell which was which.

I interrupted myself here, to drop a line to Shirley Brooks & suggest a cartoon for Punch.[4] It was this. In one of the Academy salons (in the suite where these pictures are), a fine bust of Landseer stands on a pedestal in the centre of the room. I suggest that some of Landseer's best known animals be represented as having come down out of their frames in the moonlight & grouped themselves about the bust in mourning attitudes.

Well, old man, I am powerful glad to hear from you & shall be powerful glad to see you & Harmony. I am not going to the provinces because I cannot get halls that are large enough.[5] I always felt cramped in Hanover Square Rooms, but I find that everybody here speaks with awe & respect of that prodigious place, & wonder that I could fill it so long.[6]

I am *hoping* to be back in 20 days, but I have *so much* to go home to & enjoy with a jubilant joy, that it seems hardly possible that it can ever come to pass in so uncertain a world as this.

I have read the *novel* here, & I like it.[7] I have made no inquiries about it, though. My interest in a book ceases with the printing of it.

With a world of love,

Saml.

1. Twain had quickly returned to London after taking Livy home to Hartford.

2. The American edition of *The Gilded Age*, published on 23 December 1873, a day after the British edition.

3. Popular Victorian painter Edwin Henry Landseer, best known for his anthropomorphic, sentimental, and moralistic animal paintings. Landseer had died on 1 October 1873.

4. Charles William Shirley Brooks, editor of *Punch.* Nothing came of this suggestion.
5. For Twain's highly popular lectures.
6. Hanover Square Rooms, the main concert hall in London with seating for nine hundred plus. Twain lectured there some twenty-nine times in October and December 1874.
7. *The Gilded Age.*

18. Twain to the Twichells

11 June 1874. Elmira, New York

Elmira, June 11.

My Dear old Joe & Harmony:

The baby is here & is the great American Giantess—weighing 7¾ pounds, & all solid meat. We had to wait a good long time for her, but she was full compensation when she *did* come.[1] The labor pains fooled along during the evening, after a fashion; became more pronounced at midnight & so continued till 7 AM; then *very* severe for 15 minutes, & the trouble was over. Mrs. Gleason & Della came up early in the evening & went to bed right away, up stairs, & neither of them were ever called till 15 minutes before the babe was born.[2] Livy don't call for people till she needs them. She waltzed through this ordeal, walking the floor & sewing baby clothes in the bravest possible way. And even I was cool—slept a good part of the time. I *am* ashamed of that, but I couldn't keep my eyes open. And besides, this baby has fooled along so much that I hadn't much confidence in it. It is an admirable child, though, & has intellect. It puts its fingers against its brow & thinks. It was born with a caul, & so of course possesses the gift of second sight.[3] The Modoc was delighted with it, & gave it her doll at once.[4] There is nothing selfish about the Modoc. She is fascinated with the new baby. The Modoc rips & tears around out doors, most of the time, & consequently is as hard as a pine knot & as brown as an Indian. She is bosom friend to all the chickens, ducks, turkeys & guinea hens on the place. Yesterday as she marched along the winding path that leads up the hill through the red clover beds to the summer-house, there was a long procession of these fowls stringing contentedly after her, led by a stately rooster who can look over the Modoc's head. The devotion of these vassals has been purchased with daily largess of Indian meal, & so the Modoc, attended by her body-guard, moves in state wherever she goes.

Susie Crane has built the loveliest study for me, you ever saw. It is octagonal, with a peaked roof, each octagon filled with a spacious window,

& it sits perched in complete isolation on top of an elevation that commands leagues of valley & city & retreating ranges of distant blue hills. It is a cosy nest, with just room in it for a sofa & a table & three or four chairs—& when the storms sweep down the remote valley & the lightning flashes above the hills beyond, & the rain beats upon the roof over my head, imagine the luxury of it! It stands 500 feet above the valley & 2½ miles from it.[5]

However, one must not write all day. We send continents of love to you & yours.

Affectionately

Mark.

Mrs. Gleason's father, whom she worshiped, died the morning of the day she had to come up here to look after Livy.[6]

1. Clara Langdon Clemens had been born on 8 June. The birth had at one point evidently been expected earlier, in May. Joe and Harmony by now had three children. David, their second son and fourth child, would arrive four months after Clara, on 9 October 1874.

2. Livy's doctor, Rachel Brooks Gleason, was the fourth American woman to get a medical degree. Her daughter Della (Adele) would be awarded her medical degree from the University of Michigan in 1875.

3. Popular superstition. If the caul covered the head of the child at birth it signified second sight—and other gifts (good luck, etc.).

4. Susy. Her nickname, the Modoc, was a reference to the style of her hair—at a time of recent warfare in the California-Oregon border country between the U.S. Army and the Native American Modoc tribe.

5. The study has since been moved to the grounds of Elmira College. This was to protect it from vandalism at Quarry Farm and to make it more accessible. It is still possible to visit the original site, but trees and bushes now mask the view Twain once enjoyed.

6. Mrs. Gleason's father was Reuben Brooks, a wealthy farmer from Vermont and sometime member of the Vermont state legislature. He had moved to Elmira some twenty years before his death.

19. Twain to Twichell

29? July 1874.[1] *Elmira, New York*

My Dear Old Joe:

Stop our postman (I would have written him if I had been sure of his name) & tell him somebody keeps carrying my letters to the Courant office. I telegraphed the postmaster the other day, but it didn't do any good. I suppose he thought I was in a petulant humor—which was not the case.[2]

Livy doing *tolerably* well. Little baby has the peculiarity of crying, & Livy sits up till 2 in the morning to marvel at the novelty. We shall institute a change in the nurse-department right away. We must have a nurse that has a native faculty for soothing little people. We must have one that breathes ether from her nostrils & oozes chloral hydrate from every pore. We must have one who is worthy to stand in the pulpit.

How about the Beecher Scandal *now*?[3] If Mr. B. had done this in the *first* place no doubt it would have been better. And by George it's *Tilton* that is on trial, at last!—& before a packed jury. Beecher's own people say it is Tilton that is on trial. I like the idea of a man insulting my wife & then I being tried for the heinous offense of complaining about it. But I have no sympathy with Tilton. He began by being a thundering fool & a milksop, & ends by being a hopeless lunatic—& a lunatic of that poor kind that hasn't even spirit enough to be interesting. Mr. Tilton never *has* been entitled to any sympathy since the day he heard the news & did not go straight & kill Beecher & then humbly seek forgiveness for displaying so much vivacity.

Love to you all.

Ys always

Mark.

1. This is an approximate dating given by the Mark Twain Papers.

2. Earlier that summer, when Twain was in Hartford, Livy's letters to him had been addressed to the *Courant* office—thus the postman's later mistake.

3. The ongoing Henry Ward Beecher adultery trial was a matter of keen interest to both Twain and Twichell, and to the whole Nook Farm community (which included Beecher's sisters, Isabella Beecher Hooker and Harriet Beecher Stowe, author of *Uncle Tom's Cabin*). Theodore Tilton, with whose wife, Elizabeth, Beecher was accused of having an affair, had been arrested on 28 July on charges of libeling Beecher. The adultery case finally ended in a hung jury with Beecher's ministerial reputation relatively undamaged.

20. Twichell to Twain

13 August 1874. Franklin Park, New Jersey

Franklin Park, N.J.
Aug 13th 1874.

Dear Mark,

Day after tomorrow, at 12 o'clock, noon, I sail, God willing, for the land of Incas and—guano, *Peru*. You have doubtless heard of it before now.[1]

I am going with Yung Wing on Celestial business, and expect to be absent two months.[2] We journey by way of the Isthmus. A doctor is going along to tackle and at once annihilate any presumptious malady that may dare to so much as wink at us.

I write just to say good-bye and God bless you. Harmony will return to Hartford in about a month, and I want you to comfort her forlornness a little, by looking in upon her now and then. With cords of love to Livy and Susie and the other one.

Yours as ever

Joe.

P.S. *Gov. Fuller* called on us in Hartford a few days ago and we had a delightful talk with him.[3]

1. Twain, indeed, had written about guano and Peru in chapter 50 of *Roughing It* (1872).

2. Twain and Livy were out of Hartford until September, when they would finally move into the Farmington Avenue house. Twichell refers here to a visit to Peru with fellow Hartford resident Yung Wing (the first Chinese person to receive a degree from an American university and, by this date, a U.S. citizen) to look into the conditions of the Chinese workforce in that country. They were accompanied by Dr. Edward W. Kellogg, brother of Yung's fiancée, Mary Kellogg. Yung's Chinese Educational Mission (which brought young boys to New England to educate them and—though this was not a stated purpose of the mission—to Christianize them) was strongly supported by Twichell, who would later enlist Twain's help when its existence was put in threat by the Chinese government. For more on this, see Courtney, *Joseph Hopkins Twichell*, 144–48, 201–7. Yung's U.S. citizenship would be revoked with the Chinese Exclusion Act of 1882.

3. Frank Fuller, a close friend of Twain's from his Nevada days, was the former acting governor of Utah.

21. Twichell to Twain

22 August 1874. At sea.

P.M. SS. "Colon."
Approaching Aspinwall.[1]
Aug. 22nd 1874

Dear Mark,

Who of all possible candidates should a kindly Providence give me for a fellow passenger on this ship but your old friend Capt. Wakeman![2] I could hardly have had a better. I first saw the Ancient Mariner in the company's office in New York and took an immediate interest in him. After we came on board I overheard a couple of gentlemen speaking of him. That informed me who and what he was. Presently, watching my chance, I encountered him making his way across the deck with considerable difficulty—the ship was rolling and he is badly paralyzed, you know—gave him my arm, got him a seat and opened conversation with him; which conversation has remained open a good share of the time ever since. He hadn't said ten words before I tasted richness, and I have had a rare feast of it, as you will easily believe. I never was more entertained in my life. Really, I hate to think of parting from him as I must to-night or tomorrow. You'll be glad to hear of this lucky hap, and that's why I write to tell you of it.

He led off with a chapter or two of nautical adventure—in fact that subject occupied our first session. And he gave me certain documents of his own composition to read which I presume you have seen. I took a few notes however to show you. But later, he branched off into other discourse taking a wide range. What a delicious old misanthrope he is—what an entertaining denunciator! And, oh Mark, what a titanic commentator of the Old Testament!! I've heard of men who were "mighty in the Scripture," but I never had the privilege of meeting such an expounder as he. There are no difficulties to him.

Well, well, I didn't set out to describe him to you—, which were quite superfluous,—but only to tell you of my adventure. The thought that you had heard the same fascinating and unspeakably amusing talk, added to my relish of it. But I mean to tell him before I say good bye, or *when* I say good bye that I am a minister. I think it will tickel [*sic*] him to recall certain of his remarks on the profession.

It transpired almost as soon as we got together that he knew you. He had a good deal to say about your books, which he admires enthusiastically. By and by he told me of his having written to ask you to write up his career and expressed himself as much disappointed that you declined the job. And really, I was sorry myself that you had to refuse him. 'Twould have done him so much good to have you for his chronicler.

He says that Ross Browne is going to do it for him, but you would have been better.[3]

I have got up an immense affection of the dear old gentleman who I can see has a gentle and true heart and is harmless as thunder. It was fun to hear him change off from his wrath against missionaries and Copernicus and Isaac Newton and all the whole race of humbugs that have combined to spoil the glories of the ancient world and corrupt the South Sea Islanders to the tender tone of husband and father in speaking of his own family, the tricks and sweet sayings of his children &c.

We have had a most charming voyage to this point and I have enjoyed every minute of it. I haven't had the slightest qualm of sea-sickness. I have read novels, perused the passengers, smoked, colleagued with Capt. Wakeman and written love letters to Harmony. It is nine years to-day since I proposed to that dear girl, and God knows, it was the wisest act of my life. If ever I was inspired it was then. What happy, and for my part I own undeserved fortunes, have fallen to our lot. But I must drop that, for I begin to snivel at once,—I'm so far from home you know.

I send my love unfeigned to Livy. Bless her dear heart. There's none truer. To you, old fellow, I waft from these summer seas the best wishes of which I am capable. Yes, Mark, and a kiss,—of which I am not ashamed. I anticipate with something akin to rapture the good times we'll have next winter at our respective firesides. No, I'll work next winter i.e. I'll confine myself to one hour's loafing a week.

As ever

Joe

1. Aspinwall is now named Colón (Panama).

2. Twain had met Edgar ("Ned") Wakeman in 1866 on his way from California to New York, via Panama, on the side-wheeler *America.* Wakeman was the ship's captain and his personality and eccentricities greatly appealed to Twain. He figured in various guises in a number of Twain's works, including the unfinished *Captain Stormfield's Visit to Heaven.* See *Autobiography of Mark Twain,* 2:192–95.

3. John Ross Browne, best known for his *Etchings of a Whaling Cruise* (1846). Wakeman's biography was published in 1878 as *The Log of an Ancient Mariner,* with the help not of Browne but of Wakeman's daughter, Minnie Wakeman-Curtis.

22. Twichell to Twain

27 January 1875. Hartford, Connecticut

Wed a.m.

Dear Mark,

You see how badly the padre feels, and also what a pleasant humor he is of. We mustn't give up visiting him. His heart is evidently set upon it.[1]

Joe

1. A reference to one of the visits Twichell and Twain tried to make to Father Joseph O'Hagan, Twichell's Civil War comrade and, at that time, president of Holy Cross College in Worcester, Massachusetts. See the letter from O'Hagan to Twichell on 26 January which is excerpted in Michael B. Frank and Harriet Elinor Smith, eds., *Mark Twain's Letters,* vol. 6: 1874–1875 (Berkeley: University of California Press, 2002), 367.

23. Twichell to Twain

29 March 1875? Hartford, Connecticut[1]

Monday Morning

Dear Mark,

If you had only let me know that you were dead (which considering our past relations would have been no more than decent) I would have attended the funeral *with pleasure*.

It would have been much as ever though that I could go for I really believe I was never so busy in my life as I have been since I got home from New York ten days ago. I had to go to New Haven Sunday last week, I had to preach Good Friday, spend Saturday afternoon at a funeral, and preach three times yesterday. But I have been wanting to see you all the while intensely, for I had a budget of fresh matter of various kinds from New York to open, most of which has now evaporated I fear. I had a notion that you might possibly drop in on us, but finally fell back on our seeing you at church (or after) yesterday. I was too dog tired to come over after evening service or I would have done it. I would come over this morning but I have another funeral to go to at 10 o'clock, the other side of the city. I shall hope to meet you at the Club tonight, if you are there.[2]

My sister has been here for a fortnight with her two children—another reason that has kept me at home.[3]

But what I want to know *now* is—Would you like to go down with me Wednesday to New Haven and spend the evening with the boys? I have to attend a College Corporation meeting at 3 p.m., but the evening will be free and we can have a good time. Please make up your mind about it as I want to send down word. It will do to tell me tonight, but answer now if you can just as well.

Yours, (rather grieved, yet disposed to accept any excuse you may invent)

Joe

1. Almost certainly this date. Twichell had been in New York (with Twain) at the Beecher trial, 16–19 March ("ten days ago"), had preached at Yale on Sunday 21 March, and was to attend a Yale Corporation meeting on 31 March (Wednesday). All noted in Twichell's journal.

2. The Monday Evening Club.

3. Twichell's younger sister, Sarah Jane Twichell, had married Edward Asa Ware, first president of Atlanta University, in 1869. Their two children were Edward Twichell Ware and Gertrude Huntingdon Ware.

24. Twichell to Twain

Circa 10 April 1875. Hartford, Connecticut

Tuesday

Dear Mark,

Heaven knows I don't want to bore you, and that I am truly grieved to add a feather to the burden of manuscript reading that must be one of the trials of your life. But what else can I do? Here Dean Sage sends me this MS (he said nothing about it when I was down there) with the enclosed notes explaining why he sends it.[1] Now *I'm* no judge of such a matter. The piece is to me very interesting, in its facts especially, and the style seems suited to those facts. But what the performance is in a literary point of view, I can't say. And I feel rather embarrassed. I don't want to inflict upon Howells the discomfort of saying "no" if it is a cock sure thing that he must say it.[2]

Will you, Mark, like a good fellow, just run the thing through when you have a chance—to-day or tomorrow—so that you can tell me when I call what I'd better do.

I enclose (my modesty mildly protesting) a notice the College journal gives me, which I don't want you to lose. Be so kind however as to peruse it. I don't suppose you can guess how sweet a morsel it is to me, but maybe it will help you to appreciate me.[3] That's what I want. I don't think you are as proud of me as you ought to be. When the world finds me out and does me justice you will (too late) be sorry that, having had a better chance than almost anybody else, you failed to see my "p'ints."[4] We do hope Livy is better.[5]

Yours ever

Joe

1. Dean Sage was one of Twichell's oldest and closest friends. He was the son of successful lumberman and businessman Henry S. Sage, who, incidentally, was a friend and business associate of Jervis Langdon. Dean Sage's own considerable wealth (he worked in the family business) would fund the Yale University education of three of Twichell's sons.

2. The date on this letter is earlier than that suggested by the Mark Twain Papers (8 May 1876). Sage had left a second manuscript with Twichell around that time for possible publication in the *Atlantic*, thus the Mark Twain Papers date. But Howells—in a letter to Sage himself—then refers back to an earlier Sage piece ("Ten Days' Sport on Salmon Rivers," *Atlantic Monthly*, August 1875, 142–51). See *Mark Twain–Howells Letters*, 139. Internal evidence suggests it was this earlier submission that Twichell is writing about here. And see the Twichell Journal entry excerpted in *Mark Twain's Letters*, 6:453.

3. Twichell writes in a journal entry for 21 March 1875, "March 21 preached at College Chapel in exchange w/ Dr Porter: Yale Record comment 'the sweetest sugarplum I have

had in a long time.' 'It was a simple, earnest discourse, amply illustrated, admirably delivered and treating the subject in such a manner that its application to each individual could be readily understood. . . . [T]his man seemed to understand his audience better and to know what they needed. . . . [T]he sermons which are best remembered and oftenest quoted are not those which deal in metaphysics, but those which appeal strongly and personally to that better nature which exists somewhere in every man'" (Beinecke). All Twichell Journal references henceforth are courtesy of the Beinecke Rare Book & Manuscript Library, Yale University.

4. In "The Celebrated Jumping Frog of Calaveras County," perhaps his best-known story, Twain has the owner of one frog in a jumping competition say of his opponent's frog: "I don't see any p'ints about that frog that's any better'n any other frog."

5. On 28 March 1875, Twain wrote to David Gray, co-owner of the *Buffalo Courier*, saying that Livy was regaining her strength but that she was "threatened by diphtheria" (Mark Twain Papers).

25. Twichell to Twain

18 April 1875. Hartford, Connecticut

THE COURANT.
HAWLEY, GOODRICH & CO., PUBLISHERS
HARTFORD, CONN. 187_[1]

Sunday Night

Dear Mark,

Perhaps I shall not see you at Concord tomorrow, and so I write to tell you—and I grieve to do it—that you will in vain expect me in Cambridge Tuesday.[2] I must return home by the earliest train Tuesday morning.

The cause is funerals.

One of the Chinese boys Ts'au Kia Tsioh died last night and [Yung] Wing has asked me to give him a Christian burial. Poor little fellow—he's a long way from home, and I feel a tender kindness for him. The service is to be at the Mission Headquarters at 1 o'clock. Then at 3 o'clock I must officiate at the funeral of old Mr. Root, A. C. Dunham's father-in-law.[3] So I must give up the ornamental and luxurious feature of the trip entirely. But it hurts, I assure you.

My love to the Howellses, every one of them. I hope you have been behaving yourself.

My love [to] Mr. & Mrs. Howell, Amen.

Yours aff.

Joe

P.S. Livy was in church today looking—oh my!—beautifully!!

1. Twichell's stationery has the letterhead of the *Courant.*

2. Twichell had traveled to Concord to attend the centennial celebrations commemorating the 1775 revolutionary battle against British troops, and had been scheduled to meet up with Twain and Howells in Cambridge the following day. See *Mark Twain's Letters,* 4:451n1, for an account of Twain and Howells's own unsuccessful attempt to reach Concord.

3. Austin Cornelius Dunham was a prominent Hartford businessman and philanthropist. Mr. Root is James Root, once a pioneer and Indian fighter, who had returned to his Hartford home in middle life. He was a wealthy man due to his property holdings out West.

26. Twichell to Twain

21 May 1875. Hartford, Connecticut

Friday Morning

Dear Mark,

Here is a letter from Dean Sage. What do you say?[1]

Harmony is ailing and if she keeps it up I can't leave home next week of course. But if she is on her pins again shortly I will go with you any day you may fix.

Is Tom Beecher at your house? If he is give him my love and tell him that he *must* preach for me Sunday morning, I implore him.

By the way won't his visit interfere with your Trial going?[2]

My love to dear Livy. I've been swelling with gratitude to her ever since I knew that she had invited poor Mrs. P. to the club. But I'll never ask her to do it again. Now that it is too late to help it, I begin to think that I went too far, even with her, in proferring such a request—for I suppose that in her eyes it amounted to a request.

Yours aff

Joe

1. Sage's letter, enclosed, invites Twichell and Twain to revisit the Beecher trial (they had attended in April) and also invites Twichell to go salmon fishing in Canada. The former invitation was not taken up, but Twichell did go fishing with Sage in July.

2. Another reference to Henry Ward Beecher's adultery trial (see Letter 19, note 3), which Twain and Twichell had attended 13–15 April. Both men took an ongoing interest in the case and stayed with Sage during these Brooklyn visits.

27. Twichell to Twain

16 June 1875. Hartford, Connecticut

Wed. morning

Dear Mark,

I am just back from a wedding (my sister's) in the country.[1] It would appear that the Hartford public have somewhat got the notion that I am the proper medium of approach to you, which beyond a certain limit is unpleasant—to me any how.

Here is a note I received yesterday from the Supt. of the H.P. & F.R.R. inviting us (but you more especially I suppose) to go to Boston to-morrow on an excursion—leaving here at 5 a.m. and getting back at 10.30 p.m.[2] He enclosed tickets (free) corresponding. I suppose a very pleasant company of Hartford men will go along. I mean to go, and of course shall be made happy by your company which is always my delight. But, mind, I don't *ask* you to.

May be I'll be over this evening, but I thought I would send this right over that you might have time to consider.

Harmony is better.

Yours aff.

Joe

1. Twichell's half-sister, Mary Delight Twichell, married Alfred Henry Hall on 15 June 1875.

2. Almost certainly the Hartford, Providence and Fishkill Railroad. Twichell's journal for 17 June speaks of the Bunker Hill centennial: "invited M.T. to go with me but he being immersed in the new story he is writing [i.e., *Tom Sawyer*] declined."

28. Twichell to Twain

22 December 1875. Hartford, Connecticut[1]

Wed. morning

Read (if you haven't) the extracts from Omar Khayyam on the first page of this morning's Courant.[2] I think we'll have to get that book. I never yet came across anything that uttered certain thoughts of mine so adequately. And it's only a translation. Read it, and we'll talk it over. There is something in it very like the passage of Emerson you read me last night, in fact identical with it in thought.[3]

Surely this Omar was a great poet. Anyhow he has given me an immense revelation this morning.

Hoping that you are better,

J.H.T.

1. This "post-card," as Twain describes it, was transcribed as part of his autobiographical dictations of 7 October 1907. See Benjamin Griffin and Harriet Elinor Smith, eds., *Autobiography of Mark Twain*, vol. 3 (Berkeley: University of California Press, 2015), 158–59. Twain described it there as an item "out of the long ago." In fact, the extracts to which Twichell refers in the card were printed on Wednesday, 22 December 1875, making this, as good as certainly, its date.

2. "Omar Khayyam: The Astronomer-Poet of Persia," including forty-two quatrains from *The Rubáiyát of Omar Khayyám*, was published in the *Hartford Courant* of 22 December 1875. An accompanying article noted the publication by Bernard Quaritch, London, of an edition of the famed Edward FitzGerald translation. Twain and Twichell remained interested in the Rubáiyát all their lives—and see Twain's bitter parody of it in his 1898 "AGE—a Rubáiyát."

3. Ralph Waldo Emerson, American Transcendentalist poet, philosopher, and essay writer.

29. Twichell to Twain

23 December 1875. Hartford, Connecticut

Thursday Morning

Dear Mark,

Andy Hammond (West Point cadet) is coming home Christmas bringing some fellows with him.[1] I have invited him and them to dinner Monday. I don't know yet that they will come, but if they do I want you to come over—you and Charley Warner—and dine with us also. It will be *such* a treat to the boys if you can.

I will see you again about it. I write now to give you the chance to plead a previous engagement in case you are asked to do something you would like to escape next Monday night. It was one thing that I called to see you about yesterday and I couldn't remember it. Yet I knew there was something *omitted* and went away conscious that the business I had done had not discharged my mind. Queer, isn't it?

Yours aff.

Joe

1. Andrew G. Hammond, who would go on to have a long military career and to lead troops in Cuba during the Spanish-American War. Twain came to have a close relationship with the United States Military Academy at West Point, New York, sometimes lecturing there

and, in a fifteen-year period starting in 1876, visiting at least ten times. See Philip W. Leon, *Mark Twain and West Point* (Toronto: ECW Press, 1996). Twichell would accompany him on some of these visits.

30. Twain to Twichell

29 or 30 December 1875. Hartford, Connecticut

Religious Conundrum suggested by my present disease.[1]

Question: If a Congress of Presbyterians is a PRESBYtery, what is a Congress of dissenters?

Answer: A DYSentery.

Joe, you can sell the above to some religious paper or get it off on Dean Sage as original.

Yrs Ever
Mark

1. The word "Religious" is an insertion here. On 30 December 1875, Twichell noted in a journal entry that this note had been sent by "M.T. being sick with an attack of *dysentery*."

31. Twichell to Twain

3 February 1876. Hartford, Connecticut

Thursday a.m.

Dear Mark,

I have just refused to ask you to lecture or read in a case in which I would have hardly refused anything I could do but that. Mrs. G. F. Davis of Washington St. representing the Orphan Asylum now caught in a pecuniary crisis, is the party I turned away, not without regret and I confess, considerable compunction.[1] But I have sworn not to let my personal relations to you be utilized in that way. I had to do it in self defense, and in decency.

<u>But</u>, if this most excellent lady gets at you through any other channel, I advise you to grant her at least an audience. I almost wish I had excepted orphans when I made my vow.

There is no trick in this note i.e. I did not tell Mrs. Davis I would write it.

I shall be vastly grieved to miss dear Howells' visit if he is here over Sunday. I am going out of town.

To Father [David] Hawley's funeral, now with a sorrowful heart.[2] How glad you must be, how *very* glad to think of the comfort you gave him. Today it is worth to you a thousand times more than all the trouble it cost.

Yours aff

Joe

1. Lucy Strong Davis, wife of Gustavus F. Davis (president of the Hartford City National Bank). She was the Hartford Orphan Asylum's corresponding secretary.

2. Hawley had died on 31 January.

32. Twichell to Twain

8 February 1876. Hartford, Connecticut

Tuesday a.m.

Dear Mark,

I have chosen the 28th for our visit to West Point, and written to Andy Hammond accordingly. That's the best time for us, and the boys ought to conform to our convenience. It is only reasonable that they should.

What do you mean about one of Patrick's children? Or you mean that it has the scarlet fever? If so, what do you mean by saying it was all right the next day? That's not the kind we give. However, I don't suppose that makes any difference. If any body hereabouts should break a leg within the next six months, we should no doubt be held accountable for it.[1]

The hospital is lively and happy this morning.

We shall know by the latter part of the week, probably, how much longer it is to be kept up.

Yours aff

J.H.T.

1. These paragraphs refer to the Twichell family's being placed in quarantine for scarlet fever during January and February, though Twichell says in his journal, "our visitation was of the mildest type." Patrick McAleer was Twain's coachman.

33. Twichell to Twain

19 February 1876. Hartford, Connecticut

Sat a.m.

Dear Mark,

Home last night at midnight.

Here is a letter from Kozima.[1] The news concerning House (if it be news) concerns you as his friend.[2]

As for Kozima, may be (though I hope not) we shall have yet to consider the expediency of raising the means of keeping him here till he is through college.

Love to Livy. I suppose I shall see you Sunday eve.

Joe

1. Noriyuki Kojima and Kakichi Mitsukuri were two students brought to the United States by Edward H. House. Both were boarded and otherwise aided by members of the Nook Farm circle. Kojima studied at Cornell University and became a noted architect in Japan. Mitsukuri gained his doctorates in the United States, going on to become a zoologist, diplomat, and academic.

2. This "news" is unknown.

34. Twichell to Twain

8 May 1876. Hartford, Connecticut

Monday Morning

Dear Mark,

Dean and Sarah are coming tomorrow and to our house.[1] As they will arrive quite early in the morning, (coming by boat) and as Sarah is sick, and as Harmony is in such a plight, I must give up going to Boston with you.[2] I'm mighty sorry for it for I had luxuriated in the prospect of the trip. But there's no help for it that I can see. I ought to be on hand when Dean comes. I hope you'll have a good time. Give my love to Howells and his wife, also, the enclosed photograph of Dr. Bushnell.

I hope we shall want you and Livy to come over here to tea in the course of the week. It will depend on Sarah's condition.

Anyhow you must come over and see Dean.

We'll go together to a good game of base-ball, if there is one.[3]

Yours aff.

Joe

1. Dean Sage and his wife.

2. The Twichells' fifth child, also named Harmony, would be born on 4 June 1876: thus, presumably, the "plight" of Harmony (senior). On 26 April Twain had written to Howells that he and Livy "think of going to Boston May 7th to see Anna Dickinson's *debut* on the 8th." (Dickinson was a reformer and lecturer known for her work on abolition and the rights of women. She was at this stage of her life planning to become a playwright and actress.) By 4 May he had changed his plans slightly, aiming to arrive on 8 June without Livy but with Twichell. See *Mark Twain–Howells Letters*, 133, 134, 136.

3. Twain and Twichell went periodically to watch the Hartford Dark Blues play at the Ball Club Grounds near the Colt factory. In May 1875 a boy stole Twain's umbrella at a game. Twain placed an advertisement in the *Courant* offering a five-dollar reward for the umbrella and "$200 for [the boy's] remains."

35. Twain to Twichell

25 December 1876. Hartford, Connecticut (Inscription in The Adventures of Tom Sawyer*)*

To Joseph H. Twichell
from his true friend
S. L. Clemens

Christmas 1876[1]

1. Twain gave Twichell the book at a carol concert in the Twichell house. It was apparently Twichell's son, Edward, who would later say, "Mark often said that writing *Tom Sawyer* was fathers idea but that he was determined not to corrupt us by sharing the proceeds" (Mark Twain Papers).

36. Twichell to Twain

25 June 1877. Hartford, Connecticut

Hartford, June 25

Dear Mark,

I send you by mail to-day [Sabine] Baring-Gould's novel "In Exitu Israel", which it has taken me longer than I thought to procure.

And I seize the occasion—in fact I have been waiting for it—to tell you again how much I value our late trip to Bermuda and how grateful I am to you for your kindness in inviting me to it.[1] Ever since we got home I have felt that it would be necessary for me to shed a little ink on the subject before I was done with it i.e. as a matter between you and me.

The more I think it over, the more impressed I am with the fact that we (or I) had a splendid time—the more conscious I am of having enjoyed it, as I have enjoyed few things in all my life. I had to work so for a fortnight after our return that I could not fairly compose my mind to a review of what we saw and did. But now that I am somewhat less intensely occupied, it comes over me night and day as a dream of delights. What a happy four days we spent ashore—how innocent and mirthful! I was more like a boy in my feelings than I remember being for many a year.

I find that I derived very marked physical benefit from the recreation and rest I had, and furnished my mind with a rich stock of new impressions as well. Put it down as an oasis! I'm afraid I shall not see as green a spot again soon. And it was *your* invention and *your* gift. And your company was the best of it. Indeed, I never took more comfort in being with you than on this journey; which, my boy, is saying a great deal.

Well, Mark, I thank you for everthing, and may God bless you and yours for your goodness to me and mine. Amen.

A rumor has reached us that Clara was sick on the way to Elmira. We judge, however, that her illness was brief, or we should have heard more about it.

Dean Sage got home a fortnight ago and a few days after had a violent attack of his malady, from which he is slowly recovering and expects to come up this week or next to spend a day or two with us. Will Sage—to whom I wrote making inquiry—says that they are all a good deal discouraged about Dean, as it is plain that he cannot endure many attacks like this last.[2]

All of us are well. Six weeks more and we are off for the Adirondacks—six groaning weeks—while you repose like gods on the heights of your calm cool Hill.[3] Tell me what you think of "In Exitu." With love to Livy & the girls.

Yours aff.

Joe

1. Twain and Twichell had visited Bermuda together 16–24 May 1877. Always generous to his much poorer friend, Twain paid Twichell's way, writing up the holiday as "Some Rambling Notes of an Idle Excursion" (1877). Twain reported to Howells in its aftermath, "Joe Twichell and I roamed about Bermuda day & night & never ceased to gabble & enjoy." *Mark Twain–Howells Letters*, 178 (29 May 1879). On this trip, see Courtney, *Joseph Hopkins Twichell*, 193–95.

2. William Henry Sage, Dean's brother. He, too, was in the family lumber business and, like Dean, a benefactor of Cornell University.

3. That is, at Quarry Farm.

37. Twain to Twichell

27 June 1877. Elmira, New York

Elmira, June 27

Dear old Joe—

Your letter came today—thanks for it, & thanks for the generous thanks you filled it with, & which I do not deserve in the least, but accept & enjoy just as happily & gratefully as if I did. It was much the joyousest trip I ever had, Joe—not a heartache in it, not a twinge of conscience. I often come to myself out of a reverie & detect an undertone of thought that had been thinking itself without volition of mine: viz: If we had only had ten days of those walks & talks instead of four!

I sent those 2 articles to Howells & have completed our trip in 2 more since I came here. I like the last two ever so much; but I have written to Howells & suggested the destruction of the 2 I read to you. In my closing chapter I have got in your story of the 2 dying soldiers & the coffin; if that doesn't travel the rounds, then this is an unappreciative world. I got in the cabbage palms in due & solemn state; & the white houses; & Alfred; & the soup & chicken of St George's & that young girl there; & Moore's chair which we didn't see; & the absent tramps; & a blast at our health officer, & upwards of several other things. I like those 2 chapters.[1]

You grieve us to death with your news about Dean Sage. I am conscious of a stubborn inward refusal to accept of this impending dispensation—a sort of resentment about it that is afraid to formulate itself. There are so *many* we could spare!—& that *he* should be singled out! This is wicked, no doubt, but it is at least honest. And justifiable.[2]

We all of this household send love & God bless you's to your [*sic*] & yours.

Ys Ever

Mark.

Exitu-Israel has just come—many thanks, Joe—I'll give you an opinion. Been reading a lot of French rot here & am glad to get this.[3]

1. Twain is referring to "Some Rambling Notes of an Idle Excursion," published in the *Atlantic* in four parts beginning in October 1877. Among the incidents Twain recounts is one Twichell observed during the Civil War, of a competition between two dying soldiers for the only coffin available and its grimly comic finale.

2. Whatever the nature of this problem, Sage would live until 1902.

3. This after-note is an insertion. In his 6 August 1877 letter to Mary P. Fairbanks, Twain describes what he is reading at the time, mentioning *In Exitu Israel.* He calls it "a very able

novel by Baring-Gould, the purpose of which is to show the effect of some of the most odious of the privileges of the French nobles under *l'ancien regème* [*sic*], & of the dischurching of the Catholic church by the National Assembly in '92."

38. Twichell to Twain

25 July 1877. Hartford, Connecticut

Hartford July 25

Dear Mark,

I hear that a full and circumstantial account of last week's affair at your house has appeared in the Boston Herald.[1] I want you to understand that it has not been through me that it has attained this publicity. Charley W. says that it was written by young Richardson (son of A.D.R.) who is temporarily stopping in town.[2] He must have got his particulars from the police. I have related the matter to only a very few judicious folks, and I feel perfectly sure that the public revelation is not to be laid at my door. But I was in a sweat of misery till I happened to think of the police[,] so wretched indeed that I went down to Wethersfield to see poor Chapman and get him to cheer me up.[3]

I don't know how the fellow Richardson has told the story. If he has done it at all properly there's nothing in it to feel particularly badly about. Only it was so essentially a *private* matter that it seemed an outrage to publish it.

I suppose you are sitting on your hill like a god "careless of mankind" overlooking the Strike in the troubled world below. What a time it is! I wish I was at liberty to repair to the scene of the show and watch it a little, on the outside.[4]

Yours aff.

Joe

1. This was the story on which Twain's "Wapping Alice" would later be based. A suspected burglar breaking into the Hartford house turned out to be one Willie Taylor, let into the house by Lizzie Wills, a family servant. On discovering that Wills was apparently pregnant but that Taylor did not intend to marry her, Twain decided to intervene. With a plainclothes detective and Twichell (who would perform the ceremony) close at hand, he "persuaded" Taylor to marry Wills on the spot, giving the couple a hundred dollars to start their new life together and calling in the other servants to celebrate with cake and wine. Lizzie was, as it happened, not pregnant at all and may have been playing something of her own game as these events occurred. Unsurprisingly, this all took place when Livy was absent in Elmira. The incident was widely reported. For more detail, see Messent, *Mark Twain and Male Friendship*, 43–44. See, too, the various entries in *Autobiography of Mark Twain*, 3:24, 34–35, 38–40, 456–58.

2. Charley W. is Charles Dudley Warner. "A.D.R." is Albert Deane Richardson, one of the best-known journalists of the day and author of *Beyond the Mississippi* (1866) and other titles. His son was Leander Pease Richardson, journalist, author, and playwright.

3. James L. Chapman, a deacon of Twichell's church, whose alcoholism and consequent embezzlement of money from the bank for which he worked led to his incarceration at Wethersfield State Prison. The event cast something of a pall over Twichell's life just then (see Courtney, *Joseph Hopkins Twichell*, 192–93, 195). It seems unusual that Twichell should describe the imprisoned and disgraced Chapman's misery as cheering him up—rescuing him from the idea that Clemens would think he had betrayed a confidence. But Twichell was capable of such cattiness in unguarded moments.

4. Twichell may well be referring to the Great Railroad Strike of 1877, marked by considerable violence in the days preceding this letter. The quote is an allusion to Tennyson's "The Lotos-Eaters."

39. Twichell to Twain

12 September 1877. Keene Valley, New York[1]

Keene Valley. Essex County.
Sept 12th 1877

Dear Mark,

In Charles Kingsley's Life, American Ed. p. 407, I find the following.—"from the ship we beheld with wonder and delight, the pride of the West Indies, the Cabbage Palms—well named by the botanists the *Oreodoxa*, the glory of the mountains—grey pillars, smooth and cylindrical as those of a Doric column &c &c."[2]

I think it rather a pity that you didn't have that word "oreodoxa" for your article, to take off the flavor of the Cabbage.[3] It would have looked well inserted in brackets.

Home next week! Then we'll tell you our story and hear yours. Are you all up for long walks this Fall? I mean to go it strong in that line myself.

All of us are well.

With undying love to both of you

Joe

1. The Adirondacks, where the family holidayed.

2. Charles Kingsley was an Anglican priest, popular British novelist, and social reformer, best known for *The Water Babies* (1863). This is from *Charles Kingsley: His Letters and Memories of his Life* (1877).

3. See the version of this article, "Some Rambling Notes of an Idle Excursion," in *The Stolen White Elephant and Other Detective Stories* (New York: Oxford University Press, 1996), 86.

40. Twain to Twichell

10 April 1878. Elmira, New York (Correspondence card)

Elmira, Wed[y] Noon

Good bye, Joe dear, we are about to take the train. We sail tomorrow, 2 PM in the Holsatia. Will write you from Germany & tell you what will be the *best* time for you to come, then you can come at the time you *can* come, you see, without regard to the *best* time.[1] Good bye, & love to Harmony & you & all the friends & the babies.[2]

Mark

1. Twain and his family were about to sail for Europe on the trip that would be the basis for *A Tramp Abroad* (1880). Twain would pay for Twichell to come and join him. On 8 June, Twichell writes in his journal, "By the p.m. mail comes a letter from M.T. at Heidelberg, Germany, enclosing $300 and inviting me to join him about Aug. 1st for a two months visit, all at his expense!! Really our bounties are extraordinary. This is a most handsome offer. And I must of course, accept it." See Courtney, *Joseph Hopkins Twichell*, 196. Twichell made other trips abroad accompanying, and paid for by, his parishioners.

2. Harmony junior was now nearly two years old, while Twichell and wife Harmony's sixth child, Burton, would be born just under two months later, on 8 June (and see Letter 41 below).

41. Twichell to Twain

8 June 1878. Hartford, Connecticut

Hartford, Conn.
June 8th 1878

Dear old Mark,

By all the powers, but this has been a great day to me! In the first place my third *son* was born, and in the handsomest possible style, at early dawn. And then the mail brought your letter of the 23rd ult. Whew! I can hardly hold myself down. The two events blend most happily, however, for the advent of the boy enables me to say that I can leave so as to reach Heidelberg Aug 1st or not much later, and that I will, please God. What between the noble prince added to my house,—and his dear mother, Heaven be praised, all right—and the near prospect of such an unearthly feast of delight as you call me to, I am almost too joyful for pleasure. I labor with my felicities. They load me. How I shall get to sleep tonight, I don't know: though I have a good start in not having slept much last night. Oh, my! Do you realize, Mark, what a symposium it is to be? I'm afraid you don't appreciate the size of your own (and Livy's—bless her) invention. I do. To begin with, I am thoroughly tired, and the rest will be worth everything. Then, I shall fill up my pond. Nothing replenishes me as travel does. Most of all I am to have my fill, or a big feed anyway, of your company—and under such circumstances! To walk with you, and talk with you, and sleep with you, and say my prayers with you, and see things with you, for weeks together,—why it's my dream of luxury. I can't tell you how it "rises the cockles of my heart" to think of it. The fact is, Mark, I'm in love with you—but what's the use? I shall grow soft if I go on.[1] But look here, old fellow: this proposition of yours is something of a surprise to me. I have all along supposed that the plan as you broached it before you left was for next year. The first word I received from you disturbed that notion, for you seemed to speak of something presently to be arranged: yet I thought I might mistake your meaning. However, it is all right, and, for me, best as you now wish.

I'm going to get my Committee together right off and ask for the eight weeks, may be, ten: (or rather two or four, for I have six any how). I guess I shall get what I ask for, and easily. Then, I'll find out all about the steamers and decide which line to employ: then I'll settle on the time: and then let you know. Within a fortnight, I judge, everything will be determined. Harmony, who at sunrise this morning deemed herself the happiest woman on the continent; when I read your letter to her widened her smile perceptibly and revived another degree in strength in a minute. She wouldn't think of her being left alone, which I flatter myself is rather rough on her, but only of the great chance opened to me, and said at once that nothing must prevent my going.

I have been bothered for some days with not knowing what to reply to a church in Chicago that wants me to take its pulpit a few weeks this summer. But that business was disposed of in half-a-minute when you entered, and mighty glad I am of it. There never was anything more timely than your appearance on this occasion. It cuts a number of knots, and sets me free.

Shoes, Mark. Remember that ever so much of our pleasure depends on your shoes. Don't fail to have adequate preparation made in that department. Recall the tears we have shed over the discomfort you suffered the day we wandered by the Bermuda shore. Perhaps I'd better fetch along a pair of mine to make all sure.

Harmony has got through this present affair, so far, most brilliantly. She displayed her accustomed gallantry throughout the action and I brevetted her on the field.[2]

Right in the middle of the fight, of a sudden, Julia appeared on the scene—her black eyes standing open to their widest extent—a startling figure in white and demanded to know what ailed Mamma. How we turned her off I can hardly tell, but we did, and she went back to bed and to sleep, and hasn't said anything about it since.

The new baby is a buster. He made more music from the word "go" than all the birds in our grove, which at that moment was ringing with their daybreak overture.

The sensation he has made among the children is simply tremendous.

Well, I won't write any more now. In a month past I have been thinking of things to tell you of in Letter No 1, but I'll keep them till we meet. Oh the gossip we will have! I have seen old Riggs, and what he said on the subject of his extortion will amuse you when you hear it.[3] It is all out in the papers,—the Riggs matter I mean,—and correctly, though I don't know who told.

I enclose a letter just received from Dean [Sage].[4] It is characteristic, yet somehow it sinks my heart. What a spirit the dear fellow has! Harmony says "give my love and greetings to darling Livy and her little girls." She is mighty fond of you, too, Mark, as you well know.

What will *be my address* while I am away? Good night. Imagine me turning handsprings as I make my exit.

Yours aff.

Joe

1. On Twichell's emotional effusiveness in male-to-male relationships here and elsewhere, see Messent, *Mark Twain and Male Friendship*, 22–23.

2. The term "brevet" refers to conferring a higher military rank, often for outstanding service, while awarding no extra pay.

3. Probably Hartford dentist John Riggs. For more on Riggs, see *Mark Twain's Notebooks & Journals*, 2:53n18. Details of the "extortion" are unknown.

4. The letter from Sage is dated 7 June 1878 from Albany. Mentioning a desire for Twichell's company on an upcoming trip to the Restigouche River in New Brunswick, Canada, he says, "I am just in that condition of mental & physical weakness wherein I could enjoy you to the utmost." He also reports sympathy received from customers (presumably of the family lumber business) "on the grounds of my impending decease." Twichell's sinking of the heart seems to be on these grounds. See Letter 36.

42. Twain and Livy to Twichell

9 September 1878. Geneva, Switzerland

Geneva, Sept. 9.

Dear Old Joe—

It is actually all over![1] I was so low-spirited at the station yesterday—& this morning when I woke, I couldn't seem to accept the dismal truth that you were really gone, & the pleasant tramping & talking at an end. Ah, my boy, it has been such a rich holiday to me; & I feel under such deep & honest obligations to you for coming. I am putting out of my mind all memory of the times when I misbehaved toward you & hurt you; I am resolved to consider it forgiven, & to store up & remember only the charming hours of the journeys, & the times when I was not unworthy to be with you & share a companionship which to me stands first after Livy's. It is justifiable to do this—for why should I let my small infirmities of disposition live & grovel among my mental pictures of the eternal sublimities of the Alps?

Livy can't accept or endure the fact that you are gone. But you are—& we cannot get around it. So take our love with you—& bear it also over sea to Harmony—& God bless you both.

Mark

[Inside, the letter also contained a note from Livy:]

Dear Joe

I wont [*sic*] mar Mr Clemens note except to say that we do miss you *desperately*, that we want some one to knock on the door & waken us in the morning, that we want many things that you used to do when you were here, but at any rate there is one thing left to us and that is a stronger affection for you than when you came to us—

With deepest love to Harmony, affectionately

Livy L. C.

1. The letter marks the conclusion of Joe's part of the *Tramp Abroad* trip.

43. Twichell to Twain

13 September 1878. Liverpool, England

North Western Hotel
Liverpool
Sept. 13th 1878.

Dear old Fellow:

I have the evening before me, and on the whole I think I can pass it, or part of it, less lonesomely than in any other way that offers, in writing to you.[1] There is a concert (sacred) with a chorus of 1000 children's voices to be given in St. George's Hall which I might innocently attend, but somehow I am glad that it isn't my duty to do so.

My heart was mighty heavy, I can tell you, when the train moved out of Geneva after I bade you good bye. That I was starting for home I could not make seem the fact. I had not got far enough. I felt only what I was leaving behind. After brooding a while in my corner, which was sunny, I found that I was growing very uncomfortably warm in all those extra underclothes. Now grief and heat do not go so well together, so, as I couldn't get rid of the heat, I took up arms against the grief and resolved on a soothing smoke. Opposite me sat a real pretty girl, whom, spite of my sadness, I had been regarding with furtive admiration, and as I drew out one of those overgrown cigars I waved it toward her with a smile which signified at once a request and the conviction that it was granted before it was made. Judge my emotions when that little stuck up thing delivered herself, with mechanical distinctness, pausing between the words, as if she had committed it to memory and it was all the English she knew, as follows: "It—is—not—allowed—to—smoke—here." In an instant she was transformed into a hag. Here was a nice situation! No smoke from Geneva to Paris (for her party I saw were booked for Paris) unless I got into another carriage, which upon reflection I was afraid to risk an effort to do. I thrust the cigar unlighted into my mouth, pulled my hat over my eyes and fell to reading sulkily, i.e. Mark, I was rude to the girl. I let her see that I didn't like her response, which of course she had a perfect right to make, and in twenty minutes I would have given one of the under-shirts I had on, cheerfully, for the privilege of tendering her an abject apology. I was so ashamed before her that I wished for night to hide me from her sight. And my shame mounted to remorse when at the first stopping place, she and her sister after a conference with their father left their good end places in our compartment, and went to some other part of the train,—got out of *my* way. The old gentleman came back, red in the face, as if he had had hard work to find them seats. I declare I never felt meaner in my life. But a nemesis arrived in the shape of the person who presently became my vis-a-vis, in the young lady's room. It was a man of a forbidding and even revolting aspect—as homely as the man we have heard of who had to take a nap in the day time, to rest his face. He took snuff. O, ye kind angels of oblivion, grant me this boon,—to forget that handkerchief!! From the look of his hands he might have been the party from whom Leech made the study for that wash stand picture.[2] And he perspired like an ice pitcher. Some time before daylight he got down a lean bag—of the 12th century—and after a rustle in what seemed a rat's nest of paper began to feed. You couldn't see him eat, but you could hear him. He threw something against the window, which for the moment he evidently supposed to be open, and it stuck there. I judged it to be the fat rim of a piece of cold ham. He removed it from the glass with his fingers. I took a sort of satisfaction in all this for it avenged my affront to the young girl. Only I wished she knew it.

I slept a good deal during the night, although I shouldn't have thought it but for the unexpected arrival of dawn, and the signs that we were nearing Paris. I not only had not been at all chilly, but had had to keep my vest open most of the time for comfort. The weather had grown mild as we proceeded. [At day break I was washing at a pump, at a station, and I saw a *nun* looking wistfully on the operation. I looked friendly at her, she came timidly up, and I pumped for her while she washed.][3] The train was nearly half-an-hour late in reaching Paris, so that it was not possible to catch the early train to Calais, and when I had deposited my luggage at the Northern R.R. Station, I had the day, till 4 p.m., on my hands to dispose of somehow. It was a burning hot day. And what a pickle I was in with all those confounded underclothes on. There was no way of getting them off except by going to a hotel and taking a room, and that I didn't want to do for a matter of six or seven hours. I am sure you would have pitied me, if you had seen me seated on the pedestal of a statue in the Place de la Concorde mopping my streaming visage. Whew, how I sweltered. And then I felt the effects of my broken rest. I went at about noon into a restaurant in the Palais Royal and ordered a substantial lunch. When they brought it I was fast asleep and they had to wake me up. Thus your poor friend became the sport and gibe of fools. Still I managed to enjoy the day a good deal looking around, and had considerable pleasure mingled with my pain. I was out of luck in finding the Louvre closed.

There I had purposed to spend most of my time and there I could have kept cool with a fan.

I won't attempt to relate the particulars of my second night's journey. It was a wretched (but not unhappy) experience, and next to no sleep at-all. However I brought up in London all right Tuesday morning early, (had to pay duty on my cigars) and after bath and breakfast felt fresher and jollier than the facts warranted. I spent the day actively and went home at night with Mr. Dawson.[4] Did I tell you he was a wholesale boot and shoe dealer? I need not repeat or add to what I have already written about my visit with those dear people. It was altogether delightful.

I called on Johnson, my pedestrian friend, at the stock Exchange.[5] I told you that, but I didn't tell you of a recent stroke of his, as he related it to me. He lives at Seven Oaks, a small place, an hour from London, on, I think, the Chatham and Dover road—anyway a road by which you go from Dover to London. When he was in Paris last week he wrote to the management of that road asking that the "tidal" train leaving Dover at 4 a.m. on which (day named) he should journey from Dover returning from Paris, might stop at Seven Oaks and let him off, *and* received answer by mail in due time *that his request would be complied with*, and so it was.[6] This "tidal" train, I understand, is the most important mail express in the Kingdom. You or I would as soon think of trying to get the moon to stop for us. I asked him if he knew the authorities of the road personally, or if he brought any influence to bear upon them. No, he said, he only happened to think that it would save him two or three hours time if the train stopped for him, so he wrote saying that he had long been a patron of the road and had never sought a favor, and that now he *had* a slight one to ask. He is a character, that Johnson, and no mistake. Such noble cheek! We shall hear from him yet. He went with me to help me buy an overcoat, and I havn't been so supported in a business transaction since I came of age, as I was in that.

Oh, I nearly forgot. The Dawsons had learned all about *Mr. Eden*. Livy was right. Her instinct or insight, was true, perfectly so. He *did* have an unhappy domestic experience. He ran away with his wife, in the first place. After they went to Lausanne, he took private pupils, and with one of these private pupils—the son of some aristocratic house, she eloped. He made every effort to get her to come back to him, went after her, offered her forgiveness, but in vain. She is now dead. Poor, poor, Mr. Eden. No wonder he had that look about him. But Livy is a seer.

Wednesday I went to Polesworth, and to Polesworth you and Livy must go, for sure, when you are in England.[7] The vicar, who is the nicest fellow, has house and heart room for you all. To my surprise he proved a bachelor, so that Livy will have no women to bother her. Polesworth is a specimen of Old England as nearly preserved as can be. 'Twas a nunnery, you know, and there are Norman arches in the church still. At morning service yesterday (there is a service *every* morning) I sat against the effigies of an abbess of the 13th century. And I went to Pooley Hall built in the 15th century and still inhabited—had a cup of tea there.[8] And Tamworth church will ravish you with its venerableness. And in Tamworth you will see a Saxon wall.[9] Lichfield Cathedral a little way off has infinite riches of tombs and mural tablets. There you will see, on a tomb, Chantrey's sleeping children.[10] No work of art ever gave my in'ards such a turn as that did. I couldn't leave it. How I did want you to see everything there with me. But it is for Livy's sake most of all that I hope you will manage to spend a day or two or three with Mr. Madan.[11] I understood what it was that made the place so enchanted to Sarah Sage, and what she liked, Livy will. Mr. Madan says that he'll esteem it the greatest piece of good fortune he ever had to have you pay him a visit, and he means it. He is a great admirer of yours—kept me talking about you all the while. But there you smell odors of England—the country England—of a former age. Write to Mr. M. anytime. You don't need any further introduction than you have, or if you do, Dean will furnish it, and I'll add a postscript.

As soon as I got here [Liverpool] this p.m. I went to the Cunard office to see if your boxes had arrived. No, they have not, and the freight clerk said that it is *perfectly certain* that anything shipped from Geneva last Saturday will not arrive in time to go on the "Bothnia."[12] Now listen to what I did and will do and see if it is all right. I gave the freight clerk the marks on the two boxes, and asked him (wrote it all down) to notify me by mail when and by what ship they do, in the event, go, which he agreed to do.

When I get to New York I will deposit also with the Custom House officer in chief at the Cunard wharf a description of the boxes i.e. their addresses, and ask him not to open them, but to put them where they can readily be got at. I'll tell him all about them, you know, and whose they are &c. Additionally, I will instruct him to notify H. W. Sage & co. of their arrival.

Then I will go to Will Sage and leave with him the invoice with your statement on it and ask him when he hears that the boxes have come to go and pay the duty on them and forward them to their respective destinations, and send me his bill which Charley Perkins will pay.[13] Will Sage will be only too glad to render this service. When I get the Cunard notice from here, I'll send Will Sage word, in case I haven't heard from him before. That covers the chance that the Custom House officer at New York forgets or omits to do it.

Now I suppose you are gnashing your teeth over this plan of mine as a piece of tomfoolery all through, but, though of course I suspect there is a fatal flaw in it somewhere, it is the very best I can study out alone. The freight clerk said he thought the boxes would be two whole weeks getting here. "By express?" I asked. "Yes," he said "by express." So much for that. I am very sorry that the delay deprives me of the opportunity of suffering the tid bit of torture for your sake I had anticipated in New York among those Custom House ogres.

Now, Mark, what I *really* sat down to do this evening was to say at some greater length than I have yet said, how earnestly I thank you for the never to be forgotten pleasures of the past few weeks. Not that I hoped to do the subject justice, but I wanted to shed some ink on it anyhow. But, as you see, I have fooled away my time and I must sing my gratitude on another occasion. No danger that it will cool. How we *have* enjoyed ourselves. I was never more satisfied with any vacation. I love you all with a new affection. God bless you everyone, and give us the delight of meeting again and tasting the cup of friendship together many years. And so standing on the edge of departure I bid you Good bye.

Joe

1. Twichell was on his way home. He had not yet received Twain and Livy's letter of 9 September.

2. Possibly cartoonist and literary illustrator John Leech.

3. This sentence is written in the margin of the page with an arrow indicating its proper location in the body of the letter.

4. Most likely John Dawson, of Joseph Dawson and Sons, Wholesale Boot and Shoe Manufacturers, 23, London Wall, London. The editors of *Mark Twain's Notebooks & Journals* note, "[Twain] and Twichell met the Dawson family in Leukerbad on August 26 [1878]. They also met Mr. Eden [see below], rector of the English church in Lausanne, at about the same time" (2:161n9).

5. Probably someone Twichell also met on the *Tramp Abroad* trip.

6. "'Tidal' train": the London to Paris boat train docked at irregular times dependent on tides.

7. Polesworth, a twelfth-century abbey church in Warwickshire.

8. An early sixteenth-century manor house on the outskirts of Polesworth village.

9. Tamworth, Staffordshire, ancient capital of the Anglo-Saxon kingdom of Mercia, originally protected by fortifications.

10. Sir Francis Chantrey's marble statue of *The Sleeping Children* is in Lichfield Cathedral, Warwickshire.

11. Rev. Nigel Madan, vicar of the Abbey Church, Polesworth, between 1866 and 1881.

12. The passenger ship SS *Bothnia*, built in 1874, was the largest steamship then con-

structed for the Cunard Line. The forty-five-hundred-ton ship could carry up to fourteen hundred passengers.

13. Charles Perkins, a lawyer who served as city attorney in Hartford and who represented Twain.

44. Twichell to Twain

22 October 1878. Hartford, Connecticut

Hartford. Oct 22nd 1878

Dear old Mark,

I'll make a start on a letter any how, though I can do little more today. I had devoted the forenoon to you, but bit by bit it has been filched from me by all sorts of time plunderers till the lunch bell is about due.

I have been thinking of you all the morning. It is one of those golden, perfect autumn days, when one's desire to be off somewhere among trees, mounts to a passion and can hardly be refused. Had you been home I should have been after you betimes, and by now we should be bathing our souls and bodies in the delicious tinted light of the wood paths of Talcott Mountain, kicking the yellow and red October leaves before us, (oh, the sweet rustle of 'em!) and, having a *talk*, old fellow. There never *was* such weather as is upon us now. It really seems ungrateful and wicked not to give all the time to it one possibly can. When Davie and Harmony went out after breakfast, I noticed that for quite awhile they stood still and silent, drunk with the rapture of such sunshine.

Now, Mark, let's make a vow, that when we are once more together, we will use these heavenly days as they were meant to be used, and as we shall wish we had when we come to look back on life. But I think we may well despair of producing another chapter of life so barren of matter for conscience to work up into gimcracks of remorse, as that composed by our late six weeks together.

The astounding note I received from you on the Bothnia at Liverpool, which made me, and still makes me laugh and cry by turns, is a dainty bit of literature—it's so natural—just precisely as if it was something that had happened.[1] You surely didn't mean it for irony, assuming with feigned humility, acknowledgments that were rather due from me? Yet, really, I can't make *any* sense of it on any other hypothesis. Confound me, don't I remember the day I got mad at you—and you so mild and unresenting under it? Oh, you dear long suffering Mark, there's nobody that I want to travel with henceforth but you, even at my own charge and if I were a "coupon cutter" of high grade.[2] My goldenest earthly day dream now is of a summer of twelve weeks strolling with you through Switzerland.

I suppose you would like to hear something of my journey home. It was a great disappointment to me to miss Parker's company.[3] However, Beilstein was something of a compensation.[4] He was my room-mate, or one of my room-mates, for I had two. No 1. was a quiet, small man—a doctor, in poor health. I had supposed him to be the only sharer with me of the spacious state-room I was assigned to, till, as we were undressing the first night, a burly, red-haired form appeared in the door, rather aggressively yet not at-all ill-naturedly announcing his right to a place with us. He had the documents to prove his title; so into the top berth he went, with the Doctor below him, and I on the sofa under the port-hole. It took Beilstein about a quarter of a minute to make his toilet for the night. Spite of the fact that he was an unexpected and unwelcome presence, there was a kind of vigor and heartiness about him and a natural good will that showed in his manner, that conciliated me toward him almost immediately. During that first night we struck a heavy sea. I was awakened before day by being half thrown out of bed. It was really fearful the way the ship was rolling and quivering under the blows of the great waves. To add to the effect our luggage was all in motion over the floor and the crash of breaking crockery was heard on every side. For myself down there under water (for we were in the 2nd Cabin) and with such infinite forces playing around me, though not scared, I did feel awe-struck, and inclined to send my thoughts upward.[5] While I lay thus silently confessing that I was a poor weak helpless creature &c I heard Beilstein in his berth, in a soft whisper, so as not to disturb the rest of us whom he supposed to be asleep, expressing *his* sentiments, somewhat as follows: "Blank blank the blank blanked sea to H.!!!" His tone was low and suppressed but exceedingly *feeling*. There was an unction in it that made each word tell. You saw that he was sincere: that there was no affectation in him.

Presently he started to get up. Very quietly he reached down his leg till he stood on the edge of the under berth, holding with one hand to his curtain rod, and meaning to make no particle of noise. But at that moment the ship gave a lurch, and down he came onto the floor fetching away the rod and all the curtain gear with him, and *then*—well, the elements that were exhibiting themselves so handsomely outside couldn't hold my attention at all, there was so much finer a show of its kind going on within. The man lying there on the floor amid the debris of the avalanche that brought him down or that he brought down was a very great artist as his manner of meeting this emergency proved. His resources and his command of them, were simply amazing. Oh, forgive me, Mark. It's too bad, of course I *didn't* take pleasure in Mr. Beilstein's profanity. I speak of it in this light way, under the influence of other impressions and memories of the man, later formed, that *are* pleasurable. He didn't suspect at this time that he had a minister in his audience. He never so much as said "Oh, my." after he found that out.

Nothwithstanding so unpromising a beginning, he was destined to do more to beguile the tedium of our voyage than any other of my fellow passengers.

He was a butcher from Pennsylvania. Here are his name and address cut from the outside of an envelope. (We have been correspondents)

[Twichell pasted here a picture of a bull in profile with a return address, presumably cut from an envelope from Beilstein. It reads:

If not called for in 10 days return to
J. F. BEILSTEIN
203 Spring Garden Ave.
ALLEGHENY CITY, PA.

The "cut" in the next sentence is used in the sense of an "illustration."]

The cut and all, seem somehow to represent and reflect the man—or rather, the cut does i.e. as I view it. It appears to be, not simply an open, but a triumphant confession of the business it indicates.

Such at-any-rate was the manner of Beilstein's confession of his trade of butcher. His whole thought was upon it: his interest in it amounted to a burning enthusiasm: he had no desire, pride, or ambition that was not connected with it. He had acquired considerable wealth but he told me with unconcealed vanity that his wife, of whom he appeared exceedingly fond, could "tend shop" just as well as he himself could.

I can't begin to report all the entertainment he afforded me. Everyday I had a long talk with him on some head of his invariable theme. He was always charming. He used to go to the cook's galley and borrow a sharpener and stand for half an hour whetting his pocket knife and looking dreamily out upon the sea, as if [he] had a vision of slaughtered beeves that he was soon to enjoy the heavenly rapture of cutting up.

He told me one morning about a match in which he engaged with eight other competitors, in Chicago three years ago, where the prize was a Champion Belt to the man who dressed a bullock best, in shortest time.[6] He described the whole affair—the different theories of the true mode of dressing bullocks that obtained among the highest authorities—his *own view* and the reasons for it, as against the other views—reasons of his own failure to win the Belt—the local and to some extent corrupting influence that Chicago brought to bear to affect the result—Chicago, *determined* that the Belt should not leave the city, if by hook or crook, it could be retained:—the agony of the match itself—the passions of hope, fear, suspense that agitated alike competitors and spectators: it was all splendid, first class *literature,* and I often felt that I would give anything if you could hear it with me. I never can reproduce it, but I can give you something of an idea of it, perhaps, when we meet. He chanced on a California man one day who knew something about cattle and soon they were in a discussion that grew hotter and hotter, till the Californian fled from the scene, not so much intellectually as physically vanquished. Beilstein pursued him around the deck as a conquering rooster does a conquered one, his face blazing with delight—trying to get him to make one more stand. But the Californian had had enough. Nor could Beilstein bring him to the scratch again. I occasionally saw him after that hanging around wistfully in his neighborhood, waiting to see if he wouldn't give him a round or two, and when I approached him he would say, "Wish I could get that fellow talking about cattle again. He didn't know *me*—thought I didn't know much when he begun—I *would* like to have one more chance at him!" Yet he had not the least malice in the would.[7] The only thing about him that I *couldn't* enjoy was a habit he had of greasing his hair. After he had washed in the morning, he would deposit on the palm of his left hand a lump of some soft pomatum-like substance, and *slap* his right hand onto it and proceed to rub and grind it for a long time between his palms, which gave a kind of sucking sound when he opened them. At last he would smear it all over his short-cropped red head with the expenditure of an amount of force that shook the stateroom. This operation appeared to yield him great delight. He also seemed to consider it as a point of elegance in style, and often urged me to adopt it, offering me, most cordially the free use of his huge bottle of unguent.

But I did like Beilstein. There were plenty of highly civilized people on board, clergymen and such like, but none of them gave me half the pleasure he did with his talk of butchering. Morning, noon and night we communed on that great—to him supreme—matter. And really I got interested in it.

We parted at New York almost with tears. If ever I get into his neighborhood it is agreed that I am to pay him a visit and see his slaughterhouse and market with my own eyes.

I was very sick the day after we left Queenstown—sea-sick I mean.[8] There was a tremendous sea, and it fetched almost everybody. During the prevalence of this misery a scene occurred (or rather *some* of it occurred and the whole was suggested to me) which I thought wouldn't be so bad to put into a book.

Scene. A company of sea-sick passengers all alike wretched reclining in various attitudes around the Smoking Room.
1st Sea-sick Passenger (J.H.T.) "Gentlemen, in reading the other day I came across a line of poetry descriptive of sea sickness, but I can't remember whether it was,

'Heaving o'er the sickening wave'

or,

'Sickening o'er the heaving wave'

Which should it be?[9] Which is the most felicitous expression? Let us beguile these sad moments by lifting our minds to the plane of literary interest."
2nd Sea-sick Passenger is about to speak on the point, when suddenly he bursts from the door and rushes to the rail. As he returns, and sinks into his place, all inquire "Well, how is it?" He answers feebly "I think *'Heaving o'er the sickening wave'* is what he wrote: he did anyhow if he was a true poet."

3rd Sea sick passenger, under precisely the same circumstances, thinks the other rendering preferable.

4th Sea-sick passenger returning from *his* excursion to the rail and staggering to his corner, after a silence, remarks eagerly, but in, a so to speak, haggard voice, "I've got it! It's—'*waving oer the sickening heave.*' That's what 'tis. You're all wrong! That's it, depend upon it."

5th Sea sick Passenger, nearly dead and out of sight rousing himself and whispering "Oh, my God, that's it: that's it. He's got it."
I think that's quite a choice bit of sea sick comedy i.e. in its *elements.*

Mark *is* that Switzerland notebook lost?[10] Haven't you found it? I can't be reconciled to such a calamity. Why *think* of all the treasure we had garnered in it! I prophesied (to myself) that the forthcoming book would storm the world. I shall never cease to judge (in case it isn't written) that M.T. missed his best chance.

On my way home I read Disraeli's "Vivian Grey," and felt a great throb of pleasure when I came across a reference to our old friend Göetz of Berlichingen, in it.[11] Oh Heilbronn!! Why didn't I know how happy I was in those days!

By the way Consul Smith has sent me the Corn Flower seed, like a good fellow, and next spring if God will, we'll try it.[12]

—But I must stop right here—for now. Since the Custom House business is out of the way at last, I feel that the regular business between us may be resumed.

Harmony supposes that I have sent her thanks to Livy for the gloves and the childrens' thanks for the music box, long ago. The gloves have been a constant source of rapture, ever since I got home, and extract a blessing every time they are put on. And the music box has been worked to death almost. [I have made your desires about the big music box known to Susie W.][13] My love to Livy—*our* love. How we long to see her—we and a good many besides. And the girls—my nieces, give them a fond uncle's hug and kiss on my behalf—same to Clara S.[14]

All of us are well and home never was so happy. I often wonder if I should enjoy my blessings any better if I felt I deserved them. I don't believe I should so well. I am very hard at work—to what purpose I know not. Life never seemed so short, or the other world so near. God save us all and bring us together in the *Fathers* House above.

Thine most affectionately

Joe[15]

P.S. *What* a mess of bosh I have written. I'm ashamed of it.

1. See Twain's 9 September letter [Letter 42].

2. Person of some wealth and leisure whose main occupation is to cut and cash bond coupons. Such coupons—part of the bond certificate—marked each scheduled interest payment during the bond's life, to be detached and presented for payment as it fell due.

3. Edwin Pond Parker, close friend of Twichell and minister of South Congregational Church, Hartford.

4. John F. Beilstein, butcher of Allegheny City (now part of Pittsburgh). Of German birth, Beilstein came to the United States with his parents in 1838. His father was also a butcher. See *History of Allegheny County* (Chicago: A. Warner, 1889), 536.

5. That is, intermediate class (or "cabin") between first class and third (or steerage, sometimes called "emigrant") class.

6. A champion or championship belt: a trophy awarded for a winner, now most particularly associated with boxing.

7. That is, not the least malice in the word "would."

8. Queenstown, Ireland (known now as Cobh), where the *Bothnia* made a stop before crossing the Atlantic.

9. Bret Harte's condensed novel, "The Hoodlum Band," serialized in *Godey's Magazine* in early 1878, introduces a character called "Bromley Chitterlings—the Boy Avenger." Commenting on this sobriquet, Harte writes:

> "Let us not seek to disclose the awful secret hidden under that youthful jacket. Enough that there may have been that of bitterness in his past life that he '*Whose soul would sicken o'er the heaving wave,*' or 'whose soul would heave above the sickening wave,' did not understand."

The origin of the "heaving wave" quotation is Byron's *The Corsair.*

10. The notebook was later found. See Letter 48.

11. Benjamin Disraeli published *Vivian Grey,* his first novel, in 1826, when he was just twenty-one years old. Gottfried (Götz) von Berlichingen (1480–1562) was legendary as a type of German Robin Hood. He engaged in multiple military activities, including fighting for the rebels during the Peasants' War of 1525. Goethe wrote a play about him.

12. Possibly Dr. William Smith, U.S. consul in Weymouth, 1861–78.

13. Susie Warner. See Twain's 20 November letter (Letter 46).

14. Clara Spaulding, an Elmira school-friend of Livy's and close family friend who accompanied them on the *Tramp Abroad* trip.

15. Twichell started to write "J. H. Tw" and then crossed it out.

45. Twain to Twichell

3 November 1878. Rome, Italy

Rome, Nov. 3/78.

Dear Joe—I am disgusted with myself for having put all that work & vexation upon you & Will Sage, but you know we couldn't foresee it. If the cursed boxes had reached Liverpool in time, no doubt the matter would have been simpler. But after all, the thing that mainly hurts *me* is, that after I had fortified you and those boxes with a written oath sworn in the presence of the Holy Trinity, my country should deem that group not august enough without the addition of a U.S. Consul. I am sensitive about these things. However, it is all right, now. I have sent to Geneva for the clock-maker's certificate, & as soon as I get to Munich, (Nov. 18 or 20,) I shall swear once more by the Trinity, adding the Fourth Personage, & immediately transmit the document, thus sublimely freighted, to Will Sage. And at the same time I will thank Sage for taking the trouble this matter has cost him.

I have received your several letters, & we have prodigiously enjoyed them. How I do admire a man who can sit down & whale away with a pen just the same as if it was fishing—or something else as full of pleasure & as void of labor. *I* can't do it; else, in common decency, I *would,* when I write to *you.* Joe, if I can make a book out of the matter gathered in your company over here, the book is safe; but I don't think I have gathered any matter before or since your visit worth writing up. I do wish you were in Rome to do my sight-seeing for me.[1] Rome interests me as much as East Hartford could, & no more. That is, the Rome which the average tourist feels an interest in; but there are *other* things here which stir me enough to make life worth the living. Livy & Clara are having a royal time worshiping the old Masters, & I as good a time gritting my ineffectual teeth over them.

A friend waits for me. A power of love to you all. Amen.

Mark

1. See chapter 30 of *A Tramp Abroad*, "Harris Climbs Mountains For Me." Here "Mark Twain" sends his agent (Harris, the Twichell stand-in) to visit "noted places" on his behalf, bringing back "a written report . . . for insertion in my book." The narrator, meanwhile, judges it "best to go to bed and rest several days, for I knew that the man who undertakes to make the tour of Europe on foot must take care of himself."

46. Twain to Twichell and Susan L. Warner[1]

20 November 1878. Munich, Germany

No. 1[a] Karlstrasse
(2[e] Stock,)
Care Fraülein Dahlweiner,
Munich, Nov. 20.

Dear Joe:

By George but the clocks have been an elephant, haven't they! I am supremely grateful that the taking care of him fell to you & Will Sage instead of to me. I am greatly obliged to you both for allowing me to inflict the animal upon you. I think I will ship *all* my purchases through you.

Well, I have lost my Switzerland note-book! I have written to Rome and Florence, but I don't expect to find it. If it remains lost, I can't write any volume of travels, & shan't attempt it, but shall tackle some other subject. I've got a work-room, a mile from here, & am all ready to go to work, but shall lie on my oars till I hear from Rome & Florence.

Tell the Warners we are delightfully situated here & have fallen in love with the Fraülein. She gives us the very best cookery, (& the widest variety) we have had in Europe. I have the sort of appetite which you had at the Hotel du Soliel [*sic*] in Visp. It is a charming novelty. The food is all as good as it can be; & the maid who serves it carries such a depth of soil on her hands that at short range you can't tell her from real-estate.

The Boyesens have been in Munich ten days.[2] I saw their names on the banker's books, & that they were to leave today for Italy; so Livy & I drove to their lodgings yesterday afternoon; by my translation, the landlady said they had left town. But after we had returned home the German sediment gradually settled to the bottom & the correct translation was revealed—to-wit: the Boyesens were simply *nicht zŭ haŭse.* However, it was too late to try again—so we didn't get to see the Boyesens.

[A section of the letter is here addressed to "Dear Mrs. Susie (Warner.)" It concerns Twain's purchase of "a perfect love of a music box in Geneva" and his attempt "to select the 10 tunes for it." He asks for her help, saying: "Its best hold is not loud, or staccato or rapid music, but just the reverse—a soft, flowing *strain—its strong suit is the plaintive. I have selected 4: The Lorelei, the Miser[e]re from Trovatore, the Wedding March from Lohengrin, & the Russian National Anthem—& at that point I* stuck." *He continues: "You are just the person who can suggest some tunes to get the wanting 6 out of. This box is great on rich chords—pours them out like the great god Pan—or any other man. She's not one of the thumping or banging or tinkling sort, with castanets & birds & drums & such-like foolishness—no, her melody is low-voiced, & flows in blended waves of sound. Her forte is to express pathos, not hilarity or hurrah. Come, will you help me? I shall wait to hear from you."[3]]*

Dear Joe (again.)—There is nothing like saying a thing when it occurs to you—hence the above parenthesis to Susie Warner. We staid a day or two in Chambery & Turin, a week in Milan, several days at Bellagio on the lake of Como, three weeks in Venice, a week in Florence, a fortnight in Rome—then flew northwards, only stopping to rest & sleep at Florence, Bologna & Trent (in the Austrian Tyrol.) I discharged George at Venice—the worthless idiot—& have developed into a pretty fair sort of courier myself since then.[4]

The children are well—so well that there is hardly any possibility of enduring their awful racket. The stove-heat here keeps Livy's head splitting with headache, but otherwise she is well—Miss Clara also.

With a power of love to you & the family & the friends,

Yrs Ever

Mark.

1. Susie Warner, Charles Dudley Warner's wife.

2. Hjalmar Boyesen and wife, Lillie. Boyesen, a Norwegian-born American author, translator, and college professor, was a friend of William Dean Howells.

3. Susan Warner was a gifted amateur musician. For more on this matter, see Kerry Driscoll, "Mark Twain's Music Box: Livy, Cosmopolitanism and the Commodity Aesthetic,"

in *Cosmopolitan Twain,* ed. Ann M. Ryan and Joseph B. McCulloch (Columbia: University of Missouri Press, 2008), 140–186.

4. George Burk, Twain's courier.

47. Twichell to Twain

23 December 1878. Hartford, Connecticut

Hartford. Dec. 23rd

Dear, dear Mark,

There's a letter coming one of these days. I'm big with it. In fact, I have begun it. But before I stretch myself out at mental ease for a chat, I want to get this Custom House business out of the way.

I enclose a note received from Will Sage yesterday, which will soothe your poor heart.

I enclose also a lot of newspaper clippings which I have stored for you. Gov. Hubbard's rhetoric is one of your delights, I remember, as it is mine.[1] I send you a specimen or two.

The news of the loss of the Switzerland Note Book is simply appalling. I can't bear to think of it yet. It musn't be so.

Thanks to dear Clara S. for her note. 'Twas a real sugar plum. *Where* in the world did she get hold of that sermon!

With love to all of you, and assurances that you are *missed, missed, missed* seven days in every week.

I am

Yours most aff.

Joe

1. Enclosures missing. Richard Dudley Hubbard, governor of Connecticut from 1877 to 1879 and a noted lawyer and orator. As a Democrat, he would have been a natural target of Twichell's scorn.

48. Twain to Twichell

23 January 1879. Munich, Germany

Munich, Jan. 23.

Dear Joe—

I've got to write to Mr. Bliss & Frank through you, for I don't know their address.[1] I have the idea that Frank said they might leave the publishing company during the summer.

I only want to say to them this: I am doing my very level best, but I don't want to attempt any more prophecies as to date of completion of the book [*A Tramp Abroad*]. My prophecies seem to fail, every time. I work *every* day that some member of the family isn't sick. This does not give me a great deal of time, but I make the most of what I *do* get.

Very well, then,—as to items: I have torn up 400 pages of MS, but I've still got about 900 which need no tearing. They suit me very well. So the book is half finished. If anybody will tell me how long it will take me to write the other 900 in a way which shall satisfy me, I shall be under many obligations to him. I know *one* thing,—I shall fool away no time—*I* want to get through.

I have found my lost Swiss note-book.

I shall make from 10 to 20 illustrations for my book with my own (almighty rude & crude) pencil, & shall say in the title page, that some of the pictures in the book are from original drawings by the author. I have already made two or three which suit me. It gives me the belly-ache to look at them.

When the MS is done, I shall ship it right along, without copying, & run the risk.

I can't venture to ship any of it yet, for I may want to alter the first part in several important particulars.

That's all. Now as to *you* Joe, I'm going to write you presently.

We thought our youngest child was dying, three days ago, but she is doing pretty well, now.[2]

Yrs Ever

Mark.

1. Frank E. Bliss was Elisha Bliss's son. He also worked for the American Publishing Company until 1878, when he set up his own subscription publishing company. Twain had initially contracted with him to publish the *Tramp Abroad* book, but the book in fact went to his father's company (which Frank was in the process of rejoining).

2. That is, Clara. The nature of her illness is unknown. K. Patrick Ober, author of

Mark Twain and Medicine, comments, "The girls got sick fairly frequently. [Twain] tended to make little of their illnesses, Livy tended to be overly worried about everything that came along, and [Twain] would sometimes go along with it. In fairness, they had lost Langdon from diphtheria, which started off as a nonspecific upper respiratory disease (we would call it 'a cold'), and so any illness was potentially worrisome" (e-mail correspondence).

49. Twain to Twichell

26 January 1879. Munich, Germany (Three transcripts by Albert Bigelow Paine and Dana S. Ayer)

Munich, Jan. 26/79.

Dear old Joe—

Sunday. Your delicious letter arrived exactly at the right time.[1] It was laid by my plate as I was finishing breakfast at 12 noon. Livy & Clara arrived from church 5 minutes later; I took a pipe & spread myself out on the sofa, & Livy sat by & read, & I warmed to that butcher the moment he began to swear. There is more than one way of praying, & I like the butcher's way because the petitioner is so apt to be in earnest. I was peculiarly alive to his performance just at this time, for another reason, to-wit: Last night I awoke at 3 this morning, & after raging to myself for 2 interminable hours, I gave it up. I rose, assumed a catlike stealthiness, to keep from waking Livy, & proceeded to dress in the pitch dark. Slowly but surely I got on garment after garment—all down to one sock; I had one slipper on & the other in my hand. Well, on my hands & knees I crept softly around, pawing & feeling & scooping along the carpet & among chair-legs for that missing sock; I *kept* that up;—& still kept it up & kept it up. At first I only said to myself, "Blame that sock," but that soon ceased to answer; my expletives grew steadily stronger & stronger,—& at last, when I found I was lost, I had to sit flat down on the floor & take hold of something to keep from lifting the roof off with the profane explosion that was trying to get out of me. I could see the dim blur of the window, but of course it was in the wrong place & could give me no information as to where I was. But I had one comfort—I had not waked Livy; I believed I could find that sock in silence if the night lasted long enough. So I started again & softly pawed all over the place,—& sure enough at the end of half an hour I laid my hand on the missing article. I rose joyfully up & butted the wash-bowl & pitcher off the stand & simply raised —— so to speak. Livy screamed, then said, "Who is it? what is the matter!" I said "There ain't *any*thing the matter—I'm hunting for my sock." She said, "Are you hunting for it with a club?"

I went in the parlor & lit the lamp, & gradually the fury subsided & the ridiculous features of the thing began to suggest themselves. So I lay on the sofa, with note-book & pencil, & transferred the adventure to our big room in the hotel at Heilbronn, & got it on paper a good deal to my satisfaction.[2]

I've found the Swiss note-book some time ago. When it was first lost I was glad of it, for I was getting an idea that I had lost my faculty of writing sketches of travel; therefore as the loss of that note-book would render the writing of this one simply impossible & let me gracefully out, I was about to write to Bliss & propose some other book, when the confounded thing turned up, & down went my heart into my boots. But there was now no excuse, so I went solidly to work—tore up great part of the MS written in Heidelberg,—wrote & tore up,—continued to write & tear up,—& at last, reward of patient & noble persistence, my pen got the old swing again!

Since then I'm glad Providence knew better what to do with the Swiss note-book than I did, for I like my work, now, exceedingly, & often turn out over 30 MS pages a day & then quit sorry that Heaven makes the days so short.

One of my discouragements had been the belief that my interest in this tour had been so slender that I couldn't gouge matter enough out of it to make a book. What a mistake. I've got 900 pages written (not a word in it about the sea voyage,) yet I stepped my foot out of Heidelberg for the first time yesterday,—& then only to take our party of four on our first pedestrian tour—to Heilbronn. I've got them dressed elaborately in walking costume—knapsacks, canteens, field-glasses, leather leggings, patent walking shoes, muslin folds around their hats, with long tails hanging down behind, sun umbrellas, and—*Alpenstocks.* They go all the way to Wimpfen by rail—thence to Heilbronn in a chance vegetable cart drawn by a donkey & a cow; I shall fetch them home on a raft: & if other people shall perceive that that was no pedestrian excursion, they *themselves* shall not be conscious of it. This trip will take 100 MS pages or more,—oh, goodness knows how many! for the mood is everything, not the material, & I already seem to see 300 pages rising before me on that trip. *Then,* I propose to leave Heidelberg for good. Don't you see, the book (1800 MS pages,) may really be finished before I ever get to Switzerland?

But there's *one* thing I want you to tell Frank Bliss & his father to be charitable toward me in,—that is, let me tear up all the MS I want to, &

give me time to write more. I shan't waste the time—I haven't the slightest desire to loaf, but a consuming desire to work, ever since I got back my swing.[3] And you see this book is either going to be compared with the Innocents Abroad, or *contrasted* with it, to my disadvantage. I *think* I can make a book that will be no dead corpse of a thing & I mean to do my level best to accomplish that.

My crude plans are crystalizing. As the thing stands now, I went to Europe for *three* purposes. The first you *know*, & must keep secret, even from the Blisses; the second is to study *Art*; & the third to acquire a critical knowledge of the German language. My MS already shows that the two latter objects are already accomplished. It shows that I am now moving about as an Artist & a Philologist, & unaware that there is any immodesty in assuming these titles. Having three definite objects has had the effect of seeming to enlarge my domain & give me the freedom of a loose costume. It is three strings to my bow, too.

Well, your butcher is magnificent. He won't stay out of my mind. I keep trying to think of some way of getting your account of him into my book without his being offended—& yet confound him there isn't anything you have said which he would see any offense in,—I'm only thinking of his friends—*they* are the parties who busy themselves with seeing things for people. But I'm *bound* to have him in. I'm putting in the yarn about the Limburger cheese & the box of guns, too—mighty glad Howells declined it.[4] It seems to gather richness & flavor with age. I have very nearly killed several companies with that narrative,—the American Artists' Club, here, for instance, & Smith & wife & Miss Griffith (they were here in this house a week or two.) I've got 3 other chapters that pretty nearly destroyed the same parties, too.

O, Switzerland! the further it recedes into the enriching haze of time, the more intolerably delicious the charm of it & the cheer of it & the glory & majesty & solemnity & pathos of it grow. Those mountains had a soul; they thought; they spoke,—one couldn't hear it with the ears of the body, but what a voice it was!—& how real. Deep down in my memory it is sounding yet. Alp calleth unto Alp!—that stately old Scriptural wording is the right one for God's Alps & God's ocean. How puny we were in that awful presence—& how painless it was to be so; how fitting & right it seemed, & how stingless was the sense of our unspeakable insignificance. And Lord how pervading were the repose & peace & blessedness that poured out of the heart of the invisible Great Spirit of the Mountains.

Now what *is* it? There are mountains and mountains & mountains in this world—but only *these* take you by the heart-strings. I wonder what the secret of it is. Well, time & time again it has seemed to me that I *must* drop everything & flee to Switzerland once more. It is a *longing*—a deep, strong, tugging *longing*,—that is the word. We must go again, Joe. October days, let us get up at dawn & breakfast at the tower. I should like that first rate.

Livy & all of us send deluges of love to you & Harmony & the children. I dreamed last night that I woke up in the library at home & your children were frolicking around me & my Julia was sitting in my lap; you & Harmony & both families of Warners had finished their welcomes & were filing out through the conservatory door wrecking Patrick's flower pots with their dress skirts as they went. Peace & plenty abide with you all!

Mark.

I want the Blisses to know their part of this letter, if possible. They will see that my delay was not from choice.

I'm not stopping this letter because I'm done but because dinner is ready.

P.S. Why did you go in second cabin?

1. Twichell's 22 October 1878 letter has clearly only just caught up with Twain.

2. See *A Tramp Abroad*, 118–21. "Harris" becomes here the sleeping partner.

3. Both Frank and Elisha Bliss were involved in the publication of *A Tramp Abroad*.

4. "The Invalid's Story," published as part of a reworked version of "Some Rambling Notes of an Idle Excursion" in 1882. Howells evidently persuaded Twain not to include it as part of *A Tramp Abroad*.

50. Twain to Twichell

24 February 1879. Munich, Germany (Two transcripts by Albert Bigelow Paine)

Munich, Feb. 24.

Dear old Joe—

It was a mighty good letter, Joe—& that idea of yours of sending newspaper slips is a rattling good one.[1] But I have not sot down here to answer your letter,—for it is down at my study,—but only to impart some information.

For 2 months I had not shaved without crying. I'd spend ¾ of an hour whetting away on my hand—no use, couldn't get an edge. Tried a razor strop—same result. So I sat down & put in an hour thinking out the mystery. Then it seemed plain—to-wit: my hand can't give a razor an edge, it can only smooth & refine an edge that has already been given. I judged that a razor fresh from the hone is this shape V—the long point being the continuation of the edge—& after much use the shape is thus v—attenuated edge all worn off & gone. By George I *knew* that was the explanation. And I knew that a freshly honed & freshly stropped razor won't cut, but after stropping on the hand as a final operation, it *will* cut. So I sent out for an oil-stone; none to be had, but messenger brought back a little piece of rock the size of a Safety match box—(it was bought in a shoe-maker's shop) bad flaw in middle of it, too,—but I put 4 drops of fine Olive oil on it, picked out the razor marked "Thursday" because it was never any account & would be no loss if I spoiled it—gave it a brisk & reckless honing for ten minutes, then tried it on a hair—it wouldn't cut. Then I trotted it through a vigorous ten minute course on a razor strop & tried it on a hair—it wouldn't cut—tried on my face—it made me cry—gave it a five minutes' stropping on my hand, & my land, what an edge she had! We thought we knew what sharp razors were when we were tramping in Switzerland, but it was a mistake—they were dull beside this old Thursday razor of mine which I mean to name Thursday October Christian in gratitude. I took my whetstone, & in 20 minutes I put two more of my razors in superb condition—but I leave them in the box—I never use any but Thursday O. C. & shan't till its edge is gone—& then I'll know how to restore it without any delay.

Everybody well but the children & Livy, though Clara S. & Rosa are ailing slightly & I have a cold in the head & a sore leg.[2] We all go to Paris next Thursday—address, Monroe & Co., Bankers.

With love—
Ys Ever
Mark.

1. The letter may be a reply to Twichell's 23 December 1878 letter (Letter 47).

2. Rosa (Rosina Hay) had been hired as Susy's nursemaid in January 1874. German by birth, she tutored the children in that language on this trip.

51. Twichell to Twain

6 May 1879. Hartford, Connecticut

[There are several clippings attached to this letter, one about Wong Shin, A Chinese national who had visited the United States in 1847.[1] *Twichell adds a note to the clipping saying that Shin had come as "a boy with Y[ung] Wing." He goes on to say that Shin, after a career in China, was now "interpreter of the Chinese Legation*

at Washington, but temporarily on duty at the [Chinese Educational] Mission here. He has been for 30 years a member, and for 15 years a faithful and beloved deacon *of the native church in Hong Kong. 'Twas a becoming and beautiful thing, in my eyes anyhow, to see him serving at the Lord's table. It meant much." Other clippings treat minor local events, including the death of "the wife of Mr. Ngeu Noh Liang, one of the Chinese commissioners."]*

Hartford. May 6th 1879

Dear Old Fellow,

On this sweetest May morning, with the smell of flowers and an innumerable blackbird chorus, and the yells of children in the ecstasies of snake hunting and slaughter, wafted in at my study window, I greet you. I have no news to tell, but you are in my thoughts.

My love to Livy and the girls. God grant that all are well. I'm going to Cornell U. next week to preach, and Dean S. [Sage] is going with me. But I have told you that before.

All of us are well, but Aunt Dora. She has had a rough winter of it.

The Inebriate Asylum is closed: Cause: lack of funds.[2] Cause of that: the superintendent a failure, *I think.* Yet new drunkards are blooming all around. I've got another awful secret or two of impending ruin and disgrace, loaded onto me, and it is a sick business, I can tell you.[3]

I wish I loved any good things half as much as I hate Rum, now that I have found it out. Mark! Mark!! *Do you look out for it!* It is the arch deceiver. It *fools* men.

How impatient I am to have you get home!

Yrs. Ever

Joe

1. Shin was, with Yung Wing, one of the earliest Chinese to study abroad in the United States. Journalist, teacher, and businessman, he was also at one time a member of the Legislative Council of Hong Kong.

2. The Walnut Hill Hospital in Hartford, known variously as the Asylum at Walnut Hill and Walnut Hill Asylum for Inebriates and Opium Takers.

3. Twichell took an interest in the cases of alcoholism among his congregation and (in his view) the resultant criminal activity. He sometimes noted the progress of such cases—without identifying the person involved—in the flyleaf of his journal.

52. Twain to Twichell

10 June 1879. Paris, France (In pencil)

(Care Monroe & Co).
Paris, June 10.

Dear Old Joe—I ought to be at work instead of gossiping, even with you; but I'm barred for an hour anyhow, for they've put a woman in next to my work-room, who I think will last about that length of time, judging by the rate at which she is coughing & hawking and spitting. When it's all over with her I will go back to work.

We are mighty hungry—we want to get home & get something to eat. I can't quite make out how Americans live on this flat infernal European food several years at a time without a run home now & then to fill in with something wholesome & satisfying.[1] We have engaged passage in the "Gallia" for Aug. 21.

I'm still pegging steadily away; have written matter enough for the book, but have weeded out & discarded a fourth of it & am banging away to supply the deficiency. My artist is banging away on the pictures, at the same time.

Boyesen & wife staid in our hotel 2 or 3 weeks, but as we should leave here before their confinement & they would be friendless, they concluded to go home & take young Boyesen along in the original package. If there's a duty on such goods they will have to pay, for they can't play it on the Custom house for fat—people don't get fat here, & the inspectors know it.

Boyesen spent a pleasant evening with Tourguèneff, & he spent an evening here with us—a fine old man.[2] [Written in top margin: "*This page is private to Joe. Mum!*"] Boyesen called on Renan & Victor Hugo, also, & had a good time with both of those old cocks, but I didn't go—my French ain't limber enough.[3] I *can* build up pretty stately French sentences, but the producing of an erection of this sort is not my best hold—I make it too hard & stiff—& so tall that only a seaman could climb it, or a monkey—but the latter would have to 'tend to business: couldn't carry his nuts up in his hands, or any other provender—but you will be asking how can a monkey have connection with a subject of this kind anyway? He can't. Nobody can. However, let that pass. I leave all this French business to Livy & Clara. They are studying hard every day, & I greatly pity them. A language ain't worth half the trouble it costs to learn it. Aldrich was here a week or so, & what a rattling time we did have. That fellow is blindingly bright.[4]

Oh, Switzerland! I have finished writing it, a few days ago. I have made the burlesque of Alp-climbing prodigiously loud, but I guess I will leave it so. The German legends which I manufactured to fit the ruined castles along the Neckar seem to read very well. I tore up two or three of them, but the rest have the right ring to them. I've got in that veterinary student who said "O, *hell*-yes!" too—& if it comes handy I think I will run across him again in the closing chapters.

Well, that woman is no more—I will go to work. Love to you all.

Ys Ever

Mark.

1. See *A Tramp Abroad*, 570–76.

2. The famous Russian author, Ivan Turgenev (or Tourguèneff), was living in Paris at this time and at the center of its literary life.

3. Ernest Renan was a noted French philosopher and historian. French novelist, playwright, and poet Victor Hugo is best known for *The Hunchback of Notre Dame* (1831) and *Les Misérables* (1862).

4. Thomas Bailey Aldrich, novelist, playwright and poet, and editor of the *Atlantic Monthly* from 1881 to 1890.

53. Twain to Twichell

2 October 1879. Elmira, New York

The Farm, Oct. 2/79.[1]

Dear Joe:

George retains his place with us.

His disposition to gallantry has made us say once or twice that we wanted no more colored cooks around until he should experience a change of heart; but we hanker for them, nevertheless, & your letter makes us want to try the one you mention.[2]

1. Will you give us an idea of her wages, Joe?

2. Is she *tidy*?—because when a colored cook is untidy she is likely to be intemperate in it.

Now if you don't mind answering these two questions, Joe, favorably, Livy will tackle the candidate by letter & do the rest of the thing herself.

[In pencil, boxed on three sides: OVER]

[On the reverse, in pencil:

3. Can Harmony recommend her as a good cook? Never mind her morals; is she a good cook?*]*

And there is one question which *I* would like answered: Is she old enough, or grave enough,—or above all, strong enough & wise enough, to resist George's fascinations?

You see, George is going to live with his wife again,—unless we get a cook to his taste. I *want* him to live with his wife; it curtails her immoralities, by diminishing her time for them.

I am revising my MS. I did not expect to like it, (the MS) but I do. I have been knocking out early chapters for more than a year, now,—not because they had not merit, but merely because they hindered the flow of the narrative; it was a dredging process; day before yesterday my shovel fetched up three more chapters & laid them reeking on the festering shore-pile of their predecessors, & now I think the yarn swims right along, without hitch or halt. I believe it will be a readable book of travels. I cannot see that it lacks anything but information.

The newspapers say Mr. Francis Gillette has passed away; but as we have received letters from you, & Charley Warner, & Lilly Warner, & Mrs. Perkins since the newspapers said it (I believe,) we are fain to hope it was some one else of the same name.[3]

You have run about a good deal, Joe, but you have never seen any place that was so divine as the Farm. Why don't you come here & take a foretaste of heaven?

With love to Harmony & yourself & the seven little ones,

Yrs Ever

Mark.

2 hours later. The fields and woods down in the ravine took fire & climbed the hill, sending such a great & threatening firmament of smoke through my windows that I gathered my MSS together, tied strings around them & prepared for a speedy desertion of my study. I saw Livy, Sue, & all the farm folks carrying water down the hill, meantime. By the time I was ready to help, the danger was over.

1. Quarry Farm was commonly referred to as "the Farm."

2. George Griffin, the Clemenses' African American butler, whose romantic proclivities Twain refers to here.

3. Seventy-one-year-old Gillette, politician and one of the original founders of the Nook Farm community, had died on 30 September. Mrs. Perkins was Lucy Maria Perkins, the wife of Charles E. Perkins, the lawyer who acted as Twain's attorney during the Hartford years.

54. Twain to Twichell

16 March 1880. Hartford, Connecticut (Inscription in A Tramp Abroad*)*

My Dear "Harris—" [Twain has then crossed out this line]

No, I mean

My Dear Joe—Just imagine it, for a moment: I was collecting material in Europe during 14 months for a book, & now that the thing is printed, I find that you, who were with me only a month & a half of the 14, are in *actual presence* (not imaginary) in 440 of the 531 pages the book contains! Hang it, if you had staid at home it would have taken me 14 *years* to get the material. You have saved me an intolerable whole world of hated labor, & I'll not forget it, my boy.

You'll find reminders of things, all along, that happened to us; & of others that didn't happen, but you'll remember the spot where they were invented. Somewhere in the book is mention of that bridge & that elephant ("keepsake") & O, lots of such things. You will see how the imaginary perilous trip up the Riffelberg is preposterously expanded. That horse-student is on page 192. The "Fremersberg" is neighboring. The Black-Forest Novel is on page 211—I remember when & where we projected that, in the leafy glades, with the mountain sublimities dozing in the blue haze beyond the gorge of Allerheiligen. There's the "new member," p. 213; the dentist yarn, 223; the true chamois, 242; at p. 248 is a pretty long yarn spun from a mighty brief text—meeting, for a moment, that pretty girl who knew me & whom I had forgotten; at 281 is "Harris," [Twain initially wrote "yourself" but deleted it and inserted "'Harris'" instead] & should have been so entitled, but Bliss has made a mistake & turned you into some other character; 305 brings back the whole Rhigi tramp to me at a glance; at 185 & 186 are specimens of my art; & the frontispiece is the combination which I made by pasting one familiar picture over the lower half of an equally familiar one—this fine work being worthy of Titian, I have shed the credit of it upon him. Well, you'll find more reminders of things, scattered through here, than are printed, or could have been printed in many books. All the "legends of the Neckar" which I invented for that unstoried region, are here—one is in the Appendix. The steel portrait of me is just about perfect.

We had a mighty good time, Joe, & the 6 weeks I would dearly like to repeat, *any* time—but the rest of the 14 months, *never.*

With love,
Yours,
Mark

Hartford, March 16, 1880

55. Twain to Twichell

24 March 1880. Hartford, Connecticut

EDITORIAL OFFICE OF
THE ATLANTIC MONTHLY
———
47 FRANKLIN STREET,
BOSTON

Remail this
to me, Joe
Mark

*[Twain encloses a 22 March letter from William Dean Howells which describes how the latter had "been feebly trying to give the Atlantic readers some notion of the charm and the solid delightfulness" of Twain's new book—*A Tramp Abroad. *Among other things, Howells also says that "I must tell you privately what a joy it has been to Mrs. Howells and me. . . . Mrs. Howells declares it the wittiest book she ever read, and I say there is* sense *enough in it for ten books. That is the idea which my review will try to fracture the average numbscull [*sic*] with.—Well, you are a blessing."*[1] *]*

1. See *Mark Twain–Howells Letters,* 293.

56. Twichell to Twain

25 March 1880. Hartford, Connecticut

Thursday p.m.

Dear Mark,

Thou art a good fellow to show me Howells' letter. It was something I wanted to see.

I have felt a considerable modesty about the book, because it was so much mine (so I have been pleased to view it) i.e. I was so personally involved in it.

And now I am mighty glad that so preëminent a taster is so nearly of my own mind about it.

Mem. Next week *Friday* night (Apr. 2nd) I want you at the Chapel. Do you hear?

Thine ever aff.

Joe

57. Twichell to Twain

17 July 1880. Hartford, Connecticut

Hartford. July 17

Dear Mark,

Do you remember my speaking of some articles by Tom Lounsbury of Yale College about a mediaeval worthy? Well here they are by mail accompanying this.[1] I think they will entertain your Highness.

How are you, dear old fellow, and how's Livy? I think of you daily up there under the sky like the gods on Olympus,

"careless of mankind"[2]

and wish as intensely as one can in such a languid clime that I have a taste of your comforts with you.[3]

Harmony and the children went off to the Adirondacks two weeks and a half ago, leaving me here in a solitude which I am ill-fitted to support. If there were two of us, I could turn it into a picnic, but hollow echoes enlivened only by mice and water bugs are scant material to deal with. A good sociable bed-bug would be a relief. But patience! A fortnight more and *my* harness drops.

Dean Sage has just returned from salmon fishing. He had for fellow-sportsmen, and guests at Camp Harmony (as he styles his lodge on the Restigouche) the Duke of Beaufort, Sir FitzRoy Somerset, another Sir—I forget his name—and Florence the actor.[4] In that gilded society he ate, drank and sat up nights till he was pretty nearly laid out. But it was for his country's sake, and a noble cause to die in.

Hurra for Fiske![5] How nobly he has conquered his weaknesses. Now he can have any medical counsel or treatment he may want to try, no matter how expensive. Charley, Susie and I went up to Mt. Holyoke a week ago and passed a delightful day in the breeze.[6] Do you know that my two sisters, Mrs Hall, and Olive, are at Mrs Gleason's?[7] My love to T.K.B.[8]

I am glad that I have been to the Farm, for I know just how to picture you both at work and at play. Do for pity's sake write to me.

Susie and the Ba are all right I hope and getting the full benefit of your immense stock of sun and air.[9] And, if it please God—and you—I hope the next one will *be* son and heir.[10] The Lord be kind to Livy, who has our best wishes and prayers continually.

Yours affectionately, indeed, indeed.

J.H.T.

1. Thomas R. Lounsbury's pamphlet, *A Scholar of the Twelfth Century*, was reprinted from the *New Englander* for November 1878, January 1879, and January 1880. Lounsbury was at Yale with Twichell.

2. From Tennyson, "The Lotos-Eaters."

3. Twichell apparently means "might have" or "had" here.

4. William J. Florence, one of the most popular actors of the period and also a playwright and songwriter. He was also co-founder of the Shriners, a Masonic order.

5. Daniel Willard Fiske, Cornell librarian and language scholar. Fiske had married heiress Jennie McGraw in Berlin four days previously. His new wife would soon die (on 30 September 1881), embroiling Fiske in a complicated struggle with Cornell over her inheritance. See *Autobiography of Mark Twain*, 2:34–37. Fiske was of generally weak health; thus, perhaps, the "weaknesses."

6. Charles and Susan Warner.

7. Mary Delight Hall and Olive Twichell, both half-sisters to Twichell. Silas and Rachel Gleason ran the Elmira Water Cure, opened in 1852, with its sulphur spring and the healing properties it was said to contain. See, too, Letter 18.

8. Thomas K. Beecher.

9. Bay was Clara's nickname as a small child (she was now six), based on the mispronunciation of "baby" by Susy shortly after she was born. Twichell's version of this was "the Ba."

10. Livy was pregnant with Jean Clemens, the couple's third daughter. Twichell's emphasis implies that the Clemenses hoped for a boy. Note also Twichell's bad pun, "sun and air."

58. Twain to Twichell

19 July 1880. Elmira, New York (Two independent typed copies prepared for Albert Bigelow Paine)

Quarry Farm, July 19.

Dear old Joe:

We have been up here 10 days, now, & I have been on the sick list pretty much all that time, with lumbago. Mrs. Gleason was here a few days ago, & told us your sisters were at the Cure, but neither Livy nor I have fairly been in condition to go down there since then. I have spent part of my time in bed; but yesterday evening Livy & I determined to get to the Cure this morning—but there's another failure: I'm bedridden again—a decided case of rheumatism; I shall not be out again for some days I guess. We have twice sent verbal messages to Olive, begging her to waive ceremony & run up here, but she don't waive worth a cent. It is cold & stormy to-day; but Livy & Sue will go to the Cure as soon as the weather moderates.

Have just finished the Scholar of the 12th Cent. & am delighted with the amusing & pathetic story. Suppose Giraldus had been politic; he might have reached the primacy; then imagine poor Henry II saddled with this *second* Beckett [*sic*]![1] I wish I could read the original; those marvels charm me—such as the spring running with milk, the man breached like a bull, & that soldier's immaculate conception of a calf. I will re-mail the pamphlet to you to-day or to-morrow.

I am writing with a stylographic pen.[2] It takes a royal amount of cussing to make the thing go, the first few days or a week; but by that time the dullest ass gets the hang of the thing, & after that no enrichments of expression are required, & said ass finds the stylographic a genuine God's blessing. I carry one in each breeches pocket, & both loaded. I'd give you one of them if I had you where I could teach you how to use it—not otherwise; for the average ass flings the thing out of the window in disgust, the second day, believing it hath ne virtue ne merit of any sort, whereas the lack lieth in himself, God of his mercy damn him.[3]

I have writ one or two magazine articles & about 100 pages on one of my books, since we left Hartford—been idle the rest of the time.[4]

"1601" is on its travels again; John Hay has been handing it around, in Washington, & took it out & left it in Cleveland, the other day, in the hands of an antiquary who will memorize it & then return it.[5]

(I hear the mellow German tongue out yonder:

"Clara, where art thou?"

"Here above. We wait for thee, Susie"[6]

It seems to me our tongue lost a good deal when the gentle thee & thou departed out of it.)

Tom Beecher & family are up in the woods at Jim Beecher's; Mrs. Langdon is at Avon Springs; Charley Langdon, with his family, is at Waukesha, Wisconsin, suffering horribly with dyspepsia.[7] This household is well & flourishing, except me. I think we are growing doubtful about the son & heir. Sometimes we say, "He cometh not at all, & is a delusion & a fraud;" at other times we be dimly hopeful, & say, "Mayhap this is not so; peradventure he cometh by slow freight."

Well, old man, we all send a power of love to you & Harmony & the kids—& I am

Yours Ever

Mark

1. In 1175, the young Gerald of Wales (Giraldus) was elected Bishop of St. David's by his supporters there. King Henry II, however, realized the political implications of such an appointment and blocked it. Just five years previously Thomas Becket had been murdered in Canterbury Cathedral as a result of conflict with the king concerning the power of the church.

2. The stylographic pen was the first successfully functioning fountain pen available on public sale.

3. Twain falls into a mock medieval diction here.

4. Twain was working on *The Prince and the Pauper* at Quarry Farm this summer.

5. *1601*, an Elizabethan parody Twain had composed in 1876. It was written, partly at least, to amuse and perhaps shock Twichell with its moves between the elaborate formality of Elizabethan speech and its down-to-earth subject matter (flatulence, masturbation, etc.). See *Autobiography of Mark Twain*, 2:155–57. John Hay, journalist, author, and politician, Lincoln's private secretary and secretary of state under McKinley and Roosevelt.

6. Rosina Hay, the children's German tutor, was still with the family.

7. Rev. James Chaplin Beecher was the youngest of the numerous Beecher siblings.

59. Twichell to Twain

23–25 August 1880. Keene Valley, Essex County, New York

Keene Valley.
Essex Co. N.Y.
Aug. 23rd. 24th. 25th somewhere
along there

Dear old Mark;

I send you goods by mail as follows: a copy of a California journal lately come to me from some unknown source which may afford you—as a Californian—two or three minutes entertainment. And a small book which I carried away from Charley Warner's on account of its title "Adirondack Stories."[1] I have found it so interesting that I feel the impulse to pass it on to you. The habit of years of communicating every sensation experienced forthwith to you is very strong upon me. So as soon as I began to taste the flavor of this book, the idea of asking you to taste it too followed naturally. I do not know who the author is. I never heard of him before. But if I am not mistaken he is a mighty promising writer. I'd like to have your judgment on him anyhow. Just read for a specimen "John's Trial" and tell me if you do not think it equal to anything of Bret Harte's.[2] There's no dialect to garnish the simple dish it sets before you, and no apparent *effort* to produce effect, but it takes hold—of me anyway. I do not think it is an ordinary man who takes such material and handles it so delicately. Fetch the book back to Hartford with you when you come.

But really I am making the book serve as an occasion and excuse for writing to you. We are anxious to learn how you are—particularly Livy. A letter from Susie Warner a few days since said that you had reported to somebody—Mrs. Perkins I think—that she (Livy) was not getting on as well as you would like to have her. How is it now? Pray God 'twas nothing serious. But do send us just a bulletin to relieve our anxiety. And we would like to have a general statement of the p'ints of the new baby.

I wish that Susie and the Ba were here for a few days to join the festivities—the revelries—that are constantly going on in and about these premises. It is an incessant picnic and I am taking a world of pleasure in looking on.

All of us are well. Harmony walked fourteen miles one day last week, and the younger ones are tanned black as Indians with out of door life. Are you at work? I am not, except at fishing and reading novels. I have been having a delicious time with Thackeray.

I passed a night with Dean S. on the way hither and heard all about his fortnight with the Duke of Beaufort & Co, I will rehearse the tale to you when we meet.

I live over again daily our glorious tramp of two summers ago. That was my Golden Vacation, for which I must thank you as long as I live.

An invoice of love to Livy and to all of you.

Yours ever aff.

J.H.T.

1. Philander Deming, *Adirondack Stories* (1880).

2. Bret Harte was a highly successful short-story writer, perhaps best known for his "The Luck of Roaring Camp." A literary colleague of Twain's in California in the 1860s, Twain fell out with him during Harte's 1876 visit to Twain's Hartford home and would thenceforth speak of him with contempt.

60. Twain to Twichell

29 August 1880. Elmira, New York (Transcript by Albert Bigelow Paine)

Quarry Farm, Aug. 29.

Dear Old Joe—

Concerning Jean Clemens, if anybody said he "didn't see no p'ints about that frog that's any better'n any other frog," I should think he was convicting himself of being a pretty poor sort of observer.[1] She is the comeliest, & daintiest & perfectest little creature the continents &

archipelagoes have seen since Bay & Susie were her size. I will not go into details; it is not necessary; you will soon be in Hartford, where I have already hired a hall; the admission fee will be but a trifle.

It is curious to note the change in the stock-quotations of the Affection Board brought about by the throwing this new security on the market. Four weeks ago the children still put Mamma at the head of the list right along, where she had always been. But now:

Jean
Mamma
Motley } cats.
Fraulein }
Papa[2]

That is the way it stands, now. Mamma is become No. 2; I have dropped from No. 4, and am become No. 5. Some time ago it used to be nip & tuck between me & the cats, but after the cats "developed" I didn't stand any more show.

I've got a swollen ear; so I take advantage of it to lie abed most of the day, & read & smoke & scribble & have a good time. Last evening Livy said with deep concern, "O dear, I believe an abscess is forming in your ear."

I responded as the poet would have done if he had had a cold in the head—

'Tis said that abscess conquers love,
But O believe it not.[3]

This made a coolness. For the one thing which Livy cannot stand, is wit.

I have read "John's Trial," & like it very much indeed. It has the advantage of Bret Harte's rot, that it is sincere. I mean to read the rest, to-day. The papers say that Harte & William Black are bumming around together in the Highlands.[4] I suspect that at bottom these two are kindred spirits.

I am more than charmed to know that John T. Raymond has made a most complete & pitiful failure in London with Col. Sellers. Still, it doesn't do me half the good it could have done if it had come sooner. My malignity was so worn out & wasted away with time & the exercise of charity that even Raymond's death would not afford me anything more than a mere fleeting ecstasy, a sort of momentary pleasurable titillation, now—unless, of course, it happened in some peculiarly radiant way like burning, or boiling, or something like that.[5] Joys that come to us after the capacity for enjoyment is dead, are but an affront.

Been reading Daniel Webster's Private Correspondence.[6] Have read a hundred of his diffuse, conceited, "eloquent," bathotic (or bathostic) letters written in that dim (no, vanished) Past when he was a student; & Lord, to think that this boy who is so real to me now, & so booming with fresh young blood & bountiful life, & sappy cynicisms about girls, has since climbed the Alps of fame & stood against the sun one brief tremendous moment with the world's eyes upon him, & then—*f-z-t-!* where is he? Why the only *long* thing, the only *real* thing about the whole shadowy business is the sense of the lagging dull & hoary lapse of time that has drifted by since then; a vast empty level, it seems, with a formless spectre glimpsed fitfully through the smoke & mist that lie along its remote verge.[7]

Well, we are all getting along here first-rate; Livy gains strength daily, & sits up a deal; the baby is five weeks old and—— but no more of this; somebody may be reading *this* letter 80 years hence. And so, my friend (you pitying snob, I mean, who are holding this yellow paper in your hand in 1960,) save yourself the trouble of looking further; I know how pathetically trivial our small concerns would seem to you, & I will not let your eye profane them. No, I keep my news; you keep your compassion. Suffice it you to know, scoffer & ribald, that the little child is old & blind, now, & once more toothless; & the rest of us are shadows, these many, many years. Yes, & *your* time cometh!

Mark.

1. Jane Lampton (Jean) Clemens was born in Elmira on 26 July 1880.

2. Motley and Fraulein were the family cats.

3. These are a distorted version of the first two lines of a song by Frederick William Thomas.

4. William Black was a highly popular Scottish novelist known especially for his portrayals of Highland characters and scenery.

5. John T. Raymond had successfully played Sellers in Twain's own stage version of *The Gilded Age,* first produced in 1874. At this point he had leased the play from Twain to take to England (where it did badly). In 1883, Twain would write of Raymond that he "would stand with his foot on the steps of the throne of God & lie" (*Mark Twain–Howells Letters,* 619). He nonetheless approached him in 1884 to play the lead in *Colonel Sellers as a Scientist.* Raymond would, in fact, die in an Evanston, Indiana, hotel while on tour in 1887.

6. *The Private Correspondence of Daniel Webster* had been published by Little, Brown & Co. (Boston) in 1857.

7. Bathotic is an archaic form of "bathetic."

61. Twain to Twichell

Dated by telegraph operator 14 October 1880. Boston, Massachusetts

THE WESTERN UNION TELEGRAPH COMPANY.[1]

DATED Boston Mass 14 1880
RECEIVED AT Octo " 730
TO Rev J H Twitchell [*sic*]

I want you to dine with us saturday half past five 5 and meet Col Fred Grant no ceremony[2] Wear the same shirt you always wear

S. L. Clemens

1. Further information here and at foot of telegram specifying the conditions under which messages are sent, etc., omitted here.
2. Frederick Grant was the son of Ulysses S. Grant.

62. Twichell to Twain

3 November 1880?[1] Hartford, Connecticut

Wednesday

Dear Mark

If this divine weather holds, we Twichells, i.e., Julie, Sue and Ed (and maybe a friend or two of them) propose to kick leaves to the Tower Saturday.[2] If you will join us we shall have all the better a time. I think we will telephone Bartlett to make ready a lunch.[3]

Yrs aff

Joe

1. Provisional dating on the basis of postmark (3 November) and day (Wednesday), the ages of Twichell's children, and the 1877 date of the installation of Twain's phone (Twichell would have been dependent on a neighbor's phone). 1886 is the only other possibility if the match of date and day above is correct.
2. Twichell variously refers to his daughter Julia as Julie in her childhood, Judy later.
3. Matthew H. Bartlett, *Hartford Republican* publisher and builder of Talcott Mountain Tower.

63. Twichell to Twain

28 January 1881. Hartford, Connecticut

Friday evening

Dear Mark,

Monday Feb. 21st will do for West Point so far as I am concerned, unless it finds me tied up by scarlet fever circumstances, which I hope and believe will not be the case.[1] But why must you be back Tuesday night? That will put us on a mighty short allowance of time. We shall not get there till toward night, and shall have to dig out early the next morning. Can't we have a day there?

You're the most immoderate person about this scarlet fever business I've seen yet. I haven't been near a horse car since the last time I saw you. Yes, I have, I rode up on the platform with the driver once afterwards. I tapered off with that and now I'm a total abstainer. But, my gracious, what's the use of abstaining from the pulpit? The thing don't throw like a skunk. You can't give it where you don't *go.* The next minister I exchange with is the only possible victim.

If I was on the top of Matterhorn in my shirt it wouldn't satisfy some people.

Our patients are so jolly, that the "outs" are hoping their turn will soon come.

With love to all of you.

Yrs ever

Joe

1. The Twichells were quarantined for scarlet fever about this time. Joe writes in his journal at the time that, despite "our visitation [being] of the mildest type, . . . I found so many people in fear of me, that for a month and more I attended no meeting or service whatsoever, except that of Sunday mornings."

64. Twichell to Twain

16 February 1881. Hartford, Connecticut

Woodland St.
Wednesday morning

Dear Mark,

Will you read for us—and for me in particular—in the chapel next week Friday evening, Feb. 25th? It will be for you a preparation for West Point, and for our good folks a service that will be much appreciated.[1]

Please send me word by Julie who will wait outside (she is commanded not to go in) to receive it. I want to know today.

The accompanying parcel for Livy I charge you to deliver unopened unto her hand.

Yours aff.

Joe

1. The West Point reading had been put back to 28 February. See Bush, *Mark Twain and the Spiritual Crisis of His Age*, 167.

65. Twain to Twichell

16 February 1881. Hartford, Connecticut

---

*[Twain sends on a 15 February letter from Charles Dudley Warner, the start of the final paragraph of which reads: "Just this minute going to take journey for Brooklyn to talk tonight to the Young Men of Dr Storr's [*sic*] church—[*same such lecture humbug as Joe gets up in his.*] "[1]*

Twain has circled the phrase within the square brackets, with a drawing of a hand pointing to the circled phrase.]

Dear Joe—All right, I'll do your lecture-humbug for you the 25th. Keep it quiet, you know; no printer's ink. The way we did it before was right.

Yrs Ever

(in dreadful haste—just leaving for New York——both of us—couple of days—

Mark

[Written to the left of the signature with a horizontal rule above and a vertical rule on the right:]

I told Howells [to] send you the pen—did he?[2]

[New page:]

Please return this letter of Charley's to me.

---

1. Rev. Richard Salter Storrs was pastor of the Congregational Church of the Pilgrims in Brooklyn, New York.

2. Twain had gifted one of the new fountain pens on which he was so keen to both Howells and Twichell. Neither evidently kept them long. See *Mark Twain's Notebooks & Journals*, 2:396.

66. Twichell to Twain

18 February 1881. Hartford, Connecticut

Friday Eve.

Dear Mark:

All right, and I'm a thousand times obliged to you. Stevens (the Committee on Entertainments) says I had better not advertise you on Sunday, as that makes it next to impossible to keep it out of the papers.[1] I'll speak of it at the Thursday evening meeting. But there'll be folks enough there, no fear of that. Governor Bigelow is going to be invited, for one.[2]

We are all well now.

Yours aff.

Joe

No. I haven't got the Stylograph yet.

1. Stevens was presumably a member of Asylum Hill Congregational Church.

2. Hobart B. Bigelow, then governor of Connecticut.

67. Twichell to Twain

March 1881?[1] Hartford, Connecticut

Dear Mark,

Wing wants to see you. More business for Gen. Grant.—*big* business—bigger than the other. Can you stop work for an hour this p.m.—say at 3 o'clock—and give the Mandarin and me an interview?[2] Please answer.

Yrs. Aff.

Joe.

1. Provisional dating. The envelope is addressed "Mark Twain | Present | By the hand of Miss Twichell" and Twain has annotated it in blue ink: "General Grant & the Chinese Educational Mission."

2. There was an ongoing crisis concerning the future of the Chinese Educational Mission at this time. In a 10 March letter, Yung Wing wrote Twichell, "Could you go over & see our friend Mr. Clemens & tell him confidentially what good he is capable of doing." Twain had, with Twichell, been to see ex-President Grant the previous December to use his influence on this matter, and with good results. But on 9 July 1881, Twichell would write in his journal, "*The Mission is doomed!*" This present letter, however, seems to have more to do with Wing's desire for the United States to provide both men and financing (ahead of England) for a new Chinese railroad project, perhaps attempting to use the Twain-Grant connection for this purpose while it was still active. In his journal for March 25–28, Twichell writes of this project, saying that "Yung Wing arrives from Washington full of business." See, too, *Mark Twain's Notebooks & Journals*, 2:389–90.

68. Twichell to Twain

13 July 1881. Hartford, Connecticut

Hartford.
Wed. morning.

Dear Mark:

We got home all right, and found Harmony and the small fry well. Now we desire to waft back our formal, deliberate, and most hearty thanks for the hospitality that will always add sweetness to the memory of our golden little excursion. It but forms the latest item of that long and ever lengthening, and never-to-be settled account, Twichells,—Due—to Clemenses. Well, for my part, I am a good deal resigned to it. In fact, I sometimes wonder if I don't take it a little too easily—as a matter-of-course. If I do, the fault is all yours and Livy's—who do not give your kindness to us the chance ever to be a fresh sensation.[1]

But, by the powers, we are not insensible to it, for all that.

In a burst of more than ordinary stupidity after buying at the Branford Station the additional ticket and a half required (after you gave me those two) to get us to New H. [New Haven] I bought three and a half to Hartford, and didn't see that I was doing the business from Branford to N.H. twice over. So I have the enclosed left on my hands and send them to you—to go with you on your River trip in the fall and travel around a little.[2]

With no end of love to all and every one of you—yours aff—but before I close, remember us to the delightful Whitmores.[3] I shall long remember with satisfaction that wicked, wicked evening in my room.

I thoughtlessly omitted yesterday to bestow the courtesy of a good bye on the landlord of the Montowese, who stood there with you seeing us off. Queer! It came to me like a shot when we were about half way to the Station. If you think it best to repair the injury by anything said, do so: if not, not.

I know that I was very dull and unprofitable company yesterday and Monday, but the fact is I have got below the point of spontaneity for this year i.e. working year, and it would have been such a mockery of our mutual friendship and confidence, for me to have tried to rouse myself. I didn't try, and the consequence is, I love you to-day as well as ever.

But, my sakes, how lame my arm is. I can hardly write. Likewise my back and side and legs—all from those blessed ten pins.

We have had many and many a good time together, my dear old fellow; it has been a bright streak experience to me all through; but, oh dear me, how I do wish I had been a better pastor to you. God bless you, spite of me.

Yours aff.

Joe

1. Twain and Livy had invited Twichell and Harmony to the Branford, Connecticut, coastal resort where they were staying. Harmony had declined the invitation (due to the "'boiling machine' of perpetual nausea"—she was pregnant with her seventh child), so Twichell had presumably taken three of the elder children with him. Something of the intimate relationship between the two wives is illustrated in Harmony's letter to Livy at this time, writing in a heartfelt and negative way about the pregnancy—and, by implication, about Joe's unwillingness to ease up on this reproductive front. Toward the end of the pregnancy (in January 1882) she would ask (secretly) to borrow money from Livy to meet her household needs, but it is likely the money was given as a gift ("Livy, I have had a good '*joyful*' cry over your goodness to me"). Sarah Twichell was born in February 1882, with Harmony pregnant again by the following August. See Courtney, *Joseph Hopkins Twichell*, 223–24. Annie Moffett Webster, Twain's niece, would later comment, "Someone once asked Uncle Sam how many children Mr. Twichell had. He said 'I don't know. I haven't heard from him since morning'" (Mark Twain Papers).

2. A reference to Twain's plans to return to the Mississippi River as he researched *Life on the Mississippi* (1883). Twain in fact made this trip a little later, in April 1882.

3. Franklin G. Whitmore, Twain's Hartford business agent, and wife, Harriet G. Whitmore.

69. Twichell to Twain

17 August 1881. Hartford, Connecticut

Hartford. Aug. 17th

Dear Mark,

I send you by mail a periodical containing an article by our friend Lt. Wood.[1] You will see by the postal card accompanying it that he desired me to do so.

Next week, I'm off to Keene Valley. My month alone has been dreary.[2] All the news from Harmony and the regiment is good.

Parker got home day before yesterday.[3] He says that he was more than ever impressed with your prodigious popularity in England. On one or two occasions where the talk was of you, he ventured diffidently to say that he knew you personally, but was so evidently thought to be lying for effect, that he did not venture to say so any more—thus, in a manner, practicing untruth to save his reputation for veracity.

But I can't stop to write a letter this morning. Besides, the dark look of things at Washington has taken my spirits all away.[4]

With much love to Livy, and the bonnie lasses, your daughters.
Yours ever affectionately
Joe

1. Twain and Twichell met Lieutenant Charles Erskine Scott Wood, adjutant to the commanding general at West Point, on their visit there in 1881. It was Wood who arranged for West Point Press to secretly publish fifty copies of Twain's *1601* in 1882. Wood's first known publication is "Among the Tlingits in Alaska" (*Century Magazine*, July 1882), based on an 1877 trip to that newly acquired territory. This may just possibly have been an early copy. Wood's career was not only as a soldier, but also as lawyer, painter, reformer, and philosophical anarchist.

2. Harmony and the family would already have been in the Adirondacks.

3. Edwin Pond Parker, Twichell's close friend and fellow minister.

4. No doubt a reference to President James Garfield's state of health after the 2 July 1881 assassination attempt. Garfield would die on 19 September.

70. Twichell to Twain

26 August 1881. Keene Valley, Essex County, New York

Keene Valley. Essex Co. N.Y.
Aug. 26th 1881

My dear Mark:

Alex Holley is abroad,—went in July and won't be back till Christmas.[1] I don't suppose you can wait to hear from him about the stock, if, indeed, he could tell you under the circumstances. Anyhow I don't know his address, though I could find out.

I can't at this moment myself think of anybody to refer you to for an opinion unless it is John C. Wyman.[2] He would be likely to be posted, and you might trust him. Boston, Mass would find him, I guess.

If I think up anybody else that you can inquire of, I'll let you know right off.

[Dean Sage knows a Mr Hine who is Alex Holley's friend, and in the same general line with him. He might know.][3]

I got here Tuesday (this is Friday) and found all hands well, and mighty glad to see yours truly. Sally, Molly and Cornell Dunham are our near neighbors, and nobody else.[4] If you and yours were as near on the other flank we should have all that heart could desire.

Dean Sage *was* here last week, but I missed him. His wife and three young children are in the neighborhood. They have had a sick summer of it amongst 'em, but are now better.

Oh, my, how good it seems to get a flannel shirt on, and stretch out on the veranda, novel in hand, pipe in mouth, a big cool mountain up against the sky yonder, and six clear weeks of unalloyed indolence ahead. To lie thus at sweet lawful leisure, and resolve to live a better and more useful life in that remote future when I shall have my neck again under the foot of the Ogre Duty—what bliss it is!

The President—here the news from Washington is two days old before it reaches us. I found that hard to put up with at first, but what difference does it make after all? It takes off the strain a little, I find. But I quite sympathize with the state of mind you reveal, produced by this long eternal, weary lift of suspense in which we have lived of late.[5] That remarkable and unprecedented feature of the situation—the universality, the *conscious* universality of the attenuating experience of hope and despondency which we have shared, I touched upon in a sermon I preached just after the Tragedy opened, only I did not have your brush to color it with. What helpless creatures we nations of men are! Spite of our united pull of wishing—yes, and praying—world wide as it is—and his own most gallant and strenuous will and struggle to live, there he is sinking away, as it seems, and nothing can by any means deliver him.

This is a spectacle, as I view it, to worship God by, for His Greatness somehow shines out of it, adorably.

Dear old fellow, how I do love you, and wish and wish and wish all manner of good to you. Well, I'll stop here. Give dear Livy a brother's embrace for me, and Uncle Joe's blessing to the Misses Clemens. Harmony is out and everybody else or there would be a general round of messages. Thine aff.

Joe

P.S. Pres. Porter of Yale Coll. has just dropped in, and he says that Judge Hale of Elizabethtown (12 miles distant from here) will know all about that stock.[6] Maybe I shall have a chance to ask him about it myself. He sometimes comes this way in the summer.

1. Alexander Lyman Holley was the brother of one of Twichell's Yale classmates. The Holleys' father had been governor of Connecticut from 1857 to 1858. Holley was a mechanical engineer particularly important for his bringing of the Bessemer process to the U.S. steel industry.

2. Former abolitionist and Boston businessman.

3. These two sentences are written in the left-hand margin of the text, with a line showing where they should go in the body of the letter. An 1884 memorial volume to Holley lists a D. S. Hines of Pittsburgh among Holley's friends.

4. The (numerous) Dunham family were Hartford residents. Sarah (Sally) Dunham was a close Twichell family friend; Molly was Mary Elizabeth Dunham, her sister; and "Cornell" was a nickname for Austin Cornelius Dunham. The families were staying in a section of Keene Valley known as the "Dunham [or Hartford] plateau."

5. Twain had presumably written Twichell about the Garfield assassination. His letter is now missing.

6. Noah Porter (philosopher and lexicographer) was president of Yale from 1871 to 1886. Judge Robert S. Hale was a lawyer and served as a U.S. congressman from 1871 to 1875.

71. Twichell to Twain

2 October 1881. Keene Valley, New York

Keene Valley N.Y.
Oct. 2nd 1881

My dear Mark:

Here is a discourse of George Eliot's which I would like you to read at your leisure, not because I think it hits you, (for I do not think it does: If I thought it did I probably should not have the courage to send it to you: and if I had the courage I should not deem it best.) but because it seems to me to put some things of practical concern to you very truly and forcibly in a manner that you will both approve and appreciate.[1]

I would *carry* it to you: for we are going home in three days more; only when I read it I *said* I would send it, and now I'm going to.

My, how I have wanted to see you the last ten days—to see you and talk with you or rather, hear you talk. It has been a strange time with me, this whole season of tragedy and tribulation. I have been, so to speak out of the world, hearing all as from afar, dreamily yet sadly enough. I was away in the woods and did not know that Garfield was dead until Thursday night![2] The last news I had heard before that was favorable. Can you imagine one being so out of the flood as that? Oh, the cruel, cruel fate of that man!

A letter from Mrs. Langdon to Harmony informs us that you are back in Hartford.[3] We hope to be there Friday. All of us are well and have been, save Harmony, who, poor woman, is enjoying a period of general discomfort. I'm mighty sorry for her all the while.

Let's walk out to the Tower some afternoon next week, if the weather serves.

Week after next I'm going to St. Louis to attend a Missionary meeting. It would be a chance to make that down river trip with you if I had been home the past fortnight, as I naturally should have been, but for having postponed my vacation. As it is I shall have to hurry back directly or the parish will mutiny.

Our love unfeigned to dear Livy and the girls. I do hope we shall see a good deal of one another all round the coming year.

I'll try to be a better minister than ever to you, Mark, i.e. I'll try to *be* one, which I often fear I haven't been at all. I've got the affection anyhow, whatever else is wanting.

Yrs ever

Joe

1. George Eliot (pen name of Mary Ann Evans), English novelist. The article or essay is no longer with the letter, and its identity is unknown.

2. Garfield had died on Monday, 19 September; Twichell had not heard the news until 29 September.

3. Livy's mother was a frequent guest in the Twain household.

72. Twain to Twichell

9 October 1881? Hartford, Connecticut (Transcript by Albert Bigelow Paine)

Hartford, Sunday Afternoon.

Rev. J. H. Twichell—

Dear Joe: When you notified the congregation, this morning, that your chapel would be open, next Friday, for the reception of various rehabilitating supplies for Michigan's unfortunates, it seemed to me that in specifying the articles needed, you omitted a class of quite important necessities.[1] Through you, I beg to contribute an article which belongs to that ignored class: therefore, accompanying this letter, please find a deck of cards & a cribbage board. When a man has lost his all, & his heart hangs like a lump of lead in his body, there come times when an hour's innocent amusement is more worth to him than bread & meat & clothes: it unbinds him from the rack of his thoughts, it charms his troubles to sleep, it refreshes his spent forces, it is balm to his bruised spirit.

I am not actuated by any frivolous or unsympathetic impulse in doing this—as you would know, without my telling you—but by a much better & worthier motive: one which more than one stricken & despondent man & woman in Michigan will understand and appreciate. I want this box & the cards to go to the burned district; they will find a friend there, somewhere.

I enclose, also, some money, to buy more cards with. No—to buy what you please with.

Your friend

Mark.

1. A gale had hit Michigan in early September, followed by a severe forest fire (a million acres devastated in the Sanilac and Huron Counties alone). There were 282 lives lost and more than $2.25 million in damage.

73. Twichell to Twain

Most probably February 1882. Hartford, Connecticut

Wednesday morning

Dear Mark,

Your remembrance of dear Alex Holley, and your liking for him will give the enclosed eulogy and notice of the works he wrought some interest to you.[1] It is a scientific journal, as you see.

Please keep it for me, I want it to preserve.

Isn't that extract from his speech at Pittsburg [*sic*], exquisite?

Hope Jean and House are better this morning.[2] We are just about the same;— had a long forlorn night, but sunshine seemed to bring relief— like St. Jacobs oil or Lydia Pinkham's sweet swill.[3]

Yrs ever

Joe

1. Holley had died on 29 January 1882. The enclosure is now missing.

2. Edward H. House had fallen ill while staying with Twain and his family. In 1883 he would suffer a disabling stroke and was thenceforth confined to a wheelchair.

3. The lineament, St. Jacob's Oil, was a common remedy for rheumatism and other aches and pains at the time. Lydia E. Pinkham's Vegetable Compound was a well-known treatment for "female complaints" but was also said to cure all manner of illnesses.

74. Twichell to Twain

17 February 1882. Hartford, Connecticut

Friday morning

Dear Mark

My sin, as a total abstainer, now finds me out. I haven't a beer bottle in the house.

I have the idea that we cannot *buy* the kind we want for our Koumiss.[1] Will you kindly spare us a few of your empty ones? We are nothing but a Koumiss factory this morning. A specimen bottle which Lettie brought home from Mr. Holbrook's proves quite agreeable to Harmony's taste right off, i.e. *the little of it we succeeded in saving.*[2] The most of it is on the wall, and in Burton's hair—who, or which happened to get in the way. As to the *Malt Extract*,—while we are sending for the indispensable "Loefland's," pray tell me gently what we are to do with this "Trommer" variety which you sent over yesterday?[3] What is *it* for?

Harmony, I am sorry to say, passed a most wretched night. I wish you'd write a sermon.

Yrs aff.

Joe

1. Kumis (variously spelled by Twichell and Twain) was a fermented mare's milk product used as a general remedy for a number of illnesses at this period. The remedy is for Harmony, who then had some (unspecified) problem with her health. The bottles to which Twichell refers appear to be necessary for the decanting of the medicine.

2. Lettie Lockwood, a servant to the Twichell family.

3. Loefland's Extract of Malt, a common health remedy. Trommer's Extract of Malt was a similar "medicinal cure."

75. Twain to Twichell

18? February 1882. Hartford, Connecticut

Dear Joe—

The Holbrooks always lose ⅔ of their Koomiss, too, I believe, in unbottling. Now there is no sense in *all* people being idiots: take a big 2-quart pickle-jar, up-end your Koomis-bottle, & uncork *downwards* into that. Then you'll save it all.

Patrick says he asked, at Moses's, for Loefland's Extract of Malt, & showed them my spelling of the name—& they said "all right" & handed him the bottle which reached you.[1] Maybe it *is* all right; still, the first time you are sending down town, you better get Loefland's.

I always *told* you to keep a few sermons ahead—write them in the woods instead of always loafing. If I knew the channel I'd write you one, cheerfully.[2]

House is getting better & better.

Very very sorry Harmony had a bad night, but mighty thankful that she takes to the Koumiss.

Yrs Ever

Mark

1. Most likely, Moses's is S. G. Moses & Co., Druggist, at 587 and 605 Main Street, Hartford.

2. Deletion of "ropes" with "channel" then written to replace it.

76. Twichell to Twain

10 May 1882. Hartford, Connecticut

Hartford. May 10

Dear old Mark:

I suppose you have heard from Livy how the lightning of my peculiar sort of luck has struck me again, and this time from a most unexpected quarter. For your neighbor Case was the last man, on Asylum Hill anyhow, that I should have thought would treat me so—the very last.[1] I hardly know what to make of it. However, I will try to make the dear old gentleman glad of his venture.

And I suppose you have heard, too, of what Livy is up to, in sending Julie along with me. I can't begin to tell, and she will never know, what gratitude Harmony and I are overflowing with, for her generosity. For to tell the truth, Mark, the prospect of a three months campaign in foreign parts with Mr. Case and party, was not altogether blissful,—you can understand why. My tender affections were all going to be subjected to the torture of a long fast from their objects. There was nobody in the crowd that I wanted to sleep with, as it were. I couldn't help thinking of the contrast with the *last* time, in that respect. And it was with this aspect of the affair before my mind, and rather oppressing me, that I exclaimed to Livy, whom I chanced upon down town and was telling what had happened, "My! what wouldn't I give, if one of the children was going to be along!" And that started up the notion in the luxuriant soil of her kind heart, of doing what she has done.

I won't pretend that I wish I hadn't said it, though I do feel somehow a little guilty of the consequences. Yet I had no more idea that I was planting the seed of action in her mind, than I should have had if I had uttered the same sigh upon the empty air here alone in my study. But I tell you what, Julie's going makes the trip a very different thing to me in anticipation, and will in experience, from what it had been, or (confound this English language) would be. And it must be that she will derive great benefit, as well as pleasure, from it. The dear girl is dazed with the vision so suddenly let down out of the skies before her. How I shall enjoy her company—and in those very places where you and I were together, and where I had been thinking I should be most occupied with the discomfort of missing you.

I have been suffering these three weeks past, hearing of your delights on the River, pangs closely, I fear, resembling those of jealousy.[2] Your junketing with other fellows is to me, by turns, sweet (?) as those kisses Tennyson speaks of

"By hopeless fancy feigned
"On lips that are for others.[3]

Well, my boy, may I never love you less, and I don't think I ever shall.

I have comforted my self in my regret that I couldn't share the rich enjoyment of your present excursion, with looking forward to a walk to the Tower with you some shining June day, and hearing the whole yarn from beginning to end. But that will have to go over now, for I shall probably be off before you are back, and I don't suppose I shall see you till September. Meanwhile, dear Mark, God bless you, and bless us both—and all, and make us thankful for His goodness—thankful enough to observe His wishes.

Harmony sends you her love. Poor girl she's got to stay by her cares.

Yours ever aff.

Joe

1. Twichell returned to Europe in 1882 with a group from Hartford which included one of his wealthy parishioners, Newton M. Case. Case paid for Twichell to go, while Livy (as noted in the letter) paid for Joe's fourteen-year-old daughter, Julia, to accompany him. See Courtney, *Joseph Hopkins Twichell*, 214.

2. Twain had made his Mississippi trip in April and May 1882 in the company of his publisher, James R. Osgood, and Hartford stenographer Roswell Phelps.

3. From Tennyson's "The Princess: A Medley."

77. Twichell to Twain

11 July 1882. Paris, France.[1]

Paris. July 11th 1882.

Dear Mark:

We have seen the Gerhardts—twice, though a blank call was scored on each side before we met.[2] Last Sunday morning they came over (to the Hotel Continental) and went to Church with us and took lunch with us; and today we i.e. Julie and I, have paid them a visit. They have seemed mighty glad to see us, as we certainly have been to see them. Julie and Mrs. Gerhardt (*isn't* she the dearest little woman?) flowed together like two drops of water, and got to hugging one another right off, girl fashion. On the way to church they separated themselves from [the] rest of us and went chatt[ing] [har]d up the Champs Elyseés [*sic*], [the m]atter being, as Julie subsequently informed me, mostly about Livy, of whom they are both confessed worshipers, in common with some adults.[3]

(Now, Livy, how are the folks out there in Elmira, any-way?) Before we leave here the two children are going to spend a day together on a lark: I to furnish the money for unlimited cabs, a dejeuner [*sic*] where they will, and anything else that may be required to complete their bliss.[4] It will be a great refreshment to them both—to Julie any how.

I can't tell you how much I like these Gerhardts. They've carried me quite by storm. What a nice fellow he is, and how immensely in earnest, and she too. I havn't seen in many a day so beautiful a thing as her look in telling me of the "honorable mention" he won in the late "Concours,"—if that is it.[5] God bless her: she's a colossal wife—that young girl.[6]

He took me into the Atelier this morning—I'll tell you all about it when I get home—and showed me the work that [earne]d him the "honorable mention"[. It's spl]endid, ——Mercury meditating, or in a sitting figure, half life size—a reduced copy of the antique, *lovely*.[7] You ought to see it. It is going to be cast, and I wish to goodness it could be sent to you. He let it out very modestly, in the course of our talk, that he had been much encouraged by various commendations from high sources his work had received during the year. I never was more certain of anything in my life, than that it was a most felicitous liberality that sent him over here. You'd better believe he is in an exalted state of mind about you and Livy. Gratitude is no name for it. I let him come upon the topic of what had been done for him several times—you know I wouldn't *shove* him on to it—just to hear it in his voice. I'm sure he prays for you, for I judge, by signs, he's that kind of a man, and you'll think none the worse of him on that account. But enough of the Gerhardts for now. They have made a great impression on me, though: and seeing them has recalled my thoughts to you to that degree that I am at last at the writing pitch. I've been going to write ever since I landed, but I havn't [felt] up to it hitherto.

[I st]ruck you, however, before I go[t] fairly out to sea. The day after we sailed, I think it was, a gentleman addressed me on deck and asked me if my name was Twichell, and introduced himself to me as Gifford the artist, saying that he and friends of his had passed a charming evening in your company not long before, in the course of which you enchanted them with stories in some of which I had place.[8] I will not deny, Mark, that it produced an agreeable sensation in me to hear this. Mr. Gifford evidently regarded me with favor by reason of the setting up you had given me, and presently introduced me to certain other artists, his traveling companions, as the man who figured in those stories of Clemens', whereat they all greeted me with extreme cordiality, and I had no end of a good time with them the whole way to Liverpool. With one of them, Abbey, a delightful fellow, I fell deep in love.[9] He was a pure-hearted confiding youth—a kind of pet of his comrades, he seemed to be—who told me his secrets—clean secrets all of them—and did me good. Then I struck you again in old Chester, and in a queer way. One evening Mr. Case, Julie, and I were peering about the Cathedral, and while peeping through a high board fence within which some work of excavation and restoration was in progress we were sallied out upon from one of the residences pertaining to the establishment by a bare-headed clergyman who advanced upon us as if to warn us off. Mr. Case had mounted something and putting on his spectacles was looking *over* the fence, and I felt that the situation was somewhat awkward. However, our clergyman turned out nothing to be afraid of. He came with a key in his hand, and asked us if we would like to go in, and let us in, and went with us, and with patient kindness led us all about and showed us the old crypt that was being uncovered, and took us up a ladder, and into a room filled with recently exhumed relics, and told us all about things, till we were so delighted and thankful that something had to be said. Accordingly I made him a little speech of acknowledgment and remarked that he couldn't appreciate how exceedingly interesting to us all that sort of thing was, coming as we did from a country that had nothing old in it &c. To which he responded that we had some things that England didn't have. "I take one of your magazines," he said, "*and there's Mark Twain.*" Mr. Case looked at me, and quietly remarked "Why, he is a near neighbor of mine: and this gentleman (pointing to me) is his minister." And Julie put in "and at our house we call him Uncle Mark." Well, the man was radiant in a minute. He roused right up and proceeded to hump himself, and I'll be blowed if he didn't call a sexton and order a light and conduct us in and out and up and down for an hour.[10] He took us by a dark passage into the Cloisters, moonlit and with ravishing effects of light and shade,—and I can't tell you all he did. But 'twas an evening to remember, and Julie never will forget it. Her face, as we emerged into the cloisters, hung with ivy, and bathed in moonlight, was a study. Our benefactor proved to be the Rev. Mr. [George] Preston, Master of the King's School, connected with the Cathedral, and when I get home I want a photograph of you with your name on the back of it to send him, with mine, to let him know that we told him the truth and that we have not forgotten his kindness to us, largely for your sake. So you see, Mark, you are a sort of a providence, after a manner, to those who can conjure with your name the world over. You are an immense convenience.

Perhaps you would like to know what sort of a time I am having. I declare, I can hardly tell. It is needless to say that it is very unlike the time I had in this Europe four years ago. But there couldn't be another of that specie anyhow. That was the only one there was. It wouldn't be quite the same bliss to you and me again. I am both enjoying and suffering a good deal. Our party is of a singular make up—singularly uninteresting, all save the old man. (I don't count Julie in.) It is preëminently a non-humorous crowd. I've long since given up attempting to lighten our solemn dimness by such poor regales in the way of anecdotes &c as I can furnish, finding myself unable to support the tasks of explanation involved in the effort. Now we simply discuss the Hartford news contained in the latest Courant received. As a party we are haloed by the densest ignorance. This you will easily credit when I assure you that I am the most intelligent person in it—by far the most intelligent. We have a woman who is a mixture in equal parts of self-complacence and vulgarity (I don't mean coarseness)—who wonders audibly at the table, so that the waiters may hear, why people stare at us so, when, heaven knows, she'd make an Egyptian mummy stare at her. She's a perfectly good-natured soul, though, and good as she can be, and does my mending for me most maternally, and I ought not to speak ill of her; but I am talking to you confidentially.

And then there's a helpless woman, who don't know what she wants to do, or where she wants to go, or what she wants to see, or what she wants to eat, or anything—she wants to do, go, see, &c "what the rest do," and she drives me wild for the rest want to do what pleases *her.* I indicate a variety of things to which the day may be devoted, and tell 'em I'll be back in half-an-hour to hear their decision and make arrangements accordingly: and come back in half-an-hour and find 'em just where I left 'em.

And we've got a boy of eighteen who is absolutely without qualification for deriving either enjoyment or profit from the present tour, being wholly devoid of historical information—*wholly*—or of the slightest interest in anything, but machinery: and without enough gumption to enable him to hunt up machinery. He sat down, bored, in a chair in Westminster Abbey while the rest of us went in to view the royal tombs, saying that he didn't care to see them. You show him a venerable structure, place or relic, and tell him what it is, and he remarks simply, "Well, what of it?" And to complete his charm, he is a boor in manners, and improves every chance he gets to practice the art of incivility. Religious principle alone has often restrained me from killing him. I must in fairness, however, say that his intentions are well enough: there's nothing bad about him, and much as I dislike him, I respect him. I believe he is honest to the core, and pure-minded as a girl, and that mitigates his case, and renders him not quite intolerable. Poor fellow, he's not to blame for his yawning gulfs of deficiency; he is quite unaware of them and can't help them. The fault is in his make, or his bringing up, or both. I ought to have entire patience with him and try to mend him. And I *have* taught him to wash himself. He is not nearly so ill-deserving as I am, after-all; and now that I come to write him out, I am overtaken by compunction for having felt *so* uncharitably toward him. (He has just been looking over my shoulder to see what I am writing—a way he has.) I must resist my impulse to murder him, and try to act the pastor toward him. One happy circumstance is that he has no sensitiveness whatsoever, and my frequent sarcasms have inflicted no pain upon him or given even momentary offense. He is very fond of me, poor lad. When he draws up a chair beside me to read my newspaper with me, and I, with a withering look and lofty air, hand him the paper, as one who would say "when you are done, I'll go on," he calmly accepts it, and sits there in serene composure turning the pages, commenting on the news, and does not know that aught is amiss. When he has occasion to expectorate, as for instance in the cars, he chooses a good place on the floor, fires his shot, contemplates the result a minute or so, and then looks up and smiles at the audience. I'm now only reminding myself of the work laid out for me, in compassing his improvement.

Finally there's the old gentleman. To begin with, he is the sweetest tempered man I ever knew. Nothing since we left home has seemed to ruffle or discompose him for a single instant, and I am conscious of a daily increasing esteem and affection for him. He bears with the women, and the boy, like a saint—and with me too. But he is the *slowest* human being I ever fell in with. I never knew a man who was so long in getting hold of a fact or an idea. We shouldn't have left the wharf at Liverpool, yet, if our movements had depended on him. It takes him hours to play a game of backgammon.—but then he *wins*. He has some little ways that are engaging. For example, he went to the Bank at Liverpool and drew £100. In the change he received there were a couple of well worn sixpences. The old man turned them over and over and studied them, and finally said "Aint they rather smooth?" "I'll give you new ones if you prefer," answered the cashier. "Well, I wish you would," said Mr. Case. You can fancy, Mark, the rapture with which I listened to this conversation. There's a deal of entertainment in him. We visited Furness Abbey. He walked around and surveyed the ruins for half-an-hour or so without uttering a word, and then gravely said "Did I understand you to state that the Roman Catholics built this?" And when we were going to Dryburgh Abbey, after I had read him all that the guide book said about it, he mused awhile and inquired "Are there any monks there *now*?"[11]

I wouldn't have you infer from his prudence in the matter of the sixpences that he is close fisted, for he isn't. He is very liberal with his money—insists on the best hotels and carriages—keeps my pocket furnished with ample funds for my own use, and don't fear expense in any direction. I heard him offer £175. for the mate to an old clock he saw at Chester. He is taking us through handsomely.

But the care and responsibility of the whole expedition are on me. I have to run the concern: make the bargains, pay the bills, buy the tickets, map out the journey ahead—do everything. This is a good thing for me no doubt, in fact I feel that it is, but I get sick of it once in a while.

I have to keep an account of my disbursements for general expenses, and, my soul, what a torture it is! But *that's* valuable practice, too, I have heard.

And then this old gentleman has to urinate about once in twenty minutes, and I have to provide him opportunity for it. In fact my prevalent pursuit is hunting after a urinal. I bundle him out of the cars and snatch him along to the "Hommes," and it does seem as if he'd never get through. Lively as his kidneys are, the rest of the machinery partakes his constitutional slowness, and the whole party are in an agony for fear he'll be left. I fetch him back at last on the trot and boost him in just in time, and for fifteen minutes we are all happy. This Paris is a great place for him. He can stop like a dog at every corner.[12]

Oh dear, what a mess of stuff I have written. Pray don't understand that I have said what I have about my company in a querulous or ungenerous spirit. For I haven't. Don't think either that I am not enjoying myself. No, I am having a very fair time. What I have been getting ready to say is, that under the present circumstances, it is an unspeakable boon to me to have Julie along. If it wasn't for her I <u>*should*</u> be rather cheerless, and wish forty times a day that I was safe home again. As it is I am entirely content and more. She and I manage to get many an hour together, and when we do we take heaps of comfort. And I am sure she is profiting greatly by all that we see and experience. We are drawn very closely together in sympathy, and shall be more to each other henceforth, than we ever could have been but for just such a dependence on one another as we are now brought into.

Every hour I bless Livy and you for sending her with me. 'Twas a merciful deed. I think it is the best turn you ever did me (or us) and that is saying a good deal.

I want also to thank you both for going to see Harmony as you did before you left for Elmira. She has written me of it, and of the cheer it gave her in time of need. It was a rough thing to abandon her this summer, and I felt, and feel, badly about it, but I couldn't help it. I am unutterably in love with her, and am resolved to make her life, so far as in me lies, cloudless sunshine when I am with her again. But isn't she a true, good girl?

Oh, Julie and I went out and passed an evening with the dear *Dawsons* when we were in London![13] They gave us the warmest welcome, one and all, and shed all manner of kindness on us. They are precisely the same nice folks that they were. They asked a hundred questions about you and Susie and Clara, merrily recalling the incidents of our and their encounter and companionship in Switzerland.

But, my sakes, I must stop this tedious MS right here. Do forgive it. My love to the three Graces, and to their dear Grandmama toward whom I cherish filial sentiments, also to General Langdon and his family, also to Mr. & Mrs. Crane, and to Bro. Thomas Beecher.[14] I strongly hope to see Elmira again.

What wouldn't [I] give to spend a day or two on the farm with you! We must resume our pilgrimages to the Tower in the Fall. There's infinite talk to be unloaded.

Good bye for now. If I have forgotten any thing it is so much gain to you and by "you" I mean the two of you everywhere the sense will admit.

I shouldn't preach exactly the same sort of a sermon to Livy, though, that I should to 'tother one. Well, well, well, good bye. Clear out.

Yours ever aff.

Joe

P.S. You needn't write to me. There's no occasion. But if I can do aught for you, or there is any thing you *want* to say my address is care J. S. Morgan & Co[.] London.

1. See the previous letter. Twichell was now on the European trip, leading the Newton Case party.

2. Karl Gerhardt and his wife, Harriet. Gerhardt was a local Hartford sculptor whose work impressed Twain so much that he funded Gerhardt's study in Paris at L'École des Beaux-Arts.

3. The material in square brackets is speculative as the letter corners are torn off.

4. He refers to Harriet Gerhardt (born in 1863) as a child.

5. L'École des Beaux-Arts apparently had a concours (competition) at six-month intervals at which the students were ranked. This may well be what Mrs. Gerhardt was referring to.

6. Twichell deleted "gal" here.

7. As before, speculative, with corner of page torn off. Gerhardt's statue of Mercury is currently in the Mark Twain House at Hartford. See http://www.twainquotes.com/Gerhardt/kgworks1883.html (accessed 24 November 2015).

8. Landscape painter Robert Swain Gifford.

9. Edwin Austin Abbey.

10. "Hump himself"—this means something like "liven up" or "really put himself out on our behalf." One of the dictionary definitions of "hump" is "to exert (oneself) vigorously." Twain uses the word in the sense of "to get a move on" ("Git up and hump yourself, Jim! There ain't a minute to lose. They're after us!") in chapter 11 of *Adventures of Huckleberry Finn.*

11. The remains of Furness Abbey, founded by French monks in the twelfth century, are on the Furness Peninsula, north of Barrow, in Cumbria (England). Dryburgh Abbey, too, was founded in the twelfth century. Its remains are located in the Scottish Borders, north of Jedburgh.

12. Because of the famed "pissoirs" in that city: urinals encircled by a screen giving just enough visual protection to preserve the user's modesty.

13. See Letter 43.

14. General Charles J. Langdon, Twain's brother-in-law. The title came from his service as brigadier general (commissary) in the New York State National Guard.

78. Twain to Twichell

19 September 1882. Elmira, New York

Elmira, Sept. 19.

Dear Joe—

I honestly *meant* to write & thank you for your superb letter from Europe, but I was simply compelled to deny myself all such satisfactions, & religiously save up *every* little wayward & vagrant suggestion of intellectual activity & hurry to apply it to *work* before it weakened & died. Never was book written under such heavy circumstances.[1] I am full of malaria, my brain is stuffy & cloudy nearly all the time.[2] Some days I have been five hours writing two note-paper pages.

I must quit, now. My head is in a chaotic whirl. We all send love & welcome home to you & Julia; & the same to Harmony.

Ever Yrs

Mark.

1. *Life on the Mississippi.*

2. Twain complained in other letters of the time of malaria contracted at New Orleans during his river trip earlier in the year.

79. Twichell to Twain

20 September 1882. Hartford, Connecticut

Hartford Sept 1882

Dear Mark,

This is to tell you that Julie and I are safe home again. In fact, we have been here several days, yet not long enough to have got over the sense of a delicious novelty in the situation.

Really, I am about as happy as I *thought* I should be: and for the time as content,—utterly, thankfully, joyfully content,—with my earthly lot, as I felt I must be while contemplating it at a distance of three to four thousand miles. Oh, it is splendid. This yer' 125 Woodland St is enchanted ground, clear out to the barbed wire fence.[1] "Kings may be great, but Tam was glorious."[2] Love beats rum for that, though. Harmony and I are having just a new honey moon, and the seven children in the chorus don't seem at-all in the way.

Harmony—oh my!—but you ought to see her! I don't know as you and Livy have heard of it, but she is quite back and up to her old mark in point of physical condition. I've been out walking with her Prospect Hill way, a couple of times, and I tell you she put me through. We are thinking of the Tower Saturday, if the weather comes to its senses.

I've had [a] good fair time abroad, with Julie's help. Nothing went amiss with us from first to last, and the great sights were all in their places. But I heaved a long sigh of sweet relief when I landed the old gentleman and his party on the platform of the Hartford depot.

I will recount our various adventures some evening at your or my fireside, please God, when you are restored to Hartford, where you are rather impatiently expected. You will be glad to hear about Chamonix and Martigny and Visp and Zermatt, and the Riffel and Gorner Grat.[3] The Gorner Grat—you remember the charming afternoon we went up there. We had a good day for it this time, only it was piercing cold—so cold that my moustache froze solid,—and as for the old gentleman he lost his "holt" on his bladder entirely. My sakes, how it *did* fetch the urine out of him. I thought he'd make a new glacier. We went to Leuk Bad, over the Gemmi, to Kandersteg, to Interlaken—to Lucerne—to Heidelberg,—and found everything just as we left it, and to my feeling, so to speak, inquiring for you.[4] Like the western member of Congress I traveled incognito most of the time, but on one or two occasions the ladies managed to let it out that I was "Harris," and I tasted the sweets of reflected glory.[5] Julie's modesty, however, was so sensitive, that I couldn't take much satisfaction in it i.e. the glory. Julie and I did some good walking, but having a company ahead of us or behind us to worry about, we didn't have the sense of freedom and independence that pedestrians need, to be happy.

We hear, from George, who came into our yard this morning on a grocer's wagon, that you are coming pretty soon.[6] Hurry up. We are hankering for you. Love to each and all.

Yours ever.

Joe

1. Twichell's Hartford home address.
2. From Robert Burns, "Tam o' Shanter": actually "Kings may be blest."
3. All sites in the French and Swiss Alps visited earlier by Twain and Twichell together.
4. Leuk Bad is another form of Leukerbad.
5. "Western member of Congress" is an unknown allusion.
6. George Griffin. Twain and his family returned to Hartford in late October.

80. Twichell to Twain

21 November 1882.[1] *Hartford, Connecticut*

[Twichell enclosed two letters sent to him by R. P. Hibbard, pastor of the New England Congregational Church on South Ninth Street, Brooklyn. In the second—written on 18 November 1882—Hibbard asks if he might use a letter Twichell had written to him in order to approach Twain. This was in regard to a proposed lecture Hibbard wished Twain to give in Williamsburg (a Brooklyn neighborhood) on behalf of what he calls "a downright good and needed service." Twichell had evidently already been discouraging about any such approach, but Hibbard, clutching at straws, wished to use Joe's letter in a new, more "direct appeal." It was far from unusual for people to use Twichell as a conduit to Twain in this way.[2]*]*

Tuesday morning

Dear Mark,

I sympathized with this fellow-minister, and really *couldn't* say "no" to the second request he made me, it seemed so little a thing to ask and to grant.

I send you both his letters that you may see how the case stands before you hear from him.

If you feel disposed to do the work of charity he craves (I suppose you can get him a thousand dollars) and if it is any inducement to you, I will agree to go to Williamsburg with you, and sleep with you the night you lecture or read. By the way, *read* by all means, if you do anything.

Yours aff.

Joe

1. Provisional dating.

2. Hibbard's second letter is the only one now extant. There is no record of Twain following up on Hibbard's request.

81. Twichell to Twain

30 November 1882. Hartford, Connecticut

30 Nov 1882 Thursday morning

Dear Mark

We are going to have a company of six or eight young apprentices and mechanics to dine and spend the evening with us *Saturday*—these fellows to whom you gave membership in the Young Men's Institute, among them.[1]

Now if you are at leisure or liberty that evening, and feel disposed to do a lordly thing, step over and sit a half hour with these boys. It will be a great delight to them both then and afterwards.

Of course I know that you are quite likely to be otherwise engaged.

We are off for the country this noon.

Yrs aff.

Joe

1. This Hartford institution for the improvement and education of young men—and (despite its name) of women—was a predecessor of the Hartford Public Library.

82. Twichell to Twain

17 July 1883. Hartford, Connecticut

Hartford. July 17.

Dear Mark,

The papers say that you are getting up from an attack of rheumatism and malaria. We are mighty glad to know that you are getting up but if we had known that you were down we should certainly have made some sign of our interest and sympathy.

How sick have you been? We had been thinking of you and Livy up there, "on the hills like gods together: careless of mankind" inhaling the odorous breeze, cured of all mortal ills, rid of life's every misery for the time: and to find that you have been, if this newspaper tale is true, worse off than we weltering and sweltering in bondage here, is—*not* comforting I vow and protest, but—painfully disappointing.[1] 'Twas half a vacation to us to contemplate your sweet repose in the lap of Quarry Farm after Livy's hard winter and your fretted year.

I was thinking that by now you, Mark, were feeling enough better to begin wishing you had gone to church more of late as having something to thank Heaven for, after all. But if you have had the rheumatism—*and* malaria—It is too bad; indeed it is—and I won't moralize, at least not this time. But I'll *tell* you something—that I guess will be rather pleasant.

Mr. J. M. Allen—I think you know him,—Pres. of the Boiler Ins. Co.—one of our deacons—a good deal of a scientific man, was guest of the old man Bowen at his great Fourth of July blow out at Woodstock.[2] At Bowen's house he met ex-Pres. & Mrs. Hayes,—also guests.[3] All hands were very busy—drivings—dining—receptions &c but Pres. H. said to Mr. A. when introduced to him "I want to see you before we break up here—when there's a chance." It wasn't till the second day they were there that they got by themselves a few minutes, and then Pres. H. said "Do you know Mark Twain?" "A little" replied Mr. A. "but not as well as I wish I did. I *see* him often. [Mr. A. doesn't stare around much Sundays—looks at the minister.][4] He goes to our church." Whereupon Pres. H. broke out in the strongest, most enthusiastic expression of interest in you and liking for your books, which he declared had been one of his chief instruments of relaxation and refreshment under the business of office. He said that there was hardly any man in the world whom he so much desired to meet as you. He wanted to know all about you, the kind of fellow you were &c &c.

Presently he asked, "Do you know *Mr. Twichell*?" "Nobody any better: he's my Pastor!" "Well, *is* he Harris?" "He probably is.—he was with M.T. on that Tramp Abroad." "I'd like to see *him*, too. What sort of a man is he?" Wasn't that queer? How did Pres. H. get hold of my *name*? Mr. Allen told him that whenever he came our way, if he would stop over at Hartford, he could see us both; and he said he believed he'd do it—with his wife—and he would let Mr. Allen know ahead, if the time ever came.

There, Mark! What do you think of that? I thought I'd tell about it, so that if you happened to run against the Ex-President anywhere, you would know the state of his sentiments. Possibly too you might like, when opportunity offered, to obtain for yourself and Livy and Hartford the honor and pleasure of a visit from him and his lovely wife.

But I have such a high opinion of the Hayeses that it did me good to learn that you had such a place in their esteem. How *can* I help suggesting, dear Boy, that there's a moral for thee in this story.

Harmony is about well: goes down to dinner: is dearer than ever. Livy, we hope and suppose, is quite restored. Loads of love to her and the girls—also to Mrs Langdon, and all the Langdons, and the Cranes, and Tom Beecher.

Our five oldest are all away and have been for several days, but are coming back this week. We are weary of peace and quiet. The new baby has a voice like a cornet though, and has done his best to soothe us.[5]

Adieu. We shall be here till Aug. 20.

Yours ever aff.

Joe

1. The quote is from Tennyson's "The Lotos-Eaters."

2. Jeremiah Allen was president of the Hartford Steam Boiler Inspection and Insurance Company. Henry Chandler Bowen of Woodstock, Connecticut, ran a successful dry goods business that specialized in silks. The Fourth of July celebrations (starting in 1870) held at Roseland Cottage, Bowen's summer home, were legendary, and the guests over the years included Ulysses S. Grant, Benjamin Harrison, Rutherford B. Hayes, William McKinley, Henry Ward Beecher, Oliver Wendell Holmes, and many others.

3. Rutherford B. Hayes, nineteenth president of the United States (1877–81) and a cousin of Elinor Mead Howells (wife of W. D. Howells).

4. Twichell's footnote is repositioned here where it makes most sense.

5. The Twichells' eighth child, named Joseph Hooker Twichell (after the Civil War general under whom Twichell had served), had been born on 15 June.

83. Twain to Twichell

*20 July 1883. Elmira, New York (*Hartford Courant, *24 July 1883)*

[Full letter now missing. This part of it was published, at Twichell's instigation.]

[Unknown amount of text missing.]

For the time that has elapsed since I came here, I've a day's work to show for every single working day. I'm not suffering in any way that I know of, except the old difficulty, only twenty-four hours in a day, & not days enough in the week.

[Unknown amount of text possibly missing.]

Day before yesterday, feeling not in condition for writing, I left the study; but I couldn't hold in—had to do something; so I spent eight hours in the sun with a yard-stick measuring off the reigns of the English kings on the roads in these grounds, from William the Conqueror to 1883—calculating to invent an open-air game which shall fill the children's heads with dates without study. I give each king's reign one foot of space to the year, & drive one stake in the ground to mark the beginning of each reign;—& I make the children call the stake by the king's name. You can stand in the door & take a bird's eye view of English monarchy, from the Conqueror to Edward IV.; then you can turn & follow the road up the hill to the study & beyond, with an opera glass, & bird's eye view the rest of it to 1883.

You can mark the sharp difference in the *length* of reigns, by the varying distances of the stakes apart. You can see Richard II., 2 feet; Richard Cromwell, 2 feet; James II., 3 feet, & so on—& then big skips: pegs standing 45, 46, 50, 56 & 60 feet apart, (Elizabeth, Victoria, Edward III., Henry III., & George III.—by the way.[1] Third's a lucky number for length of days, isn't it?)

Yes, sir, by my scheme you get a realizing notion of the time occupied by reigns.

The reason it took me eight hours was because with little Jean's interrupting assistance, I had to measure from the Conquest to the end of Henry VI. three times over—& besides I had to whittle out all those pegs.

I did a full day's work & a third over, yesterday, but was full of my game after I went to bed,—trying to fit it for *in*doors. So I didn't get to sleep till pretty late; but when I did go off, I had contrived a way to play my history game with cards & a cribbage board.

[Unknown amount of text missing.]

1. The *Courant* replaced "Richard Cromwell" with "Oliver Cromwell." See Letter 85.

84. Twichell to Twain

22 July 1883. Hartford, Connecticut

[Twain mailed this letter received from Twichell to his mother, Jane Lampton Clemens; his brother, Orion Clemens; and his sister-in-law, Mary E. Clemens—all in Keokuk, Iowa. He wrote on it, obscuring the headings: "I send this to beg that at least you *folks will avoid this damned fool's example. I shall never thoroughly like him again. S.L.C."]*

Hartford. July 22.

Dear Mark:

Your letter has just come and is most welcome for the good news it brings of your health, besides being very delightful in itself.

I'm going to let Charley print part of it,—that part about English History—and I'm going to do it before you will have time to prevent me; so don't fret a minute.[1]

And what do you say to my putting into the Courant (with judicious editing, of course) an extract from Beard's observations on Gerhardt?[2] That I won't do without your advice. It is matter of local interest, and its publication might procure him a commission. It might be explained in a prefatory note that he has been assisted by friends in Hartford, without intimating who they are. I can't think of any harm that would come of it.

All the children (except Ed.) are home again and the dreary tranquillity we have suffered is over. Make my prostrations to Livy, and wish the girls a Merry Christmas fm [from] their Uncle.[3]

Thine as ever
Joe[4]

1. Most likely Charles Hopkins Clark, part of Twichell and Twain's Hartford circle of friends and managing editor of the *Courant*, who did most of the hands-on editing at this point in time.

2. This may refer to Rev. Dr. A. F. Beard, the pastor of the American Church in Paris, a Congregationalist church. Beard presumably gave a good report of Gerhardt. In his letter of 8 September, Twichell calls him "Dr. Baird."

3. The "Merry Christmas" greeting is presumably a (poor) joke.

4. "Rev" and "Twichell" are added in Twain's hand before and after the "Joe."

85. Twichell to Twain

24 July 1883. Hartford, Connecticut

Hartford. July 24.

That History Game makes a mighty nice little piece in this morning's Courant. But, some smarty in the office changed *Richard* Cromwell into Oliver and probably thinks he ought to be thanked for it—the ignoramus.[1] It won't be noticed though by most readers, I suppose. I'm glad to have such a thing set going the rounds, on account of the pleasant impression it will make of M.T.

—Charley [Warner] and I walked to the Tower Saturday. Had a good talk,—with Julie to over hear it. She said, at night, that it had been the delightfulest day—about—she ever had—just listening. You and I must give our girls such a day once in a while. It is better than to talk *to* 'em.

Aff.

J.

Hartford

1. See Letter 83. Richard Cromwell, Oliver's son, was lord protector of England, Scotland, and Ireland for just under nine months (3 September 1658–25 May 1659).

86. Twichell to Twain

8 September 1883. Franconia, New Hampshire

Echo Farm House
Franconia N.H.
Sept. 8. 1883

Dear Mark,

Now that your wrath is presumably cooled by time and I am away up here behind the Franconia Range, I venture humbly to address you these few lines inquiring for your health and that of your family.

It is long since we heard from you. Perhaps even under these circumstances I should still hesitate to intrude myself upon your notice: but I see, by the papers, that you are presently going duck shooting upon the Sound, and I am desirous, while you are yet alive, to have, if possible, a friendly word from you, which, knowing how little used you are to handling a gun I cannot but judge may be the last.

Three weeks nearly we have been luxuriating in this glorious region, enjoying ourselves with all our might. Perhaps it isn't quite up to the Adirondacks, *for us*—we are better acquainted there—but there are splendors enough to keep us enchanted right along, and all sorts of mountain and wilderness delights—and good fishing besides. Give me mountains forever! I wish to goodness you and Livy and the children were here.

I declare to you, Mark, I *never* found such a place to smoke in.

Next week, or the week after, Julie and I are going off on a five or six days tramp among the Presidents, Washington, Jefferson, & co. and if only you were on hand to bear us company 'twould be a perfect thing.[1] The roads hereabouts are almost as fine for walking as those in Switzerland.

This Echo Farm House suits us well enough for vacation quarters. It isn't very commodious, and if one were disposed to criticize, the table might now and then be objected to in points: For instance I hear

Harmony occasionally wishing that they would strain *all* the manure out of the milk. But we get along with it in the main quite comfortably, and are one and all in a flourishing condition. You and I saw worse places in the Alps. We have received many attentions and favors from your friend Wm C. Grimes who summers at the Profile House six miles away.[2] Harmony and I spent a charming day with him and Charley Warner at his Lonesome Lake Farm. A most delightful retreat we found it, furnished out with every conceivable camp luxury, and with first-rate angling right before the door. Since then I passed two days and the intervening night time with four of the children, and we had no end of a good time.

You made a great fuss about my letting Charley print that little extract from your letter; and abused me brutally for it. I suppose it was because you wanted to pick a quarrel with me. If that was it, you'll have to try again, old fellow. Of course, if I'd got your telegram in season (I supposed, at first that it referred to Dr. Baird's letter about Gerhardt) I should have held my hand.[3] But since the deed was done I'm entirely impenitent on the subject. It was a good sin that I committed. That extract has gone and is going the rounds, as I wanted it to, and knew it would. Here it is as I cut it out of one of our best religious papers only last week. Just run your eye over it and see how nicely it reads, and what a creditable and amiable M.T. it is, who shines forth in it. I tell you what it is, it is a mighty sight better thing to have circulating than some of those confounded private talks of yours the press gave to the public out west last summer.[4] I'll show you some of 'em if you care to see 'em. You can depend upon it I was given the chance to enjoy them. People are so blamed thoughtful.

But, really, I didn't mean to say anything about this matter, when I sat down to write. You've probably forgotten all about it by this time, on top of forgiving it. If you wish I will subscribe a vow never to do anything of the kind again. I'm as safe as Howells henceforth. But *he'll* give you away sometime—anyhow if he happens to survive you.

By the way, Charley read me a delicious letter he had from H. [Howells] just after he (H.) got back from abroad. I've found nothing in any of his books so graceful and bright. Why is it that you stars write best when you don't try?

Well, Mark, I want very much to see you and Livy, and Harmony does too. We find when we come to be separated from you for a season that you have got established among the necessaries of life to us, and we are not quite our natural selves without you. I've had, first and last, since you left us ever so many things to tell you, but whether they will come at call when we meet is doubtful.

Harmony has all her strength back again, and is blooming. The new baby is gradually recovering from the confusion incident to the novelty of terrestrial existence, and getting settled in his mind, and promises to turn out well. His name is Joseph Hooker.

We hope that Livy is back to her highest mark, also, and beyond. Our love to her and the girls. Write us just a word—a bulletin—and tell us how you all are. Good bye. My! how I'd like to take a turn at the ducks with you.

Yours ever aff.

Joe

1. Mounts Jefferson and Washington are part of a long hike across the Presidential Range in the New Hampshire White Mountains.

2. William C. Grimes is Twain's pseudonym in *The Innocents Abroad* for William C. Prime, author of *Tent Life in the Holy Land* (1857), one of the travel books he parodies.

3. See Letter 84.

4. Twichell seems to contrast what he saw as his own minor lapse (publishing the history-game letter, so infuriating to Twain) with Western reporters relaying Twain's "confounded private talks" in the papers during the 1882 Mississippi River trip. Twain showed an aversion to the press on this trip, even detouring Memphis to avoid them. Even so, on one occasion a St. Louis reporter reported Twain's words in detail when he clearly did not want to be quoted. See Gary Scharnhorst, ed., *Mark Twain: The Complete Interviews* (Tuscaloosa: University of Alabama Press, 2006), 34–38.

87. Twain to Twichell

16 September 1884. Elmira, New York

Elmira, Sept 16/84.

Dear Joe—

On the contrary, the summer has been lost time to me.[1] I spent several weeks in the dental chair, coming down from the hill every day for the purpose; then I made a daily trip during several more weeks to a doctor to be treated for catarrh & have my palate burnt off. The remnant of the season I wasted in ineffectual efforts to work. I haven't a paragraph to show for my summer.

I sent for the bicycle & mounted it once; got a hard fall, & have never tried since; mainly because I had no company. But anyway there is no chance here for the art—the hills are long & steep, & one would have to walk back after riding down.[2]

Livy is just getting about from an exhausting spell of sickness; so I don't believe she will be strong enough to travel for at least a week yet. I am down town today, & she is on the hill or she would give me a date & some messages for you.

Gerhardt came here & made an excellent bust of me (*that* occupied some portion of my time every day for four weeks), then he ruined it in attempting to cast it in plaster; but went to work & made a new one, & just as good, in five days, & has gone to Philadelphia to cast it in bronze.[3] We must find somebody in Hartford or South Manchester who wants a bust made. Gerhardt can do it. I will send you a photograph from the plaster cast, & you can "leg" for him.

I am powerful glad you are all home again, & shall be gladder when we join you, & can talk. Mother was well when I saw her last—which was yesterday—& indeed all the tribes are the same—meaning the three families.[4] We shall begin to ship the live stock (cats & dogs), about a week hence, & we shall shortly follow. Consider that all of us are sending to you & all of you a power of love, & that I am

Always affectionately Yours
Mark.

1. Clearly in response to a Twichell letter, now lost. The tone of this letter shows that the friendship is again clearly back on solid ground. In the upcoming November 1884 presidential election, Twichell would join Twain in taking a public stand against the Republican candidate James G. Blaine—whose congressional record marked him out as corrupt. Twichell usually stayed clear of politics, and his actions, in what was a more-or-less solidly Republican local community, did not go down well among many of his parishioners and friends and left Twichell feeling alienated from them. See, too, the various entries in Harriet Elinor Smith et al., eds., *Autobiography of Mark Twain*, vol. 1 (Berkeley: University of California Press, 2010) (310–12, 314, 318–20, 575, 577), where Twain, however, exaggerates the negative effect this had on relations between Twichell and his congregation.

2. Twichell had taken up the new activity of bicycling in the spring of 1884 and then drew Twain into the venture. Twain proved less than adept. See *Autobiography of Mark Twain*, 2:258, 575.

3. This bust, now in the restored Mark Twain House in Hartford, would be used (when reproduced in heliotype form) as a frontispiece for *Huckleberry Finn.*

4. It may be that Orion, Mollie, and Twain's mother were visiting Quarry Farm and Twain refers to them and the Cranes alongside his own family. Or the third family could be the Langdons (albeit only represented by "Mother" Olivia L. Langdon at this point).

88. Twichell to Twain

1 August 1885. Willoughby, Vermont

Willoughby Vermont.
Aug. 1, 1885.

Dear Mark:

I think I never wanted to see you so much:—in fact, that I never wanted to see anybody so much, (unless 'twas Harmony.) as I have you the past ten days—to talk over General Grant.[1]

I'd give any thing for a day or two with you just now sitting or strolling around, and letting our converse run freely, where it would, through the whole subject. Your heart is full of it, I know: and mine certainly is. I can't get my mind off it.—and don't wish to. I wander about, mostly alone,—but if I am in company it makes no difference—all the while seeing the General lying cold and still, under the flag, yonder at Mt. M^c^Gregor, with the soldiers guarding him. There's a lump in my throat half the time.

What I lack is the relief of *utterance*. Nothing that I read; nothing that I can think or say with myself, or with anybody here, at-all suffices for it. I don't feel in the least moved to attempt it by writing: and I couldn't do any thing to the purpose in that way anyhow. I have just answered "no" to a summons to come to Hartford and make a speech at the public Memorial Service to be held there next Saturday. Well, I really had no choice about it: for Harmony is disabled by an obstinate attack of lumbago, or something of the sort, and I couldn't think of leaving her. But, then, I didn't care to go, and was rather glad I had a competent reason for declining. No speech that I could frame would be much of a vent to me. The only thing I can think of that would, would be, as I have said, a day or two of talk with you.

I suppose I have said to Harmony forty times since I got up here "How I wish I could see Mark!" My notion is that between us we could get ourselves expressed. I have never known anyone who could help me read my own thoughts, in such a case, as you can, and have done many a time, dear old fellow. I'd give more to sit on a log with you in the woods this afternoon, while we turned a wreath together for Launcelot's grave, than to hear any conceivable eulogy of him pronounced by mortal lips.[2]

But it can't be.—more's the pity. I count it a misfortune that the occasion finds us so far apart. By the time we meet the flood will have gone down in our breasts. But, oh, my General; all thoughts and all tears are yours today!

Now, Mark, I have said this to you, just because I felt like it, and it was uppermost with me, and you will please take it for whatever it may signify to you. It is a very true disclosure of my inside. We send our love to you all. With the exception of Harmony's back, which I have spoken of, we are as well as possible. She isn't sick, but only lame, and hopes soon to be in her usual sound state.

That extract from the Round Table Legend, which you sent to the Courant—'twas the fittest word yet published.[3]

Yours ever aff.

Joe

1. Ex-president Ulysses S. Grant died on 23 July 1885. Twain had been closely involved with Grant, publishing his *Personal Memoirs* (also in 1885) through his own firm, Charles L. Webster & Co.

2. The last part of this paragraph has been set apart from the rest of the letter (possibly by Twain) by slash marks (//) before "I'd give" and after "lips."

3. Twichell refers to a short piece by "S.L.C." titled "General Grant," published in the *Courant* on 24 July 1885.

89. Twichell to Twain

15 August 1885. West Burke, Vermont

WILLOUGHBY LAKE HOUSE
WEST BURKE, VT.
Aug 15. 1885.

Dear Mark:

I have just now discovered in an envelope unopened hitherto, your kind invitation to come down to New York and share your facilities for viewing the Funeral procession.[1] It is queer that I should have overlooked it: never did such a thing before that I remember. This will explain my not answering it.

I couldn't have accepted it, for, as perhaps you know, I finally went to Hartford to take part in the service held there that same day.[2] But I am as much obliged to you as if I had.

All of us are well.

With love to Livy and the girls.

Yours ever aff.

J.H.T.

1. That is, Grant's funeral.

2. Twichell gave a lengthy address on Grant at the observances in Hartford on

8 August—a performance that the *Courant* said made the eyes of many listeners "uncomfortably moist."

90. Twichell to Twain

23 October 1885. Hartford, Connecticut

[Twichell enclosed a long clipping about improvements in the aerial navigation of hot air balloons with his letter.]

Friday morning

Dear Mark,

Don't you remember how one of us said, when we last walked to the Tower, speaking of aerial navigation, that the problem was bound to be solved sometime, because it was never given up, that there were always men at work on it.

The sight of the enclosed recalled the remark.

Yrs aff

91. Twain to Twichell

24 December 1885. New York, New York

Dec. 24, 1885.

Dear Joe & Harmony:

Livy & I love you both, & fervently wish you a long & happy life, & eventually a sufficient family.

Always Yours

Mark

[In pencil:] Enclosing $200

92. Twichell to Twain

25 December 1885. Hartford, Connecticut

Dec. 25.

Dear Mark:

What to say to you on this occasion. I'm sure I don't know. Harmony and I are simply submerged; and somehow can't manage yet to get to the surface, and brush the water out of our eyes,—yes, the water out of our eyes,—so as to see where we are. We plainly perceive that there has been a conspiracy, and we are pretty clear who the chief of it is, but beyond that our thoughts are not articulate thus far.[1] Give us time, friends. We can't surround the subject in one day. We were never here before. But we'll be all right presently.

Just for now let us say that we are in a transport of love and gratitude,—and you, dear old Mark, are in the heart of a cyclone of our benedictions. We do wish our blessing was worth something more. But such as it is, it is yours; it always was, in fact, and always will be.

May all good, earthly and heavenly, now and forever, be your portion.

Yours unspeakably

Joe

P.S. I don't call this an acknowledgment. It is only a hug.

1. Twichell may here imply that Livy had been the instigator of the $200 gift.

93. Twain to Twichell

1886. Hartford, Connecticut (In pencil)

Dear Joe—

Livy sent me to see if Harmony would lend you to us for dinner Wednesday evening. I was to explain to Harmony that this shabby invitation of only one-half of the firm is not dictated by desire, but necessity, there being a vacant male seat but no vacancy in the female line; & she hopes Harmony will be charitable & let you come, for the case is urgent. Will she?—& may we expect you?

Yrs Ever,

Mark.

Here also is your Grant Memoir[1]

1. Twain sends over a copy of Grant's *Memoirs* with the letter, indicating that we can date the letter early in the year (he was sending out other copies of the book in early February).

94. Twichell to Twain

15 February 1886. Hartford, Connecticut[1]

Tuesday

Dear Mark,

This Sam Jones is a very live brother and preacher, and I like him.[2] Just see how delighfully he mixes wit and sense in this extract enclosed—and makes his points i.e. if you agree with him.[3] To me it seems strong talk.

Dear old Sherman still has to endure the penalty of existence in a world inhabited by small men—so small that they can't see the whole of a large man, or begin to. The raking up of his provisional arrangem[en]t with Johnston way back in 1864 and trying to discredit him with it now is surely the most ingenious piece of meanness and, as it were, stupidity, I ever knew of,—the whole affair having been transparently due to his big-hearted impulsive generosity.[4] But generosity is a hidden mystery to a moral skunk.

Yours aff

J.H.T.

1. Mark Twain Papers date this letter 1887. But Twain's 18 February 1886 letter makes reference to its subject matter.

2. Samuel ("Sam") Porter Jones—a crowd-pulling evangelist who led revivalist meetings all over the United States. He would publish *Quit Your Meanness: Sermons and Sayings* in 1886, but this is probably a reference to a published version of an interview, lecture, or essay.

3. Enclosure missing.

4. Twichell mistakenly says 1864 here but refers to 1865. Confederate general Joseph Johnston (in charge of the armies William Sherman had been pursuing through the Carolinas while Grant pursued Lee in Virginia) surrendered to Sherman about a month after Lee surrendered to Grant. Sherman gave him generous terms, as Grant had given to Lee. Because Lincoln's assassination had intervened and a spirit of vengeance was abroad, Sherman was criticized for this. A *Courant* editorial, also from 15 February 1886, about Confederate documents published in the *New York Sun*, repeated the charge, on the basis that the documents showed that the South was helpless at the time of Johnston's surrender and so Sherman was needlessly and unpatriotically generous in his terms. The *Courant*, however, defended Sherman, acknowledging his error but attributing it (as Twichell does) to his generosity. Quite who the "moral skunk" was is unknown.

95. Twain to Twichell

18 February 1886. Hartford, Connecticut (Transcript by Albert Bigelow Paine)

Feb. 18/86. Hartford

Dear Joe—

Yes, the Rev. Jones is bright, & slangy, & happy, & not destitute of sense, in this talk. So I suppose he is a hopeless donkey or a fetid abscess only when he preaches. (I am rather familiar with his pulpit vomit.)[1]

I have not encountered what you refer to about Sherman, thank Goodness

but I can easily imagine it, for one can easily imagine how greedily men would naturally snatch at such an opportunity to do a loathsome thing. Joe, why do you want to save men? You owe it to yourself, & to the powers that are in you, to reform.

[Signature cut away][2]

1. Twain would make his contempt for Jones clear in "A Singular Episode: The Reception of Rev. Sam Jones in Heaven" (probably written in 1891).

2. As Twichell sometimes did when asked for a Twain autograph.

96. Twain to Twichell

23? December 1886. Hartford, Connecticut

[In the top margin of "The National Holiday," Portland Morning Oregonian, *6 July 1886, containing a report of a lengthy patriotic speech by Thomas Fitch.*[1] *Fitch had been an early journalistic colleague of Twain in Nevada. Sent to Twain by Twichell on 22 December 1886.]*

It is fine, Joe. Preserve it.

Mark.

1. Fitch was a newspaperman, lawyer, and politician.

97. Twain to Twichell

14 March 1887. Hartford, Connecticut

Hartford, Mch 14/87.

Dear Joe:

It is a noble sermon, & I am glad I did not hear it.[1] The mere reading it moved me more than I like to be moved—or, rather, *would* like to be moved in public. It is great & fine; & worthy of its majestic subject. You struck twelve.

What a pity—that so insignificant a matter as the chastity or unchastity of an Elizabeth Tilton could clip the locks of this Samson & make him as other men, in the estimation of a nation of Lilliputians creeping & climbing about his shoe-soles.[2]

Yrs ever

Mark.

1. Henry Ward Beecher had died the previous week and Twain was clearly responding to a Twichell sermon on him (probably given to Twain to read—it was published in the *Courant* on the fifteenth). For extracts from the sermon, see Courtney, *Joseph Hopkins Twichell*, 220–21.

2. See Letter 19 for further information on the Beecher-Tilton scandal.

98. Twichell to Twain

16 March 1887? Hartford, Connecticut

Wednesday.[1]

Thank you, dear Mark, from my heart, for your kind expressions about my sermon. The only thing I feel concerning it was its inadequacy. And then, in the Courant there were omissions here and there, and typographical errors, that to me—and me only, I suppose,—— were sore blemishes.

But I'm mighty glad it pleased you. I guess it was a good deal because you met me more than half way in it, and between us we captured the idea I was in labor with.

Yrs aff

Joe

1. Postmark is 16 March and letter is dated "Wednesday." The 16th of March fell on a Wednesday in 1870, 1881, 1887, 1892, 1898, 1904, and 1910. The date of 16 March 1887

seems likely, given Twain's response (Letter 97) to the Beecher sermon. The letter is too informal for 1870, and Twain left Hartford in 1892.

99. Twichell to Twain

27 September 1887. Hartford, Connecticut

Tuesday a.m.

Dear Mark,

If you were coming over here this morning; come along: I'll be glad to see you. But you needn't feel obliged to come; for I have discovered since Sue was at your house last night, that it is out of the question for me to go to the yacht race Thursday.[1]

You understand I had an invitation from a gentleman of my acquaintance in Yonkers to come down and join his party on a private craft of some sort, and *bring a friend with me.* So without stopping to think it over, I dispatched Sue to find out if you would go. If you would, I would. If you wouldn't, I didn't think I cared enough for it to go alone—that was my notion.

But, as I say, on reflection I can't go anyhow, and so must beg your pardon for bothering you about the matter, and ask leave to withdraw my too hasty overture.

Yrs ever

Joe

1. This trip to watch the America's Cup race took place after all. Twichell writes in his journal (28–29 September 1887) of a Mr. Peene of Yonkers inviting him to see the race between the English yacht *Thistle* and the American *Volunteer* "and to bring a friend with me." "Accordingly," he continues, "MT and I went down on the 28th." The race was called off because of calm. Twichell continues, "M.T. went to Mr. Peene's incognito i.e. simply as Clemens, but Mr. Peene guessed him out at the dinner table, where his talk betrayed him." The race then took place the next day and was won by the American yacht. Mr. Peene was probably Joseph Peene, a yachtsman who with his brothers owned a small fleet of boats that carried freight between Yonkers and New York City.

100. Twichell to Twain

10 February 1888. Hartford, Connecticut

[Clipping pasted in at head of letter:]

A TILT ABOUT MODERN IMPROVEMENTS.

BROWN'S BOY. "We've got stationary wash-stands in our house."
SMITH'S BOY. "We've got tessellated vestibules."
BROWN'S BOY. "We've got open grates."
SMITH'S BOY. "So have we. And an elevator."
BROWN'S BOY. "Pooh! we've got electrical bells."
SMITH'S BOY. "Well, we've got something youenses hasn't got—we've got rheumatic tubes. There now!"

[End of clipping.]

This made me *think* of the speech you are pregnant with.—and which it seems to me has *great* possibilities. I don't know that "rheumatic tubes" is any-thing to your point, though. It isn't much to any point, to be sure, but, as I say, it called the speech to mind.

Yrs Joe

101. Twichell to Twain

29 May 1888. Hartford, Connecticut (Typed copy)

Tuesday Morning

Dear Old Mark:

I find myself this morning wanting to tell you how thankful to you I am and *we* are for the part you bore in our reception last night.[1]

I appreciate that it must have seemed, on some accounts, rather rough on you to be asked to *appear* on such occasion.[2] And had I been consulted about it—which I was not—I would have spared you.

All the more am I affected with gratitude toward you, that you did not spare yourself, but took up the cross and accommodated yourself with such kindly grace to the situation, with your difficulty in which, proud as I was to have you there, I was in acute sympathy.

I hope you understand that by submitting to be called out, as well as by what you said, you gave great pleasure to many worthy people.

And may I say that in the tone and air of a long familiar friendly sentiment toward me, bred and nurtured in a personal relation, that pervaded your charming talk, you perfectly met that particular propriety of the occasion which I judge you aimed to meet.

I never heard you read anything better than you read the verses with which you closed—which is saying a great deal.[3]

Dear old fellow, heaven only knows how I love you, and what unspeakable desires for your happiness live in my heart.

I have learned to what extent Harmony and I are beholden to Livy and you for our sudden elevation in point of material fortune. There again I would have had you spared. What an expense to you we are! It is too bad. But the people didn't know.

As I said last night, we can't yet quite get hold of so strange a fact as that we are worth ten thousand dollars! You had the sensation of it once, I suppose, but you have forgotten all about it now. We are trying, struggling, to climb into it. We shall get there, I guess, but it is a dizzy job.

I know we feel toward you two for your share in making us richer than we had ever thought of being, I will attempt no expression. I don't know what to say. I can only sign a blank check and ask you to fill it out for yourselves.

Yours as ever

Joe

1. This letter followed Twain's (leading) part in the celebrations organized by Twichell's parishioners to mark Joe's fiftieth birthday. Twichell's value to his congregation can be measured by their generosity to him at this point, with the gift of the deeds of his house (in other words, paying off the house mortgage) and a significant sum of extra money (probably $4,000) to enlarge and improve the property. Twain was one of the contributors, and from the letter's content, evidently a generous one. A *Courant* clipping of 28 May in Twichell's journal reports that "Mr. Twichell was taken altogether unprepared" by the gift, reporting that he said that he had expected crockery.

2. This may merely be a reference to Twain's general preference for privacy.

3. Twain read St. George Tucker's "Days of My Youth."

102. Twichell to Twain

1 June 1888. Hartford, Connecticut

[Twichell encloses a letter written by Thomas Wilson, curator of the Division of Prehistoric Archaeology at the U.S. National Museum (Smithsonian) dated 26 May 1888. Wilson thanks Twichell for his "thoughtfulness" in writing to him about Wilson's lecture, "Prehistoric Man in Western Europe," which Twichell must have heard.[1] "The praise you give," Wilson wrote, "I accept, not on my own behalf, but of that prehistoric man whom I represent. Poor devil! He must have had a hard

time of it." Twichell must have reported on the lecture to Twain—who, it seems, also found it intriguing.]

Friday morning

Dear Mark,

That pre-historic man romance in Puck, I wouldn't have missed seeing for a good deal.[2] Much obliged to you for it. How bright it is!

I enclose a letter (which you needn't return) from Dr. Wilson. I told him that my account to you of what he had shown me had so interested you, that he need not be surprised if we appeared to him together some day and asked him to repeat the lecture.

You have seen, I guess, the clipping from the N.Y. Sun.[3] If not, it will amuse you—or something.

Yrs aff.

Joe

1. Wilson had delivered this lecture at the National Museum in Washington, D.C., on 6 April 1887. It can be assumed he repeated the lecture there or elsewhere on other dates. An exhibition on the progress of prehistoric man in western Europe (with a display of some ten thousand objects) was put on at the Smithsonian at this time.

2. A one-page cartoon, "A Prehistoric Romance," by Frederick Burr Opper, appeared in the 30 May 1888 issue of the humorous magazine, *Puck* (229).

3. On 27 May the *New York Sun* reprinted part of an item from the *Courant*, "Mr. Twichell Not Going," on Twichell's trip to New York to "personally decline" the pastorate of the fashionable Presbyterian Church of the Covenant on Park Avenue. A Yale classmate had prompted the church's offer, which would have meant a significant increase in Twichell's pay.

103. Twichell to Twain

25 June 1888. New Haven, Connecticut

YALE UNIVERSITY
NEW HAVEN,
CONN.
June 25 1888

Dear Mark:

The Corporation of the Yale University, now in session, have just decreed you the honorary degree of Master of Arts (M.A.)

It will be very agreeable to all concerned (Pres. Dwight bids me say to you) i.e. all except yourself if you can be present at the Alumni Dinner; Wednesday P.M. (27th inst.) and accept the well-earned decoration conferred upon you, in a few brief remarks.[1]

Wednesday is Commencement Day. If you choose to come and pass the day here, telegraph me in *Hartford* by what train you will come to New Haven, and I will meet you at the station (I'm going home tonight to stay *till* Wednesday)

Don't think you are *compelled* as a matter of courtesy to come. But everybody would like to see you, of course. Ask Livy, for me, how it seems to have a Master of Arts for a husband after so long having only an ordinary man.

Robinson H. C. also gets haloed.[2]

Mark: I'm mighty glad this most proper act on the part of an old Connecticut College has been done. 'Twas an unanimous business.

In haste

Yrs aff.

J.H.T.

[Over]

The Honorary Degrees conferred at this Commencement are not announced till Wednesday. Till then they are a dead secret. Mind that.[3]

1. Timothy Dwight V, Congregationalist minister and president of Yale from 1886 to 1899. A typical reference here to Twain's preference to avoid public appearances where he could. We leave Twichell's original punctuation (or lack of it) in place.

2. Henry C. Robinson, Hartford lawyer and mayor from 1872 to 1874, twice Republican candidate for state governor.

3. Twain evidently chose not to attend the ceremony and wrote to President Dwight on 26 June to say so. In the letter he makes particular reference to his role as a humorist, responding to the late Matthew Arnold's rebuking "the guild of American 'funny men'," making "your honorable recognition of us . . . peculiarly forcible & timely." He goes on to defend the humorist's role as "a worthy calling; that with all its lightness & frivolity . . . has one serious purpose . . .—the deriding of shams, the exposure of pretentious falsities, the laughing of stupid superstitions out of existence; & that whoso is by instinct engaged in this sort of warfare is the natural enemy of royalties, nobilities, privileges & all kindred swindles, & the natural friend of human rights & human liberties" (Mark Twain Papers).

104. Twichell to Twain

27 June 1888. New Haven, Connecticut

Domi. Jun. XXVII[1]

Marce Carissime:

Hodie audivi Praesidem Universitatis Yalensis, coram populo, dicere: "Pro auctoritate mihi commissa, constituo Magistros Artium, honoris causa:

Samuelem Langhorne Clemens" —— et alios.

Inter laureatos tuum nomen primum in ordine fuit.[2]

And I tell you, old fellow, it sounded good. Everybody was pleased, but nobody more than I, I'm sure.

I was mighty sorry you couldn't be at the Alumni Dinner. Dear old Sherman made a fine characteristic speech of considerable length.[3] After him came Stanley Matthews: next a naval officer, Commander Goodrich, who was in the list of this year's honorary M.A.'s with you: next Lt. Gov. Howard: then the President read your letter, which, let me say, was just right, and was received with decided favor; and then, entirely without warning me beforehand, which he had the grace to state confound him, he called up *me*.[4] Heaven only knows what I said, but I blundered out something and crawled off. There were other talks, some of them fine. Your letter satisfactorily explained your absence: but your presence would have been very welcome, and I think you would have enjoyed being there.

However, next year will do about as well, and you will have plenty of time to get ready. But I am glad and proud that Alma Mater has seen fit to extend to you so clear a mark of recognition in the eyes of the world: and I trust you will set some small value on it yourself. You will & you do, I know. Gen. Sherman, with whom I talked across the table, expressed himself as warmly gratified by it. The dear old fellow was in the best of spirits, and made himself wonderfully agreeable. He sat beside the oldest living graduate, Rev. Dr. Wickham, aged 93, and showed him much attention. The old man said grace, and when he sat down I heard Sherman say to him right off, in his hearty way "That's a prayer we can all join in."

But I didn't set out to write you a letter.

My Gettysburg address is done.[5] We'll see how it goes off. Harmony thinks it not so bad. She is going to G. with me, you know. We are anticipating a big memorable time.

You have received Dean's book I imagine.[6] Isn't it splendid? It is charming *reading* to me, letting alone its other charms. The girls are at West Point, bathing in bliss no doubt. Ed. has gone to Colebrook, Conn. for the summer. Dave and Burt are camping over behind Talcott Mountain with Yung Wing's boys.[7] We are accordingly rather lonesome. But we love you and yours all the same.

Yours as ever

Joe.

1. The day of the degree ceremony.

2. "Dearest Mark, Today I heard the president of Yale say in public: 'By the authority invested in me, I award the honorary degree of Master of Arts to Samuel Langhorne Clemens'—and to others. Among those so honored your name was the first on the list."

3. General William T. Sherman.

4. Stanley Matthews, associate justice of the U.S. Supreme Court; naval officer Caspar Goodrich; James Howard, lieutenant governor of Connecticut.

5. Twichell was to speak at the Grand Reunion of the Army of the Potomac and the Army of Northern Virginia at Gettysburg in the summer of 1888. He witnessed and served at the battle in 1863.

6. Dean Sage's *The Ristigouche and Its Salmon Fishing* was published in 1888 in an edition of only 105 copies. It is now a valuable rare book.

7. Bartlett Yung and Morrison Yung, Yung Wing's sons, lived with the Twichells when their father was in China, their mother, Mary Kellogg Yung, having died in 1886. Yung Wing ultimately returned to Hartford and died there in 1912.

105. Twain to Twichell

28 June 1888. Elmira, New York

BITUMINOUS COAL CORPORATION.
MINERS & SHIPPERS OF MOSHANNON CREEK BITUMINOUS COAL.
PRESIDENTS'S [*sic*] OFFICE.

C. J. LANGDON,
CHAIRMAN OF THE BOARD.
WM. D. KELLY, PRESIDENT.
F. W. KENNEDY, VICE PREST.
M. H. ARNOT, TREAS.
L. P. MILLER, SECY. ELMIRA, N.Y. June 28/88.

Dear Joe:

How they waste their privileges—the women. That is a thought which swam through my mind as I was walking down here a moment ago. It was born of a perplexity: how in the *nation* to excuse myself from a blow-out in New York with something better than the tiresome old "circumstances-over-which-I-have-no-control" sort—something with a whang of actuality about it, something which nobody could absolutely *know* was an invention. *They*—the women—why, their noble chance is wholly wasted on them; they never in any case use it. But land! suppose we had it. We would play it 31 days in the month & 365 in the year, & in our gratitude count its temporary discomforts as nothing. To-wit:

"January 1. Gentlemen: I am sorry to be obliged to say that my monthlies having come upon me last night, etc."

Jan 2. Gentlemen: In consequence of my courses being due upon the date you name, etc"—

Jan. 3. Gentlemen: Unfortunately I shall be debarred by "the custom of men," etc—

Jan. 4. Mr. Chairman—Dear Sir: As I am expecting to be unwell upon the date named, etc"—

Jan. 5. Mrs. President—Dear Madam: I should have been quite able to accept, ordinarily, & would of course do so with pleasure, but unhappily I have gone over my time, this month, & so am obliged to decline, since I cannot now foretell when I shall be taken unwell," etc—

Jan. 6. Gentlemen: I regret to say that I have been a little irregular for some time, & my monthly period having now come upon me before due, I find myself obliged to telegraph this withdrawal of my engagement at the last moment" etc—

Jan. 7. My Dear Young Ladies: To my inexpressible regret I am flowing again; & therefore it will not be safe for me to attempt to keep my engagement to address the Esthetic Club this evening upon "The Beautiful in Art & Nature—Especially Nature."[1]

And so on, through the whole month.[2]

Thank you most cordially, Joe—& all of you. I do very greatly enjoy being a Master of Arts. I wish I could have been at the dinner. If Livy hadn't been so worn out with the heat & the trunk-packing, I would have asked for her to let me off from fetching her up here.

I send my love to you all. But I shall not tell Livy I have written, because she would want to know what it was I wrote.

Yrs Ever
Mark.

1. Quotation marks in this letter as Twain gives them.

2. Again one senses Twain's delight in pushing Twichell's tolerance for the more risqué elements of his humor to its limits.

106. Twichell to Twain

21 November 1888? Hartford, Connecticut

Hartford. Nov. 21.

Dear Mark;

At his request, made of me through Atwood Collins, I am giving Mr. E. R. Kennedy, a native (I believe) of Hartford, now a resident of Brooklyn, a note of introduction to you.—a thing, you will bear me witness, that I havn't done for anybody else in a long time.[1] What Mr. K wants of you, I gather, is to speak at a New England dinner. Please refuse him gently, as he is a good fellow. He used to be in Mrs. Bushnell's Sunday School Class when he was a boy.[2]

x x x x x

I had a letter from Charley Stowe the other day of which the following is an extract:

> "I have been reading in the volume of Dr. Burton's 'Remains,' as the old folks used to say, your remarks at his funeral. I think for beauty of diction, richness of thought, and delicacy and strength of psychological analysis it is up to any of the masters of our tongue.[3] The passage I admire most of all is that beginning:" [Here Charley evidently took down the book to copy the said passage. He continues] "Now here *is* a joke. It was, on examination, *not* your words, but *Dr. Parker's* that so filled me with admiration[.]" Then he quotes the paragraph and *goes on* and on heaping his impudent eulogy upon it, to a wearisome extent.

I sent the letter to Parker, saying that I had read it with *fluctuating* emotion, as he would; only the *order* of his fluctuation would be different from mine.

Well, old fellow; how are you? I am consumed with desire to see you. I've lots of things to tell you and to hear from you. But they will keep. We are all pretty well here. It's the same with you, I trust. By your means our path is smoother under foot than it has been for a long time, in an important respect.[4]

Yrs aff.

Joe

1. Atwood Collins was an attorney and prominent member of Asylum Hill Church.

2. Here and elsewhere, Twichell uses such marks as immediately follow to denote a change of subject.

3. Rev. Charles Stowe was the son of Harriet Beecher Stowe and Calvin Stowe. Rev. Nathaniel J. Burton's posthumously published *Yale Lectures on Preaching, and Other Writings* (New York: Charles L. Webster, 1888) was prefaced by sermons by both Twichell and Edwin Pond Parker. Published by Twain's publishing company despite Webster's own objections, the book was evidently a success. Twain refers to this matter of the funeral remarks in *Autobiography of Mark Twain*, 1:310–11 (though in the form of a conversation between himself and Twichell).

4. This reinforces the 1888 dating, remembering the fiftieth birthday celebrations and the paying off of Twichell's mortgage earlier in the year.

107. Twain to Twichell

25 January 1889. Hartford, Connecticut

Hartford, Jan. 25/89.

Dear Joe:

It is a great & admirable performance, & does you infinite credit.[1] It must have cost prodigious labor to prepare it; yet it is so thoroughly well prepared & so well digested & thought out, that the labor does not obtrude itself; there is nothing to call the reader's attention to it in the treatment, the art of it all is so fine & good. Livy buried me under reproaches last night, because I was absent, & she made me feel sorry & ashamed (for she has no just appreciation of Bulk[e]ley & Barnard as a team), but I am not sorry now; I could reflect—& leisurely reflect—as I read you this morning, whereas you would have allowed me no time for that: I should have been obliged to keep along abreast of you.[2]

I have sent a copy to Chauncey Depew.[3] He is orator at the coming Constitutional celebration, & he can't claim ignorance, now, if he fails to do justice to Connecticut.

I think you have painted Thomas Hooker for all time; it must remain the original, the master-work; all that follow will be merely copies.

Ys ever

Mark.

1. Twain is responding to Twichell's ten thousand word speech on Thomas Hooker (Puritan preacher, founder of Hartford and—for Twichell—of modern modes of democratic government) delivered to the Connecticut Historical Society. It appears from the letter that there were copies of the speech printed up. Courtney suggests that Twain's praise of Twichell's oratorical skills is of a somewhat "oblique" nature, with the emphasis more on the "prodigious labor" than its art (see *Joseph Hopkins Twichell*, 233–34).

2. Twain had evidently not attended the speech, given on the occasion of the 250th anniversary of the founding of the Connecticut colony. Governor Morgan G. Bulkeley and Henry Barnard, a prominent educational reformer and official of the society, both also spoke at the event.

3. Chauncey Depew was a well-known New York politician. He stood unsuccessfully for the Senate in 1881 but would later be elected to that body.

108. Twichell to Twain

11 November 1889. Hartford, Connecticut

Monday

Dear Mark:

The best I can do about West Point is to say that I will go with you to be there Dec. 8th if *I can.* should it suit you to fix that time.[1] The practicability of my joining you will be somewhat doubtful for a fortnight yet.

Yours aff

Joe

1. It seems this visit did not take place on this date. On 23 December, Twain asked Howells to go with him to West Point on 11 January 1890, when he planned to read from *A Connecticut Yankee.*

109. Twain to Twichell

22 or 23 February 1890. Hartford, Connecticut

[Letter enclosed, addressed to Mr. S. L. Clemens from Charles L. Webster & Co. on headed notepaper, dated 21 February 1890:]

Dear sir:—

Mr. Stedman asked us to write you, knowing that you knew Mr. Twitchell, if you would kindly find out from him in what regiment professor Thomas R. Lounsbury served during the war, and how long.[1] Also, if Mr. Twitchell knows what Professor Lounsbury's occupation was between the time of his leaving the army and taking the professorship at the "Yale."

Professor Lounsbury always declines to give any information about himself, but, as Mr. Stedman wishes to write a biographical sketch of him for the 11th. Volume of the "Library of American Literature," he would like to get some facts on which to base a biographical sketch.

Hoping this will not be any trouble to you, we remain

Yours very truly,

[Signed] Chas L Webster Co.

[Twain inserts at the foot of the letter:]

Dear Joe:

?

Ys Ever

Mark.

1. Charles L. Webster & Co., the publishing company Twain owned, was working on an ill-fated, eleven-volume *A Library of American Literature* from 1887 to 1890. Edmund Stedman, journalist and poet, was one of the editors.

110. Twichell to Twain

22 March 1890. Hartford, Connecticut

March 22

Dear Mark:

Harmony's report of a talk she had with Livy the other day (I remark in passing that there's a certain moral beauty attaching in my mind, to the idea of a conference between those two women) has suggested to me—not logically or in any direct fashion at-all.—the propriety [of] saying to you apropos of that House "Prince and Pauper" business, that I share the opinion, which must be universal with all who know you, that you are wholly and scrupulously and even fastidiously a man of your word; that nothing is more impossible than that you should evade, or otherwise than most strictly and to the last letter observe, any contract whatsoever into which you had consciously entered, whether with or without formality.[1] And now having said it I am doubtful if I ought not to ask your forgiveness for the same—it is from me, as I hope you are aware, so utterly superfluous.

Well, if I have done a left-handed and blundering thing and have affronted you, *I take it back.* I beg you to overlook it, and consider it unsaid.

If on the other hand I should have said it before—wildly improbable as I conceive that to be—I trust you will believe that my silence has been due to the fact that the House complication has not occurred to me in a light to seem to call for such an expression. That I have not even been very much alive to the intense disagreeableness to you and Livy both of the situation into which Mr. House's procedure has brought you—which, I own, has been the case—has arisen from the circumstances that of late I have been selfishly preoccupied with private troubles and care, to an unprecedented degree in my experience.[2]

One thing more I will say—that while I have for the year past been wont when in New York to call on Mr. House out of regard to his forlorn condition, I have never exchanged a syllable with him on the subject of this difficulty.[3] He did once make a remark to me, incomprehensible at the time, which I afterward understood as referring to it. But that is all.

Should he ever open the matter to me, I should certainly declare to him the judgment of you which I have set down in this note.

Yours aff.

Joe.

1. Edward H. House had brought a suit against the 1889–1890 production of *The Prince and the Pauper* (staged by Daniel Frohman and Abby Sage Richardson) on the grounds that Twain had earlier given the rights to adapt the book solely to him. The litigation stopped Twain from receiving any royalties from the play and ended the two men's friendship.

2. One such "trouble" was the death of Twichell's sister, Sarah Jane Twichell Ware, of consumption in February. She was just forty-five years old.

3. In 1888, House and his adopted daughter Koto, who had been staying with the Clemenses and others in Hartford, had moved to New York to be closer to House's physicians.

111. Twichell to Twain

28 October 1890. Hartford, Connecticut

Tuesday a.m.

Dear Mark

All that old friends ought to feel for one they love thinking such thoughts as are your sad heart's company today, Harmony and I are feeling.[1]

A boy has only one own mother in his whole life, and when she is gone this world can never be quite the same to him any more.

God bless you, and bless us all.

Yours with much affection

Joe.

1. Twain's mother, Jane Lampton Clemens, had died on 27 October 1890.

112. Twain to Twichell

15 April 1891. Hartford, Connecticut

Apl. 15/91.

Dear Joe—

Stepniak is spending the evening with us—an interesting man.[1] Come over, won't you.[2]

Ys

Mark

1. Radical revolutionary and author Sergei Stepniak-Kravchinskii was the Russian anarchist responsible for the 1878 fatal stabbing of General Mezentsev, head of the czar's secret police. By this time, he was living in London and known for his anti-czarist views and the series of books he had written about his homeland. Twain would become a member of the Society of Friends of Russian Freedom founded in the United States during Stepniak-Kravchinskii's visit.

2. Notes of this type from Twain to Twichell were, one would guess, fairly commonplace. One imagines Twichell may have been taken out of his comfort zone by some of his friend's guests.

Mark Twain—Samuel L. Clemens—in the early 1870s, the period during which he and Rev. Joseph Hopkins Twichell cemented their friendship in Hartford. (The Mark Twain House & Museum, Hartford)

Twichell—shown here at age fifty in 1888—retained a youthful quality that seemed to match a similar element in Twain. (The Mark Twain House & Museum, Hartford)

Twichell served as pastor of Hartford's prosperous Asylum Hill Congregational Church from 1865 to 1912. Twain called it "The Church of the Holy Speculators," but attended regularly during his early Hartford years. (The Mark Twain House & Museum, Hartford)

Twichell's Italianate home on Woodland Street, Hartford, was a center of family life for the minister and ultimately a refuge for Twain, who completed *A Connecticut Yankee at King Arthur's Court* there in 1888. (The Mark Twain House & Museum, Hartford)

Twain's elaborate mansion on Farmington Avenue was completed in 1874 and the family lived in the home until 1891. Maintained as a museum today, its gables, chimneys, and whimsical balconies still overlook the busy thoroughfare. (The Mark Twain House & Museum, Hartford)

In his letters, Twichell frequently yearns for a walk with Twain to Bartlett's Tower on Talcott Mountain, west of Hartford. The pair made the eight-mile conversational walk frequently in the fall and spring. (The Mark Twain House & Museum, Hartford)

Twichell turns up most prominently in Twain's work in *A Tramp Abroad*, his sometimes fanciful recounting of time spent in Central Europe in 1878–79. In this illustration the narrator and "Harris"—a version of Twichell, who actually accompanied him on the trip—witness a near-disaster in the Swiss Alps.

The Clemens family gathers on the porch of the Hartford house in 1885. From left: Clara Clemens, Livy Clemens, Jean Clemens, Samuel Clemens, and Susy Clemens. The dog is Flash. (The Mark Twain House & Museum, Hartford)

The large Twichell family, plus one, in 1892. From left, front row: Harmony Twichell Jr., Joseph Hopkins Twichell, Joseph Hooker Twichell, Burton Parker Twichell, Harmony Cushman Twichell, Louise Hopkins Twichell (on her lap), and Edward Twichell Ware, a nephew. Rear row: Susan Lee Twichell, David Cushman Twichell, Julia Curtis Twichell, Sarah Dunham Twichell (peering over her mother's head) and Edward Carrington Twichell. (Yale Collection of American Literature, Beinecke Rare Book and Manuscript Library)

On 29 November 1895 Twain wrote to Twichell that he "vastly" liked a photo taken by H. Walter Barnett in Sydney, Australia, two months before, saying it was the "best one that was ever made of me." (State Library of New South Wales, Australia)

Samuel and Livy Clemens in 1903, shortly before departing for Europe, where Livy died in 1904. (The Mark Twain House & Museum, Hartford)

Joe and Harmony Twichell in later life maintained their close relationship with Twain. (Asylum Hill Congregational Church)

In 1905 Twain's daughter Jean took a picture of the old friends in Twain's New York house. The Twichells were on their way from Hartford for a seaside visit to Atlantic City, New Jersey. (Yale Collection of American Literature, Beinecke Rare Book and Manuscript Library)

During their 1907 visit to Bermuda, Twichell and Twain had secretary Isabel Lyon take a snapshot in front of the boardinghouse where they had stayed on their previous visit in 1877. They found that their landlady, Mary Ann Kirkham, had passed on, but her daughter Emily still kept boarders. "We were white-headed, but she was not," Clemens wrote in his autobiography; "in the sweet and unvexed spiritual atmosphere of the Bermudas one does not achieve gray hairs at forty-eight." (Henry W. and Albert A. Berg Collection of English and American Literature, The New York Public Library, Astor, Lenox, and Tilden Foundations)

In 1907 Twain and Twichell revisited Bermuda, which they had last seen together thirty years before. On shipboard they posed, coatless, in January weather for the redoubtable Isabel Lyon, Twain's secretary. (The Mark Twain Papers & Project, Bancroft Library, University of California, Berkeley)

PART 3
1891–1900

Twain and His Family as Peripatetics; Business Failure; the Death of Susy; Continued Exile

Twain and Livy closed the Hartford house down in June 1891 when the family went to Europe. The move seems to have been spurred by a variety of factors. Twain had suffered throughout the year, with his arm "crippled with rheumatism" and accordingly unable to write.[1] Livy, so often on the verge of invalidism, was suffering from rheumatism, too, but also, and more seriously, from the early symptoms of heart disease and—it seems—depression. The death of her own mother, Olivia, in 1890, a month after the death of Twain's mother, may have been a factor here. Other factors included the increasing financial difficulties caused partly by the high costs of running the Hartford home, the ups and downs of Twain's publishing firm, Charles L. Webster & Co., and the increasing drain on resources resulting from Twain's huge investments in the Paige Compositor, an invention for setting type automatically that looked to revolutionize the print industry but which in fact could never quite be brought to work effectively. Twain sank a fortune into this last venture. One strong factor in the European move, indeed, was that it was a cheaper place to live.

Generally, during this period, life was on a downward spiral for Twain and his family. Susy had enrolled at Bryn Mawr in 1890 but had lasted only a term, her intense relationship with fellow student Louise Brownell perhaps leading her parents to end her time there. Jean's health, too, was poor: she was already possibly suffering from the epilepsy that would be officially diagnosed in 1896, when she was fifteen. Thenceforth her health would always be a source of anxiety to her parents, and the letters of this period reflect that. They reflect, too, the temporary relief following Jean's treatment by Henrik Kellgren and his Swedish Movement Cure, a manipulative therapy similar to osteopathy.

Twain's publishing business, Charles L. Webster & Co., also went belly up at this time, partly as a result of poor business practice, partly because of the economic panic of 1893. Webster's was consequently declared bankrupt in April 1894, with catastrophic results for Twain himself. If he and Livy had initially put no fixed time limit on their stay in Europe when they left Hartford, they certainly had no idea that it would signal the start of a period of long-term exile. They would be based in Europe for most of the next nine years, spending time in France, Italy, Sweden, and Germany, and especially in Austria (a twenty-month stay, mainly in Vienna, from September 1897) and England.

During this period, and soon after Twain's 1895–96 world lecture tour made to recoup some of his lost fortune, the couple faced devastation in the death of Susy from spinal meningitis in August 1896. Susy was visiting Hartford and staying in the family house at the time—with her parents meanwhile resident in England. That tragedy made it impossible for the family ever to return to Hartford (they would sell the house in 1903), and indeed the town became synonymous with "Heartbreak" in Twain and Livy's minds.[2] The family remained in Europe in the years following Susy's death, and only in 1900 were they ready to return to New York and American life. Twain did, however, make frequent business trips back home, mainly to New York, during these years.

Twichell, meanwhile, stayed mainly in Hartford, writing to Twain about events taking place in the town and in the nation, helping to keep him connected to both communities, and offering him emotional support and continued close friendship despite their distance. Twichell would also see Twain on his New York business trips. The two families, too, would meet up in Germany—at Bad Nauheim, a spa near Hamburg—when Twichell and Harmony came to Europe in the summer of 1892. It was here that Twain, while in Twichell's company, was invited to meet the Prince of Wales, the future Edward VII. Twichell takes some relish in describing the "notably cordial" meeting between prince and celebrity commoner and the "striking and even comical contrast" they made as they "fell talking and laughing together like old friends . . . the prince solid, erect, stepping with a firm, soldier-like tread; Mark waving along in that shambling gait of his, in full tide of talk, brandishing, as an instrument of gesture, an umbrella of the most scandalous description."[3] The Twichells made another European trip in 1899, but this time failed to meet up with Twain and Livy, though they did briefly rendezvous with their daughter Clara.

Back in Hartford, in 1896, Twichell would be with Susy at the time of her death and would comfort Twain as best he could in its aftermath, never wavering in his commitment to his friend. What had been a relationship based on proximity turned into something rather different in these years as letter writing rather than frequent close personal contact became its base, and as Twichell became one of Twain's main intimate ties to his American homeland.

It is noticeable in sections of this correspondence that at times there is little sense of ongoing dialogue. This speaks of other missing letters and also, perhaps, of delayed mail between the two continents. But what is also noticeable is the changing tone of the correspondence as, inevitably, the impact of the wider world on each of the two men, as well as the impact of the transatlantic world they shared, played an increasingly significant part in the letters.

As one might expect, what we might call Twain and Twichell's "domestic" lives continue to feature in the letters—Susy's death, Jean's illness, Harmony Jr.'s state of health and her nursing career, and Dave's volunteering for military service at the time of the Spanish-American War (1898). But there is also increasing focus on the lives (and demises) of their fellow Hartford residents, as, with the passing of time, death started to take its inevitable toll. Twain also used Twichell as his man-on-the-spot for research needed for his writing—and especially in the case of his growing and sardonic interest, from 1899 on, in Mary Baker Eddy and Christian Science.

In terms of the wider world, events in the Austro-Hungarian Empire (which, not so long afterward, would play a major part in the lead-up to the First World War) are a center of interest in Twain's Vienna letters and Twichell's response to them. The colonial policies of the Western powers, too, come increasingly under scrutiny, with America's intervention in Cuba and the Philippines, Twain's particular interest in South Africa and the South African (Boer) War, and both men's concern with the situation in China at the time of the Boxer Rebellion. Partly as a result of such matters, the worldviews of both men start to draw more obviously apart, with Twain becoming increasingly misanthropic and Twichell resisting such a position. It is, then, significant that in the last few letters in this section Twain should be making such remarks as "Oh, the human race!—what a ridiculous invention it is. . . . Let us hope there is no hereafter; I don't want to train with any angels made out of human material"; significant, too, that Twichell should come back at him with a counter-response: "Mark, the way you throw your rotten eggs at the human race doth greatly arride me.[4] We preachers are extensively accused of vilifying human nature, as you are aware; but I must own that for enthusiasm of misanthropy you beat us out of sight."[5] As the correspondence continues, the two men's philosophical, theological, and political differences would become increasingly pronounced, with the—usually friendly—sparring that resulted becoming one of the most fascinating and revealing of its aspects.

1. See, for instance, his letter to Richard Watson Gilder of 21 July 1891. Mark Twain Papers, Bancroft Library, University of California, Berkeley (henceforth Mark Twain Papers).

2. See Letter 153.

3. Quoted in Steve Courtney, *Joseph Hopkins Twichell* (Athens: University of Georgia Press, 2008), 245. For Twain's account of the meeting, see Benjamin Griffin and Harriet Elinor Smith, eds., *Autobiography of Mark Twain*, vol. 2 (Berkeley: University of California Press, 2013), 181–82.

4. "Arride": an archaic word meaning delight or gratify.

5. See Letters 176 and 179.

113. Twichell to Twain

4 July 1891. Hartford, Connecticut

[Twichell forwards a letter to Twain (now in Aix-les-Bains, a health spa in eastern France) from the chaplain of the Hartford County Jail, E. B. Dillingham, dated June 1891, appealing for donations of books for the jail's library. Dillingham details the number of inmates and explains the function of the library, then adds, "This jail serves the whole County. Many even of the churches have been represented among the inmates." Twichell has underlined that last sentence. There is no accompanying letter from Twichell himself, but scribbled at the bottom of Dillingham's letter is this note:]

Dear Mark

Here's a gem "of purest ray serene"—as you see.[1] I send it to you for a Fourth of July present. With love and greetings to all—

Yrs aff—

Joe

1. The quote is from Thomas Gray's "Elegy Written in a Country Churchyard."

114. Twichell to Twain

17 August 1891. Hamilton, Bermuda

Hamilton. Bermuda.
Aug. 17. 1891

Dear Mark,

I knew as soon as I got here that I should have to write to you before I left.[1] For I saw that being here was bound to keep you incessantly in mind. In fact, the moment we landed and stepped into the glare of the white street I was back again in 1878 (was it?) and in your company.[2] And through the whole fortnight since I have had a deal of silent converse with you. At sight of that colonnade of palms (now happily called royal instead of cabbage) that so ravished us, I said "There they are, Mark!"—and so it has been all the while. Well, as I say, I was going to write to you sure; but to prick the sides of my intent, here is Livy's letter to Harmony passed on to me by mail, and come to hand this morning, with just the news of you all I wanted to hear—except that plaguy [*sic*] rheumatism which I hadn't supposed was so bad.[3] Dear me, I hope you will manage to dispose of it somehow shortly. You have less use for it where it is (or has been) than almost anybody I can think of. Had you been here with us it would have been *fried* out of you. We expected warm weather. It was advertised at 85° on the average. But it will take a fortnight of not much above zero to make that the average *this* month. I cool off with a hot bath, being wary of violent changes at my age. However, the news is (or are) that they have been roasted at home; which lends some degree of probability to the testimony borne on all hands that we have struck the most torrid streak Bermuda has experienced for many a year. Yet we have enjoyed ourselves hugely nevertheless i.e. the majority of us. You know my company—Young Dean Sage, aet. 15; Walter, red-headed son of my classmate Prof. Tom Lounsbury of Yale, aet. 19, and Dave; three as fine youngsters as you will seldom get together.[4] (or often get together—which is it?) Spite of the temperature the lads have been in unquenchably high spirits every single hour since we sailed from New York, and have kept [me] by contagion, in pretty much the same mood. Though I havn't been caught up into quite their skylarking pitch, I have gone everywhere with them, and sunned my soul in their cheerfulness. We have visited all nooks and corners of the islands, by carriage and by boat; explored the reefs with their amazing under-water splendors, have bathed and fished; observed the customs of the country and its institutions. (yesterday we attended a session of the miniature parliament [.]) Evenings we have played whist (poor whist—the poorest no doubt) on the veranda. Sundays we have worshipped at the garrison church, where they march the red-coats of the King's Regiment in to the music of a band of sixty pieces, which afterward leads all the responses and accompanies the hymns (on the bass drum I read, from where I sit, Blenheim, Oudenarde [*sic*], Malplaquet, Ramillies, Dettingen, *Niagara,* Lucknow, Delhi, Afghanistan, Egypt).[5] No sermon to speak of. The boys never enjoyed church half so much before. Really they have had a splendid time spite of the swelter—which they don't particularly mind. There. e.g. just now go Dean and Dave rattling down the street in a donkey cart en route for the beach and a tumble in the surf, laughing and shouting, and all Hamilton on the grin to look at them. In fact Hamilton is well aware of us, in the season's dearth of more important subjects of interest. The enclosed newpaper clipping will indicate how our trivial doings are noted. You should have seen the boys' faces when they saw it. They had to swim about a rod.[6]

I don't know how you would manage if you came here again. Modern history dates from your visit. Were you to repeat it the whole Colony would be immediately on top of you with attentions. We have suffered somewhat on your account. It transpired soon after our arrival—through my calling on our landlady Mrs. Kirkham, I suppose—that I was the man who was here with you. Forthwith the invitations began, I might almost say to pour in on us. But we excused ourselves, with one or two exceptions only. By George, I was of half a mind to hire a hall and advertise a lecture on M.T. and carry home a ship load of shillings. One of the invitations we didn't decline was that of a lady (wife of the speaker of the Colony parliament) who wanted us to go with her and see a notable garden in her neighborhood. The day was a broiler, but we went. The lady ordered her carriage, which was presently announced. Though the coachman was in livery with a rosette on his hat, the vehicle was one-horsed and quite light. "There will be room for *two* of you to *ride*" (emphasis on "ride") said the lady with much sweetness of manner. So Walter Lounsbury and I got in (being the elders) and Dean and Dave pedestrianized behind. It was a good distance we had to go, and the way those luckless boys "larded the lean earth" in their efforts to keep up was a caution.[7] When we came to a cross road, we'd stop till they hove in sight, and point the direction, then rumble on. I can't describe the comical expression their steaming countenances wore responsive to the glances (triumphant) Walter and I now and then cast back at them over our shoulders. They brought up dripping at our destination a quarter of an hour or so after us, and then we were escorted together to see the interesting vegetation the spectacle of which was to reward our venturing out in such frightful heat. Garden? I'm blessed, if it wasn't a *Conservatory*—a wide low-roofed, air-tight, glass furnace full of equatorial plants that cannot bear exposure in this climate. Well, the boys were just liquefied. To see them so well-mannered and polite as the slow show went on, with the rivulets of sweat running down their cheeks! Stewed as I was, I *had* to laugh. They will long remember their Bermuda *ride*.

Harmony said that she was going to give Livy a full account of little Harmony's condition.[8] Till she had Livy's letter she thought (so she alleges) that I had written to you before I came away. But I was too much occupied with finishing my scrap of a book to attend to such duties.[9] You'll never catch me authoring again—once I'm out of this scrape.

Harmony tells me that the first instalment of proof has come. How I hate the thought of it. I can't correct proof, and had relied on you to teach me the art. You are saved that trouble, and I guess that generally you are no loser by remoteness from the subscriber. Somehow of late the conceit has all gone out of me, Mark, which I regret, for I hold it one of the friendliest infirmities.

But I have had a good refreshing of spirit in the fountain of youth, in the companionship of these boys, honest, ingenuous fellows, full of nature and of truth, knowing little of evil. I hope they will be as good men as they are boys. God grant it. Is it too much to ask? I won't believe it—though I am not myself an example of that blessedness, through my most grievous fault. I have marked nothing whatsoever to show, or suggest, or by the faintest sign betoken, any lowness of mind in any of them, no most distant approach to coarseness; nothing but generosity and refinement and modesty, and respect for things that ought to be respected, though they are so full of noise and motion.

There, Mark, I'll let up on you now. This is no sort of a letter, as you perceive.—nothing to bring you in debt. You need not think yourself obliged to answer it—ever. I wouldn't if I were in your place, i.e. if I had anything else to do.

I will write again one of these days, if I have anything to communicate.

God send you a sound arm soon. My true love to Livy, whom I esteem the crown of womankind—she and one other—and to her dear girls who are promising candidates for the same rank. As for me, I am your no account, though inveterately affectionate friend

Joe

1. The first three weeks of Twichell's annual vacation were spent in Bermuda with his son David and the two other young men mentioned in the letter.

2. His previous visit to Bermuda with Twain was in May 1877.

3. Twain was suffering from rheumatism in his right arm. "Prick the sides of my intent" is from *Macbeth*, act 1, scene 7.

4. Aet: *aetatis suae*, of his (or her) age.

5. Various British battle names, presumably written on the drum-face. Twichell emphasizes the one (Niagara) that took place on American soil in 1859, during the French and Indian War.

6. The clipping reports that Dean Sage and David Twichell capsized in a local harbor: "As both were good swimmers, nothing worse than a good wetting resulted."

7. See the description of Falstaff's sweat in *Henry IV, Part 1*, Act 2, scene 2.

8. On 5 April 1892 (Letter 118), Twichell reports that Harmony Jr. has had a long-term disease that includes "a morbid shrinking from the resumption of activities." Members of the family were prone to depression.

9. Twichell had written *John Winthrop: First Governor of the Massachusetts Colony* for Dodd, Mead's Makers of America series. He completed it in 1891.

115. Twain to Twichell

1 October 1891. Nîmes, France

Nimes, Oct 1/91.[1]

Dear Joe:

I have been ten days floating down the Rhone on a raft, from Lake Bourget, & a most curious & darling kind of a trip it has been. You ought to have been along—I could have made room for you easily—& you would have found that a pedestrian tour in Europe doesn't begin with a raft-voyage for hilarity, & mild adventure, & intimate contact with the unvisited native of the back settlements, & extinction from the world & newspapers, & a conscience in a state of coma, & lazy comfort, & solid happiness. In fact there's *nothing* that's so lovely.

But it's all over. I gave the raft away yesterday at Arles, & am loafing along back by short stages on the rail to Ouchy-Lausanne where the tribe are staying at the Beau Rivage & are well & prosperous.

However, that isn't what I started out to say. But *this* is: I stumbled on the whole lovely Dawson family one evening two or three weeks ago at Interlaken, & they were brim full of questions about you & Julia.[2] I told them everything I knew, & made up the balance. Now wasn't it nice to run across them in that pleasant, unexpected way?—& right in Switzerland, too—just the same as before.

Love to you all—

Mark.

1. While in Europe, Twain had evidently planned to write a series of (well-paid) commissioned travel sketches. The plan did not quite work out, and "The Innocents Adrift," the (unfinished) piece based on this raft trip, would only appear posthumously—in edited form as "Down the Rhône"—in Albert Bigelow Paine's 1923 *Europe and Elsewhere* collection.

2. See Letter 43.

116. Twichell to Twain

18 November 1891. Hartford, Connecticut

Hartford. Nov. 18.

Dear old Mark:

I am mailing you today a copy of the poor little baby book of which I have been guilty.[1] You will not read it, of course: and I do not expect you to. Your time is too valuable. And, besides, my subject is to you a *de*-viting one. The opinion you hold of the people of whom I write is, to say the least, not a flattering one.

I send you the book to occupy the only chance—*though small*—I shall ever have, of making you a return, in kind, of the bounty with which you have long time been wont to bestow upon me the fruit of your pen.

It occurs to me that John Winthrop may be of service to you as an instrument of family discipline. For instance, if Susie or Clara, or Jean should at any time so misbehave as to require punishment, you might award the penalty of a compulsory reading of ten or (if it were a case for severity) twenty pages of Uncle Joe's book. In that wise I might as an author be, though not pleasurable, profitable to you. But I should be sorry for the girls.

Your bulletin of last month from Nimes "rose the cockles of my heart." The raft-voyage: the luck meeting with the good Dawsons, the names Ouchy and Beau Rivage: all were enchanting in their suggestions. Thank you heartily for so sweet a morsel.

One of these days I'll write you a letter, but not now. Loads of love to you all. Harmony keeps getting better. Julia keeps getting worse;—but bless the child all the same. The rest of us are in excellent condition.

Yours ever aff

Joe

[I wrote to you from Bermuda. Did you get it? Small loss if you didn't.][2]

1. The *John Winthrop* book: "the people of whom [Twichell] write[s]" are Winthrop and his fellow Puritans.

2. This is written in the left-hand margin of page four of the letter.

117. Twichell to Twain

2 February 1892. Hartford, Connecticut

Hartford. Feb 2. 1892

Dear Mark: Dear Boy:

Old Dr. Hamlin the Missionary was lately here passing a day and a night with us—to our great pleasure; for no man I know, but you, equals him as a raconteur.[1] In the morning after breakfast he spied Flagg's portrait of you which hangs in our parlor over the book-case, and looked at it long, close to, then further off: with his spectacles, then without them. Finally he turned to me and said, "Twichell, that is an excellent likeness of you. It is lifelike; and reproduces one of your characteristic expressions perfectly."[2] Whereupon I made no remark whatsoever; best let it go; for what was the use? He being purblind to such a degree, what would have been gained by setting him right—to his mortification? But—the incident was of this effect—whether in your eyes happy, or otherwise, I will not judge, or give you the benefit of my doubts—to make me resolve to write to you without delay.

I had something to tell. And having something to tell has these many years sent me hunting you up. How I did miss you when I got back from Bermuda in the summer! (By the way I guess you had a letter from me written there, didn't you?) We had for a fellow passenger coming home an old U.S. Navy Surgeon, Dr. Martin; who entered the service in 1848; and was literally crammed with recollections, thrilling, informing, pathetic, humorous—all sorts—of men, of events, side-lights of history, which it was his evidently keen pleasure to impart, and which were more charming to hear than I can express.[3] He was a tender hearted veteran—nearly 80 years old he was—who cried easily—you know the kind—and always carried his audience with him—a simple, guileless, unaffected, octogenarian boy. The lads with me were wholly fascinated by him, and we spent a large part of our time from Hamilton to New York around his chair. So that I landed fit to burst with fresh yarns some of which it would have risen the cockles of your heart to hear, and no Mark on the continent! I was sorry. The matter will keep—the substance of it, or of much of it—but the dew will be off. It will be more like canned stuff. However, Dr. Martin was not the end of the world by any means.[4]

Well; as I was saying, Dr. Hamlin's observation upon my portrait gave my intent to write to you a sharp prick. But it has required this pleasing double note, from Livy and you, just arrived, to get me actually in motion.[5] The fact is, I do so much work-writing and corresponding, that epistles of friendship, for love's sake, get atrociously postponed waiting for a disengaged free hour in which I can feel a bit leisurely as suits that intercourse.

I am delighted and proud—as I ought to be—that you managed to pull through "John Winthrop," and could say that you found it interesting. Thank you much for your generous judgment. I much doubt if you are ever called on again to read a book of mine. That little volume cost me a heap of time and toil. So long as I have the duty of a parish for my *first* obligation, I do not think I can be persuaded to venture on another such job. Had I been other wise unoccupied I should have enjoyed it. As it was, I was harrassed by it. But I think it has profited me for my professional writing to turn my pen into another road, out of the didactic rut, awhile. Harmony protests that I grow less dull in the pulpit—and she ought to know, poor woman.

Professional: that brings up something I lately read that reminded me of you. It was in a volume of lectures by the late Prof. Hatch of Oxford on the Influence of Greek Ideas and Usages upon the Christian Church—one of the big books, fascinating as a novel.[6] He is speaking—in his lecture on Greek Education—of the decay of the *profession* of Philosophy, and to illustrate cites from an author (Greek) named Timon, his description of a certain eminent member of that profession, distinguished for his discourses in praise of virtue and his severity against the votaries of pleasure. Still "there is not a man to beat him in the way of lying and braggadocio and avarice," and at feasts he habitually "goes on preaching all the time about temperance and moderation, until he is so dead-drunk that the servants have to carry him out." x x x[7] "In fact (says Timon) he is *clever all round*, doing to perfection *whatever* he touches" which instantly suggested the accomplished hero of your poem "He done his level best," and dated him back to the beginning of our era.[8]

And, maybe, it yielded me further suggestions—but never mind: they did not concern you.

Henry Robinson showed me a letter from you the other day in which you said—referring to my New England dinner talk—that it was Frederick the Great who demanded of his troops holding back from a charge if they wanted to live forever.[9] Now, its queer, but in reading Carlyle's Frederick twice last year I never noticed that i.e. so as to remember it.[10] And it certainly was during the war (in the papers) attributed to an officer of our federal army: but that, of course, is no evidence whatsoever of the fact. I had a suffering time at that New England dinner, though I got along with my business pretty well, for me. I'm on the point of swearing off from that sort of pleasure: it is too painful—to sit sweating with fright three or four hours, your heart heavy as lead. I saw a number of your friends there, who inquired for you: among them Horace Porter.[11] He begged me to come and see him and we'd "cut a watermelon." I'll go with you sometime, when you get back, if you say so. I like that fellow very much; he must be stuffed full of talk that it would be a treat to hear.

Judy's approaching marriage necessarily takes up our family mind in a rather wholesale measure these days.[12] Yet we don't say much about it. We are omnipresently conscious of the shadow of it, though. It stalks, a ghost, amongst us from morn to eve.

Mark, I feel *bad*, by turns downright ugly. But I try not to show it. The young man is well enough—in fact, he is very well; which is only a mitigation; it does not cure the disease. I haven't yet the faintest glint of a paternal sense of him. I couldn't even say that I'm a friend of his. Toward Judy I observe a systematic and laborious dissimulation. "Hello, Howard" I exclaim, with counterfeit cordiality, when he appears; and then I give his hand a scr-e-e-unch that sends a spasm across his confounded grin; and wish I could twist it off him.[13] But then we have temporary reliefs of one kind and another. One we had very early in the trouble—the first hour indeed. Upon the announcement of what had befallen, in the domestic circle, (it was an entire surprise) before the shock was off, Sally and Louise scuttled out to the kitchen to tell Old Jane the black cook about it and (according to their wont) receive consolation. They got it this time, for by and by they returned with shining faces, and Louise rushed up to Judy and most eagerly asked "Say, Judy. *Will* you get a little baby and bring it home?" A dynamite bomb couldn't have scattered that crowd quicker. How Judy looked I don't know, for I didn't look at her. No one did. All had something requiring immediate attention out of the room. But the sensation was immense: and it really relaxed the strain that we were under.

I wish the obsequies were over. I wish they had eloped. Are you keeping a suitable watch on your girls? They are in danger. Do have out your pickets against those foreigners![14] If you don't bring all my nieces with you when you come home I don't want to see you. But in that case, you would probably stay over there and buy a lot in some German cemetery. I should hope you would.

There, I have written enough—and more.

Next summer Harmony and I hope to go abroad ourselves—though we may not be able to manage it. If we succeed, however, and are so fortunate as to come across Livy and you, we'll surely cut a watermelon. Tell Livy that half this letter is hers. That is the reason why it is so long.

We have delighted in hearing every way we have been permitted to do. Your letters to the papers have been fine, every one of them. That about the Bayreuth Festival was one of the best things you (or anybody) ever wrote, in my opinion.[15]

Goodbye. Peace be with you. I love you both like a boy.

Yours forever

Joe.

1. Cyrus Hamlin, a longtime friend of Twichell who served as a missionary in Turkey. From 1880, he was president of Middlebury College (Vermont).

2. Artist Charles Noel Flagg, who lived in Hartford, painted Twain in 1890. Twichell evidently had the painting hanging in his house. Hamlin was not alone in mistaking rep-

resentations of the one man for the other. Flagg also painted an 1895 portrait of Twichell, now in Asylum Hill Congregational Church's Twichell Room.

3. Charles Martin, appointed as navy surgeon on 5 September 1848.

4. The meaning here is obscure, perhaps that it is not the end of the world if Twain did not hear this account of Martin.

5. Now missing.

6. Edwin Hatch, theologian, gave the 1888 Hibbert Lectures at Oxford on "The Influence of Greek Ideas and Usages upon the Christian Church." They were published in book form in 1890.

7. Twichell is probably using the *x*'s as ellipses.

8. In "Answers to Correspondents," in Mark Twain, *Sketches, New and Old* (Hartford, Conn.: American Publishing Co., 1875), 74–75, Twain offers a poem sent to him about a preacher who would "cuss and sing and howl and pray / And dance and drink and jest, / And lie and steal—all one to him— / He done his level best."

9. There is no record of this letter. Twichell gave a speech titled "The Soldier Stamp" at the annual dinner of the New England Society in New York on 22 December 1891. In it, he related the story of a Union colonel in the Civil War who urged on his men with the cry, "Great heavens, men, do you want to live forever?" Frederick the Great was supposed to have asked his troops, "Rogues, do you want to live forever?" at the battle of Kolín in 1757. The words have since been attributed to various commanders in various wars.

10. Thomas Carlyle's *History of Friedrich II of Prussia, Called Frederick the Great* was first published in 1858.

11. Horace Porter served under Ulysses S. Grant in the Civil War and, when Grant was president, became his personal secretary. Later, he was vice president of the Pullman Palace Car Company and then U.S. ambassador to France.

12. Julia Twichell was to marry attorney Howard Ogden Wood in April 1892.

13. See Peter Messent, *Mark Twain and Male Friendship: The Twichell, Howells, and Rogers Friendships* (New York: Oxford University Press, 2009), 157–59, on Twichell's reaction to the 1891 engagement of daughter Julia (then 22) and the general difficulty he (and Twain too) had in letting their daughters separate out from the family to an independent life. At the time of this letter, Sarah ("Sally") Twichell was nine years old and Louise Twichell was seven.

14. Clara Clemens would later marry a "foreigner," the Russian-born pianist and conductor Ossip Gabrilowitsch.

15. "Mark Twain at Bayreuth," published in the *Chicago Daily Tribune*, 6 December 1891—often retitled "At the Shrine of St. Wagner."

118. Twichell to Twain

29 March 1892. Hartford, Connecticut

Hartford March 29.

Dear Mark:

It pleases me much that you have got an angle of vision on Walter Phelps that gives his good points their proper show.[1] Many people distaste him because they have chanced to plant their camera in the back yard or too squarely in front, with consequences that in [the] case of most living men—or the Church even—are unfortunate. But I always liked Walter, and I have known him thirty three years.[2] Isn't he a lad of fluid speech, though? Two weeks ago last Sunday we had a call from his wife, whom I have also known since my college days. She was visiting her sister in the neighborhood, and stopped in to hear and tell the news, doing both in a charming manner.

Last Friday night I went down to New Haven to make a speech at the banquet following the Yale-Harvard public debate—in which, by the way, Yale didn't come off first, in my judgment.[3]

Chauncey Depew presided at the debate and banquet both, and was at his best.[4] Which he isnt [*sic*] always; e.g. he came near spoiling a big athletic dinner in New York (where, again, I was on the programme) by talking 38 minutes by the watch—and dull talk too, which the audience didn't finally attend to much, and was ruined, of course, for the rest of us. But at this New Haven feast he was as fine as possible. How he keeps up the quality of his performance, however, to its prevailing level, is a wonder of the world. Three times a week, he told me, on the average, all winter through, he's on tap. I am obliged to say, though, that there are signs of the saturation of the New York ear with his oratory, good as it is. An invitation I lately had (and declined) to squeak my penny trumpet there, said "We want to get along without Depew, if we can." The "if *we can*" to be sure, was mighty complimentary to him, but significant, I took it, of a belly full of his particular article of eloquence.

For my part, I am sick of making speeches and propose to stop it. It involves too much misery. The grind of writing'em and learning'em, and the torture of waiting for your turn when the scaffold is reached, and the heart-sinking uncertainty of how your performance will take—no outcome of agreeable result can compensate the greater sum of that suffering. i.e. to a man like me who can't escape it. Wherefore henceforth, with exceedingly rare exceptions, I must be excused. Besides it's all a kind of hollow fraud. It aims at nothing worth while.—has no object that a fifty-year old minister should covet. "Hello"—you say—"he's out of stories!"

Mark, I'm sorry to be obliged to tell you that the old naval surgeon is dead.[5] I sent him John Winthrop soon after it was published, had a very hearty and charming acknowledgment of its receipt, and the next news was that he had gone aloft, on abrupt but not unwelcome orders. I did fervently hope to meet him again on the deck of Mortality and get another banquet of his sea tales—partly for your sake. But that book is closed. President Smith says that he knew him—sailed with him once—

that he was a gossip who sometimes bred quarrels among his ship mates.[6] I think it quite likely. He naturally had the faults of his virtues. But I profited by the virtues. The yarn dripped with an ease and continuousness that suggested the pull of a law of gravitation. He couldn't help telling all he knew. Goodbye, old man.

April 5.

Since I let up on you a week ago we have had a Joy Day in our house, viz. last Sunday when little Harmony went to Church for the first time in nearly a year and a half. It was her own idea, which was an assurance (the doctors say) of its safety—for one of the consequences of her disease is a morbid shrinking from the resumption of activities. Anything she wants to do she may do; but she must not be urged.[7] We all felt glad and triumphant "to a degree," (what a queer expression that is!) and the congregation seemed to share our happiness. The child had quite a reception at the close of the service—with not the least ill effect that we could see. God give us grateful hearts for all his tender mercies.

Last night one of your mechanics (Parker) and his wife called on me to say farewell. They are off to Chicago with the machine in high enthusiastic confidence of the greatest results. Parker was fairly eloquent in the statement of the grounds of his faith in an infallible and world-echoing success—which will evidently be to him a heart felicity. The Type setter is to him as a living object of pride and affection.[8]

Your letter from Mentone [*sic*]—and by the way I had no idea of making you write to me when I dispatched my fool screed—I thought only to show my feeling for you as a person whom I love, under the weather;—your letter from Mentone, I say, was right cheerful reading, for it bore signs of the passing of your eclipse.[9] But it drew from me many a sigh of longing for my own escape into the free air. However my time is coming. Four months of liberty, please Heaven, lie before me not far off. As I told Livy, it is not yet settled that we go abroad. I don't know when it will be. But we are going somewhere out of reach of the octopus tentacles of Duty—which is, after all, the main point. Till the hour of our blessed emancipation strikes, I am climbing my tread-mill as usual, doing the same old things, not unhappily, but on the edge [of] being too tired to take a proper interest—unelastic, dull.

But things happen, now and then, to vivify me—in my common round, I mean.

The other day I had a funeral—not a funny one this time—that had color to it—a baby's funeral, and a very small baby 3 or 4 weeks old only—so small that going to the burial the little casket was laid on the front seat of the carriage in which I rode with the father. The father was a youth scarcely out of his teens—a dudish kind of fellow: inclining to be trivial in his nature—but all his heart was in the little casket, about whose scrap of a tenant he ran on—and I let him—with incessant tender garrulity the whole way to the grave.

"Now that little chap, Mr. Twichell—if youll [*sic*] excuse me—he knew a good deal more than you'd think. He liked me from the day he was born—and he *was* like me—had the same ways and the same tastes. Now one thing about me is that [I] want plenty of light; I can't bear blinds and curtains. Well, that little chap—*he* wanted plenty of light. And when he was crying and they couldn't stop him, I'd say 'I know what he's crying for; it's too dark here; fetch in some more lamps, a lot of 'em, all we've got'; and then I'd set 'em on chairs and tables all round the bed; and you ought to see the way he'd quiet down. O, there wasn't any body that understood him like me. (Sobs) I could tell in a minute just what he was thinking of. Now there's another thing about me. When I'm not doing anything I always hold my thumb this way—between my first and second finger—I always *did*, mother says. Well, that little chap, *he* did—just precisely the same—and if you'll look into the casket, you'll find his little mite of a thumb (sobs) between his first and second finger—exactly as I tell you"—and so on and so on, till the "little chap" and we got to the cemetery.

I havn't had any thing stir me under the vest so in a good while. Somehow I felt the pathos of our humanity in it. Partly on the hint of it I am writing a sermon on the text "Like as a father pitieth his children, so the Lord pitieth them that fear him."

But I may as well stop here. We are having beautiful April days at present. Our woods are full of birds and our yard full of boys tearing the turf to shreds with their athletics. Goodbye. The Lord love us all, as Charles Lamb used to say.[10] Blessings on every one of you.

Yours ever aff.

Joe.

1. Walter Phelps, a prominent New Jersey Republican, was ambassador to Germany under President Benjamin Harrison. While Twain was staying in Berlin, in the winter of 1891–92, the two men became firm friends.

2. From Twichell's days at Yale. Twichell graduated in 1859, Phelps in 1860.

3. The second Yale-Harvard debate, held on 25 March 1892. The motion (affirmed by Harvard) was that "Immigration to the United States should be restricted."

4. Chauncey Depew was at this time president of the New York Central Hudson River Railroad Company. He had also stood for the Republican presidential nomination in 1888.

5. See Letter 117.

6. The Rev. George Williamson Smith was president of Trinity College in Hartford and had been a naval chaplain from 1864 to 1876.

7. The only reference found to Harmony Jr.'s illness in Twichell's 1891–92 journal is in the description of his 1892 European trip: "Of course the first condition was a leave of absence which—14 weeks—had been granted by our parish at its annual meeting in 1892, the same being the renewal of a leave granted the previous year, which young Harmony's sickness forbade us to use." Chase Twichell (poet and great-granddaughter of Twichell) has referred to the history of depression in the family. Such, too, can be inferred from later Twichell letters and journal entries (see Courtney, *Joseph Hopkins Twichell*, 260–62). David, Twichell's son, would end his life by suicide.

8. In 1892, manufacture and testing of the Paige Compositor model was moved from Hartford to Chicago, in part for the opportunity to demonstrate the machine at the 1893 Chicago World's Fair. This goal was not met. As Twain's role in the typesetter saga dragged on, it would at times seem as if all outstanding issues had been resolved, but they never were.

9. The missing letter perhaps expressed hope about Twain's financial condition, which would not in fact be restored until the late 1890s.

10. Charles Lamb, English poet and essayist. He was a close friend to Coleridge, and would end his letters to him with "God love you; God love us all."

119. Twain to Twichell

25 April 1892. Rome, Italy

Rome, Apl. 25/92.[1]

Dear Joe:

Your delightful letter came yesterday. I am not going to try to answer it, because my arm will allow me to write only a little, & I must try hard to make that little hold out till I can tell you the adventure which was vouchsafed to two Englishmen in the Campagna yesterday.[2]

The dogs of the Campagna (they watch sheep without human assistance) are big & warlike & are terrible creatures to meet in those lonely expanses. Two young Englishmen—one of them a friend of mine—were away out there yesterday, with a peasant guide of the region who is a simple-hearted & very devout Roman Catholic. At one point the guide stopped, & said they were now approaching a spot where two especially ferocious dogs were accustomed to herd sheep; that it would be well to go cautiously & be prepared to retreat if they saw the dogs. So then they started on, but presently came suddenly upon the dogs. The immense brutes came straight for them, with death in their eyes. The guide said in a voice of horror, "Turn your backs, but for God's sake don't stir—I will pray—I will pray the Virgin to do a miracle & save us; she will hear me, oh, my God she surely will." And straightway he began to pray. The Englishmen stood quaking with fright, & wholly without faith in the man's prayer. But all at once the furious snarling of the dogs ceased—at three steps distant—& there was dead silence. After a moment my friend, who could no longer endure the awful suspense, turned—& there was the miracle, sure enough: the gentleman dog had mounted the lady dog & both had forgotten their solemn duty in the ecstasy of a higher interest!

The strangers were saved, & they retired from that place with thankful hearts. The guide was in a frenzy of pious gratitude & exultation, & praised & glorified the Virgin without stint; & finally wound up with "But you—you are Protestants; she would not have done it for you; she did it for me—only me—praised be she forever more! & I will hang a picture of it in the church & it shall be another proof that her loving care is still with her children who humbly believe & adore."

By the time the dogs got unattached the men were five miles from there.[3]

We all love you—every one of you. Good-bye.

Mark

1. The family were in Rome from late March to late April.
2. His rheumatism was clearly still bothering him.
3. This story clearly appeals to Twain's delight in anything slightly off-color—especially when it can be, as here, combined with a satire of narrowly faith-specific and human-centered modes of religious thinking.

120. Twichell to Twain

5 June 1893. Hartford, Connecticut

[Enclosed with the letter is a newspaper report of the general court martial of a Private Mark Twain, Company I, 10th Infantry, found guilty of a "Violation of the 62d Article of War," which included actions prejudicial to "good order and military discipline." Private Twain, while drunk, had seized an arresting officer by the throat.]

Hartford. June 5.

Dear Mark,

Mollie Dunham told us of her chance meeting with you at the Murray Hill Hotel in April—was it?—and that you reported yourself sick.[1] Beyond that we learned nothing whatsoever of your wretched experience while in the country till you had taken your departure. Had I known how it was with you in New York, I should certainly have gone down to see you, (or at-any-rate have asked you if I might) and to stay with you as long as you wanted me to. I can't help feeling as if you must have thought it strange that I didn't appear to you in some fashion; though probably it wasn't so at-all. But what a miserable time you had of it! God grant you are well by now.

It is great good news to hear that you are soon coming home.[2] Your house looks as though it was going out of mourning. I saw the gleam of new paint on the quarter deck as I came by the other day.[3] Here are some things we might keep for you, but I guess I will send them along. The Court Martial report came to Sue from some West Pointer of her acquaintence [*sic*].[4]

We are all pretty well, though Harmony has considerable room for improvement yet. Judy is here for a fortnight with her kid.[5] Sally is in the last stages of recovery from a broken collar bone. Should any thing happen to detain you abroad do ship Susie over to pass a few months with us. We shall have lots of room to spare when Dave and Ned Ware are gone to college by and by.[6]

The day is hot and I am in a state of extreme debility after a hard Sunday; so goodbye,

Yours aff.

Joe.

1. Mary "Mollie" Dunham, see Letter 70, note 4. The Murray Hill Hotel is in New York. Twain was then back in the United States on business as the financial situation threatened the future of Charles L. Webster & Co. Meanwhile, despite the odd moment of optimism, work on the Paige machine was failing to show any long-term positive result. Twain stated his intentions to go to Hartford in correspondence during this trip, but in a letter to Pamela Moffett on 26 April says he has been "very close to the pneumonia" and ordered to bed for more than a week (Mark Twain Papers).

2. This must have been either a false rumor or a plan that Twain would later drop.

3. The extended porch on the Clemenses house, often referred to as the "ombra" by the family, was also called the "deck" or "quarter-deck."

4. Enclosures missing.

5. Helen Ogden Wood, born 17 February 1893.

6. Edward [Ned] Twichell Ware was Twichell's nephew, who lived with the family after the death of Sarah Jane Twichell Ware (his widowed mother) in 1890.

121. Twain to Twichell

9 June 1893. Florence, Italy

VILLA VIVIANI
SETTIGNANO (FLORENCE)
June 9/93.

Dear Joe:

The sea voyage set me up & I reached here May 27 in tolerable condition—nothing left but weakness, cough all gone. I was ill in bed eleven days in Chicago, a week in Elmira & 3 months in New York (seemingly) & accomplished nothing that I went home to do.

The packing to leave here is going on, & this house looks like chaos come again. But Livy will resolve it to perfect order with a sure hand—that I know. We leave for Germany five days hence—3 of us. Susy will probably go to Paris for a while with the Mademoiselle. We perceive that this 9 months of semi-seclusion has been good for Livy. She is a great deal better than she was when she left America, & I feel very well contented about her now. She is going to improve right along. This is not judgment biased by love, it is dispassionate opinion.

I want to call your attention to one matter—you want to enthuse a little more over the grandchild. It is scandalous—your disinterested attitude toward that annex to the Nation. We send it our love & admiration, & to its mother our love & sympathy.

I do not find it easy to imagine Harmony an invalid—it seems so out of character. I hope she is well, now, & that this will not happen again.

Old Sir Henry Layard was here the other day, visiting our neighbor Janet Ross, daughter of Lady Duff Gordon, & since then I have been reading his account of the adventures of his youth in the far East.[1] In a footnote he has something to say about a sailor which I thought might interest you—viz:

"This same quartermaster was celebrated among the English in Mesopotamia for an entry which he made in his log-book—after a perilous storm: 'The windy & watery elements raged. Tears & prayers was had recourse to, but was of no manner of use. So we hauled up the anchor & got round the point.'" There—it isn't Ned Wakeman; it was before his day.

With love,
Mark.

1. Austen Henry Layard, archaeologist, art historian, diplomat, and author. Twain refers to his *Early Adventures in Persia, Susiana, and Babylonia* (1887). Lucie, Lady Duff Gordon, who died in 1869, was an author and translator. Her daughter, Janet Ross, traveler and writer, spent most of her adult life in the Florence area. It was she who found the Villa Viviani for Twain to rent, and the two became friends.

122. Twain to Twichell

9 October 1893. New York, New York

THE PLAYERS,
16 GRAMERCY PARK.
Oct. 9/93.

Dear Joe:

I am likely to run up [&] tie up with you a while before very long, though I can't guess the day yet, nor indeed guess very near it; but I'll give you notice beforehand, & then if you ain't at home I'll visit around till you come. I want Clara to have a good visit with your girls. Charley Warner is just & kind & cordial as he can be & wants her to make her headquarters at his house, but I want Clara to be with young people—it is a luxury she can't have much of, in Europe.

I am living here at the Players, but the Murray Hill people sent your letter to me.

You don't need to urge me, b'gosh, I'm willing enough to come and sweat you with a large visit without that.

I am powerful anxious to see you all, & have a lot of talks & several walks, & am not going to be cheated out of these things this trip.

Livy seems to be getting along well. She is probably in Paris by this time.

With love to you all

Mark.

123. Twain to Twichell

20 November 1893. New York, New York (Typed transcript)

THE PLAYERS,
16 GRAMERCY PARK.
Nov. 20/93.

Dear Joe:

It is delicious, delicious! It couldn't have happened to anybody but you. It has done me lots of good & I think it will be better medicine for Livy, when she gets it on her birthday the 27th. This adventure & the dyed hair of a year & a half ago—well, they make a sparkling pair![1]

Warner & I met Henry Irving at dinner last night, & he made a lot of appreciative inquiries after you & remembered the dinner at our house & the good times there & then.[2] He asked me to ask you if you wouldn't call on him at the Plaza Hotel the first time you are in town; & thought you would like Becket, & wants to invite you to see it. And you *must* see it, Joe. It's an ideal picture of what we all imagine the England of seven & a half centuries ago to have been.

With lots of love to all of you,

Mark.

1. Twain appears to be replying to a letter from Joe referencing one more of the ludicrous scrapes in which Twichell would occasionally get involved. In this particular incident Twichell was visiting two "fluttery old ladies" when—while waiting to see them—his back started itching. To relieve the itch, he picked up a long ivory paperweight and pushed it down the back of his collar. The length of ivory, however, broke off at its handle, and one of the elderly sisters had to help retrieve the fragments. Details from Joseph Hooker Twichell (Joe's son) to Dixon Wecter, July 1947 (Mark Twain Papers). As for the "dyed hair," Harmony had bought her husband a tonic (also a type of dye) to remedy hair loss. Twichell did not read the instructions properly and when he next spoke from his pulpit, it was with "bright green" hair. See Harriet Elinor Smith et al., eds., *Autobiography of Mark Twain*, vol. 1 (Berkeley: University of California Press, 2010), 290.

2. British celebrity and actor-manager Sir Henry Irving was playing the title role in Tennyson's play, *Becket.*

124. Twichell to Twain

1 January 1894. Hartford, Connecticut

Hartford. Jan 1. 1894.

Dear Mark:

Indeed, you *may* put up with us Jan. 10th and as many more days as you like before or after, or both; and occupy two rooms, or three, or a whole floor—we are that superabundant in vacant space since our young folks began to leave us. As for *interior* accommodation—there's no limit to it. We have supposed that you were *promised* to us the next time you fared this way. You can say that to Charley W. [Warner] or anybody else who claims you.

I had already been advised by the witness of Livy's own dear hand that the Hartford P.O. had triumphantly stood the test we put it to.

I judge that my chance of seeing Mr. Irving is gone by now. But I have not been able the past month or six weeks to get away from Hartford. I have (by gift) some of the best cigars you ever saw in your life, and you will have a royal smoke anyhow while you you are with us. They are perfectly delicious, but not so strong but that you can keep at 'em all day long with pleasure.

God's blessing on you and yours for the New Year.

Yrs ever aff.

Joe.

P.S. I'm going to write to Livy *now.*

125. Twain to Twichell

12 April 1894. SS New York *en route from Southampton, England, to New York, New York*

U.S. M.S. "NEW YORK"
At Sea, Thursday.

Dear Joe:

I am on my way back alone.[1] Livy couldn't leave her doctor as yet, & she can't spare a child. Besides, Susy is getting into better shape, now, & we hope she is on the road to health.[2] I hope you'll be down & let me have a sight of you, for I probably shan't get to Hartford. Livy allows me only 3 weeks on this side—so I suppose I must return in this ship May 7.

I bring a lot of love for all of you, & add my own.
Mark.

1. Leaving his family this time in Paris.
2. Susy's Paris music teacher evidently spoke of the nervous and highly emotional young woman's "voluntary self-starvation." This, at least, according to Edith Colgate Salsbury, who looks to recreate a collage of voices both of and surrounding the Twain family, in *Susy and Mark Twain: Family Dialogues* (New York: Harper, 1965), 339.

126. Twichell to Twain

10 April 1895. Hartford, Connecticut

Hartford. Apr. 10. 1895

Dear Mark:

I have been so sure that the desired boarding-house address I sent to you at New York two or three days after you left here, reached you about the time you (urged by telepathic influence) were writing to ask for it, that I havn't judged it in the least necessary to repeat the information. But this morning happening (in connection with yearning for your return) to think of it, I am seized with a doubt and a qualm. What if you chanced not [to] pass the day before you sailed at Mr Rogers' house? and what if your letters were not sent to you on board ship? and what if they were not forwarded to Paris? &c &c &c.

In short, it seems prudent to duplicate my former epistolary dispatch. The address, then, is as follows

Mrs Rufus McHard
61 West 17th St.

Sally D. said that it would be advisable to apply some time in advance, as the place is likely to be found full otherwise.[1] She also said that for her quarters there she had paid $25.—pr. week.

The situation with us is unchanged, except that Young Harmony is home for the Easter Recess. Your call on her at Farmington, she declares, improved her social consequence there in a marked degree.[2]

Dave writes from Nassau that his neuritis is on the wane.

Livy and the girls are well or getting well we hope. I trust that the first named received a longish letter I wrote to her (Care of Drexel, Hayes & Co) some weeks since.[3] I don't want her to answer it; but I do want her to know I mailed it.

"Pudd'nhead Wilson," appears to have been successfully launched. We sent a delegation to see it (I couldn't go) and it was reported delightful.[4]

"Joan of Arc" seems also to have struck the public attention favorably. I notice that you are already guessed as the writer of it.[5]

May be, old fellow, your best days as author are yet ahead of you. Why shouldn't they be, with your fruit ripening on the bough?

Any how, with whatever temporary pebble in your shoe, you are still one of the most fortunate of men. Do think of that—occupy yourself with that side of the case. A. C. Dunham said "Tell 'em (the Clemenses) to come home and give themselves a chance to see how we all love 'em." So say I.

Yours never more affectionately,

Joe

1. Most probably Sally Dunham.

2. Harmony was attending Miss Porter's School at Farmington, Connecticut. This was thanks to the generosity of Albert A. Sprague, a friend and former Yale colleague of Twichell, now a Chicago merchant and philanthropist.

3. Drexel, Hayes & Co. were a Paris banking firm.

4. *The Tragedy of Pudd'nhead Wilson,* based on Twain's 1894 novel, was dramatized by American actor Frank Mayo and opened (prior to its New York run) in Hartford in April 1895.

5. Twain's *Personal Recollections of Joan of Arc* was published anonymously in serial form in 1895 in *Harper's.* Twain published it anonymously because he did not want his reputation as a comic writer to affect the text's reception.

127. Twain to Twichell

29 November 1895. Napier, New Zealand

FRANK MOELLER'S
MASONIC HOTEL,
NAPIER.
New Zealand.[1]

November 29/95

Dear Joe: Your welcome letter of two months & five days ago has just arrived, & finds me in bed with another carbuncle. It is No. 3.[2] Not a serious one this time. I lectured last night without great inconvenience, but the doctors thought best to forbid to-night's lecture. My second one kept me in bed a week in Melbourne, & had to be dressed every day afterward on the road for about 3 weeks. Livy is become a first-rate surgeon, now; she has been dressing carbuncles once & twice a day almost without a holiday ever since the 25th of last May.

1. Livy thinks she would rather you wouldn't use the first incident you mention—the courting-incident.[3]

That is the *only* objection offered. Bang away with a perfectly free hand as regards to everything else.

Yes, I like the idea of the Flagg portrait.[4] And I also vastly like a photo which was made in Sydney lately—I ordered one to be sent to Harper. Best one that was ever made of me.[5]

No doubt Livy will suggest some house-views—it's just in her line, & her taste is a sure thing to depend on. She can write, or she can tell me.

Any cyclopedia, (or annual annex to the same) or Men of the Time, or Biographical dictionary in my library or yours or Warner's will give you the few facts of my life. I believe I know of no pleasant new ones except that I am one of the founders of the Players; & was made a life member of the Lotos Club 30th of last March.[6]

We are all glad it is you who are to write the article, it delights us all through.

I think it was a good stroke of luck that knocked me on my back here at Napier, instead of in some hotel in the centre of a noisy city. Here we have the smooth & placidly-complaining sea at our door, with nothing between us & it but 20 yards of shingle—& hardly a suggestion of life in that space to mar it or make a noise. Away down here fifty-five degrees south of the equator this sea seems to murmur in an unfamiliar tongue—a foreign tongue—a tongue bred among the ice-fields of the Antarctic—a murmur with a note of melancholy in it proper to the vast unvisited solitudes it has come from. It was very delicious & solacing to wake in the night & find it still pulsing there. I wish you were here—land, but it would be fine!

Livy & Clara enjoy this nomadic life pretty well; certainly better than one could have expected they would. They have some tough experiences, in the way of food & beds & frantic little ships, but they put up with the worst that befals [*sic*] with a heroic endurance that resembles contentment.[7]

No doubt I shall be on the platform next Monday. A week later we shall reach Wellington; talk there 3 nights, then sail back to Australia. We sailed *for* New Zealand October 30.

Day before yesterday was Livy's birthday (underworld time), & tomorrow will be mine. I shall be 60—no thanks for it.

I & the others send worlds & worlds of love to all you dear ones.

Mark.

1. Twain was on his round-the-world lecture tour, organized to rebuild his financial situation and pay off the debts still owed by his (now bankrupted) Charles L. Webster & Co. business.

2. Twichell's letter is missing.

3. Twichell had that summer been asked to write a biographical article on Twain and had "reluctantly consented to undertake it"—reluctantly, most likely, due to the fact that he never found such writing easy (Twichell Journals). He had obviously been running his ideas by Twain. The essay, "Mark Twain," would appear in *Harper's New Monthly Magazine* of May 1896. Twain here starts to number the points he is making, but no other numbers follow.

4. See Letter 117.

5. The photograph had been taken by H. Walter Barnett on 16 September, and can be seen in the photo gallery. An engraving from the Barnett photograph was used to illustrate Twichell's essay.

6. After "Players;" the phrases "am an early Kinsman; and am an early Lotos" are deleted.

7. This is, most likely, a reference to the *Flora*, on which the family sailed from Australia to New Zealand. See *Following the Equator*, chapter 32.

128. Twain to Twichell

24 and 25 May 1896. Pretoria, South Africa (Two typed transcripts by Albert Bigelow Paine)

Pretoria, South African Republic,
The Queen's Birthday, '96.

Dear old Joe—

Harper for May was given to me yesterday in Johannisburg [*sic*] by an American lady who lives there, & I read your article on me while coming up in the train with her & an old friend & fellow-Missourian of mine, Mrs. John Hays Hammond, the handsome & spirited wife of the chief of the 4 Reformers, who lies in prison here under a 15-year sentence, along with 50 minor Reformers who are in for 1, and 5-year terms.[1] Thank you a thousand times, Joe, you have praised me away above my deserts, but I am not the man to quarrel with you for *that*; & as for Livy, she will take your very hardest statements at par, & be grateful to you to the bottom of her heart. Between you & Punch & Brander Matthews, I am like to have my opinion of myself raised sufficiently high; & I guess the children will be after you, for it is the study of their lives to keep my self-appreciation down somewhere within bounds.[2] And how little they know how to go about it. Why, it does me good to furnish them new & frequent aggravations, just for the joy of hearing them make a fuss about it. I allowed that American lady to drive all the way from her home, early yesterday morning, & pack my bag for me, just so that I could drop the fact to Livy & Clara in Durban in an innocent casual way, as if it did not occur to me that there was anything wrong in allowing that poor woman to go to all that trouble about a thing which I or the call-boy could have done in fifteen minutes & done plenty well enough. But it will make those two sweat when they get the letter.

I had a note from Mrs. Rev. Gray (nee Tyler) yesterday, & called on her to-day. She is well.

Yesterday I was allowed to enter the prison with Mrs. Hammond. A Boer guard was at my elbow all the time, but was courteous & polite, only he barred the way in the compound (quadrangle or big open court) & wouldn't let me cross a white mark that was on the ground—the "death-line," one of the prisoners called it. Not in earnest, though, I *think.* I found that I had met Hammond once when he was a Yale Senior & a guest of Gen. Franklin's.[3] I also found that I had known Capt. Mein intimately 32 years ago.[4] One of the English prisoners had heard me lecture in London 23 years ago. After being introduced in turn to all the prisoners, I was allowed to see some of the cells & examine their food, beds, etc. I was told in Johannisburg that Hammond's salary of $150,000 a year is not stopped, & that the salaries of some of the others are still continued. Hammond was looking very well indeed, & I can say the same of all the others. When the trouble first fell upon them it hit some of them very hard; several fell sick (Hammond among them,) two or three had to be removed to the hospital, & one of the favorites lost his mind & killed himself, poor fellow, last week. His funeral, with a sorrowing following of 10,000, took the place of the public demonstration the Americans were getting up for me.[5]

These prisoners are strong men, prominent men, & I believe they are all educated men. They are well off; some of them are wealthy. They have a lot of books to read, they play games & smoke, & for a while they will be able to bear up in their captivity; but not for long, not for very long, I take it. I am told they have times of deadly brooding & depression. I made them a speech—sitting down. It just happened so. I don't prefer that attitude. Still, it has one advantage—it is only a *talk,* it doesn't take the form of a speech. I have tried it once before on this trip. However, if a body wants to make sure of having "liberty," & feeling at home, he had better stand up, of course. I advised them at considerable length to stay where they were—they would get used to it & like it presently; if they got out they would only get in again somewhere else, by the look of their countenances; & I promised to go & see the President & do what I could to get him to double their jail-terms.[6]

We had a very good sociable time till the permitted time was up & a little over, & we outsiders had to go. I went again to-day, but the Rev. Mr. Gray had just arrived, & the warden, a genial, elderly Boer named Du Plessis explained that his orders wouldn't allow him to admit saint & sinner at the same time, particularly on a Sunday.[7] Du Plessis—descended from the Huguenot fugitives, you see, of 200 years ago—but he hasn't any French left in him now—all Dutch.

It gravels me to think what a goose I was to make Livy & Clara remain in Durban: but I wanted to save them the 30-hour railway trip to Johannisburg. And Durban & its climate & opulent foliage were so lovely, & the friends there were so choice & so hearty that I sacrificed myself in their interest, as I thought. It is just the beginning of winter, & although the days are hot, the nights are cool. But it's lovely weather in these regions, too; & the friends are as lovely as the weather, & Johannisburg & Pretoria are brimming with interest. I talk here twice more, then return to Johannisburg next Wednesday for a fifth talk there; then to the Orange Free State capital, then to some towns on the way to Port Elizabeth, where the two will join us by sea from Durban; then the gang will go to Kimberly [*sic*] & presently to the Cape—& so, in the course of time, we shall get through & sail for England; & then we will hunt up a quiet village & I will write & Livy edit, for a few months while Clara & Susy & Jean study music & things in London.[8]

We have had noble good times everywhere & every day, from Cleveland, July 15 to Pretoria May 24, & never a dull day either on sea or land, notwithstanding the carbuncles & things.[9] Even when I was laid up 10 days at Jeypore in India we had the charmingest times with English friends. All over India the English—well, you will never know how good & fine they are till you see them.

Midnight & after! & I must do many things to-day, & lecture to-night.

A world of thanks to you, Joe dear, & a world of love to all of you.

Mark.

Curtis is at the Cape in very bad health—has not had his trial yet.[10]

1. John Hays Hammond, American engineer in charge of Cecil Rhodes's mining operations in South Africa, was a main member of the Johannesburg Reform Committee—looking to bring more stable and fairer government to the South African Republic (the name of the Afrikaner [Boer] country occupying the Transvaal region). After the failure of the Jameson Raid of December 1895, a British-led attempt to bring down Paul Kruger's Afrikaner government, the reformers were put on trial and their leaders, including Hammond, sentenced to death. They were, though, then released after the payment of large fines. Twain was fascinated by the political situation in South Africa, as evidenced in *Following the Equator* (1897) and the (slightly different) British version of that book, *More Tramps Abroad*, published the same year.

2. Possibly referring to the praise in *Punch* magazine (4 January 1896) for *Adventures of Huckleberry Finn* as a "Homeric book." The May 1896 issue of *Harper's New Monthly Magazine*—the same issue that contained the profile of Twain by Twichell—included an article on American humor by literary critic Brander Matthews that praised Twain.

3. William Franklin, Union general in the Civil War. After the war, Franklin became vice-president of the Colt's Fire Arms Manufacturing Company in Hartford.

4. Californian Captain Thomas Mein, wealthy American mine owner who went to South Africa to develop the British mining operations there. One of the main figures in the Jameson Raid.

5. Frederick Gray, a member of the Reform Committee, committed suicide while in Pretoria jail on 16 May 1896. His death was partly responsible for a softer response by the Transvaal government to the remaining captives.

6. This joke did not, evidently, go down well with the prisoners.

7. Rev. James Grey, a Scot and Presbyterian minister in Pretoria. J. C. du Plessis was to become acting chief of the Johannesburg prison service in 1898.

8. The Orange Free State was the second of the two independent Afrikaner republics (Transvaal being the other). The remainder of what is now South Africa was composed of British-ruled colonies.

9. Twain is referring to his entire lecture tour here. He lectured in Cleveland, Ohio, on 15 July 1895.

10. Mining engineer J. S. Curtis, one of those charged with high treason for endangering the safety of the South African Republic.

129. Twain to Twichell

27 September 1896. London, England (Two typed transcripts by Albert Bigelow Paine)

Permanent address:
c/o Chatto & Windus
111 St. Martin's Lane,
London, Sept. 27/96.[1]

Through Livy & Katy I have learned, dear old Joe, how loyally you stood poor Susy's friend, & mine, & Livy's: how you came all the way down, twice, from your summer refuge on your merciful errands to bring the peace & comfort of your beloved presence, first to the broken mind of that poor frantic child, & again to the broken heart of her desolate mother.[2] It was like you; like your good great heart, like your matchless & unmatchable self. It was no surprise to me to learn that you staid by Susy long hours, careless of fatigue & heat, it was no surprise to me to learn that you could still the storms that swept her spirit when no other could; for she loved you, revered you, trusted you, & "Uncle Joe" was no empty phrase upon her lips! I am grateful to you, Joe, grateful to the bottom of my heart, which has always been filled with love for you, & respect &

admiration; & I would have chosen you out of all the world to take my place at Susy's side & Livy's in those black hours.

Susy was a rare creature; the rarest that has been reared in Hartford this generation. And Livy knew it, & you knew it, & Charley Warner, & George, & Harmony, & the Hillyers & the Dunhams & the Cheneys, & Susy Warner & Lilly, and the Bunces, & Henry Robinson & Dick Burton, & perhaps others.[3] And I also was of the number, but not in the same degree—for she was above my duller comprehension. I merely knew that she was my superior in fineness of mind, in the delicacy & subtlety of her intellect; but to fully measure her I was not competent. I know her better now; for I have read her private writings & sounded the deeps of her mind; & I know better, now, the treasure that was mine than I knew it when I had it. But I have this consolation: that dull as I was, I always knew enough to be proud when she commended me or any of my work—as proud as if Livy had done it herself—& I took it as the accolade from the hand of genius. I see now—as Livy always saw—that she had greatness in her; & that she herself was dimly conscious of it.

And now she is *dead*—& I can never tell her.

God bless you Joe—& all your house.

S.L.C.

1. The firm of Chatto and Windus was Twain's official English publisher from 1875 onward. Andrew Chatto himself would become a close friend of Twain.

2. Susy, who had stayed in Elmira with Jean while the round-the-world tour took place, died in Hartford on 18 August 1896. This was before her mother (who had been sent news of her illness), and Clara, who was accompanying her, could get back home. Twain himself stayed in Guildford at the time—the quiet English village in which he intended to write up the travel book of his lecture trip—so he had to cope with the blow of Susy's death without Livy's support. Katy is Katy Leary, family servant 1880–1910, who was with Susy at her death. Twichell would meet Livy as her ship docked.

3. All Hartford area neighbors and friends. George was George Griffin. Lilly was Lilly Warner (wife of George Warner, Charles Dudley Warner's brother).

130. Twain to Twichell

19 and 20 January 1897. London, England (Mourning border)

London, Jan. 19/97.

Dear Joe—

Do I want you to write to me? Indeed I do. I do not want other people to write, but I do want you to do it. The others break my heart, but you will not. You have a something divine in you that is not in other men. You have the touch that heals, not lacerates. And you know the secret places of our hearts. You know our life—the outside of it—as the others do—& the inside of it—which they do not. You have seen our whole voyage. You have seen us go to sea, a cloud of sail, & the flag at the peak; & you see us now, chartless, adrift—derelicts; battered, water-logged, our sails a ruck of rags, our pride gone. For it *is* gone. And there is nothing in its place. The vanity of life was all we had, & there is no more vanity left in us. We are even ashamed of that we had; ashamed that we trusted the promises of life & builded high—to come to this!

I did not know that Susy was part *of* us; I did not know that she could go away; I did not know that she could go away, & take our lives with her, yet leave our dull bodies behind. And I did not know what she was. To me she was but treasure in the bank; the amount known, the need to look at it daily, handle it, weigh it, count it, *realize* it, not necessary; & now that I would do it, it is too late; they tell me it is not there, has vanished away in a night, the bank is broken, my fortune is gone, I am a pauper. How am I to comprehend this? How am I to *have* it? Why am I robbed, & who is benefitted?

Ah, well, Susy died at *home*. She had that privilege. Her dying eyes rested upon no thing that was strange to them, but only upon things which they had known & loved always & which had made her young years glad; & she had you, & Sue, & Katy, & John & Ellen.[1] This was happy fortune—I am thankful that it was vouchsafed to her. If she had died in another house——well, I think I could not have borne that. To us, our house was not unsentient matter—it had a heart, & a soul, & eyes to see us with; & approvals, & solicitudes, & deep sympathies; it was of us, & we were in its confidence, & lived in its grace & in the peace of its benediction. We never came home from an absence that its face did not light up & speak out its eloquent welcome—& we could not enter it unmoved. And could we now? oh now, in spirit we should enter it unshod.

20th I approve all that Brander Matthews said; & I thank him cordially.[2] You must tell him so for me—& I will tell him again when I see him. I am very glad you sent it to me.

I am trying to add to the "assets" which you estimate so generously. No, I am not. The thought is not in my mind. My purpose is other. I am working, but it is for the sake of the *work*—the "surcease of sorrow" that is found there. I work all the days; & trouble vanishes away when I use that magic. This book will not long stand between it & me, now; but that is no matter, I have many unwritten books to fly to for my preservation; the interval between the finishing of this one [*Following the Equator*] & the beginning of the next will not be more than an hour, at most. *Continuances,* I mean; for two of them are already well along—in fact have reached exactly the same stage in their journey: 19,000 words each.[3] The present one will contain 180,000 words—130,000 are done. *I* am well protected; but Livy! She has nothing in the world to turn to; nothing but housekeeping, & doing things for the children & me. She does not see people, & cannot; books have lost their interest for her. She sits solitary; & all the day, & all the days, wonders how it all happened, & why. We others were always busy with our affairs, but Susy was her comrade—had to be driven from her loving persecutions—sometimes at 1 in the morning. I have done it often. To Livy the persecutions were welcome. It was heaven to her to be plagued like that. But it is ended now. Livy stands so in need of help; & none among us all could help her like you.

Some day you & I will walk again, Joe, & talk. I hope so. We could have *such* talks! We are all grateful to you & Harmony—*how* grateful it is not given us to say in words. We pay as we can, in love; & in this coin practicing no economy. Good bye, dear old Joe!

Mark.

1. "Sue" was Susan Crane. John and Ellen O'Neil were caretakers of the Hartford house.
2. Matthews had published an article, "Mark Twain—His Work," in the January issue of *Book Buyer.* Presumably Twichell sent this in a letter now missing.
3. One of the manuscripts on which Twain was working was "The Chronicle of Young Satan."

131. Twichell to Twain

9 February 1897. Hartford, Connecticut

Hartford. Feb. 9. 1897

Dear Mark:

Your letter received a few days ago did me a lot of good. I am glad that you love me,—as you *must,* old fellow, to the end of the chapter. Thank you for telling me about your work. I perceive, by your way of telling it, and the gait of your pen altogether, that your literary power is *all* with you still,—as I am certain the book, and the books, will prove. I only wish that there [was] something that Livy could do to give her respite also. If she were here I would take her, with her consent, to a mother heart worse broken than hers is—with *nothing* left,—to balm with her tears and tender sympathy. That would be medicine to her pain, and it is the divinest way of comfort.

x x x x x x

But I am not going to write about you this time. I have a matter to relate. It seems to me that never in my life before, in the same space of time, have I had so many *Cases* revealing the wo[e]ful tragical aspects of human experience, brought to my knowledge, as in the past few months. Of one of them I want to give you some account,—and the more because I have so often wished I might consult you upon it.

In September I had a letter from a young woman whom I never met who lives at a distance from Hartford, but of whom I knew; with whose father I am acquainted, telling me that a young man to whom she had been engaged, whom I well knew, who was once my parishioner, as his parents—very excellent people—now are, but who has been away from here a good while, had betrayed her, and wouldn't marry her. It was a letter of thirty closely written pages, in a fine lady-like hand, wonderfully well expressed, and, Mark, literature doesn't contain the equal of it for the pathetic, pitiful, heart-rending utterance of the thoughts of such a forlorn spirit. Harmony and I both cried over it. Sometime I will show it to you. It was a very humble letter; there was no anger in it; she did not in the least acquit herself of blame for what had happened; she only said that it was partly through her ignorance, and largely through her perfect trust, that she had gone astray. But, oh, the suffering she had endured and was enduring! It was terrible,—her story of it. But the point of it all was,—would I try to help her i.e. try to induce that fellow to do his duty by her? Well; Harmony and I talked it over and over and over, and there was further correspondence with the girl,—voluminous on her part, for, as she said, having spoken and meeting kindness, she couldn't resist letting the tide of her long pent up agony of distress flow through the outlet thus opened—for which again and again she begged our forgiveness.

I thought, at first, that I would make a journey and see the man in person. We also discussed the policy of operating on him through his father. (and I have a letter she wrote, addressed to his father, to be used in case that plan were adopted.) But finally, it was decided that it was best I should write to him. Which I did, and soon got a reply, which was (quite unconsciously to him) the most amazing exhibit of moral perversion and baseness I ever saw, and which brought to light the fact that the infernal skunk was engaged to another woman!

Now you may open my enclosed envelope.[1] It contains copies of my two letters to him, and of one I wrote to the woman he is now engaged to.

x x x x
And what do you think of them, Mark? Of course you may, if you like, show them to Livy. By the way, I want them back sometime. You will have seen referred to in them several particulars I had not mentioned. My second letter to him has given you, by intimation, the salient features of his reply to my first.

As to letter No 3. I might say, that the girl to whom it went is the head-nurse of a hospital (to whom I therefore felt free to state the facts) and is not living at her home, which is somewhere in the South;—so the scoundrel, her lover, told me. She replied to it very briefly and curtly, saying that what I had communicated to her she had for some time known; seeming to imply that it made no difference with her.

Thus the business, so far as I have to do with it, ends. Between you and me I think it well that it so ends. i.e. I feel sure that nothing but untold further misery could have resulted to the other girl from marrying that villain.

In a cruel, brutal letter he wrote her at my command announcing his new engagement (which I have) he taxes her with malignity in injuring his standing with me, *who baptized him.* But consider the position of that young woman! She is evidently a cultivated person. Harmony, who pities her infinitely and has written to her, says "She knew better"—and she herself says so and no doubt it is so. But she is in the best of society in the great city where she lives, a member of its literary circle—and there she moves about, her dread secret ever in her thoughts at home and abroad, her conscience torturing her, her soul ashamed day and night and in all company.—and a good woman, I'm sure. Where's your novel that equals it?

With love unbounded

Joe

P.S. I meant to say further of Letter No. 3. that it was written at the instance of my poor client—and rather against my advice—who felt that it would be wrong not to let the other young woman know what kind of a man it [was] who proposed to marry her. She took the chances of exposure involved in the offer to prove the facts. She thought it likely, however, as I did, that the beast had told *who she was.* She knew from him that he had told one man—to get an opinion from him, he claimed, regarding his *duty* to her!

My gracious, Mark, I have to look down every Sunday from the pulpit on that reptile's father—but especially mother—a sweet woman. They are totally unsuspicious of his infamy—are proud of him. She spoke to me the other day of his broken engagement with a smile and a sigh, as if it was one of the things bound to happen now and then, and nobody much the worse for it.

1. Missing.

132. Twain to Twichell

10 April 1897. London, England (Mourning border)

London, April 10/97.

Dear Joe:

Mrs. Plunkett's letter is most pleasant & acceptable reading. It is not my disposition to let those newspaper-libels pass unchallenged, but it is my policy to do it. To answer them would but widen their currency & breed others. If the scene were England I would take hold of them at once in the courts & make their propagators very sick; but America has no libel law; there, a man's character is legally the prey of any journalistic assassin that wants it.[1]

I don't like to see the family dragged in & slandered, but they don't seem to mind it, & I don't very greatly mind it myself. The fifteen or twenty people who really know Livy & the children, need no denials of that slander; what the rest think, could not be a matter of consequence unless Livy & the children were public characters, & that they are not. As for my own reputation I care not a damn for any smirch upon it not put there by myself.

I am finishing my book. In it I find 61 things which would stand the sharp test of the lecture-platform; the most of them humorous, perhaps, the others of various qualities. If there are 61 in all the rest of my books put together, I—but there are not. This book comes near to satisfying me; & to satisfy myself is of course the thing which I would prefer to do, first & last & all the time.

With all our loves,
Mark

1. Twain writes in his notebook, on 28 March, that Twichell "sends me a vast newspaper heading, the breadth of five columns 'Close of a Great Career' in which it is said that I am living in penury in London and that my family has forsaken me. This would enrage and disgust me if it came from a dog or a cow, or an elephant or any of the higher animals, but

it comes from a man, and much allowance must be made for man" (Mark Twain Papers). The identity of Mrs. Plunkett is unknown.

133. Twain to Twichell

8 July 1897. London, England (Mourning border)

London, July 8/97.

Dear Joe:

Susy Crane & Julie Langdon have just arrived from home, & you will not doubt that we were glad to see them. We shan't see *much* of them, though, till we get launched for Switzerland (Lucerne) day after tomorrow; for this present day, & this night, & all day tomorrow & tomorrow night are absolutely "full up" as the 'bus conductors say—oh, a whole world of things to do, & not time enough.

I see I can't write you a letter—there isn't time—so I will enclose a stranger's that has just come, & which I have been answering.[1] I send it because it is in the line of what you were saying in your last, about what reason I have to be proud & thankful for my cloud of witnesses, my affectionate invisible friends. Such letters come every few days, & they make me want to turn out & go lecturing through these isles.

With a power of love to you all,

Mark.

1. The enclosure is a letter from a Jessie E. MacDonald of 15 Broughman St., Edinburgh, dated 6 July 1897. She thanks Twain "Not only for the bright and picturesque pages of the 'Tramp', but for dear 'Huck' and Tom Sawyer[,] for 'King Arthur';—for all, I think, that you have ever published." She also speaks of the "unpayable debt of gratitude" she owes him, concluding with some words from a young doctor friend: "How he opens all hearts,—this dear 'Mark' of ours!"

134. Twain to Twichell

31 July 1897. Weggis, Switzerland

On the Rigi-side
Above Weggis, July 31/97.[1]

Dear Joe:

In this came some clippings from German papers; & the same day comes from Pennsylvania the enclosed cutting, with the suggestion that

I sue upon it for libel. But no, I've no such disposition. I like the picture. I would rather be picturesque than pretty, any time, & it seems to me that this portrait answers the requirements.[2]

A couple of days ago Livy had the grand luck of running across President Smith of Trinity on the Lucerne boat—a great find, & welcome as the flowers of May.[3] I [*sic*] came up yesterday & lunched, & stayed with us three hours; & it was more refreshing & uplifting & enjoyable than any sixty hours we have known for months. A wonderful man in all ways, & unspeakably lovable; it was a lucky day when Hartford captured him. I am going to Lucerne this afternoon to see him & Mrs. Smith.

This is the charmingest place we have ever lived in, for repose, & restfulness, & superb scenery whose beauty undergoes a perpetual processional change from one miracle to another, yet never runs short of fresh surprises & new inventions. We shall always come here for the summers if we can.

Yesterday Clara & Jean climbed to the Rigi-culm with Susy Crane's butler. They walked up in 3 hours, & down in half the time, & brought plenty of skinned feet & blisters. Susy Crane & Julie Langdon went up the ladder railway & the gang dined at the summit.[4] Clara & Jean got down in time to go with Livy & me in the row-boat to Viznau, & there we picked up Susy & Julie & rowed them home. I've a notion to go up the Rigi myself some day—particularly if you come & participate.

All hands here are in sufficiently good health, & all send lots of love to you & Harmony.

Mark.

Our address till toward October is *not* the above (which is private & not to be used or divulged), but just Chatto & Windus, London.

1. Weggis is on the northern shore of Lake Lucerne.

2. In his letter Twain sends an enclosure with the "clippings"—a 26 July letter from the Austrian travel writer Ernst von Hesse Wartegg. Wartegg speaks of a Twain lecture tour in Germany as one which "would be remunerative and very interesting for you" and encloses "an article [titled "Mark Twain's Plans"] published in the Berlin *Tagblatt* which will amuse you, all about your financial affairs." He notes, "Strange how all the Germans are bothering themselves about your purse." Wartegg also requests "a line from your hand . . . signed Mark Twain" for "a sweet Lady here, the wife of the Austrian Consul General at Zurich." The Pennsylvania "cutting" is missing.

3. See Letter 118, note 6.

4. A cog-railway leads to the top of the 1,800-meter summit. Twain and Twichell had visited the Rigi previously. See *A Tramp Abroad*, 284–303.

135. Twain to Twichell

22 August 1897. Weggis, Switzerland (Typed transcript by Albert Bigelow Paine)

Lucerne, Aug. 22/97.

Dear Joe:

Good for Davy. Send him to West Point; there's the stuff in him for a good soldier.

Livy made a noble find on the Lucerne boat the other day on one of her shopping trips—George Williamson Smith—did I tell you about it? We had a lovely time with him, & such intellectual refreshment as we had not tasted in many a month.

And the other night we had a detachment of the Jubilee Singers—6.[1] I had known one of them in London 24 years ago. Three of the six were born in slavery, the others were children of slaves. How charming they were—in spirit, manner, language, pronunciation, enunciation, grammar, phrasing, matter, carriage, clothes—in every detail that goes to make the real lady & gentleman, & welcome guest. We went down to the village hotel & bought our tickets & entered the beer-hall, where a crowd of German & Swiss men & women sat grouped around tables with their beer mugs in front of them—self-contained & unimpressionable-looking people, an indifferent & unposted & disheartening audience—& up at the far end of the room sat the Jubilees in a row. The Singers got up & stood—the talking & glass-jingling went on. Then rose & swelled out above those common earthly sounds one of those rich chords the secret of whose make only the Jubilees possess, & a spell fell upon that house. It was fine to see the faces light up with the pleased wonder & surprise of it. No one was indifferent any more; & when the Singers finished, the camp was theirs. It was a triumph. It reminded me of Lancelot riding in Sir Kay's armor & astonishing complacent knights who thought they had a struck a soft thing. The Jubilees sang a lot of pieces. Arduous & painstaking cultivation has not diminished or artificialized their music, but on the contrary—to my surprise—has mightily reinforced its eloquence & beauty. Away back in the beginning—to my mind—their music made all other vocal music cheap; & that early notion is emphasized now. It is entirely beautiful, to me; & it moves me infinitely more than any other music can. I think that in the Jubilees & their songs America has produced the perfectest flower of the ages; & I wish it were a foreign product, so that she would worship it & lavish money on it & go properly crazy over it.

Now, these countries are different: *they* would do all that, if it were *native.* It is true they praise God, but that is merely a formality, & nothing in it; they open out their whole hearts to *no* foreigner.

The musical critics of the German press praise the Jubilees with great enthusiasm—acquired technique, etc., included.

One of the Jubilee men is a son of General Joe Johnston, & was educated by him after the war.[2] The party came up to the house, & we had a pleasant time.

This is paradise, here—but of course we've got to leave it by & by.

The 18th of August has come & gone, Joe—& we still seem to live.[3]

With love from us all.

Mark.

1. The Fisk Jubilee Singers were (and still are) an a cappella group of African Americans, founded at Fisk University in Tennessee in 1871. They first traveled to Europe in 1873.

2. Joseph E. Johnston (1807–1891) was a senior Confederate general. An 1895 portrait of the Jubilee Singers includes a Charles Johnstone, but information on this alleged paternity is elusive.

3. The first anniversary of Susy's death.

136. Twain to Twichell

7–10 September 1897. Weggis, Switzerland (Two typed transcripts by Albert Bigelow Paine)

Weggis, September ? 1897.

Dear Joe:

I must enclose you another letter, (you are mentioned in it) which I have just been answering.[1] Isn't it a wonderful gift?—the gift to rightly word a compliment. Over here they possess it. You have it; I haven't it. I think Livy has it. I am familiar, these many years, with complimentary letters whose intention was a compliment, but whose unfortunate form pretty nearly concealed it. In incompetent hands, compliments are damaging things; they scorch, where they only meant to warm. That Edinburgh girl has the gift.

Which reminds me again, that the world is small. Last week I ran down to Lucerne—for the third time in 6 weeks—with some errands to do, & exactly 2 hours (in Lucerne) to do them in: one for Livy, the others for myself. I set them down on a paper—putting each in its proper place, so as to economize time & travel:

1. Pay 45 francs for 3 weeks' rent of our row-boat—(Livy's errand.) 2. Get a library book. 3. Leave a note at the Schweizerhof. 4. Make an appointment with the dentist. 5. Get my hair cut. 6. Get 200 cigars. 7. Get pair of suspenders. 8. Get a ream of writing paper. 9. Get a new shaving-brush. Fifty minutes required for these; then an hour to wait for the one o'clock boat.

I went first to the row-boat man—whom I had never seen before—& told him I had come to pay for Mrs. Clemens's boat. "Dank' schön." Then I said I had forgotten to bring the money. He thanked me again, & I went my way. Do you know, that was the only errand I accomplished in my list.

For as I started down the Esplanade a gentleman with 3 ladies in charge said, "It is Mr. Clemens, I believe; you will remember spending an hour in my house in Pietermaritzburg—Sir James [*sic*] Robinson, Premier of Natal."[2] I remembered him, then, & we all stood there & talked a good while. Then parted, & I turned around & a lady put out her hand & said, "You don't remember me, after these 19 years." It was Mrs. General Fairchild, whose husband was minister or consul-general in Paris in '78.[3] She had a daughter with her whom I had known when she was a baby. We stood there & talked a long time. Then a young woman passed along—waited a little, then begged pardon & said she only wanted to say a word. It was Miss MacDonald, the Edinburg [*sic*] girl whose letter I sent you.[4] We all talked a few minutes, standing in the same old original tracks, across the road from the Schweizerhof, then I shook hands & rushed for the one o'clock steamboat, & just caught it. It is a small world; & its smallness obstructs erranding.

Here is a curious case. Last week, at midnight in the dark, down near the Weggis pier, a traveling Frenchman quarreled with a hotel porter & shot him dead. The quarreling was heard, but the fight not *seen*. It was a violent quarrel, but it was done in French, & not a witness understood that tongue— except one word, a despairing cry of the porter, "Help! help!" A court can do nothing with that case.

Our love to you all.

Mark.

1. Missing.
2. Sir John Robinson was premier of Natal, South Africa, from 1890 to 1893.
3. General Lucius Fairchild was U.S. consul-general in Paris from 1878 to 1880.
4. See Letter 133.

137. Twain to Twichell

23 October 1897. Vienna, Austria (Typed transcript by Albert Bigelow Paine)

Hotel Metropole,
Vienna, Oct. 23/97.[1]

Dear Joe:

Dave seems to be having his full share of adventures—& prime ones they are, too. The Canadian one was fine.[2] He inherits his talent for getting into picturesque situations from you. You are the boss at that.

When we first reached here & the German letters & newspaper-mentions began to accumulate, I thought I would forward these things to you; but I neglected it, & then presently gave it up. However, I think I can get a magazine article out of the material by & by.

We are gradually getting settled down & wonted.[3] Vienna is not a cheap place to live in, but I have made one small arrangement which has a distinctly economical aspect. The Vice Consul made the contract for me yesterday—to-wit: a barber is to come every morning at 8.30 & shave me & keep my hair trimmed for $2.50 a month. I used to pay $1.50 per shave in our house in Hartford.

Does it suggest to you reflections when you reflect that this is the most important event which has happened to me in ten days—unless I count-in my handing a cabman over to the police day before yesterday, with the proper formalities, & promise to appear in court when his case comes up.

If I had time to run around & talk, I would do it; for there is much politics agoing, & it would be interesting if a body could get the hang of it. It is Christian & Jew by the horns—the advantages with the superior man, as usual—the superior man being the Jew every time & in all countries. Land, Joe, what chance would the Christian have in a country where there were 3 Jews to 10 Christians! Oh, not the shade of the shadow of a chance. The difference between the brain of the average Christian & that of the average Jew—certainly in Europe—is about the difference between a tadpole's brain & an Archbishop's. It's a marvelous race—by long odds the most marvelous that the world has produced, I suppose.[4]

And there's more politics—the clash between Czek [*sic*] & Austrian. I wish I could understand these quarrels, but of course I can't.

Oh, before I close this, I must tell you a part of last night's dream—*mind, it has an indelicate place in it*—be warned. I woke up in a rage with somebody, & with this remark falling from my lips: "You humiliate me—&

publicly. You make me feel like an exposed & conspicuous person whose legs a dog has been surreptitiously pissing on whilst he was absorbed in looking at a procession."

I think it rather vividly photographs the situation.

With the abounding love of us all

Mark.

1. The family arrived in Vienna on 27 September and stayed for twenty months, partly to accommodate Clara's wish to learn the piano. Twain was welcomed to the city as a celebrity, though Livy, who was still mourning Susy, was far less socially active.

2. David and Burton Twichell had gone on a hunting trip in Canada that summer, and had been unjustly accused of poaching. Earlier, David Twichell had captured a burglar in the Twichell home (Twichell Journals).

3. "Wonted" meaning accustomed to our surroundings.

4. Twain's "Concerning the Jews," an essay in praise of Jews that has been criticized for its own perpetuation of stereotypes, was published in 1898.

138. Twichell to Twain

2 November 1897. Hartford, Connecticut

Hartford. Nov. 2.[1]

Dear old Mark;

We have been reading, and re-reading, and again reading your "In Memoriam" with the accompaniment of a gray autumn sky and the falling leaves to blend with its unspeakable heart-breaking sadness; its aching, choking pathos.[2] It sets all chords of memory and of love atremble. It renews the pain of the sense of Life's inscrutable mystery, and of the mystery of human experience. It renews, also, (may I say?) the deep and solemn gladness of the faith that God in whose awful Hand we all are held, is, when you get to the end of things, Love. But I will not talk about it: in fact it seems to impose hush and silence upon me. This, however, I would say: if there be those who are thinking "Can this be Mark Twain?" I am not one of them. I have long known that it was in you to chant the music of the hidden soul conversing with the Fathomless Elements, and as I followed your yearning throbbing song of Grief and inextinguishable Regret, my inward comment was "It is he: none other than *my* Mark Twain." Mark: it made me love you so that it hurt; and, of course, I felt Livy and the girls behind you; the whole dear group was there; with the beloved Shadow in the midst; and bending over all, the angel of Tears and Sorrow. "Weeping may endure for a night, but joy cometh in the morning," says the Old Book. God send you the dawn of that fulfillment soon. But I trust He is already sending it.

x x x x x

'Twas a happy, as well as a kind thought of yours, Mark to write that word of hearty tribute to the genius and generosity of Dr. Trumbull, printed in the last Century Magazine. It was copied into yesterday's "Courant."[3] I have not yet seen Mrs. Trumbull and Annie since I got home from vacation; (they have been away) but it cannot fail to have gratified them exceedingly. I thank you for it on my account. I havn't had the chance yet to speak with Pres. Smith of his meeting with you, but I'm going tonight to hear him read a paper before the Historical Society, and hope to have a word about it with him there. I saw him, as chaplain of the day, praying at a distance, at our recent big Farragut blow out.[4] Which reminds me: You know what that blow out was, I suppose. The U.S. Navy presented the city with the figure-head of Farragut's flag-ship: *The Hartford*, heroine of The River Forts and of Mobile Bay. We made a grand parade (in which your humble servant appeared mounted, on the staff of the Marshal) to escort that glorious relic to the Capitol.[5] My first sight of it gave me a great shock. As it had come off the ship—so I was informed—it had been in a *beautifully* battered and weather-stained condition, looking as if it had *been* through storm and battle. Well, if you will believe me, they had taken it and puttied up all the cracks and holes in it, and covered up every wound and every trace of its exposure to winds and seas with a coat of dazzling white paint and a blaze of fresh gilding!!! Which enormity, crime, outrage, profanity, desecration, I beheld with what disgust and wrath, you can imagine. Gracious, I can't do it justice in any language I am permitted to employ; and so I'll drop the subject. The only alleviation is that the thing was not done by Hartford, but at the Navy Yard. Thank Heaven for so much.

> Mr. Clemens will be a proud man when he learns that at the dinner to Mr. Anthony Hope at the Lotus [*sic*] Club, the other night, Dr. Chauncey Depew named *Quo Vadis* and Mark Twain's *Joan of Arc* as the two great novels of the year.[6]

You will have seen this, no doubt. There are ever so many things about you in the paper now-a-days pleasant to read: some of them commercial, I suppose, but not all. I think the book is going to have an immense success. Would it might bring you home!

All things are moving on as usual with us—quiet fashion, yet I am very busy. I have a Forefathers day speech to make at Pittsfield next month, and a lecture on Benjamin Franklin to give in a patriotic course for the schools, before that.

Harmony sets out tomorrow on a fortnight's visit in Chicago; and I'm glad of it, for vacation didn't rest her much.

I send you a letter from one of my young men, who is a rising artist (his people live on Gillette St.) that may afford you entertainment for an idle moment.[7]

If you "are a mind to," you may send me an order of admission on your account to the Players, next Ladie's [*sic*] Day.[8] Judy wants to see the place.

But I'll end here. Good bye. Loads of love to Livy and my nieces. I see that you are settled in Vienna, but I don't know your address there.[9] So this goes to London.

Yours everlastingly

Oh, I've got lots to tell you! Joe

1. The issue of *Harper's Weekly* from which the clipping attached to this letter is taken is dated 7 November. While it is possible that the letter was written on that date (with Twichell's "7" looking like a "2") the reference to "the other day" (not "yesterday") in his 8 November letter supports the present dating. It is possible that the magazine was available before the printed publication date.

2. Twain's poem, "In Memoriam," commemorating Susy, written at Lake Lucerne on the anniversary of her death, was published in the November *Harper's Monthly*. For more on the way Twain and Livy responded to Susy's death, see Peter Messent, "Coda" to *Mark Twain and Male Friendship*, and Harold K. Bush, *Continuing Bonds with the Dead: Parental Grief and Nineteenth-Century American Authors* (Tuscaloosa: University of Alabama Press, 2016).

3. Twain's Nook Farm neighbor, James Hammond Trumbull, had died on 5 August. Twain's obituary notice can be found in *Mark Twain: Life As I Find It*, ed. Charles Neider (Garden City, New York: Hanover House, 1961), 234.

4. David Farragut, who achieved fame as an admiral in the U.S. Navy during the Civil War.

5. The parade marshal was Francis B. Allen. His staff was made up of twenty-one men (all listed in the 7 October *Courant* with their Civil War rank and regiment), including Twichell. The *Hartford*'s figurehead is still in the State Capitol.

6. This clipping from the 7 November (1897) *Harper's Weekly* is attached to the top of page six of this letter. *Quo Vadis*, an 1896 novel of Roman and early Christian history written in Polish by Henryk Sienkewicz, had been translated and published in America in 1897. It remained immensely popular for decades.

7. The letter referred to, dated only the "27th," is from Charles Allan Gilbert, who had submitted illustrations to Frank Bliss for *Following the Equator* on Twichell's recommendation. Some were indeed used in the book.

8. Twain was a member of the Players Club in Gramercy Park in New York. An all-male club, it allowed women on the premises on certain days.

9. Twain's 23 October letter had evidently not yet reached him.

139. Twichell to Twain

8 November 1897. Hartford, Connecticut

Hartford. Nov. 8. 1897

Dear Mark:

Yours of Oct. 23 from Wien has come—to my extreme comfort and delectation. Circumstance plays the tyrant over us, and life crowds us more as we get on, and you and I are a long way apart: but don't let's drop one another[.] I havn't been so tickled for a year as I was by the speech you found yourself making when you woke out of the dream. But you needn't have called it *indelicate*. To be sure, I wouldn't have repeated it to a lady. Neither would I pump ship before a lady; yet there is nothing *indelicate* about that process.[1] The sacred historians do not shy the mention of it. See I Samuel 25:22.[2] Nor the prophets: See Isaiah 36:12.[3] But this isn't Sunday, and I'm not going to preach you a sermon.

You refer to the political mix and confusion around you there in the Austrian Capital. That reminded [me] of a series of articles written some while since by that odd but accomplished genius Forrest Morgan for "The Travelers," while he was Editor of it, which I read at the time with interest, but with more amazement that any man should be able to thread the labyrinth of the subject treated in them—*Austria and the Hungarian Revolution*.[4] The series was not completed, for Morgan took the losing side in the Batterson-Dennis fight, and the winner (Batterson) fired him out. But they brought the story nearly to an end; and impressed me as an astonishing piece of work. I have obtained them for you and here they are. If you, at leisure moments, can get any sort of a grip on their contents you will know more of what is behind their politics than most of the native Vienna fellows do, I'm confident, and can talk 'em blind.

What you say of the Jews recalls talk I used to hear about them from dear old Prof. Stowe.[5] He was wont to affirm that their survival and masterfulness—due to an inextinguishable and incomparable Vitality—was a phenomenon without parallel and a *miracle*.

That, again, reminds me of something I meant to tell you when I was writing to you the other day, but forgot it. A lady in my parish lately had this story from an old negro woman in her kitchen—a story of the times before the war: as follows: Sam, a slave in Virginia used often to ask and receive a permit on Sundays to go to Church. His master suspecting, after a while, that he didn't go to Church, began to demand the text of him, which Sam never could give. Finally Massa told him that the next time, if he didn't have the text, he'd flog him. Next time came, and on the text being inquired for, Sam said. "Mas'r, I disremember de tex', but I remember de *sermon.*" "Well, what was the sermon?" "Ol preacher (quoth Sam)—he tole—how de Lord—fed twelve men five thousan' loaves and seven thousan' fishes—an' dere didn' nary one on 'em *bus'*.[6] And de preacher—he say—dat dat was a *Mir'cle.*"!!

That picture of you in the Nov. McClure is far and away the best yet.[7] I wish I'd had it to go with my Harper article. It is mighty fine. It couldn't be improved. Withdraw all others from circulation. Give this universal right of way.

And that picture of Frost's illustrating the mate's frozen shadow is perfectly delicious.[8] How could he do it?

Harmony has gone to Chicago on a fortnight's visit. I'm glad of it, for vacation, in which she had to keep house for a crowd, was not restful to her.

Has Mrs Crane returned home? I suppose so, but I havn't heard of it.

Good morning. Love to Livy and my dear nieces.

Yours ever aff.

Joe

1. "Pump ship": a euphemism for urination.

2. "So and more also do God unto the enemies of David, if I leave of all that pertain to him by the morning light any that pisseth against the wall." 1 Samuel 25:22 (Authorized [King James] Version).

3. "But Rabshakeh said, Hath my master sent me to thy master and to thee to speak these words? Hath he not sent me to the men that sit upon the wall, that they may eat their own dung, and drink their own piss with you?" Isaiah 36:12 (Authorized [King James] Version).

4. Forrest Morgan edited the *Travelers Record,* published by the Hartford-based Travelers Insurance Company. Twichell refers here to an attempted coup by the secretary of the company, Rodney Dennis, against the president, James Batterson, in February 1896. Morgan later became an assistant librarian at Watkinson Library in Hartford. Twain would quote him in "Stirring Times in Austria."

5. Calvin Stowe, Biblical scholar, educationalist, husband of Harriet Beecher Stowe, and the Clemenses' next-door neighbor.

6. That is, "bust."

7. Accompanying Twain's "From India to South Africa," *McClure's* 10 (November 1897): 3–18.

8. Arthur Burdett Frost's illustration in *Following the Equator,* "The Mate's Shadow Froze Fast to the Deck." Excerpts from the book were then appearing in *McClure's Magazine.*

140. Twain to Twichell

19 November 1897. Vienna, Austria

Vienna—
Hotel Metropole, Nov. 19/97.

Dear Joe:

Above is our private (and permanent) address for the winter. You needn't send letters by London.

I shall be very glad to have a look at the illustrations of the Irish-Dog-Daly story. That is a favorite yarn of mine, & I wrote it out the best I knew how.[1]

I am very much obliged for Forrest's Austro-Hungarian articles. I have just finished reading the first one; & in it I find that his opinion & Vienna's are the same, upon a point which was puzzling me—the paucity (no, the absence) of Austrian celebrities. He and Vienna both say the country cannot afford to *allow* great names to grow up; that the whole safety & prosperity of the Empire depend upon keeping things *quiet*; can't afford to have geniuses springing up & developing ideas and stirring the public soul. I am assured that every time a man finds himself blooming into fame, they just softly snake him down & relegate him to a wholesome obscurity. It is curious & interesting.

Three days ago the New York World sent & asked a friend of mine (correspondent of a London daily) to get some Christmas greetings from the celebrities of the Empire. She spoke of this. Two or three bright Austrians were present. They said "there *are* none who are known all over the world! none who have achieved fame; none who can point to their work & say it is known far & wide in the earth: there are two *names*, Kossuth (known because he had a father) & Lecher, who made the 12-hour speech; two names—nothing more.[2] Every other country in the world, perhaps, has a giant or two who[se] heads are away up & can be seen, but not ours. We've got the *material*—have always had it—but we have to suppress it; we can't afford to let it develop; our political salvation depends upon tranquillity—always has."

Poor Livy! She is laid up with rheumatism; she had a perfectly terrible 24 hours, to start with—oh, intolerable pain! But she is getting along, now. We have a good doctor, & he says she will be out of bed in a couple of days, but must stay in the house a week or ten.

Clara is working faithfully at her music, Jean at her usual studies, & we all send love.

Mark.[3]

1. Twichell's young friend Charles Allan Gilbert's illustration of this incident, in which Twain was barred from a visit to a theater manager by an Irish porter, ultimately appeared in *Following the Equator*. See Robert Pack Browning, Michael B. Frank, and Lin Salamo, eds., *Mark Twain's Notebooks and Journals*, vol. 3: *1883–1891* (Berkeley: University of California Press, 1979), 232.

2. Ferenc Kossuth was one-time president of the Hungarian Party of Independence. His father, Lajos Kossuth, was a Hungarian revolutionary hero who addressed Congress while on his fund-raising and consciousness-raising visit to the United States in 1851. Otto Lecher was an Austrian politician who spoke for twelve hours in a filibuster against the renewal of the Ausgleich (an agreement for a dual Austrian-Hungarian monarchy) on 28 October 1897. See Twain's "Stirring Times in Austria."

3. Below his signature Twain writes, and then deletes, "['Sh! Is Isa there?'"

141. Twain to Twichell

10 December 1897. Vienna, Austria

Hotel Metropole,
Vienna, Dec. 10/97.

Dear Joe—

Pond sends me a Cleveland paper with a cablegram from here in it which says that when the police invaded the parliament & expelled the 11 members I waved my handkerchief & shouted Hoch die Deutchen! & got hustled out.[1] Oh dear, what a pity it is that one's adventures never happen! When the Ordner (sergeant-at-arms) came up to our gallery & was hurrying the people out, a friend tried to get leave for me to stay, by saying "But this gentleman is a foreigner—you don't need to turn him out—he won't do any harm."

"Oh, I know him very well—I recognize him by his pictures; & I should be very glad to let him stay, but I haven't any choice, because of the strictness of the orders."

And so we all went out, & no one was hustled. Below, I ran across the London Times correspondent, & he showed me the way into the first gallery & I lost none of the show. The first gallery had not misbehaved, & was not disturbed.

Later. I have been interrupted & now my time is short. I will shove other people's letters in—that will fill up.[2] The small note is from a handsome young girl who sat in the next box to the one occupied by Clara & the Letchititchkis & me at the opera the other night.[3] The penciled noted is the rough draft of the answer I sent her. A very pretty letter came back, but Livy is keeping it.

Some of the letters that come are just too lovely—the enclosed one from Hamburg, Germany, for instance. *That* is the way to say the pleasant thing to the stranger.

Here—as in London—Livy & the girls find that the name Clemens is no sufficient disguise. They have pleasant adventures. Yesterday Clara was out with Katy hunting for theatre tickets & was sent to the wrong place. Outside, when they were about to enter the cab, a man stepped up to Clara & said "What were you looking for?" Clara was startled, but told him. He said she would have to go to the theatre itself. She asked him to give the address to the cab-driver, which he did. As he closed the cab door upon her, he said, "Pardon—it is the daughter of Mark Twain?"

At the theatre, the box office man was a little impatient & a trifle gruff, & said "What NAME?" (falling inflection.)

"Clemens."

Then he softened in his manner. The woman-assistant said "Ah yes—Hotel Metropole."

Livy has adventures, too. And Katy—but you know Katy. If I should start in on Katy's adventures with this family's name, a certain amount of time would be consumed.

We cannot persuade Livy to go out in society yet, but all the lovely people come to see her; & Clara & I go to dinner parties, & around here & there, & we all have a most hospitable good time. Jean's wood-carving flourishes, & her other studies.

Good-bye, Joe—& we all love all of you.

Mark.

1. Pond is James Pond, lecture manager, who arranged the first (American) engagements in Twain's round-the-world tour. The German phrase means (roughly) "Up the Germans." The disruption of Parliament on 26 November followed from the deal Count Badeni (the prime minister) made with the Czechs replacing German with Czech as the official language in Bohemia. The German-speaking opposition to this measure jeopardized the ratification of the Ausgleich, the treaty that formally held the Austro-Hungarian Empire together.

2. Twichell's next letter notes that this material was not, in fact, enclosed.

3. The Leschititchkis: Theodor Leschetizky, Polish pianist and one of the most influential piano teachers of the time. Clara studied under him in Vienna. Transliterations from the Russian tend to be variable and Twain may be playfully engaging with the spelling here.

142. Twichell to Twain

27 December 1897. Hartford, Connecticut

Hartford. Dec. 27.

Dear Mark:

Sh-h-h! No, Isa is *not* here.[1] But she *was* a month ago, or so, and gave us a great fright. Harmony and I went over to Charley's one evening suspecting nothing. On the threshold Sue met us with agitation in her face and whispered something to Harmony which I did not hear.[2] But I soon found out, for when we went in there the critter was! I will say to her credit that she looked a trifle blank at seeing us, and greeted us without effusion, and kept pretty still the half-hour we were there, not even once bursting out in that horse laugh of hers. I conjecture that a reason of her subdued manner was that she knew I knew (what I never told Charley and Sue) of her having been on a royal old drunk one night at my classmate Bob Stiles', in Richmond, *after* she left Hartford.[3] Bob's daughter had invited her out to his summer lodge in the outskirts of Richmond, and she was to meet Bob at the train and go thither under his escort. Arriving at the station, Bob saw a crowd of hackmen, negroes &c in a state of high amusement over something. He edged up to see what it was all about, and, lo, Isa in the midst crazy as a loon making a circus for 'em. Bob, like a gentleman, took her under his wing and carried her home i.e. to his lodge aforesaid, and there she kept them up till near morning.—just as she used to do at Charlie's. We hear that she is now reformed, has joined the Catholic Church, and is at work as editor on a new magazine or periodical of some sort; and I hope it is true, though I doubt the reformed part of it. But I confess I can think of few things I less desire than to meet her at the house of a friend—or anywhere else. Yes, there is one thing a good deal unpleasanter. And it happened yesterday. Right in front of me in Church, close up, sat that scoundrel, my correspondence with whom I sent you awhile since;—sat there with his unconscious *proud* father and mother, and—Heaven help us—his new *bride*![4] Well, Mark, it put a strain on me, as you will believe. If he had once looked at me, I couldn't have stood it; but he didn't. From doxology to benediction I didn't meet his eye. He had the grace to preserve the attitude of inattention throughout the service. I suppose the infernal whelp couldn't avoid bringing his bride home Christmas, and being there couldn't avoid coming to Church with the family. I trust he suffered some natural torture, and I guess he did. The bride was hid behind a spray of Christmas greens, and I hadn't a fair sight of her. I don't imagine, however, that the black secret bothers *her* much, or, of course, she wouldn't have married him. But to see that mother's smiling, happy face—by George, Mark, it was terrible. But you ought to have seen Harmony! The group was in plain view to her, and her countenance was a study. She says that she experienced for several minutes after they came in, the actual physical sensation of nausea and that she couldn't tell at-all what the sermon had been about. Oh, sister Twichell was inspired with a holy wrath, I can assure you. And in her case it was all the more lurid, because the day before she had received a Christmas present from the poor, forlorn *victim*! Such a sad, grateful note came with it: which Harmony has this morning answered, saying, as I am confident you would allow might you read it, *exactly* the right thing, in the right way—a good woman's kind word to a heart-broken girl who had been wronged, yet had done wrong too.

x x x x x

But *what* a time you are having there in Austria! What luck that you are on hand to see it! I wish I was. I know of no other place in the world so interesting to a philosophical spectator just now. The illustration I enclose will suggest the popular acquaintence [*sic*] here with the fact of a great row in progress in your Reichsrath. How will it eventuate? It seems to me that Austria is in great danger of mortal disaster. Your letters are hugely interesting, every one of them. Many a time I have wished to goodness I could give passages out of them to the press. But I havn't and I won't—unless you grant me leave, and then I would do it *very* judiciously. Your correction of the false rumor of your violent expulsion from the parliament e.g.— what harm in letting Charley Clark print that? By the way, in yours of the 10th inst. you spoke of some other people's letters you were going to send me with it, but you forgot them finally.

The boys are home for the holidays and we are having no end of a good time with them.

The [Monday Evening] Club meets to-night at Gen. Franklin's and he is to talk on "The Army in 1840," and it is certain to be interesting. The report is that the new book is having a great sale.[5] I thought it would be so. I'm going to get my copy of Bliss today i.e. as a present.

So your brother Orion has ended his pilgrimage.[6] Our memory of him is of a gentle and amiable spirit—remarkably disposed to the things of good will. May he rest in peace.

Our Christmas love to dear Livy and the girls—and we do love them, and must, forever. But we hunger and thirst to see them.

With boundless affection,
Yrs ever
Joe

1. Probably Isa Carrington Cabell, a writer from Richmond, Virginia, who was close to the Warners but whom neighbors and friends found prone to upsetting behavior. Grace King, the Southern writer who visited both the Warners and Clemenses during this era, believed she was Warner's mistress. Jean Clemens, attending Warner's funeral in 1900, described Cabell's "histeria" [*sic*] and other inappropriate behavior.

2. Charley and Sue: Charles Dudley Warner and his wife Susan.

3. Robert Stiles was a Confederate veteran and Yale classmate of Twichell's; his daughter was Mary Evelyn Stiles.

4. See Letter 131.

5. *Following the Equator* had been published in November.

6. Orion Clemens died on 11 December 1897.

143. Twain to Twichell

3 February 1898. Vienna, Austria (Two typed transcripts by Albert Bigelow Paine)

(Private.)

Hotel Metropole,
Vienna, Feb. 3/98.

Dear Joe:

There's that letter that I began so long ago—you see how it is: can't get time to finish anything. I pile up lots of work, nevertheless. There may be idle people in the world, but I'm not one of them.

I say "private" up there because I've got an adventure to tell, & you mustn't let a breath of it get out. First I thought I would lay it up along with a thousand others that I've laid up for the same purpose—to *talk* to you about, but—those others have vanished out of my memory; & that must not happen with this.

The other night I lectured for a Vienna charity; & at the end of it Livy & I were introduced to a princess who is aunt to the heir apparent of the imperial throne—a beautiful lady, with a beautiful spirit, & very cordial in her praises of my books & thanks to me for writing them; & glad to meet me face to face & shake me by the hand—just the kind of princess that adorns a fairy tale & makes it the prettiest tale there is.[1]

Very well, we long ago found out that when you are noticed by supremacies, the correct etiquette is to go within a couple of days & pay your respects in the quite simple form of writing your name in the Visitors'

Book kept in the office of the establishment. That is the end of it, & everything is squared up & ship-shape.

So at noon to-day Livy & I drove to the Archducal palace, & got by the sentries all right, & asked the grandly-uniformed portier for the book & said we wished to write our names in it. And he called a servant in livery & was sending us up stairs; & said her Royal Highness was out but would soon be in. Of course Livy said No—no— we only want the book; but he was firm, & said, "You are Americans?"

"Yes."

"Then you are expected—please go up stairs."

"But indeed we are *not* expected—please let us have the book &—"

"Her Royal Highness will be back in a *very* little while—she commanded me to *tell* you so—& you must wait."

Well, the soldiers were there close by—there was no use trying to resist—so we followed the servant up; but when he tried to beguile us into a drawing-room, Livy drew the line; she wouldn't go in. And she wouldn't stay up there, either. She said the princess might come in at any moment & catch us, & it would be too infernally ridiculous for anything. So we went down stairs again—to my unspeakable regret. For it was too darling a comedy to spoil. I was hoping & praying the princess *would* come, & catch us up there, & that those other Americans who *were* expected would arrive, & be taken for impostors by the portier, & shot by the sentinels—& then it would all go into the papers, & be cabled all over the world, & make an immense stir & be perfectly lovely. And by that time the princess would discover that *we* were not the right ones, & the Minister of War would be ordered out, & the garrison, & they would come for us, & there would be another prodigious time, & *that* would get cabled too, &——well, Joe, I was in a state of perfect bliss. But happily, oh, so happily, that big portier wouldn't let us out——he was sorry, but he must obey orders—we must go back up stairs & wait. Poor Livy—I couldn't help but enjoy her distress. She said we were in a fix, & how *were* we ever going to explain, if the princess should arrive before the rightful Americans came? We went up stairs again—laid off our wraps, & were conducted through one drawing room & into another, & left alone there & the door closed upon us.

Livy was in a state of mind! She said it was too theatrically ridiculous; & that I would never be able to keep my mouth shut; that I would be sure to let it out & it would get into the papers——& she tried to make me promise———;

"Promise *what*?" I said—"to be quiet about *this*? Indeed I won't—it's the best thing that ever happened; I'll tell it, & *add* to it; & I wish Joe & Howells were here to make it perfect; I can't make all the rightful blunders by myself—it takes all three of us to do full justice to an opportunity like this. I would just like to see Howells get down to his work & explain, & lie, & work his futile & inventionless subterfuges when that princess comes raging in here & wanting to *know.*" But Livy couldn't bear fun—it was not a time to be trying to be funny——we were in a most miserable & shameful situation, & if——

Just then the door spread wide & our princess & 4 more, & 3 little princes flowed in! Our princess, & her sister the Archduchess Marie Therese (mother to the imperial Heir & to the 2 young girl Archduchesses present, & aunt to the 3 little princes)——& we shook hands all around & sat down & had a most sociable good time for half an hour—& by & by it turned out that we *were* the right ones, & had been sent for by a messenger who started too late to catch us at the hotel. We were invited for 2 o'clock, but we beat *that* arrangement by an hour & a half.[2]

Wasn't it a rattling good comedy situation? Seems a kind of pity we were the right ones. It would have been such nuts to see the right ones come, & get fired out, & we chatting along comfortably & nobody suspecting us for impostors.

We all send lots & lots of love.

Mark.

1. Identified as Princess Adelgunde, Countess of Bardi, in Benjamin Griffin and Harriet Elinor Smith, eds., *Autobiography of Mark Twain*, vol. 3 (Berkeley: University of California Press, 2015), 478–79.
2. See, too, ibid., 68–71.

144. Twichell to Twain

28 March 1898. Hartford, Connecticut

Hartford. March 28. '98

Dear old Mark:

Should any of your Vienna friends inquire of you concerning the state of religion in this country you can show him (or her) the above, as evidence that we are not, in that department, in a stagnant condition any way. The pistol of the Lord is on cock. What fun for that parson!—compared with my dull Sundays.[1]

By the way, speaking of religion,—I had the pleasure, a few weeks ago, while en route to a Yale blowout down in Pennsylvania, of falling in with Brer Bob Ingersoll and of being introduced to him and of having a lot of talk with him (it was in the smoking closet of a parlor car) in the course of which he said not a word that was out of order, though he knew that I was a minister.[2] He was exceedingly entertaining and altogether amiable. I didn't guard my speech in the slightest degree; in fact by things I said without thinking I laid myself open to him several times; but however tempted he was, he held his peace and was only charming [. . . here but the same old things. . . . d "Private" in which you . . . all that might have been . . . sit, was delightful reading. . . . ur hearts too; for, somehow, . . . impression that Livy was . . . dear Livy. How we do . . . ace and hear her kind . . . est news we have had for] many a day was a report in the papers of your having said that you were expecting to get home to your own house after a time.[3] It is true isn't it?[4] If it isn't, don't tell me so. You must be gratified with the verdict passed, by the best judges, on your book. In the flavor of ripeness, it certainly excels all your previous work. It is the *strongest* thing you have done both intellectually and in point of literary execution—so I hear said, and so I say myself. Which means that you are still a *growing man*, and if that doesn't "rise your heart," what can? I'll write again pretty soon. With lashins of love to each one,

Yrs ever aff.

Joe

1. An item, attached above Twichell's heading of place and date, has been torn from the letter, obliterating some text on the opposite side of the page.

2. Robert Ingersoll was a lawyer, orator, and freethinker, well known for his agnosticism. He was admired by Twain.

3. The left-hand side of the page is torn off (see above note), thus the ellipses.

4. Only in 1900 would the Clemenses finally decide not to return to the Hartford house, which was sold in 1903.

145. Twain to Twichell

Before 26 May 1898. Vienna or Kaltenleutgeben, Austria

[This letter is excerpted in a Hartford Courant *newspaper clipping of 27 May 1898 attached at the head of Letter 146. The original Twain letter is missing.*[1]*]*

Have you read "Old Sile's Clem?" (May "Harper.") I feel sure that it must be the best back-settlement study that was ever printed. O, the art of it! How well Coggins knows his ground, & what a sure & reserved & delicate touch he has. I knew his people, personally & intimately, every one of them, when I was a boy. I knew them in the West, you knew them in the East—they are national. How true their back-settlement wit rings; it is so good, & it is so bad—just the genuine thing, the correct border line. No bright intelligence would say those things & no dull intelligence could. They are too nearly perfect for inventions; Coggins must have heard them uttered. There are some things which the finest genius cannot counterfeit with exactness, cannot perfectly imitate, & back-settlement wit is one of these, I think. Do you remember Captain Ned Wakeman's letter to you? The genius never lived that could counterfeit that. It seems to me that Coggins's sketch is flawless, with one unimportant exception; apparently his boy utters thanks for a kindness shown him. I know the boy well. He felt his thanks, but I doubt if he allowed any detectable sign of that to appear on the outside. Watch out for Paschal H. Coggins; he is valuable & entitled to a grateful welcome.

1. Twichell had passed on to the *Courant* Twain's comments on "Old Sile's Clem: A Story," by Paschal H. Coggins, published in *Harper's New Monthly*, May 1898. The piece starts: "In a private letter to a friend in this city Mark Twain pays this high compliment to a recent contribution in 'Harper's,' and its author." Coggins was a Philadelphia attorney and author of popular handbooks on law as well as short stories such as the above, a somewhat saccharine tale of a backwoods boy and his horse.

146. Twichell to Twain

1 June 1898. Hartford, Connecticut [Clipping attached: see Letter 145]

Hartford. June 1st 1898

Dear Mark:

So you see I set your eulogy—and a choice bit of criticism it is—circulating; for which Mr. Coggins ought to be, and will be, a grateful man. But he deserves it. For on reading his article (which I shouldn't have done but for you) I saw that every word you had said about it was true. I wonder if he is a young fellow just beginning to try his wings. If he is, there are certainly great possibilities in him. *For* a tyro his *restraint* seems to me most remarkable. His story is short, and the ingredients are simple, but it is suffused with an atmosphere of feeling that fills it with life. He does make your heart ache so for that boy! Yet he doesn't in the least *strain* for that, or any other effect.

Things are moving on with us as usual. Well, no, not quite. Dave has enlisted in the army and is, at the present writing, a sergeant of artillery!![1] His battery, one platoon of which, *his* platoon, is entirely composed of

Yale men, is in camp at Niantic, near New London. I saw him at the Scroll and Key initiation in New Haven Tuesday night.—a strange figure among the collegians in his red-faced artillery uniform, but shining bright in my eyes—a proper soldier to look at, as you will believe. It was Dave's own idea to take the step. All we did was not to forbid him. He was very much in earnest about it. What especially set him on was a sort of talk that was considerably current to the effect that the fittest persons to volunteer were the loafers and bummers, and that there would be enough of them to furnish the force the President had called for. Master David dissented indignantly from that view; saying that in his opinion those who were favored and priviliged [*sic*] in their circumstances, for whom the country had done most and who had most stake in it, should be among the foremost to offer their service to it. To which Harmony and I had nothing to say, for that was the sentiment in which we had brought him up, and we felt that we must take the consequences. What is before the lad we do not know; though we *hope* that the war will be short, and that his campaign will consist of a few months of Light Artillery drill, which will only do him good. But we are well aware that something far more serious than that may be in store.

Another item of our family news that will interest Livy is that Young Harmony will in the Fall enter a hospital—the Hartford hospital probably—to study the science and art of Nursing. She arrived at the desire and purpose thereof quite by herself, and there again, all that we did was not to withhold our consent. What will come of it, we shall see. We scarcely think, however, that she will in the event practice the profession of Trained Nursing. But she may; and surely she might do worse. If Dave is a doctor, as he means to be, she may work with him. They would make a good firm.

Charlie and Susie [Warner] are back from Mexico: both well but the former sunk in black depression over the public situation—as pessimistic almost as Charley Clark. He thinks the country is gone to the dogs and has no men able to save her. Well, I *don't* think so—not by a good deal.

People in many places are all the while asking us when the Clemenses are coming home. When *are* you? Why don't you *say* something about it? The desire of you is quenchless. Time seems only to intensify it. By the way Cornelius Dunham and Dr. Parker sailed for Southampton yesterday—to be gone till August.[2] I shouldn't wonder if you saw them.

Mark, I was sixty years old last Friday!! I'm afraid it is now too late for me to think of amounting to much. Mine is a case mainly for the divine clemency—in which I hope.

As I was en route Memorial Day (May 30th) for Sali[s]bury [Connecticut] to make an address, passing through Bloomfield, I followed with my eye the path we have so often trodden going for a walk to the Tower, and thought on us two young fellows as we meandered along up the road and through the fields, and the memory of it was all golden. What talks we used to have on those cheerful excursions!

'Tears, idle tears, I know not what they mean, x x[3]

Get out your Tennyson and read the rest of it, and feel with me the sweet pathos of "the days that are no more."

But Good morning, dear old boy.

I send you Dean's comment on Will's new nuptials. Also a clipping from *The Sun*.[4] Love to dearest Livy, and the girls.

Yrs ever aff.

Joe.

The Savage Club! My![5]

I'm going to tell the Courant.

1. David Twichell, a senior at Yale, had signed up in the Connecticut Voluntary Battery of Light Artillery as a response to the outbreak in April of the Spanish-American War. The war ended too quickly for him to see service overseas. See Courtney, *Joseph Hopkins Twichell*, 249.

2. See Letter 148, note 10.

3. Twichell seems to be using these crosses either as a type of et cetera, or signaling that he cannot remember what follows. "Tears, Idle Tears" is a section of Alfred Tennyson's narrative poem *The Princess* (1847).

4. Clipping missing. William Henry Sage, brother of Dean Sage, married Isabel Whitney on 9 April 1898.

5. This may have been a reference to a planned Twain visit to London, perhaps mentioned in the rest of the "Old Sile's Clem" letter. See Twain's 31 May letter to Henry Rogers in Lewis Leary, ed., *Mark Twain's Correspondence with Henry Huttleston Rogers, 1893–1909* (Berkeley: University of California Press, 1969), 348.

147. Twain to Twichell

17 June 1898. Kaltenleutgeben, Austria (Two typed transcripts by Albert Bigelow Paine)

P.S. Has major Burbank gone to the war?[1]

Kaltenleutgeben (near Vienna)[2]

June 17/98.

Dear Joe—

You are living your war-days over again in Dave, & it must be a strong pleasure, mixed with a sauce of apprehension—enough to make it just *smeck,* as the Germans say.[3] Dave will come out with two or three stars on his shoulder-straps if the war holds, & then we shall all be glad it happened.

We started with Bull Run, before. Dewey & Hobson have introduced an improvement on the game this time.[4]

I have never enjoyed a war—even in written history—as I am enjoying this one. For this is the worthiest one that was ever fought, so far as my knowledge goes. It is a worthy thing to fight for one's own freedom; it is another sight finer to fight for another man's. And I think this is the first time it has been done.[5]

Oh, never mind Charlie Warner, he would interrupt the raising of Lazarus.[6] He would say, the will has been probated, the property distributed, it will be a world of trouble to settle the rows—better leave well enough alone: don't ever disturb *any*thing, where it's going to break the soft smooth flow of things & wobble our tranquility.

Livy let fly viciously over the news of Will Sage's second marriage—I was up, shaving, in my night-shirt at the time, & she was back of me on the other side of the room in bed—& I followed her lead with sympathetic emphasis, & that pleased her.[7] But you know how it is with a charitable man who is argumentative: after a moment of reflection it comes so natural to begin to cast about for an argument on the other side. I did that. As I went along I began to be surprised, myself, to see how much there was to say on the other side; & I grew more & more interested, & less & less conscious that there was anything left in the world but me & my argument; & at last happened to say, "Why, I see now that I ought to begin to be looking around, myself, because—"

Then a Bible or something whizzed past my cheek & broke the glass; & that adjourned the subject.

Company! ('Sh! it happens every day—& we came out here to be quiet.)[8]

Love to you all,
Mark.

1. This P.S. is an insertion. The sixty-year-old Major James Brattle Burbank of Hartford was a Civil War veteran who also fought in the Spanish-American War.

2. The family stayed here from late May till mid-October in a villa set beside a pine forest.

3. *Schmeck* is a gastronomic term referring to a small whiff arising from food, with the connotation "tasty."

4. The first battle of Bull Run on 21 July 1861 was the first important battle of the American Civil War. In the Spanish-American War, Commodore George Dewey, commanding the U.S. Asiatic Squadron, speedily defeated a Spanish squadron at Manila Bay on 1 May 1898. Lieutenant Richmond P. Hobson led the failed but valiant 3 June attempt to block the

Spanish fleet in Santiago harbor by attempting to sink the collier *Merrimac* in the harbor's narrowest exit point.

5. Twain would change his mind about U.S. foreign interventions with the Philippine-American war starting in the following year, when America then acted, in his mind, like a colonial power rather than a liberator.

6. Warner opposed the war, telling Twichell ironically that perhaps the Christian religion should be "postpone[d] . . . to a more convenient season." Quoted in Twichell, "Qualities of Warner's Humor," *Century Magazine*, January 1903.

7. William H. Sage, brother of Dean Sage, had lost his first wife, Jane Gregg Sage, in 1893. His April 1898 marriage was to Isabel Whitney, sixteen years his junior. Whitney had been listed in the 1880 census as a twenty-four-year-old boarder living with the Sages, which may hint at Livy's outrage over the marriage and Twain's joke about looking around (for a younger woman).

8. As with "Sh! Isa is not here!" in Letter 142, "'Sh!" is a way of introducing a confidence that other readers (for example, Livy or Harmony) are not supposed to read.

148. Twain to Twichell

13 September 1898. Kaltenleutgeben, Austria (Typed transcript by Albert Bigelow Paine and Mark Twain's Letters, *Volume 2: 666–68)*

Kaltenleutgeben, Sept. 13/98.

Dear Joe:

You are mistaken; people don't send us the magazines. No—Harper, Century & McClure do; an example I should like to recommend to other publishers. And so I thank you very much for sending me Brander's article.[1] When you say, "I like Brander Matthews; he impresses me as a man of parts & power," I back you, right up to the hub—I feel the same way—. And when you say he has earned your gratitude for cuffing me for my crimes against the Leatherstockings & the Vicar, I ain't making any objection.[2] *Dern* your gratitude!

His article is as sound as a nut. Brander knows literature, & loves it; he can talk about it & keep his temper; he can state his case so lucidly & so fairly & so forcibly that you have to agree with him, even when you *don't* agree with him; & he can discover & praise such merits as a book has, even when they are merely half a dozen diamonds scattered through an acre of mud. And so he has a right to be a critic.

To detail just the opposite of the above invoice is to describe me. I haven't any right to criticise books, & I don't do it except when I hate them. I often want to criticise Jane Austen, but her books madden me so that I can't conceal my frenzy from the reader, & therefore I have to stop every time I begin. Every time I read that mangy book, "Pride & Prejudice," I want to dig her up & beat her over the skull with her own shin-bone.

That good & unoffending lady the Empress is killed by a mad-man, & I am living in the midst of world-history again.[3] The Queen's jubilee last year, the invasion of the Reichsrath by the police, & now this murder, which will still be talked of & described & painted a thousand years from now.[4] To have a *personal friend* of the wearer of two crowns burst in at the gate in the deep dusk of the evening & say in a voice broken with tears, "My God the Empress is murdered!" & fly toward her home before we can utter a question—why, it brings the giant event home to you, makes you a part of it & personally interested; it is as if your neighbor Antony should come flying & say "Caesar is butchered—the head of the world is fallen!"[5]

Of course there is no talk but of this. The mourning is universal & genuine, the consternation is stupefying. The Austrian Empire is being draped with black. Vienna will be a spectacle to see, by next Saturday, when the funeral cortège marches. We are invited to occupy a room in the sumptuous new hotel (the Krantz) where we are to live during the Fall & Winter & view it, & we shall go.[6]

We are *very* sorry to hear that about that dear Libbie Hamersley.[7] It does not grieve me to hear that a friend has been set free; but to be *partly* released, then halted—that is another matter.[8]

Speaking of Mrs. Leiter, there is a noble dame in Vienna, about whom they retail similar slanders.[9] She said in French—she is weak in French—that she had been spending a Sunday afternoon in a gathering of the "demi-monde." Meaning that unknown land, that mercantile land, that mysterious half-world which underlies the aristocracy. But these Malaproperies are always inventions—they don't happen.

Yes—I wish we *could* have some talks; I'm full to the eye-lids. Had a noble good one with Parker & Dunham—land, but we were grateful for that visit.[10]

(Joe—suppose you "take the liberty" of sending those first 2 pages to Brander—they are framed for that.)

Yours with all our loves,

Mark.

[There is a note from Livy on the back of page 2 which reads:]

Dear Joe:

I feel that I ought to explain that "Sumptuous", it looks rather questionable for poor people.

As Mr. Clemens says, the Krantz is a new hotel, and for some reason they evidently felt that it would be a great advantage to them to have Mr. Clemens there for the Winter, so they made us a very advantageous offer which was naturally very gladly accepted

I thank you and Harmony for thinking of us as the sad season comes around to us. I am trying very hard to carry out the first part of the advice that the dying father gave his little boy (in Miss Deland's story "Justice & the Judge") "Don't cry—and play fair."[11]

My deepest love to Harmony. Good bye dear Joe. I am unfailingly grateful to you for all you did for me two years ago & for your comforting presence at that time.[12]

Yours always in love
Livy

1. There is no obvious trace of any 1898 article by Matthews that would fit. It is possible Twain had requested one of Matthews's previous articles (see Letters 128 and 130). Twain was at this time considering having Matthews write the biographical introduction for his *Collected Works*, to be published by Harper, and may have been doing some homework. Matthews ultimately wrote this introduction.

2. Twain's attacks on James Fenimore Cooper's prose are well-known. In *Following the Equator* (Hartford: American Publishing Co., 1897) he had described Oliver Goldsmith's *The Vicar of Wakefield* as a "strange menagerie of complacent hypocrites and idiots" (612). In his "Fenimore Cooper's Literary Offences" (1895), Twain would lightly critique Matthews's praise of the author.

3. Empress Elisabeth of Austria, wife of Franz Joseph I, was assassinated on 10 September 1898, stabbed by Italian anarchist Luigi Lucheni.

4. Queen Victoria's Diamond Jubilee in 1897 marked her sixty-year reign.

5. This "personal friend" who passed on the news of the Empress Elisabeth's assassination cannot be identified.

6. There is an insert after "hotel" in Livy's hand, reading, "(see back of page 2)."

7. Elizabeth Hamersley was an educational reformer in Hartford and her family (including her brother, attorney and politician William H. Hamersley, an early investor in the Paige typesetter) were regular summer denizens of Keene Valley's "Hartford plateau." In Twichell's journal of August 1898 he reports on Libbie's "sudden prostration by paralysis" in Keene Valley.

8. To be set free is the way Twain viewed death.

9. Mary Theresa Leiter, Washington hostess and wife of Chicago millionaire Levi Z. Leiter. An author, she was apparently known for her malapropisms.

10. Rev. Edwin Pond Parker and Austin Cornelius Dunham visited Twain in Vienna on 2 July. Both were close friends of Twichell.

11. Margaret Wade Campbell Deland's story "Justice and the Judge" had appeared in the September *Harper's*.

12. That is, at the time of Susy Clemens' death.

149. Twain to Twichell

25 September 1898. Vienna, Austria

[This letter consists of a note at the bottom of pages 21 and 22 of a Twain manuscript which reads as follows:]

21
the kind which is as old as history—
the burning of the temple of Ephesus.
Among the inadequate attempts
to account for the assassination
we must concede high rank to the
German Emperor's. He justly describes it as a "deed unparalleled
for ruthlessness," & then adds that
it was "ordained from above."
I think this verdict will not be popular "above." [Twain here deleted:
A Man is either a free agent, or he
isn't. If man is a free agent, this
prisoner is . . . responsible for what he has
done; but if man is not a free agent]
If the deed was ordained from above
there is no rational way of making
this prisoner even partially responsible
for it, & the German court cannot con-

22
demn him without manifestly committing a crime. Logic is logic; &
by disregarding its laws even Emperors as capable & acute as William
II can be beguiled into making
charges which should not be
ventured upon except in the shelter
of plenty of lightning rods.

Private. Livy edited this out, Joe, because the Emperor is a friend & has been hospitable to me; but it is theological & mustn't be wasted, so I send it to you. The Emperor wouldn't care a rap.

Mark.

[There is then an enclosure, which includes Twain's translation of the von Berger piece mentioned in it:]

34

[In pencil:]

A character in Baron [Alfred] von Berger's recent fairy-drama, "Hapsburg," tells about that first coming of the girlish Empress-Queen, & his story draws this fine picture:

[In ink:]

I saw the stately pageant pass;
In her high place I saw the Empress-Queen;
I could not take my eyes away
From that fair vision, whose soft white grace & peace
Pervasive were & subtle
Affected me Like [*sic*] moonlit snows in dreams

[In pencil:]

Subdued & soft & pure as moonlit snows in dreams.
Spirit-like & pure
That rose serene, sublime, & figured to my sense
A noble Alp far lifted in the blue,
That in the flood of morning rends its veil of cloud
And stands, a dream of glory to the gaze
Of them that in the valley toil & plod.
a dream of glory[1]

[Remainder in ink:]

P.S. Two hours later, Sept. 25/98.

Perhaps you will like this translation, Joe. I think it is rather neat. But it didn't flow: it has taken me two full hours to grind it into this perfect state.

Mark.

1. This poem has been very heavily edited as Twain looks to get his translation right. Both the prose manuscript pages and the verse translation are evidently part of a draft of Twain's "The Memorable Assassination," which was published posthumously in *What Is Man? and Other Essays* (1917).

150. Twichell to Twain

13 October 1898. Hartford, Connecticut

Hartford. Oct. 13.

Dear Mark:

I sent Brander Matthews those remarks of yours about him, saying that I could not think it *possible* you would object to his seeing them, and here is the note that came back with them. No wonder he was pleased.[1]

Here also is a leaf from a recent issue of "the Spectator" with readings on *both* sides that it struck me would interest you as a looker on in Europe the past year, and sojourner in the city that in that time has been swept by mighty tides of strangely contrasted passion.

Could I, in anticipation of the Great 1898 show, have chosen the stand from which to watch it I think on the whole it would have been Vienna. It would anyway if you were to be there. I havn't half enjoyed the Big Play because I havn't had you to talk it over with. What wouldn't I give for a few afternoons of your pedestrian company out on the country roads and into the autumnal woods just now beginning to turn. *I'm* up to it still, Mark; and so are you I guess.

Your article in the last "Forum" on Play Acting is superb.[2] I doubt if you ever did a better thing in the way of description. The art of it is really bewitching, and all the more because it is so unpretentious. You don't seem to propose any great effort, but only to give a simple account of (what's the name of it! By George, I've been hunting the house over to find that Forum and can't unearth it)—and ere the reader is aware his attention is completely fascinated and lots of thoughts are rising in his heart.

Tell Livy that I blessed her for that postscript of hers regarding The Krantz: not for the explanation, which was quite unnecessary; but because it was immediately from her hand.

I *rather* side with her in the matter of the observations on the Kaiser's holding the upper Powers responsible for the fate of the poor Empress which she wouldn't let you print.—and yet I rather wish, too, that her eye hadn't happened to light on it.

Your theology is perfectly *sound* in my opinion—so far as that is concerned; but I surely think that—not the Kaiser, but some of his subjects of the *un*humorous sort, would have taken it ill.

Libbie Hamersley was brought home last week; made the journey without any great discomfort; but is not in a hopeful way I judge. The same must, I fear, be said of Mollie Dunham. Sally Dunham, also, is far from well. Hurry back, Mark and Livy, or we'll *all* be gone.

Dave's service as light artillery man is at and [*sic*] end. His battery is to be mustered out of the U.S. service now in a few days. But the lad hasn't had enough of soldiering. And so he has sought and obtained a commission as 2nd Lieut, in the Third Conn. Vol. Infantry—one of the regiments that is to remain on duty. The chance is that he will winter in Cuba. We would have preferred his return to his studies; but he wanted a further chapter of military experience; and so we didn't object.

Young Harmony, as you have probably heard, goes into the Hartford Hospital shortly to acquire the art and mystery of trained nursing. What do Livy and Clara think of it?

The "Ladies Journal" has just printed a page and a half of alleged Anecdotes about you—a lazy lot it seems to me—hardly a good one among them: but the accompanying photographs are interesting.[3]

Isa appears completely reinstated![4] She spent the whole summer with our friends and they act as foolishly over her as ever. Doesn't that beat all? But I must quit now. Good morning, Dear old Boy, with love to the crowd.

Yours ever

Joe.

[Newspaper clipping pasted into an unnumbered page of the letter:]

The Literary Digest is authority for the following: Soon after Andy Burt was made colonel of the Twenty-first colored regiment he informed his men, then at Chickamauga, that they must play ball an hour every day in order to get hardened up.[5] "And while we are playing," said he, "remember that I'm not Colonel Burt, but simply Andy Burt." During the first game the colonel lined out what was a sure home run. "Run, Andy, run, you tallow-faced, knock-kneed son of a gun," yelled a greasy black soldier at the coaching line. The colonel stopped at first base, got another player to take his place, put on his uniform, and announced: "I am Colonel Burt until further orders."

[End of clipping. Written below the clipping:]

You remember this Andy Burt. He was commandant of a post you visited when you were starting off on your trip around the world. He has been a Brigadier General in the late war; but is now Colonel again.

1. Enclosed is a letter from Matthews dated 6 October thanking Twichell for letting him "see Mark's words of praise which warmed my heart."

2. "About Play-Acting," in *Forum,* October 1898. The play whose name Twichell was trying to remember was *The Master of Palmyra* by Adolf von Wilbrandt, the subject of Twain's article.

3. The October 1898 issue of the *Ladies' Home Journal* included an article titled "The Anecdotal Side of Mark Twain."

4. See Letter 142.

5. Twichell's friend Col. Andrew Burt was placed in command of the 25th (not the 21st) Colored Infantry at Chickamauga Park, Tennessee, in 1898. Twain visited Burt at Fort Missoula, Montana, in 1895.

151. Twain to Twichell

2 December 1898. Vienna, Austria (Mourning border)

Vienna, Dec. 2/98

Dear Joe—

I will not try to talk about it, it breaks my heart. Ned Bunce was very very near & dear to me, & to all this home-circle of mine; & he was always that, from the beginning.[1]

They have begun to fall! The charm is broken, the others will follow, now. While we are trying to imagine a Hartford without Ned Bunce in it, we are reminded to prepare to imagine a Hartford with the *rest* gone that made it Hartford to us & not Waterbury or some other mere geographical expression—& that can arrive before we see it again, short as the interval may be.

You have our love, dear Joe & Harmony, & you & Hartford & ourselves have our commiseration.

Mark.

We are keeping it from the children—& shall, as long as we can.

1. Edward Merrill Bunce, the secretary of the Connecticut Mutual Life Insurance Company, was a popular figure in Twain and Twichell's Hartford circle and a close family friend to both. See *Autobiography of Mark Twain*, 1:576. He had died on 19 November 1898.

152. Twichell to Twain and Livy

17 December 1898. Hartford, Connecticut

Hartford. Dec. 17. 1898

Dear, dear Mark and Livy:

Yours of the 2nd inst about Ned Bunce came this morning, and found me on the point of mailing you the enclosed.[1] Yes, as you say, the old fellowship is now at the dissolving stage and we are writing one another's obituaries. How could life ever have seemed anything but the stuff that dreams are made of. Only to hope and to grief is it long.

Harmony saw Libbie H.—only last Saturday. She had not walked a step alone since her stroke last summer, and she could not control her speech. Yet wrecked as she was, she was completely herself in countenance and looks and was apparently in a cheerful mind. In the end, the day broke and her shadows fled away very suddenly. All our friends were at the funeral, tender and tearful, but thinking of Libbie, not unhappy. The hour was full of the fragrance of sweet memories.

Sally Dunham is better than she was, and so is Molly, but still in a feeble state. We supposed last summer that the next farewell would be there. Now I have other things to speak of and tell, but I'm going to wait a bit. With love unbounded to you all,

Yrs ever

Joe

But you'd better come home while some are left and while you are left. If anything more happens I'm going to let somebody else tell you of it.

1. Enclosure missing: presumably, a notice of the death of Libbie Hamersley.

153. Twain to Twichell

3 January 1899. Vienna, Austria

Vienna, Jan. 3/99.

Dear Joe—

Your letter has just arrived.

A Hartford with no Susy Clemens in it—& no Ned Bunce—& no Libbie Hamersley! It is not the city of Hartford, it is the city of Heartbreak. Poor Jean. Livy let fall an unguarded word at breakfast this morning, & Jean's quick suspicions were up, at once, her eye & her tongue began a search; Livy soon saw there was no escape; she paused a moment to frame the news as softly as she might, then said in a low voice, "He is not living." (Bunce.) Jean went away crying, her breakfast untasted, & has kept her room all day, mourning. We are now wondering if concealing the bereavement from Jean softened its bitterness. We hoped for that.

In some ways time does not merely fly, now, it vanishes; it takes little or no account of intervals that are actual abysses. It seems only a few weeks since I saw Susy last—yet that was 1895, & this in 1899. On the other hand it seems many, many years since I last saw those two fine Whitmore lads that have been taken away—but it is not many, at all.[1] I think I perceive, by Howells's letters, that to him Winny's death is still recent.[2]

My work does not go well, to-day. It failed yesterday—& the day before—& the day before that. And so I have concluded to put the MS in the wastebasket & meddle with some other subject. I was trying to write an article advocating the quadrupling of the salaries of our ministers

& ambassadors, & the devising of an official dress for them to wear.[3] It seems an easy theme, yet I couldn't do the thing to my satisfaction. All I got out of it was an article on Monaco & Monte Carlo—matters not connected with the subject at all.[4] Still that was something—it's better than a total loss.

I hope Harmony jr. finds herself strong enough for the nursing, & that she likes it—but you have not told me. It is one of the high & splendid callings—nursing the sick.

We are all pretty well & comfortable, & send abundance of love to you & yours.

Mark

1. The two sons of Twain's Hartford business agent, Franklin G. Whitmore, had recently died in their twenties—Franklin G. Whitmore Jr. in 1896 and Frederick C. Whitmore in 1898.

2. Winifred Howells, W. D. Howells's eldest child, died in 1889, at the age of twenty-five, after a debilitating long-term illness.

3. See "Diplomatic Pay and Clothes," published in the *Forum*, March 1899.

4. Unpublished manuscript, "The New War Scare" (Mark Twain Papers).

154. Twain to Twichell

4 February 1899. Vienna, Austria (Typed transcript by Albert Bigelow Paine)

Hotel Krantz
Wien, I. Neuer Markt 6
Feb. 4/99.

Dear Joe:

Annie Trumbull's a duck—she does certainly turn out the cunningest & sparklingest dialogue of anybody I know.[1] The play cost me a day's work, for I lay abed till into the afternoon reading it; but no matter, it paid.

Joe, you & Harmony are too good-natured; you could just as well have sent the baby by mail; it was not worth the trouble you took, & from the way you describe it St Peter will never be able to raise it anyway, with all the other things he has to do.

Between you & me, privately, I had another of those accidents the other day. We were making a call, & the daughter of the house said, "Isn't it *too* bad that poor Mrs. X, the actress, has had all her jewels burned up in the hotel." And I responded, breezily—

"Oho, it's a wearisome old gratis advertisement, I've seen it played a thousand times; every time there's a hotel fire, all the actresses for miles around gather up their paste jewelry & flock to the place and"—

"O shut up!" (this in my ear by a male friend,) "her son is standing at your elbow!"

It is a wonderful town for taking an interest in a little thing like that. I could have uttered many wisdoms that wouldn't have traveled so far.

Joe, tell me something about Christian Science. Answer these:

1. Is it required that the membership all over America must *also* join the Mother church in Boston?

2. And pay an entrance fee?

3. And how much?

4. And pay annual dues?

5. And how much?

6. What is the "*capitation tax*?"

7. How much is it, & who pays it?

8. What is done with the money?

9. Does any of it go to charities?

10. And what *are* they?

11. Who collars the cash that comes in from "The Christian Scientist Journal" and from Mrs. Eddy's book, "Science & Health, with Key to the Scriptures?"

12. Is the business management a close corporation—& how many persons are in the management? Who are they?

13. Are many voluntary "contributions" sent in?

14. Does the Metaphysical College charge for tuition—& how much—& who gets it—& is there a profit?[2]

15. How many C. S.'s are there in America?

There's a job for you. You must know some one in Boston who can answer these questions.

The girls are out, & I am notified to adjourn to the drawing room & help Livy entertain company at 5 o'clock tea. This function costs her 2 hours of labor daily. It would soon break me down if I had to do it. Livy has the rheumatism, now, & is in poor shape for this kind of work, but I suppose she must stick to her duties.

Time! We all send love.

Mark.

1. Annie Eliot Trumbull, a Hartford author and daughter of Twain's friend James Hammond Trumbull. Her play, *A Wheel of Progress*, to which Twain may be referring, was published in 1897.

2. Mary Baker Eddy founded the Massachusetts Metaphysical College (to teach her Christian Science religion) in Boston in 1881. Twain would show considerable interest in this belief system over the coming years. He would publish his first article on Christian Science in *Cosmopolitan* later in 1899 and his book on the subject in 1907.

155. Twichell to Twain

10 March 1899. Hartford, Connecticut

[Clipping enclosed from the Christian Science Sentinel *of 2 March 1899:]*

2449 Forest Avenue, Kansas City, Mo.

I desire to express my gratitude for the souvenir spoons. The motto alone is worth the price paid for the spoons. I shall use them on my dining table at each meal, sipping from these bowls, which I know are and will always be filled with Love and Truth, from our beloved Mother.[1]

With gratitude and love for what you have done and are constantly doing for us all, I am sincerely your loving

Sallie A. Saunders.

Boston, Mass., February 16, 1899.

Am more than glad to own the souvenir spoon. That motto presented for human conception three times a day will do a great work, as even I can see.[2]

L. N. Bennett.

[Twichell enclosed, too, his letter to William B. Johnson, clerk of the Christian Science church in Boston, dated 21 February 1899, together with Johnson's 27 February reply. Johnson does not answer such questions as "What is done with the money?"—that is, the money from the "capitation tax" about which Twain asks.[3] A further note from the Christian Science Publishing Company advising Twichell that "we have no publication containing the information you desire," and advising him to write instead to the Christian Science Board of Education in Boston, is also enclosed.]

Hartford. March 10. 1899

Dear Mark:

I have found it difficult to get your Christian Science questions answered; and in the case of some of them, impossible. Harmony first took the list to a female C.S. practitioner who was operating on a neighbor and parishioner of ours—Hapgood the architect, whose baby she and I had cremated for him—who is slowly dying of cancer.[4] This healer could answer only a part of them, but she referred us to the clerk of the C.S. Church in Boston. To him accordingly I wrote. I enclose my note to him and his reply to it. I then wrote again as you see, and received the reply which you see. I then wrote to the Publishing Co. as you see and received the reply which you see. I have not yet written to the Board of Education; and perhaps I do not need to. For I have called on a man C.S. practitioner whose office is in the Hartford Fire Ins[urance]. Co's Building and have learned from him that the course of instruction in the Metaphysical College (Boston) is two weeks (with a rising inflection—as if it might not be *exactly* that) and that the fee is $100.

Also, that the schools of instruction in other places are independent concerns, though the teachers in them must be graduates of the Metaphys. Coll. Also, that the C.S. adherents in America, are reckoned at about a million in number.

The woman healer told Harmony that the course was a week—after which one was ready to practice. The man healer gave me as the name of the *business* manager of the C.S. publication department (including the book "Science and Health" which, however is Mrs Eddy's private property) Joseph Armstrong. 95 Falmouth St. Boston. The woman healer told Harmony (with a tone of satisfaction) that Mrs Eddy was very rich; also, that she (Mrs Eddy) had herself ceased from the active work of healing, turning it all over to her disciples, and had "returned to the Father." She lives in a fine house—in Concord. N.H. Of course, there is an immense sum of C.S. money handled by somebody in Boston and in other places. By the way the woman healer told Harmony that she supposed that the Boston C.S. treasury afforded assistance in C.S. Church building in other parts of the country.

That seems to be about all I have to impart as the result of my inquiries so far. What more I may find out I will communicate. If I get hold of any publication that seems informing I will send it to you.

When Harmony read your first question to the woman healer, she answered "Oh, the dear heart! he would *want* to join it, if he was here."

Mark, have you read "Science and Health"?[5] and do you get hold of its idea? I have been wrestling with it, and I confess it throws me. Yet, by the powers, I can't quite think that it is for lack of intelligence on my part. These healers I have been seeing lately seem to me people of a distinctly inferior type, but they understand it. Poor Hapgood, my neighbor, is in an ever crowing state of delight in it; but being under sentence of death he would naturally clutch at any straw floating his way,—as I would, probably, were I in his place. However, I didn't mean to express myself on the subject at-all.

Since I last wrote to you Harmony and I have been to South Carolina to see Dave, and a very delightful visit of three days with him and his comrades we had. My, but how it did bring back the things of thirty five years ago to me! The old Army of the Potomac came right up out of its grave, as I strolled about the camp or watched Dave performing in his military figure as adjutant.[6] The lad takes to soldiering naturally, and having West Pointers for his superior officers i.e. in the case of two of them, he is getting a competent training in the business so far as it goes. The ratification of the peace, will however, end his regiments [*sic*] term of service, and we expect him home before long.[7] Then we shall know what he will do next. We suppose that he can get a commission in the regular army if he wants to. Speaking of West Point—I was in New York a short time since at a banquet of the Loyal Legion, and there I met a number of elderly officers who spoke to me of our being at the Point together years ago.[8] I was called up and made a little speech that went off pretty well. The Army and Navy journal afterward spoke of it in agreeable terms; and *explained,*—or seemed to—my happy faculty &c *by my well-known relation to you*—credited you with it. And that is all the while happening.

Before I forget—I had a letter the other day from a minister named Charles J. Hill of Orange, Va, in which he said, "when you see Mr. Clemens please tell him all the donkey boys of Cairo say 'You know Markü Twain—me his donkey boy—me run up Pyramid for him!' He must have kept all Cairo busy[.]"

Another thing before I forget: A Hartford man, Mr. [Philander C.] Royce,—vice Pres. of the Hartford Fire Ins. Co—came to me and asked me to give his daughter who was going abroad an introduction to you. Of course I wouldn't do it. I told him that your family was at present not in society. But I further told him that if[,] when he knew what his daughter's address in Vienna would be, he would give it to me I would send it to you, so that you could call on her if circumstances permitted. But I havn't yet heard from him about it. However, I flatter myself I put you in the way of escaping that young woman. She is nice enough, though, and has just graduated from Smith College. But you can see that her folks are not posted in the ways of the nobility.

The Monday Evening Club has been pretty interesting this winter. I enclose a couple of its notices that I find lying about to show you what fields we have been exploring. Harmony and I went down to call on dear old Franklin a short time since and passed an hour with him most pleasantly. His legs don't serve him well yet, but other wise he seemed all right.[9]

Young Harmony is pursuing her hospital work in a mind of perfect content—and hard work it is. She is now a week on in a two month's tour of night duty, her hours in which are from 8 P.M. to 7 A.M. Sometimes she runs home to breakfast and then back to bed.—did so last Sunday morning, and looked fresh as a rose. She has gained over 10 lbs in weight since she entered the hospital in Oct. I meet no young [person] who has the appearance of a tranquil mind more marked in her countenance than she. Really she seems to be out of all the fret and stew of life, and is immensely interested in what she is doing.

And how are all of you? I came pretty near writing Livy a letter one day not long since, while undergoing a sharp attack of friendly, brotherly, pastoral affection for her. But somehow I got called off. I shall have another attack soon, however—the malady is with me all the time—and then there's no telling what I shall do. My love to her and to the girls.

Yrs ever aff.

Joe

1. The spoons bore a picture of Mrs. Eddy with, on the obverse, the motto, "Not matter but Mind satisfieth." The spoons cost three dollars; five dollars for the gold-plated version. Eddy wrote in the February 1899 issue of the *Christian Science Journal*, "On each of these most beautiful spoons is a motto in basrelief [*sic*], that every person on earth needs to hold in thought. Mother requests that Christian Scientists shall not ask to be informed what this motto is, but each Scientist shall purchase at least one spoon, and those who can afford it, one dozen spoons, that their families may read this motto at every meal, and their guests be made partakers of its simple truth." Twain refers to the spoons in chapter 7 of *Christian Science*.

2. Twichell probably offers this clipping in the spirit of male-to-male banter, given the connection between the motto imprinted on the spoon and the potential double meaning of "human conception."

3. These two letters are filed separately in the Mark Twain Papers (that is, they are not in the folder containing Twichell's current letter).

4. Architect Melvin H. Hapgood, who died on 4 July 1899. This cremation may well have been a favor for a friend and parishioner, rather than a usual practice. In his 17 January 1899 journal entry, Twichell reports on he and Harmony taking the body of an infant to Boston for cremation, the child of parishioner "MHH": "A queer errand and an experience not agreeable."

5. *Science and Health with Key to the Scriptures,* Mary Baker Eddy's foundational account of the system of healing she named Christian Science, was published in 1875.

6. Twichell served as a chaplain in the Army of the Potomac during the Civil War. See Peter Messent and Steve Courtney, eds., *The Civil War Letters of Joseph Hopkins Twichell: A Chaplain's Story* (Athens: University of Georgia Press, 2006).

7. The Treaty of Paris ending the Spanish-American War was ratified by both countries on 11 April.

8. The Military Order of the Loyal Legion of the United States was a prominent veterans' organization.

9. William B. Franklin was by now retired from the Colt's Fire Arms Manufacturing Company.

156. Twain to Twichell

22 and 23 March 1899. Budapest, Hungary (Two typed transcripts by Albert Bigelow Paine)

Mch 22.

The "set" portion of a speech which I expect to make to-morrow night at the banquet in Budapest in celebration of the jubilee of the emancipation of the Hungarian press.[1] A touch of politics will be proper, as the Government (Liberal) will be present, also many Liberal Members of Parliament.

I lecture the 25th

Mark.

[Typed on the back of this note:]

I hold it a high privilege to be permitted to assist in celebrating the anniversary of that great birth, the liberty of the Hungarian press—that rich possession, that possession which, with freedom in politics and toleration in things spiritual, makes the strength of the modern State, insures its moral and material progress, and safeguards its march toward political greatness and an honored place in the respect of the world. And you have the right and true liberty of the press: liberty without license; liberty with dignity; liberty to lash wrong-doing, but not the license to imitate it. It is an invaluable possession for any country, and may its one-thousandth anniversary be celebrated some day by your posterity and mine!!

And you have ideal toleration. They tell me that the Mohammedan pilgrim may come to this fair region out of the remotenesses of Asia and unmolested pray at the tomb of a saint of his faith who wrought in the Prophet's cause in that long-vanished time when the Turk was master here. It seems a strange thing, and beautiful, to find this large spirit here, so near to the ancient homes of Oriental intolerance and despotism that the breeze that refreshes your afternoon has visited them in the morning. One cannot overestimate its value, this ideal toleration, and I hope that when your posterity and mine shall gather here to celebrate the thousandth anniversary of the emancipation of the Hungarian press, the descendant of that Mohammedan pilgrim of to-day may be found praying unmolested at the tomb of his ancestral saint in the inviolable shelter of your magnanimous laws.

[Enclosed:]

Grand Hotel Hungaria
Budapest, March 23/99.

Dear Joe:

It was a curious experience to-night, I didn't make that speech, after all. When I got on my feet I got to talking with interest on a text dropped by the introducer, & I had a very good time; but when I got down to my "set" speech it had wholly disappeared out of my memory; so I stumbled through the opening sentences, then abandoned it & dropped back into the safer & more comfortable impromptu business. I think I will never embarrass myself with a set speech again. My memory is old & rickety & cannot stand the strain.

But I had this luck. What I did say furnished a text for a part of a splendid speech which was made by the greatest living orator of the European world—a speech which it was a keen delight to listen to, although I did not understand any word of it, it being in Hungarian.[2]

I was glad I came. It was a great night, & I heard all the great men in the Government talk.

[Signature cut off.]

1. Twain had been invited to Budapest (where he and the family stayed for a week) by the Hungarian Journalists' Association.

2. The orator is unidentified, but may have been the chairman of the event, Jenő Rákosi, the prominent conservative editor of the daily *Budapesti Hírlap,* who was also a playwright. Carl Dolmetsch in *Our Famous Guest: Mark Twain in Vienna* (Athens: University of Georgia Press, 1992) speaks of this Budapest visit in some detail (51–58).

157. Twichell to Twain

8 April 1899. Hartford, Connecticut

[Clipping from the Christian Science Sentinel *enclosed:]*

The value of Christian Science must be recognized by the world. By large fees given to doctor or lawyer people express their confidence. When Science does for them what all doctors have failed to do they show their gratitude if the Christ-spirit be there. But if that "Son of Peace" be not there they must not be allowed to preserve the mendicant spirit and get without giving in return; they must be caused to estimate the value of the help given and manifest their recognition of value in the way they would express it to others. To undervalue truth is to make it second; then Mammon is the God.

It is possible to see why a fee of three hundred dollars was required at the Massachusetts Metaphysical College. This demand was made under Truth's guidance by the teacher for a two weeks' course. No such fee was ever asked by university or college for so short a course. Only those who could rightly estimate values would be ready to pay it. They who did receive the teaching felt the fee to be as nothing to the value received. Those objecting were not ready for the truth given for they could not appreciate its value.

[Under the clipping, Twichell has written:]
(From an address or lecture by —— McKenzie at Lawrence, Mass. Nov. 1898)[1]

Hartford. Apr. 8. 1899

Dear Mark:

Your deliciously strong expressions regarding the financial phase of Christian Science, give relief to my feelings. I am thereby reminded of what I heard Lt. Col. Huntington "the hero of Guantanamo," say, at a meeting of the Loyal Legion in New York a few weeks ago, of his Cuban allies in the great fight he made last summer.[2] He spoke well of them; they were not bad soldiers at-all: but they were rather poor shots: what they lacked in marksmanship, however, they made up by an unparalleled volubility of invective—"Oh! *beautifully* obscene" he remarked in parenthesis.

Your language is not obscene, but it hath a pungent smell, suitable to the theme, and to my sentiments. It is certainly the fact,—and there can be no mistake about it,—Christian Science is yielding a rich pecuniary harvest to somebody. And you see by the above extract and enclosure how unblushingly that feature of it is handled before the public. Did you notice that communication about the *spoon* in the paper I sent you?

The question is—How long will it last? As to that, I am so happy as not to share your foreboding. I think it will have its day—*is* having it—but is destined—like many another such thing—to subside and pass away. Its principal field of prevalence is a certain *susceptible* class of people in all communities, embracing very few of trained intelligence or of natural balance. You can tell to begin with who they are that will *not* take any stock in it. It is the poor sick folk, of course, and their friends and families that have the most of an ear to hear it. There is a neighbor of ours, for instance, who has an internal cancer—a *hard* cancer,—the worst kind,—utterly incurable. And the way the Christian Science healers are fooling and bleeding that fellow is pitiful to see. They assure him that he is going to get well, and he believes it, but the cancer travels right on and he suffers horribly. He may, indeed, live a good while, as the victims of cancer often do, but he is a dying man, and (what makes me feel badly) he can't afford the money he is paying these people whose dupe he is—but they are dupes, too, I suppose. It is not surprising, to be sure that a desperate man should catch at any straw,—very likely I should do it myself—but it would be better for him to face his realities and meet them like a Christian—*without* the Scientist. No, Mark, your dark prophecy of the predestined dominion of Mother Eddy over the Protestant world (which is the Anglo-Saxon world) will not, in my judgment be fulfilled.

By the way have you seen a book by a Frenchman, Edmond Demolins, entitled "Anglo-Saxon Superiority: to what is it due?"[3] I am just reading it and find it hugely interesting.

I'm rather sorry you bolted the track on that set Budapest speech which I thought mighty strong and good.—though, of course, it's [*sic*] impromptu substitute may have been better. Did you speak in German?

The news is nothing very important. Dave is home again, in the finest possible condition, and is well content for the present to exchange military duty for the study of bacteriology. He probably could get a commission in the regular army if he wanted to, but I doubt if he will conclude to follow soldiering.

Young Harmony was gratified with your warm and kind approval of her choice of a profession. I wish you might see her. She is quite out of "the world" [of Hartford society], but her face reflects a peace and tranquillity that tea-parties do not impart. Sally and Molly Dunham are both better, though invalids still. Charley and Susy Warner have both been on a visit to Isa at Norfolk, and are apparently deeper in her toils than ever. Charley has finished a new novel—a sequel to the other two—which will soon be published.[4]

I judge from samples of the work at the stage now reached that the uniform edition of your books which Bliss is getting up will be very fine—paper, print, binding, illustrations, every thing.[5]

Come, Mark, when *are* you going to return to us? I am continually asked the question. You surely *can't* have any home but Hartford. Now that Spring weather is here I am affected with a new longing for you all. With love unbounded to Livy and the girls;

Yours ever

Joe

1. William P. McKenzie was a Scottish-American poet and university instructor who withdrew from the Presbyterian ministry and became a Christian Scientist and friend and protégé of Eddy.

2. In June 1898, Lieutenant Colonel Robert W. Huntington and his small First Marine

Battalion (with the support of Cuban patriots) took Guantanamo, Cuba, from a massively superior Spanish force.

3. Published in translation by R. F. Fenno (New York) in 1898 and a book of some renown. In this, one of an increasing number of books about racial degeneration, Demolins celebrated Anglo-Saxon individualism and its contrast to Celtic and Norman racial traits.

4. *That Fortune* (1899) was the last novel in a trilogy—following *A Little Journey in the World* (1889) and *The Golden House* (1895). All three satirized the Gilded Age that Warner and Twain had written about (and to which they had given a name) in 1873.

5. Frank Bliss's American Publishing Company would publish a Uniform Edition of Twain's works in 1899. The history of the various Uniform Editions is a complicated one due to copyright differences between the American Publishing Company and Harper's (Twain's publisher in later years).

158. Twain to Twichell

May 1899. Vienna, Austria

*[The letter begins with a printed invitation to Twain on headed notepaper from the Vienna-based "*COMITÉ FÜR KUNDGEBUNGEN ZUR FRIEDENSCONFERENZ*" (Committee for Announcements concerning the Peace Conference). The sender of this invitation was a member of the committee (all of whose names are printed on the letterhead), longtime peace campaigner Bertha von Suttner. The invitation reads (in translation), "It would be of great satisfaction to our committee and an especial pleasure to me personally if you would honor our meeting, whose results will be reported at the Hague, with your presence. This invitation entitles you to one of the places reserved for our guests of honor."[1] Twain writes below this:]*

Dear Joe:

I reckon the Peace Society must be feeling just a little sick, these days. I don't see how a bright, dear, earnest creature like Bertha von Suttner can *stand* the situation the ridiculous Tsar has put it into. I *used* to attend the Society's meetings here, although I was not interested, but it is no place *at all* for me now.[2]

Business calls me to London indefinitely; so the family have decided to go along. We leave here in a couple of weeks, stopping a day or so in Prague, the same in Dresden, a night in Bremen & go to Southampton next day per s. s. "Lahn," & thence to London.[3] The salt water will smell heavenly to me after this long privation.

Address from now on:

(Care Chatto & Windus
111 St. Martin's Lane WC.)

Love to you all
Sincerely Yours
Mark.

1. Many thanks to Elizabeth Boa (University of Nottingham) for her help with the translation.

2. Czar Nicholas II of Russia had initiated the Hague Peace Conference (which opened on 18 May 1889) to discuss an arms limitations agreement. Baroness Bertha von Suttner (who would later go on to win the Nobel Peace Prize) was a dedicated antimilitarist and president of the Austrian Peace Society. Twain's comments here may refer to the fact that the czar's initiative was not an act of pacifistic principle but financial pragmatism: the costs of keeping up in an armaments race led by Germany and Great Britain were proving prohibitive.

3. Thus marking the end of the lengthy Vienna residency.

159. Twain to Twichell

4 May 1899. Vienna, Austria (Two typed transcripts by Albert Bigelow Paine)

HOTEL KRANTZ WIEN, 1. NEUER MARKT 6
May 4/99.

Dear Joe:

I have at last finished the Christian Science article & it has gone to be type-written. Somehow I continue to feel sure of that cult's colossal future. You must remember that the human race is made up almost exclusively of people wholly destitute of anything really resembling a thinking-equipment, & that of the scattering few who have it hardly two in a million ever use it. This is not an extravagance of speech, but a cold calm fact. The Science has pirated the one feature which has kept Romanism alive & strong all the centuries—the money-lust & money-grubbing—& has added some taking things that will make for perpetuity. Among them a fresh new god to worship. That seems to me to be a mighty good asset, & that it will be a still better one when that old cow dies & her bones begin to work miracles, in presence of trains of pilgrims.[1] I would rather own her burial lot than the bank of England. Lourdes isn't going to stand any chance against her. I am selling my Lourdes stock already & buying Christian Science Trust. I regard it as the Standard Oil of the future. We are always vaporing about "human intelligence." Oh, Joe, let us humble ourselves & damn that silly phrase—a phrase which stands for an almost non-existing thing.

How lucky! the scrap which Livy made me snip out of a letter to John

Hay will come in here, ever so handy (& Livy is not by, this time, to meddle.)[2]

Yes, we are coming home in the fall.

With lots of love to you all,

Mark.

1. Mary Baker Eddy.
2. Enclosure missing.

160. Twain to Twichell

1 June 1899. London, England

TELEGRAPHIC ADDRESS 'BOOKSTORE, LONDON'

111 ST. MARTIN'S LANE LONDON, W.C. June 1 1899.

Dear Joe:

We arrived last evening after a journey of several days. Livy concluded she wouldn't split the last stage in two, but make a single bite of it—& a bite it was! All the way from Cologne to London—from 6 a.m [*sic*] till 7.30 p.m., & 4 customhouses to dig through. She is well fagged out. So am I.

I'll not try to write any more, but will enclose a very nice letter from Professor Peirce [*sic*], of Harvard.[1]

Love to you all.

Mark.

1. Possibly George W. Pierce, a physicist later involved in the development of radio.

161. Twain to Twichell

3 July 1899. London, England (Mourning border)

Address: (Chatto & Windus).

London, July 3/99.

Dear Joe:

Only a line, to say we are leaving for Sweden four days hence to be gone 3 months.[1] I have done no work since we have been in London, but I was not intending to do any. It was my purpose to take a holiday, & I have carried it out.

But shucks! there is no use in writing this—it will reach Hartford just after you have left. It is altogether too bad, too bad!—we shan't meet in London. I think it's a shame & a pity.[2]

Let me see. You are due to arrive here the 26th. So I'll send this line anyhow—there's time to catch you, maybe. I will not put much in it, but will make Clara copy a note I have been writing to Canon Wilberforce,—that will fill up. He left a luncheon-party this afternoon ½ hour ahead of the rest, & carried off my hat. When I left, there was but one hat that would go on my head; it had no name in it, but it fitted exactly & I took it. I couldn't *know* he took mine, but the circumstantial evidence was very strong, so this evening I wrote him a note. I had just finished it when a note arrived from him—which I enclose. You notice how nicely we compliment each other. A most lovely man, & the handsomest in England, I think.[3]

Come to Sweden! Chatto can tell you the road & how to find us.

We all send no end of love.

Mark

1. The family were on the way to Sweden to Henrik Kellgren's Sanna Institute for Jean to get treatment for her epilepsy (she had been diagnosed in late 1896). Kellgren was a Swedish practitioner of remedial gymnastics and massage—a type of osteopathy.

2. The Twichells were on their way to London on vacation. In fact, Twichell and his wife actually got into London just before Twain and Livy left, but, to Twain's evident frustration, they failed to make contact.

3. For more on what became an ongoing joke between Twain and Basil Wilberforce, canon of Westminster, see Twain's letter to William Dean Howells of 19 October 1899. Henry Nash Smith and William M. Gibson, *Mark Twain–Howells Letters: The Correspondence of Samuel L. Clemens and William D. Howells, 1872–1910* (Cambridge, Mass.: Belknap Press, 1960), 709.

162. Twichell to Twain

19 August 1899. Antwerp, Holland

Antwerp Aug. 19th.

Dear Mark:

I have not written to you of late for the reasons;

First, that being away from the base of those news and observations that have hitherto afforded the staple of my communications to you, I have had nothing to say;

Second; that the pace set by my Chicago friend, with whom I am obliged to keep up, has left me no time for pleasure.[1] Half an hour to a cathedral, and twenty minutes to an abbey are all he allows, for examples; and Im [*sic*] blest if we have had a single rainy day since we landed in Southampton July 5 to enable us to rest our poor feet.

Third; I have been writing to let you know when we were going to start for home; according to Livy's request in her letter to Harmony. That point has not been settled till now. We sail from Southampton Sept. 23rd; and, I suppose, shall spend the two days preceding in London. However, we have no thought of seeing any of you there, unless it should happen that business called you (Mark) there at that time. It broke our hearts to be disappointed of seeing you and Livy once more while we are still young; but the bitterness of that grief is now over. We have become reconciled to what to begin with seemed an intolerable reward of fate, and just cause for new doubts respecting the principles on which the universe is governed, which we had always believed were humane if you got far enough back into the machinery. Which is to say that we found ourselves cruelly frustrated in regard of a chief object of our coming aboard at-all, and hence, naturally, inferred that the whole world was out of joint. It was so for us, anyhow. What was left us was to hope most earnestly that the result of your going to Sweden would be Jean's better health. That, indeed, would bring things right again. Dear Jean; dear child! You and Livy may be sure that we thought more about *her* in the case than about ourselves, and if we may hear that Sweden has helped her we shall be quite content and thankful that you took her thither.

In spite of our hard work we have really enjoyed much on this trip. Our boss is the best natured fellow alive and does everything for us that he can devise.

Our Tramp Abroad, though, remains the incomparable and unapproachable vacation of all my experience. Oh, *what* a splendid outing that was!

The word we get from home is all favorable so far. The family is scattered but every member seems to be in clover—except for Judy, whose husband continues in invalid condition.[2]

We learn that Sally and Molly Dunham are both much better than when we left. That dupe of the Christian Scientists died in July. When they saw him going the C.S.'s forsook him abruptly.

Isa is now visiting the Warners.

In Edinburgh we received much kindness and furtherance from Mr. David Douglas, to whom I bore a note of introduction from Dean Sage.[3]

By the way Dean's health is greatly improved. He is somewhere in these countries, having come over with Col. Payne of N.Y. in his yacht "Aphrodite."[4]

We go hence to the Hague, then to Milan, the Tyrol, Venice perhaps—and I don't know where else. Prof. Fiske wrote asking us to Florence, if we were able to await his return thither, which we are not.[5] He said he meant to see you in Sweden.

Our old friend Dawson (you remember him,[)] I guess has passed away. Harmony is right well, and looks for another letter from Livy—whom her soul loveth. This isn't a letter, Mark, and don't pretend to be; but I simply *can't* write under present circumstances i.e. in the smoking room of a hotel.

Minister Choate, in London, spoke with warm interest of meeting you, and of a very successful speech he heard you make.[6]

We saw the Americans beaten in the athletic contest with the English collegians, but not badly.[7] We had no expectation of a different result, and wondered that our fellows did so well.

Good bye, for now, and peace be with you.

Oh, young Harmony writes that she thinks that Miss Kenealy's making up to you on the strength of their acquaintance was a "cheeky" thing.[8] And we think so too. Didn't you?

Yours ever aff.

Joe

Address as hitherto
Union Bank of London.

1. Albert A. Sprague (see Letter 126, note 2) had invited the Twichells along on this trip.

2. Twichell had reported Howard Ogden Wood's "trouble in his head—pain with vertigo" in his journal for January 1896. He again mentioned his worries about Wood's health in his 13–14 March entry.

3. Douglas was Sage's United Kingdom publisher for his book, *The Ristigouche and Its Salmon Fishing.*

4. Wealthy businessman Oliver H. Payne, one of the principal owners of Standard Oil but with major interests in other businesses too.

5. Daniel Willard Fiske of Cornell now lived in Florence.

6. Jurist Joseph H. Choate had recently been appointed U.S. ambassador to the United Kingdom.

7. In the summer of 1899 a Harvard and Yale track team were narrowly beaten (5–4) by Oxford and Cambridge Universities in what has now become the oldest continuing international intercollegiate competition in the world.

8. Apparently a friend of daughter Harmony.

163. Twain to Twichell

20 August 1899. Sanna, Sweden (Two typed transcripts by Albert Bigelow Paine)

Private[1]

Sanna, Rosendala, Sweden, Aug. 20/99.

Dear Joe:

The first of the Christian Science articles merely ridiculed the cult. I have sent it for print, but shall not use the others at present. Curiously enough this Swedish Gymnastic Cure is like that fraud in one way: it uses no medicines. Has used none since Kellgren invented it 35 years ago. Joe, you ought to come & see it—there isn't a curiosity in Europe that is its equal, for solid interest. I wish young Harmony & Daisy Warner were pupils. Few sick people take a chance in it until they have been condemned to death by a convincing procession of high-priced medical experts & there's nothing left but this or the undertaker. We took our chance in it on those terms; there was nothing left; the specialists had loaded Jean to the eyes with poisons, & in 3 years had done her not the least good, nor ever even claimed that they could.[2] Kellgren was the first man who said he could cure her. He said it without hesitation. We didn't believe it, but you may imagine that the words sounded good, anyway—they naturally would, to ears so weary of the other talk. And then Kellgren is no ignorant Christian Science village school marm out of a job, but a man whose countenance & ways compel respect at once; a man who knows the human machinery as minutely as does any anatomist that lives, & knows its *real* functions *better* than any anatomist or doctor that lives. And you presently come to recognize in him a commanding genius.

This family always carried a drug-store around, & were always calling doctors & taking medicines—often with pretty poor results. Up to July 11, Jean had taken 2 doses of bromide every day for the previous 18 months,—frequently 3, less frequently 4, on two occasions 5, & on three occasions 6,—a grand total of 1300 doses of poison. The doctors didn't allow her to venture a day without the protection of 2 doses. When we arrived here & Kellgren a stranger said he could not touch the case if she took another dose of medicine of any kind, of course we were in deep fear & dread—we did not know what might happen. Livy smuggled two doses into Jean the 11th, the day before she was to begin; then we held our breath & stood from under. We got a couple of earthquakes, so to speak, within the next fortnight, but Kellgren was not troubled; he said, "It's all right—keep your grip."

Since then we have had peace & comfort—the first in three years. Steady peace & comfort for 21 days. We shall have some more frights, but they will be light. And by & by Jean will be cured. That, I quite believe.

Every day we see the marvels that this system does. And now that we comprehend that it isn't jugglery but it is thoroughly scientific we are ceasing to marvel at the marvels. They are the results that *should* follow. They are explicable. They follow law; whereas all the other healing methods are partly law & almost mainly guess work.

Kellgren will take a chance at any ailment known to man, except surgical cases where the knife must be used, & dentistry. You understand, a limb which is a wreck of compound fractures, & swollen & black with polluted blood, is in the surgeon's line—& he will amputate. That kind of a limb is in Kellgren's line, too, but he will save it & will make it sound & good.

Livy can't abide the idea of seeing one of us go into Kellgren's hands with typhoid, diphtheria, plague, cholera, scarlet fever, or such like thing, with a temperature at 104 & no ice, no medicines, no anything but that man's two hands—the thought makes her shudder. But if I were the patient I would warn off the most illustrious practitioner in the world, & would allow none to take charge of my life but Kellgren.

It makes me sick, the prospect of having to go back to doctors & medicines again, after these weeks of emancipation. My ever-recurring curse since '93 has been racking & exasperating bronchial coughs, which stay by me 5 or 6 weeks without amelioration, in spite of the medicines—stay till they wear themselves—& me—out. That kind of a cough is merely a plaything for Kellgren; he cures it in four days, with a ten-minute manipulation per day, & in the four days he does not allow it to cost me half an hour's inconvenience or discomfort. Dysentery is another amusement for him. In fact an acute attack of any breed of disease disappears under his hands like enchantment.

It is too bad that we are to miss you again. Of course if it were not for Jean we should break up & go in time to see you; but we must stay here till the last moment (Sept. 28) on her account. I shall mark this letter Private—on account of Jean & her case.

With my deepest love to you both

Mark.

1. An insertion.
2. Jean had been taking bromides—known for their extreme toxicity and used in treating epilepsy from 1857. See *Mark Twain's Correspondence with Henry Huttleston Rogers*, 407n3.

164. Twain to Twichell

22 August 1899. Sanna, Sweden (Two typed transcripts by Albert Bigelow Paine)

P.S.

Sanna, Rosendala,
Sweden, Aug. 22/99.

Dear Joe—

Do the doctors say they can help Judy's husband? Then Kellgren can help him five times as much & ten or twenty or thirty times as speedily. Do they say he is *past* help? Their testimony is of no value—at least of very little value—being based upon vast accumulations of ignorance, with here & there a grain of knowledge. And so, no matter what they say, he ought to be taken to London & put into Kellgren's hands. Don't you doubt it for a moment. Upon my honor I think the regular physician is very nearly on a level with the Christian Scientist when it is a question of ignorance & quackery.

We remain here till Kellgren returns to London for the winter—the end of September.

His place is

49 Eaton Square, S.W.
London.

It isn't Dr. Kellgren nor Professor Kellgren, but Mister Kellgren—or Director; for he directs his assistants. He does not possess the State's license to add to the ills of the sick & the suffering.

Private. The way Jean goes on thriving is clear beyond imagination. (*Unberufen*!)[1] Six weeks ago I should have said "This is a miracle." I have learned more, now, & I recognize that there is no miracle about it. It is merely the natural result of natural laws applied by a man who *knows* those laws, (& can explain it so that *you* can see & know.) The system is wholly *scientific*—& the only system of healing that is not empirical & confessedly so. No, these are not miracles, but the results of laws as arbitrary as addition & subtraction: a simple case of 2 & 2—the result is 4, always, & no other result is possible.

Mark.

The assistants here have taken the full college course in anatomy, physiology &c; also 2 years in a London hospital; then 3 years under Kellgren learning his system & how to apply it—7 or 8 years altogether; then they are competent, & ready for business.

Everything is thorough; no Christian Science silliness.

1. Literally, "Let it not be called down upon me," but the meaning of this German expression (which Twain used frequently) is closer to the English "Touch wood!"

165. Twichell to Twain

1 September 1899. Venice, Italy

Grand Hotel
Venice Sept 1. 1899

Dear Mark:

Your glowing letter concerning Dr. Kellgren, with its following P.S., overtook us last week at the Hague. They shall be private, as you direct, except in the case of Judy and her sick husband (whom we understand *you* to except.) I would also much like to show them to one or two medical men of my acquaintance. But I will not do it without your consent; and there will be plenty of time for you to exclude Judy too if you would rather.

The hope and confidence into which you are uplifted of our sweet niece's restoration to sound health make us exceedingly glad with and for you. The relief thereof must be unimaginable. The ways have darkened around you and Livy these last years, and we are thankful that through one black cloud you see the sun shining. This we know—that we have learned to love you in your troubles with an affection otherwise impossible; and so must all other old friends; and to be greatly loved is a principal element of well-being in this world—as I look at it.

I have had many thoughts of you lately. Not that I don't always have;—but on our way from Amsterdam to Milan by the St. Gothard Tunnel route, passing through the Swiss magnificences below Lucerne, I seemed ever and anon to see you and me swinging along those glorious Alpine roads, staring at the new unfoldings of splendor that every turn brought into view—talking, talking, endlessly talking the days through;—days forever memorable to me. That was twenty one years ago! Think of it! We were youngsters then, Mark; and how keen our relish of every thing was! Well, I can enjoy myself now; but not with that zest and rapture. Oh, a lot of items of our tramp travel in 1878 that I had long forgotten came back to me, as we sped through that enchanted region;—and if I wasn't on duty with Venice I'd stop and set down some of them. But Venice *must* be attended to. For one thing, there is Howells' book to be read at such intervals as can be snatched from the quick time march on which our rustling leader keeps us.[1] He is the most amiable and generous of mortals, but is one of those unhappy people whom a pause seems to affect with a sense of something like suffocation. However in Venice, so far, we want to be gazing pretty steadily from morning to night. And by grace of the gondola we can do it without exhaustion. Really I am drunk with Venice. All impressions I had of it unseen, derived from pictures, books and talk were much further below the reality than in any other instance hitherto. We shall bide here till the middle of next week, then maybe hark back to Switzerland and hang around there till it is time to go to England to take ship on the 23rd inst. Perhaps though we shall quit the continent a few—*very* few—days earlier in order to pay a visit—as we have been urgently invited to do—to the Hawleys at Mrs. H's ancestral place in Essex.[2] We have, of course, since your letter gave the date of your return to London, quite given up the thought of seeing you; and count ourselves fortunate that we had that little sight of Clara. Our love to every one of you. Yes, Livy we *would* like to cross over to Sweden and give you and Harmony a soul filling conference; but the fates are dead against it. Mark, I'll write you a letter when I get home. Can't till then.

Yrs aff.

Joe

1. William Dean Howells had published his *Venetian Life* in 1866.

2. General Joseph Hawley's second wife, Edith Horner, was from Essex and the family were evidently resident there at this time.

166. Twain to Twichell

6 September 1899. Sanna, Sweden

Sanna, Sept. 6/99.

Dear Joe—

I've no business in here—I ought to be outside. I shall never see another sunset to begin with it this side of heaven. Venice? land, what a poor interest that is! This is the place to be. I have seen about 60 sunsets here; & a good 40 of them were clear & away beyond anything I had ever imagined before for dainty and exquisite & marvelous beauty & infinite change & variety. America? Italy? the tropics? They have no notion of what a sunset ought to be. And this one—this unspeakable wonder! It discounts all the rest. It brings the tears, it is so unutterably beautiful.

If I had time, I would say a word about his curative system here. The people actually *do* several of the great things the Christian Scientist pretends to do. You wish to advise with a *physician* about it? Certainly. There is no objection. He knows next to something about his own trade, but that will not embarrass him in framing a verdict about this one. I respect your superstitions—we all have them. It would be quite natural for the cautious Chinaman to ask his native priest to instruct him as to the value of the new religious specialty which the Western missionary is trying to put on the market, before investing in it. [He would get a verdict.][1] Love to you both!

Always yours
Mark

OVER[2]

The system is full of good, simple, common sense. Take a case of peritonitis—with a badly inflamed bladder, swollen with water which it won't give down—child of 5 years, shrieking with the pain. The M.D. would know no way but to have some people hold the struggling child while he used a catheter—& he would lascerate [*sic*] the patient with it nearly every time. These people manipulate two minutes with their hands, & bring the water. Then they teach the mother to do it & the child can have relief whenever it needs it, without having to send at midnight for the M.D. & his torture-machine. This was at a neighbor's the other day.

Jean is as fine as a fiddle. It is fifty-seven days since she has taken a dose of poison of any kind. By George, for 3 years she *lived* on it.

1. This short bracketed remark is an insertion.
2. This word is boxed in by Twain, though with a gap in the middle of the bottom line of that box.

167. Twichell to Twain

6 November 1899. Hartford, Connecticut

Hartford. Nov. 6. 1899.

Dear Mark,

Just cast your eye over the enclosed clipping.[1] Now look here, old fellow; when you come home you will be *obliged* to go to Church—evidently you will—to save me in the public estimation. It will be rough on you but you will have to stand it. But our music is fine now, every body says, and that will lighten the hardship. The first Sunday I shall expect to see somebody crawling up the aisle with a kodak [*sic*] to take a shot at you in the act, a series of shots: 1st Sitting, 2nd Standing and Singing, 3rd Listening to the sermon, 4th Sleeping &c &c.[2]

By the way the new Church opposite your house was dedicated last week.[3] It is inveigling away some of our parishoners, as was to be expected, but it wont [*sic*] capture Livy and you, I know.

Well here we are again, Harmony and I, on our old beat, working away at our same old round of duties—our summer play-spell sinking into distance and silence behind us—and we like it.[4] Yet our vacation was hugely pleasurable. Had it included a visit with you all, it would have been ever so much more a success; in fact, the best we ever had together. But we were unprecedentedly glad to arrive in Hartford and at our own door again. We had more to return *to* than ever before. It grieves us still that we missed meeting you and Livy; we can't get over it; it was a mitigation though, for which we were and are thankful, that we had a taste—a little one—a nibble—of Clara.

Your letters from Rosendale were quite the most interesting reading of the season.[5] We are eagerly waiting for more. We took unmeasured comfort in your report of Jean's betterment, and joined our hopes for the dear child to yours. The things you had to tell of Kellgren were exceedingly impressive. We wondered that the fame of him wasn't universal by this time. Must it be that *all* gospels gain ground slowly?

We did not, as you advised, consult 49 Eaton Square about Judy's husband when we got back to London, for the simple reason that we did not know at-all how to *state his case*, being ourselves greatly in the dark as to what ails him.[6] It has finally been decided, so far as we can gather, that the trouble with him is an abnormal thickening of the bone of the skull—the effect of a blow—and a consequent pressure on the brain—distinctly a case for surgery; and he is now undergoing a protracted, bit by bit, surgical operation for it, at Rochester.—though just at this present he and Judy are taking a rest between times at the Plaza Hotel in New York; after which they will return to Rochester for another turn of mallet and chisel, the access to the field of operation being through the nose. While she is in New York Judy's children are quartered on us to our great delectation. They are thoroughly agreeable kids to have in the house, overflowing with life, but good as pie. They bring back the days of our youth to us. I have no "realizing sense" in the least of *who they are.*[7] I think I will send Livy a picture of 'em one of these days i.e. if I can get hold of one.

Gracious, *what* a situation in South Africa![8] I re-read Saturday night the Boer chapter in your book. The proportion of losses on the Boer and English sides respectively that has marked previous collisions, seems to characterize the fight now on, to date. Those Dutchmen clearly know their game and they are playing it to admiration, though it *must be* they will be beaten in the event, and had better be I suppose. They are deserving and winning respect, though, which, it seems to me, will bear good results in the issue.

I hear frequent expressions, from competent sources, of praise of your Christian Science article, both of its literary skill and of its serious value.[9] Some judge it the best thing you ever did. When is the rest coming?

I attended, as guest, last week a banquet of the "Harrison Veteran Association" here in Hartford. Said Asso. is composed of men who voted for the first Pres. Harrison.[10] There were about forty at table and they averaged *eighty five* years in age. When it was formed—eleven years ago—it had 150 members; only 60 of whom are now living. It was comical to hear the old fellows chuckle over the fact that they had *survived.* Dr. Gatling presided (was there ever a more left-handed man in that function?) and he wanted me to be sure and give you his best regards.[11]

Dear old Franklin, I am sorry to say, seems to be breaking up, both physically and mentally. I havn't been to see him yet, but I am going, though I shrink from it. He will never write his book, I infer.

Sally and Molly Dunham are better, especially Molly; Charley Clark is to [be] married next week to his wife's older sister, whom we esteem a fine woman.

Charley Warner seems as well as ever, but says that he doesn't feel strong yet inside. Yet he is *doing* a good deal of work in one way and another.

Dave is in New York in the medical school and is vastly interested in his studies. Young Harmony is serenely content with her present way of life—though it is ever severely laborious. She is now on a two month's tour of night duty—her hours being from 8 oclock [*sic*] P.M. to 7 o'clock A.M. She often comes home to dinner (which is her breakfast) looking always fresh and bright after her day's sleep.

But Goodbye, my boy. Blessings on you all.

Yours ever aff.

Joe

1. Clippings included with this letter in the files kept by the Mark Twain Project include one from the *New York Sun*, 9 October 1899, on lawsuits against Eddy regarding her property, and also a poem, "Americanitis," from an unknown publication, making fun of Christian Science. Twichell only refers to a singular clipping (and one that does not seem easily to match those described here); thus, it is possible that some disarrangement in the filing system has occurred.

2. Kodak's "Brownie" camera, easy to use and affordable, made photography a leisure interest available to most Americans in the 1890s. Twain refers to the transformative power of the Kodak in his 1905 "King Leopold's Soliloquy." See *Collected Tales, Sketches, Speeches, and Essays*, vol. 2, *1891–1910* (New York: Library of America, 1992), 682.

3. The Farmington Avenue Congregational Church, the institutional descendant of several downtown Hartford churches, and later renamed Immanuel Congregational Church.

4. The Twichells had returned from Europe on 2 October.

5. Twain headed some of his letters from Sweden, "Sanna, Rosendale, Sweden."

6. The Swedish Institute, where Kellgren practiced in London, was at 49 Eaton Square.

7. "Realizing sense": a theological and philosophical term used "to express the urgency, warmth, and intimacy of a direct experience in contrast with the remote, pallid, and coldly detached quality of a representative experience." John Dewey, *Democracy and Education*, The Middle Works (1899–1924), vol. 9 (Carbondale: Southern Illinois University Press, 2008), 241.

8. The South African (Boer) War had started on 12 October. The siege of Ladysmith by the Boers commenced on 2 November.

9. *Cosmopolitan* magazine had published Twain's article, "Christian Science and the Book of Mrs. Eddy," in October.

10. William Henry Harrison, sworn in as president on 4 March 1841. He died on 4 April, having served the shortest term of any U.S. president.

11. Dr. Richard Gatling, who patented the Gatling gun and who lived in Hartford (where the Colt's Fire Arms factory manufactured the weapon).

168. Twain to Twichell

21 November 1899. London, England

London, Nov. 21/99.

Dear Joe:

The enclosed is from a very beautiful American woman 34 years old, who was never out of Chicago until she was 16.[1] She knows no language under the sun, but can chatter glibly & fascinatingly in six; & when she is talking she is obliged to draw upon her whole battery, & *does* it; & even then she can seldom pull herself past the middle of a sentence, but finishes it with the cunningest gestures, shrugs, smirks & grimaces, (borrowed from 5 of those nationalities) which sometimes convey her meaning but as a rule they don't—& she finishes with "but *I* ton't care—ain't it? n'est ce pas nicht wahr—oh indeed, yes, *I* ton't care, und I *tell* 'em so! Ain't it?" After an hour of her fireworks you feel dazed, & impotent, & all whirly, & you haven't an idea in the world of what she has been talking about. But she is as good-hearted as she can be, & very decided in her opinions about people, & admirably frank about expressing them. She hates Mme von Dutschka, (1-year widow) & the Countess Barbi [*sic*] (& these 2 hated *each other* every other week in our time in Kaltenleutgeben)—I would I could hear her discourse about them now in her 6 tongues.[2] And about Edelstein & the prince—lovely people, & Mme. Spiridon likes them; still she could discourse about them, & say the charmingest acid things, & I would dearly like to hear her.[3] I've *lost* her richest letter—I was saving it for you.

With love,

Mark.

1. Enclosure now missing, American woman unknown.

2. Madame von Dutschka hosted a Vienna salon. Twain misspells the name of the Countess of Bardi, perhaps thinking of Alice Barbi, a singer who encouraged Clara Clemens in her career. All three women were in the circle of Clara's teacher, Theodor Leschetizky.

3. Mme. Spiridon may well be the wife of painter Ignace Spiridon, who painted portraits of both Twain and his daughter Clara. Edelstein and the prince remain unidentified.

169. Twain to Twichell

1 January 1900. London, England (Mourning border)

New Years Day 1900.
30, WELLINGTON COURT, ALBERT GATE.
—'sh! *Private.*

Dear Joe: Who *is* Miss Elizabeth Alden Curtis?[1] I am afraid it is a relative of Mrs. Ned Bunce. Is it so? Have you read her Omar Khayam—with introduction by Dick Burton?[2] I have not seen such another curiosity since I was born. It is the most detailed & minutely circumstantial plagiarism that has yet been perpetrated in any century. And the author is quite innocent of crime, for it is manifest that she is not aware that she is committing one. And that is strange, for she is not a fool, but intelligent & has poetry in her somewhere. Isn't it an odd idea?—to sit down with a noble poem in front of her & proceed to recast it & degrade it line by line, stanza by stanza, straight through, & guilelessly taking credit to herself all the time for the sacrilege she is committing.[3] It is as if a Tammany Boss should wreck the Taj & then rebuild it after *his* notions of what it ought to be; & should smile around, & be pleased with himself & ask the world to take notice.[4] And should then have the daring to ask an architect of repute to publicly condone—no, praise—the crime. Dick Burton, for instance. And should get his impudent request granted. Indeed Dick, goaded by a generous impulse, & crowded into a corner where he can't help himself, braces up & lies like a hero, discharging eulogies meet for Shakspeare—blushing like sunset, meanwhile, and cursing the luck, under his breath, that compels him to spare the lash here where it is so richly deserved. It took Dick two hours to write that Introduction, & he was in a clean man's hell all the while.

Imagine that author's friends being proud of her strange crime & spreading it around in print. Why Joe, it is as if the organ-monkey should reconstruct the Overture to Tannhäuser & go discording it around town on his hurdy-gurdy happy & unashamed—yes, & the leader of the Metropolitan Opera orchestra following after him rubbing his hands & letting on to be having a hell of a time. Oh, it bangs Banagher.[5] Why, if it were a travesty, all right; but it isn't. It is a serious attempt to rise above Fitzgerald [*sic*] & take his place, or next place below, picking his pocket, meanwhile, of the materials required for the business.[6]

[Unknown amount of text missing.]

1. Elizabeth Alden Curtis, Hartford-born writer, who published her translation of selections from Omar Khayyám in 1899. Committed to the Brattleboro Insane Asylum in 1912, she would later successfully sue her former husband (and two Hartford doctors) for her abduction there.

2. Richard Burton, son of Rev. Nathaniel Burton of Hartford (one of the ministerial trio of Hartford friends: Twichell, Parker, and Burton). Richard Burton was at this point head of the English Department at the University of Minnesota.

3. Deletion of "rape" and insertion of "sacrilege."

4. Tammany was a New York City political organization. Its power was at its peak in the nineteenth century, when its "bosses" became synonymous with corruption. The Taj is the Taj Mahal in India, the story, setting, and construction of which make it perhaps the country's most famous tourist venue.

5. An Anglo-Irish expression meaning "that beats it all."

6. Edward FitzGerald, British author of the *Rubáiyát of Omar Khayyám*. See Letter 28, note 2.

170. Twain to Twichell

8 January 1900. London, England (Typed transcript by Albert Bigelow Paine)

London, Jan. 8, 1900

Dear Joe:

Mental Telegraphy has scored another. Mental Telegraphy will be greatly respected a century hence.[1]

By the accident of writing my sister & describing to her the remarkable cures made by Kellgren with his hands & without drugs, I brought upon myself a quite stunning surprise; for she wrote to me that she had been taking this very treatment in Buffalo—& that it was an *American* invention.[2]

Well, it does really turn out that Dr. Still, in the middle of Kansas, in a village, began to experiment upon this science in 1874, only five years after Kellgren began the same work obscurely in the village of Gotha in Germany.[3] Dr. Still seems to be an honest man; therefore I am persuaded that Kellgren moved him to his experiments by Mental Telegraphy across six hours of longitude, without need of a wire. By the time Still began to experiment, Kellgren had completed his development of the principles of his system & established himself in a good practice in London—1874—& was in good shape to convey his discovery to Kansas, Mental-Telegraphically.

Yes, I was greatly surprised to find that my mare's nest was much in arrears: that this new science was well known in America under the name of Osteopathy. Since then, I find that in the last 3 years it has got itself legalized in 14 States in spite of the opposition of the physicians; that it has established 20 Osteopathic schools & colleges; that among its students are 75 allopathic physicians; that there is a school in Boston & another in Philadelphia, that there are about 700 students in the parent college (Dr. Still's at Kirksville, Missouri,) & that there are about 2,000 graduates *practicing* in America. Dear me, there are not 30 in Europe. Europe is so sunk in superstitions & prejudices that it is an almost impossible thing to get her to do anything but scoff at a new thing—*unless it come from abroad*; as witness the telegraph, dentistry, &c.

Presently the Osteopath will come over here from America & will soon make himself a power that must be recognized & reckoned with; & then, 25 years from now, England will begin to claim the invention & tell all about its origin, in the cyclopedia B— [*Encyclopaedia Britannica*] as in the case of the telegraph, applied anaesthetics & the other benefactions which she urinated upon when her inventors first offered them to her.

I cannot help feeling rather inordinately proud of America for the gay & hearty way in which she takes hold of any new thing that comes along & gives it a first-rate trial. Many an ass in America is getting a deal of benefit out of X^n Science's new exploitation of an age-old healing principle—*faith*, combined with the patient's imagination—let it boom along! I have no objections. Let them call it by what name they choose, so long as it does helpful work among the class which is numerically vastly the largest bulk of the human race, i.e. the fools, the idiots, the puddnheads.

We do not guess, we *know* that 9 in 10 of the species are puddnheads. We know it by various evidences; & one of them is, that for ages the race has respected (& almost venerated) the physician's grotesque system—the emptying of miscellaneous & harmful drugs into a person's stomach to remove ailments which in many cases the drugs could not reach at all; in many cases could reach & help, but only at cost of damage to some other part of the man; & in the remainder of the cases the drugs either retarded the cure or the disease was cured by nature in spite of the nostrums. The doctor's insane system has not only been permitted to continue its follies for ages, but has been protected by the State & made a close monopoly—an infamous thing, a crime against a freeman's proper right to choose his own assassin or his own method of defending his body against disease & death.

And yet at the same time, with curious & servile inconsistency, the State *has* allowed the man to choose his own assassin—in one detail—the patent medicine detail—making itself the protector of that perilous business, collecting money out of it, & appointing no committee of experts to examine the medicines & forbid them when extra-dangerous. Really, when a man can prove that he is not a jackass, I think that he is in the way to prove that he is no legitimate member of the race.

I have by me a list of 52 human ailments—common ones—& in this list I count 19 which the physician's art cannot cure. But there isn't one which Osteopathy or Kellgren cannot cure, if the patient comes early.

Fifteen years ago I had a deep reverence for the physician & the surgeon. But 6 months of closely watching the Kellgren business has revolutionized all that; & now I have neither reverence nor respect for the physician's trade, & scarcely any for the surgeon's. I am convinced that of all quackeries, the physician's is the grotesquest & the silliest. And *they* know they are shams & humbugs. They have taken the place of those augurs who couldn't look each other in the face without laughing.

See what a powerful hold our ancient superstitions have upon us: two weeks ago, when Livy committed an incredible imprudence for a grown-up person & by consequence was promptly stricken down with a heavy triple attack—influenza, bronchitis, & a lung affected—she recognized the gravity of the situation, & her old superstitions rose: she thought we ought to send for a doctor. Think of it—the last man in the world I should want around at such a time. Of course I did not say *no*—not that I was indisposed to take the responsibility, for I was not, my notion of a dangerous responsibility being quite the other way—but because it is unsafe to distress a sick person; I only said we knew no good doctor, & it could not be good policy to choose at hazard; so she allowed me to send for Kellgren—at $16 a visit. To-day she is up & around—cured. It is safe to say that persons hit in the same way at the same time are in bed yet,—every one of them—& booked to stay there a good while yet, & to be in a shackly condition & afraid of their shadows for a couple of years or more to come.[4]

We are gradually making up our minds to go & take up life again in the Hartford house—a shrine now—where Susy fell, quite unnecessarily, by quackery, of ailments easily curable even at the stage where her doctors gave her up; & naturally, I want to know what our protections against the cemetery are to be. There are two Osteopaths in Hartford; they may be good ones, & I hope they are; but, good or bad we must use them, for I will have no doctor in the house upon any terms while an Osteopath is getable. Won't you go & talk with them, & then talk with their *patients*, which is the main thing? You can say you are not personally interested, but are only inquiring upon my account. They are not likely to object to your talking with their patients. One of them is named Underwood—see Directory.[5] He can give you the name of the other.

I wonder if you received the letter in which I enclosed a quaint epistle written by a Chicago-born girl who has lived 15 years in Europe & has forgotten her mother tongue without getting a good grip upon any other.[6] I think I never mailed that letter, but lost it. If so, it is a great pity.
[Unknown amount of text missing.]

1. Twain was fascinated by the subject of mental telegraphy. See, for instance, his 1891 essay on the subject.
2. Pamela Anne Moffett was Twain's elder sister.
3. Andrew Taylor Still, who founded the American School of Osteopathy in 1892.
4. "Shackly" means shaky or tottering, especially as applied to one in poor physical health.
5. Harvey W. Underwood and Louis C. Kingsbury had a joint osteopathic practice in Hartford.
6. See Letter 168.

171. Twain to Twichell

27 January 1900. London, England (Typed transcript by Albert Bigelow Paine)

London, Jan. 27, 1900

Dear Joe:

Apparently we are not proposing to set the Filipinos free & give their islands to them; & apparently we are not proposing to hang the priests & confiscate their property. If these things are so, the war out there has no interest for me.

I have just been examining Chapter LXX of "Following the Equator," to see if the Boer's old military effectiveness is holding out. It reads curiously as if it had been written about the present war.

I believe that in the next chapter my notion of the Boer was rightly conceived. He is popularly called uncivilized, I do not know why. Happiness, food, shelter, clothing, wholesome labor, modest & rational ambitions, honesty, kindliness, hospitality, love of freedom & limitless courage to fight for it, composure & fortitude in time of disaster, patience in time of hardship & privation, absence of noise & brag in time of victory, contentment with a humble & peaceful life void of insane excitements—if there is a higher & better form of civilization than this, I am not aware of it & do not know where to look for it. I suppose we have the habit of imagining that a lot of artistic & intellectual & other artificialities must be added, or it isn't complete. We & the English have these latter; but as we lack the great bulk of those others, I think the Boer civilization is the best of the two. My idea of our civilization is that it is a shoddy poor thing & full of cruelties, vanities, arrogancies, meannesses & hypocricies [*sic*]. As for the word, I hate the sound of it, for it conveys a lie; & as for the thing itself, I wish it was in hell, where it belongs.

Provided we could get something better in the place of it. But that is not possible, perhaps. Poor as it is it is better than *real* savagery, therefore we must stand by it, extend it, & (in public) praise it. And so we must not utter any hurtful word about England in these days, nor fail to hope that she will win in this war, for her defeat & fall would be an irremediable disaster for the mangy human race. Naturally, then, I am for England; but she is profoundly in the wrong, Joe, & no (instructed) Englishman doubts it. At least that is my belief.

Maybe I managed to make myself misunderstood, as to the Osteopathists. I wanted to know how the men impress you. As to their art, I know fairly well about that, and should not value Hartford's opinion of it; nor a physician's; nor that of another who proposed to enlighten me out of his ignorance. Opinions based upon theory, superstition & ignorance are not very precious.

Livy & the others are off for the country for a day or two.

Love to you all

Mark

172. Twichell to Twain

12 February 1900. Hartford, Connecticut

Hartford. Feb. 12.

Dear Mark:

Your last letters have been interesting "to a degree" (what an odd and absurd expression that is for a superlative, and yet I see writers of fame using it) but the feature of solar radiance in them is the news that you are coming home. I can't stop to talk about that or any thing else, though, this morning. I have other work on hand viz: to frame the address I am to make at Ward Cheney's funeral the latter part of this week.[1] He died, as you know, Jan. 7th in the Philippine Islands of wounds received in action that day. His body is now on the way hither from San Francisco.

The special reason why I write at-all is to tell you that I am mailing you a copy of a medical journal containing matter of interest (disagreeable interest) to osteopathists, which—my attention having been called to it—I thought you would like to see.[2] You will observe that in it the enemy borrows words from you with which to club your friends, little suspecting that you are of their party. I am also sending Livy a couple of photographs—one of Young Harmony, the nurse, and one of myself; both with our love. But for those occasions, I should hold my peace, for it is a season of shadow with us here such as disposes one to silence. You have heard of course of the sudden taking off of Lizzie Robinson, Molly Robinson Cheney's sister.[3] Her funeral last week was the saddest I have seen in a long time. And I suppose you are advised of Henry Robinson's probably mortal sickness. The following from Saturday's [Hartford] Times

[Pasted-in newspaper clipping follows:]

> The probably fatal illness of the Hon. Henry C. Robinson will cause a feeling of sadness not only here in Hartford, where he has so long been honored, but among people in many other places. Ex-Mayor Robinson is universally liked, and whenever he passes away his genial and helpful presence will be sorely missed.

The report this morning:

[Further newspaper clipping pasted in:]

> The Hon. H. C. Robinson, whose illness took on a critical form on Friday last, was no worse yesterday and there were some conditions which gave his physicians more hope. The report from him last evening was more encouraging than on Saturday. He is very weak and much of the time is in a semiconscious state. Mr. and Mrs. Sidney Miller arrived from Detroit Saturday [ ]ning[4]

[End of clipping]

is less despairing; yet from all I can learn I judge that the light in which we have so long rejoiced is flickering out. I am grieved for you to think of it.

Your old neighbor Charles Smith was buried last Thursday; and your neighbor Fellowes—a gentleman whom I greatly esteem, as I did Mr. Smith—is apparently soon to follow.[5] So the world melts away around us.

Charley Warner, of whom in our thoughts we were taking farewell again a fortnight ago, is convalescent—almost a miracle.[6]

Our Sue's letters from the Mediterranean (I told you, didn't I?, of her grand yacht cruise as guest of Lizzie Beach Robinson—Mrs. Colt's niece) have begun to arrive and are hugely entertaining.[7] May be you will see her in London in April, on her way home. By the way Milly Cheney Learned whose travels were interrupted by Ward's death gave me in South Manchester the other day an account of her little visit with you, which had evidently been a great pleasure to her and her husband.[8]

Good morning, old fellow. We love you all the more under these present clouds.

What we lose deepens our hunger for what is left.

Yrs ever aff.

Joe

I will write again soon. The news to-day is that the Boers in their turn are advancing across the Tugela. Any way, England is undergoing a discipline that ought to be salutary.

1. First Lieutenant Ward Cheney. The Cheney family lived in South Manchester, about twelve miles from Twain and Twichell's part of Hartford, and were in the business of silk manufacturing.

2. Missing.

3. Molly Robinson was the sister-in-law of Ward Cheney and daughter-in-law of Frank Cheney, paterfamilias of the Cheney silk enterprise in South Manchester, Connecticut.

4. Part of this last word is torn off. Robinson's daughter Lucy was Mrs. Sidney Miller.

5. Charles Boardman Smith was a saddlery manufacturer who lived in Hartford. Charles E. Fellowes was an attorney and clerk of the Court of Common Pleas in Hartford. He evidently survived this present illness.

6. Warner had been stricken with pneumonia and then facial paralysis during the winter. He was to die of heart failure in October.

7. Elizabeth Colt ran the arms business founded by her husband, Samuel Colt, after his death in 1862 and was a major philanthropic figure in Hartford.

8. Emily Cheney Learned, sister of Ward Cheney.

173. Twain to Twichell

4 March 1900. London, England

Wellington Court
Knightsbridge, Mch 4/00.

Dear Joe:

Henry Robinson's death is a sharp wound to me, & it goes very deep.[1] I had a strong affection for him, & I think he had for me. Every Friday, three-fourths of the year for 16 years he was of the billiard-party in our house. When we come home, how shall we have billiard-nights again—with no Ned Bunce & no Henry Robinson? I believe I could not endure that. We must find another use for that room. Susy is gone, George is gone, Libby Hamersley, Ned Bunce, Henry Robinson.[2] The friends are passing, one by one; our house, where such warm blood & such dear blood flowed so freely, is become a cemetery. But not in any repellant sense. Our dead are welcome there; their life made it beautiful, their death has hallowed it, we shall have them with us always, & there will be no more parting.

It was a moving address you made over Ward Cheney—that fortunate youth! Like Susy, he got out of life all that was worth the living, & got his great reward before he had crossed the tropic frontier of dreams & entered the Sahara of fact. The deep consciousness of Susy's good fortune is a constant comfort to me.

London is happy-hearted at last. The British victories have swept the clouds away & there are now no uncheerful faces. For three months the private dinner parties (we go to no public ones) have been Lodges of Sorrow, & just a little depressing sometimes; but now they are smily & animated again. Joe, do you know the Irish gentleman & the Irish lady, the Scotch gentleman & the Scotch lady? These are darlings, every one. Night before last it was all Irish—24. One would have to travel far to match their ease & sociability & animation & sparkle & absence of shyness & self-consciousness. It was American in these fine qualities. This was at Mr. Lecky's.[3] He is Irish, you know. Last night it was Irish again, at Lady Gregory's.[4] Lord Roberts is Irish; & Sir William Butler; & Kitchener, I think; & a disproportion of the other prominent Generals are of Irish & Scotch breed—keeping up the traditions of Wellington, & Sir Colin Campbell of the Mutiny.[5] You will have noticed that in S.[outh] A.[frica], as in the Mutiny, it is usually the Irish & the Scotch that are placed in the fore-front of the battle. An Irish friend of mine says this is because the Kelts are idealists, & enthusiasts, with age-old heroisms to emulate & keep bright before the world; but that the low-class Englishman is dull & without ideals, fighting bull-doggishly while he has a leader, but losing his head & going to pieces when his leader falls—not so with the Kelt. Sir Wm. Butler said "the Kelt is the spearhead of the British lance."

Love to you all.

Mark.

1. Robinson died on 14 February.

2. George was Twain's former servant, George Griffin, who had left Twain's employment in 1891 when the Hartford house was closed up, and who had died in 1897.

3. William E. Lecky, historian. Twain had been strongly influenced by his *History of European Morals* (1869).

4. Lady Augusta Gregory, Irish literary figure who co-founded the Abbey Theatre with W. B. Yeats.

5. Lord Frederick Roberts, Sir William Francis Butler, and Herbert Kitchener were all British military leaders who played important roles in the South African War. Sir Colin Campbell, who died in 1863, had commanded the relief army in the Indian Rebellion (or Sepoy Mutiny) of 1857.

174. Twain to Twichell

22 and 23 June 1900. London, England

London, June 22/00.

Dear Joe:

I attended a Kinsmen dinner to-night, the first I have "been at" since we elected you & Toole at the Players some years ago.[1] The full list of American & English members is on the back of this. I was the doyen to-night, Gilder next. E. A. Abbey could have claimed precedence of us, but he was not present.[2] It is a more respectable gang of men than I had supposed it was. I don't think there is a fault to be found with the English contingency.

It is now past midnight, but I am stealing a moment to write you this line before Livy bangs the gong.

Jean is prospering very nicely indeed; so nicely that we have given up the voyage to Sweden & have taken a country house in London for 3 months.[3] It is *called* in London, but is really just on the outer edge. The house is on high ground in the midst of several acres of grass & forest trees, & is wholly shut out from the world & noise. It is called "Dollis Hill."[4] Mr. Gladstone spent a good deal of his time in that house, resting-up & refreshing himself from his labors.[5] Jean will drive in, daily, to the Kellgren shop—40 minutes.

My! I wish Harmony was in Kellgren's hands. In three weeks (possibly two) she would be as hale as ever she was. On this I would stake a thousand dollars against a shilling, & win the shilling. In cases like hers he scores not a single failure; success results in all instances.

The gong!

With love to you all

Mark

[On the back of the letter, in another hand, is a list of names titled "ROLL OF THE KINSMEN," dated March 1899.]

1. The Kinsmen was a social club for artists and performers founded in 1882 in New York. Twain joined in 1882 and Twichell in 1894. There was also a London branch. John L. Toole was an English comedic actor and theatrical producer.

2. Richard Watson Gilder, editor of *Century Magazine*; Edwin Austen Abbey, expatriate American artist and illustrator.

3. Deletion of "cussed" before "voyage."

4. Dollis Hill was a picturesque country estate on the fringe of northwest London.

5. William Gladstone was a British nineteenth-century statesman who had served four terms as prime minister.

175. Twichell to Twain

5 July 1900. Hartford, Connecticut

Hartford. July 5. 1900

Dear old Mark;

Now you must know that I love you for I have let you alone a whole month—and more. And that for or by a man hunted from pillar to post by all creation as you are, is worthy to be credited as an act of grace and mercy.[1] You are yourself to blame for waking me up now. Your midnight report of the "Kinsman" picnic—which might have been a prohibition feast for all you show any sign to the contrary—agreeably reminds me of an honor of mine, of which, though from lack of opportunity, nothing in particular has thus far accrued to me from it, I am mighty proud—as I ought to be. I earnestly hope sometime to appear in person in some gathering of that illustrious clan somewhere and to take a realizing sense of my membership of it.

So you are to summer in England. After then what? We are booked for the hot term at Judy's new cottage on Long Island, near Easthampton. Part of us are already there and the rest are going in a few days. Our fond expectation is that the salt air will set Harmony on her feet again—since Kellgren is out of reach. By the way when I went to see Judy and hers at Watkins six weeks since I was urged by her to urge you to bring Jean home and take her to Dr. [Lewis W.] Rose of Rochester who has cured lots of such cases that all other doctors had given up—though, to be sure, Judy doesn't know in the least what Jean's case is—any more than the rest of us.[2] By the way again, I saw Poultney Bigelow at Yale last week where he was decorated with an honorary "M.A." and he sounded Kellgren's praises eloquently; told me of his (Bigelow's) rescue from death by him, and of the new life he had given you.[3] To my great regret I had to quit New Haven an hour or two after I met Mr. Bigelow to keep an appointment to speak at a Trinity college function here, and so had no chance for more than a few words with him,—couldn't even walk with him in the academic procession. I liked the look of him, and the taste of him, immensely, and saw that a good talk with him would be a prize to covet. He said that he was to be off for London (or I *think* he said so) shortly. My kindest regards to him when you meet him.

Mark, *what* a world tumult is on hand just now! And what a black appalling cloud Pekin lies under![4] Nothing like it since the Indian Mutiny. I dread the tale of shuddering horrors presently to unfold. We are wondering where Yung Wing's head is—though when last heard from he was at Shanghai, where *perhaps* he is safe.

You spoke in one of your letters of the friar question in the Philippine Islands.[5] When I was at Cornell University in May, Pres. Schurman (Chairman of the late Commission to the P.I. [Philippine Islands]) told me that in his view the right solution of that problem was the purchase of the friar holdings by the U.S. and then their sale to the natives—that so the principal part, if not the whole, of the purchase price (fixed by condemnation) would be recovered.[6] His talk on all P.I. matters was hugely interesting and informing.

Cornell Dunham, the last time I saw him, said that he was trying to get Mrs. Robinson to let Maysie go with him and young Harmony and me on our Italian excursion in October.[7] She would be a delightful addition to our party. There is nothing worth naming going on here just now. The envelope in which I deposit newspaper clippings for you affords this only—which shows that the spirit of disinterested benevolence still survives amongst us.

Our love to you each and all.

Yours ever aff.

Joe

I address this care of Chatto & Windus. You will get it I guess. Its [*sic*] not much matter if you don't.

[Pasted into letter to the left of the signature:]

Prevented a Murderer From Collapsing

Philadelphia, May 14.—A special from Williamsport, Penn., tells of an unusual action of Sheriff Miller to prevent a murderer awaiting execution from collapsing at the last moment. Wilson Hummel, who murdered his wife and two children is to be hanged on June 5. His appetite left him and the jail physician had doubts of his living until the day of execution. Sheriff Miller, fearing the man would collapse, took him in charge. A part of Hummel's daily exercise consists of jumping over a broomstick three feet from the floor and backward handsprings and walking on his hands from one end of the corridor to the other. Hummel's appetite returned under this treatment, and he is in good spirits.

1. The "or by" is an insertion above the line of text. Twichell seems not to have been sure as to how he should best express himself.

2. Julia Twichell Wood's husband apparently sought treatment at Glen Springs Sanitarium in Watkins, New York (see Twichell Journals, January 1898). The town was renamed Watkins Glen in 1926.

3. Poultney Bigelow, lawyer, traveler, author, and journalist, based in London and New York.

4. Twichell is referring to the Boxer Rebellion, an uprising by Chinese opposed to foreign and specifically missionary interventions in their country. The Boxers reached Peking (now Beijing), the Chinese capital, in June 1900. In the same month an international force was sent to China in opposition to the Boxers and other Chinese nationalists. Twain would, controversially, take the (anti-imperialist) Boxer side in this affair. "Pekin" was at this time a common alternative spelling for Peking.

5. The U.S. government was faced with the problem of what to do with the large estates owned by Spanish monastic orders once it had taken over the Philippines from Spain in 1898.

6. Condemnation: that is, legal condemnation of property—what in the United States today would be called "eminent domain," under which a government requires a property owner to sell for some greater social good. Philosopher Jacob Gould Schurman was president of Cornell from 1892 to 1920.

7. "Maysie" or "Mazy" Robinson was the daughter of the late attorney and mayor Henry C. Robinson.

176. Twain to Twichell

16 July 1900. London, England (Two typed transcripts by Albert Bigelow Paine)

Dollis Hill House,
Kilburn, N.W.
July 16, 1900.

Dear Joe—

Oh, the human race!—what a ridiculous invention it is. The duty-inspired sheriff, working that poor devil to death to keep him alive until he could be hanged. It is funny enough to make a person cry.

The ghastly news has come to-day, at last, & the Peking legations are a shambles; this news was long ago foreseen, but it did not postpone the Queen's garden party.[1] It's the human race—that explains everything; & to my mind excuses everything a man may do, too. And look at South Africa—that black blot upon England. Let us hope there is no hereafter; I don't want to train with any angels made out of human material. Europe is going to sup in hell, there in China, I think——& will richly deserve it. I believe Europe will get [it] by the ears, there; I hardly think she can escape it—unless she withdraws & leaves her booty behind her.

It's a robber-gang which will be loth to do that. I believe the human race is filthier to-day than it ever was before; & that is saying much.

Livy has at last got her tribe settled here in the country on a 3 or 4 month's lease, & most comfortably housed and bedded. It has cost her several weeks of patient hard work, & nobody in the world could have done it better. She is a person to be proud of. From the house you can see little but spacious stretches of hay-fields & green turf, with noble forest trees all about—yet the massed brick blocks of London are reachable in three minutes on a horse. By rail from our station we can be in the heart of London in Baker street in 17 minutes—by a smart train in 5. It is a roomy old house & stands high in the pure air.

But there is one tremendous defect: Livy is already so enchanted with the place & so in love with it that she doesn't know how she is going to tear herself away from it. She likes the roomy great spread of velvet lawn, & the stately trees to tea & loll & read under in the hammocks. And certainly it is the loveliest place I have ever lived in. I am the only person who is ever in the house in the daytime—but I am at work, & deep in the luxury of it. Jean drives into town every day to Kellgren's, sometimes with Livy, sometimes with the maid, but I stay at home. Visitors drive out to tea, or come by rail, as suits their taste.

With love to all of you from us—

Mark.

1. This refers to the ongoing siege of the international legations by the Boxers in Peking, where some nine hundred foreigners (mainly British, Americans, and Japanese) and almost three thousand Chinese Christians were trapped. According to Sir Claude MacDonald (the man in charge of the defense of the foreign legations), 13 July was the most difficult day of the siege, with the defending forces close to collapse. Around 9 July 1900, Twain had written a letter to C. F. Moberly Bell (manager at the *London Times*) on the subject of the Boxer Rebellion—a letter which, however, remained unsent. See Peter Messent, "Mark Twain and London," in *Cosmopolitan Twain*, ed. Ann M. Ryan and Joseph B. McCullough (Columbia: University of Missouri Press, 2008), 207–9.

177. Twain to Twichell

12 August 1900. London, England (Mourning border)

DOLLIS HILL HOUSE,
Kilburn, N.W.
London, Aug. 12/00.

Dear Joe:

The Sages & Prof. Fiske & Brander Matthews were out here to tea a week ago, & it was a breath of American air to see them. We furnished them a bright day & comfortable weather—& they used it all up, in their extravagant American way. Since then we have sat by coal fires evenings.

We shall sail for home some time in October, but shall winter in New York where we can have an osteopath of good repute to continue the work of putting this family in proper condition. But this is really on Jean's account—any osteopath, good or bad, could keep the rest of us in trim; at least in better trim than a regular physician could. We got fairly good accounts of the Hartford osteopath, but they were rather too indefinite, on the whole. I am not at all afraid of the regular physician in the ordinary run of diseases, but I would not trust him in any serious malady. To him, gastritis is a serious malady, & his results with it are ghastly; whereas in competent hands there is nothing serious about it. Three or four days ago the most eminent physicians & surgeons of London conspired together over the Lord Chief Justice's gastritis & condemned him to relief by the knife.

It would be laughable if it were not so tragic. Even [the] chuckleheadedest osteopath would have had no difficulty with that trifling disease. Livy & I dined with the Chief Justice a month ago & he was as well-conditioned as an athlete.[1]

It is all China, now, & my sympathies are with the Chinese. They have been villainously dealt with by the sceptred thieves of Europe, & I hope they will drive all the foreigners out & keep them out for good. I only wish it; of course I don't really expect it.

Why, hang it, it occurs to me that by the time we reach New York you Twichells will be invading Europe & once more we shall miss the connection. This is thoroughly exasperating. Aren't we *ever* going to meet again?

With no end of love from all of us,

Mark.

[Livy adds a note below Twain's signature: "We do hope Harmony is steadily gaining now."]

1. Charles Arthur Russell, Baron Russell of Killowen, who had died on 10 August 1900 following the operation to which Twain refers.

178. Twain to Twichell

18 August 1900. London, England (Mourning border)

DOLLIS HILL HOUSE,
N.W.
Aug. 18./00.

Dear Joe:

No, it was not gastritis alone that the Chief Justice died of—that was a journalistic error: he had a cancer. I get this from a physician.

It is 7.30 a.m. I have been waking very early, lately. If it occurs once more, it will be Habit; then I will submit and adopt it.

This is our Day of Mourning. It is four years since Susy died; it is five years & a month that I saw her alive for the last time—throwing kisses at us from the railway platform when we started West around the world. Sometimes it is a century, sometimes it was yesterday.

With love
Mark

179. Twichell to Twain

24 August 1900. Long Island, New York

Easthampton. Long Island. Aug. 24th 1900

Dear old Mark;

We are down here—all but Young Harmony of course—occupying Judy's Cottage which she didn't want this season. It is everybody's vacation but mine. I pass four days of the week here but am on duty in Hartford Sundays.—in that way saving time for the excursion to Italy in Oct. & Nov.—as I guess I have explained to you before. We are within sight and sound of the sea, and its bathing is splendid. Harmony Senior spends her days on the veranda mostly, and is steadily getting better. She is having a grand full feast of reading, both light and heavy, from The "Man who Corrupted Hadleysburg" to the "History of Civilization in the Middle Ages."[1] Today she is reviving her girlhood with "Thaddeus of Warsaw" and finding huge pleasure in it.[2] The first thing I do when I get to Hartford is go and see the Nurse.[3] The last time, she confessed herself tired. Business had been livelier than could be wished in such hot weather. Item: five babies had been born in her ward during the week. Something of a contrast that to the life of a Farmington school girl. But I meet no young woman whose face reflects a more cheerful mind than Harmony's.

Both Yung Wing's boys are with us at present, and so, as you would suppose, we breakfast, lunch and dine on the news from China, and, like yourself, we are partizans of the Chinese.[4] Y.W. is in Shanghai. His letters are wonderfully interesting, and very hopeful in tone. He is in the counsels of the native Reform Party, whose day is now coming, he thinks.[5] Some of his letters I am keeping to show you. If a manifesto of the Reform Party is presently issued, he will be the writer of it—but don't tell any body that.

You speak of Prof. Fiske's being in London. I trust he will have gone back to his country by the time we get there, for I have been reckoning much on seeing him there under his own vine and fig tree.[6]

Mark, the way you throw your rotten eggs at the human race doth greatly arride me. We preachers are extensively accused of vilifying human nature, as you are aware; but I must own that for enthusiasm of misanthropy you beat us out of sight. A favorable remark you let fall about Livy in one of your last letters was due no doubt to momentary weakness. Bless her for the kind word to Harmony she postscribed to that which has just come! For my part I think that those two good girls are a credit to our race and suggest that something may yet be made of it. But Charlie Warner will cry you Amen to every word you say. He is sure the world is going to the dogs—especially since Mr. Brockway has been forced out of the Elmira Reformatory.[7] Well, that surely was the devil's own work, but I am much mistaken if it does not soon prove that the devil lost by it.

I am mighty glad to hear that you are at some task, and I wonder what it is.[8] When shall we know? You are certainly at your best now. By the way, the Scroll and Key boys at Yale suggested to me the last time I spent an evening with them that I suggest to you that their library would be enriched and graced by a sett [*sic*] of your works.[9] But, gracious! I wouldn't do it for any thing. There's no end to the modesty of those youngsters. They even wanted *my* works.

You will not be long in New York before you see some of us, (Dave lives there, you know) nor, I suspect, before some of you venture up to

Hartford. And then, I have faith to believe, the rest, that Hartford longs for night and day, will come to pass.[10] I walked across The Deck a few evenings since and saw you there in vision. With love to Livy and the girls,

Yrs ever aff.

Joe

1. Twichell means "The Man That Corrupted Hadleyburg." The second title possibly refers to *Studies in European History: Civilization in the Middle Ages*, by Guernsey Jones, published in Chicago in 1899.

2. An 1803 novel by Jane Porter.

3. That is, "young" Harmony Twichell, in training as a nurse at Hartford Hospital.

4. Twichell considered himself pro-Chinese in the sense of supporting the Reform Party noted below. This party included Yung Wing (a fervent Christian) and Sun Yat-Sen, the venerated eventual founder (in 1911) of the Republic of China.

5. The Boxer Rebellion, which ended with the Chinese government having to pay massive reparations to Western powers, speeded demands for internal reform. Yung Wing was at this point shuttling between Shanghai and Hong Kong planning an uprising to bring about such changes with Sun Yat-Sen and others.

6. That is, in Italy.

7. Zebulon Brockway was an important U.S. prison reformer and was warden of Elmira Reformatory from 1876 to 1900. He left his job after Theodore Roosevelt brought in new appointees to the prison management board (following various accusations against Brockway, including one of brutality), affecting his autonomy as warden.

8. Twain was working on "The Chronicle of Young Satan" during this Dollis Hill summer.

9. Scroll and Key was a Yale secret society of which Twichell was a member (from his own university days). And see Letter 1, note 3.

10. The family's return to Nook Farm.

PART 4

1901–1904

The Return to America;
Livy's Illness and Death

TWAIN AND HIS FAMILY eventually returned to America in 1900. His financial situation was now once more healthy, thanks primarily to the help of businessman and increasingly close friend Henry H. Rogers. But living in Hartford was now out of the question and the family would live mainly in New York and its environs. Livy's health, never strong, went into rapid decline following what was most likely a heart attack in August 1902. Despite travelling to Italy to attempt to ease her condition, she would die there of heart failure on 5 June 1904. Twain and his daughters were devastated by the loss.

Twichell, meanwhile, remained in his Hartford ministry, giving what support he could. Though the two men would occasionally meet up in this period—mostly in New York, but in Hartford too—the friendship continued mainly at a distance. Just as Twichell had married Twain and Livy, so he would conduct the funeral services for Livy.

The letters between the two men altered and redefined themselves in this period in the light of these changing circumstances. The number of the men's friends who were dying continued to grow, with both men showing an awareness of the advancing years and their effects. Twichell, meanwhile, acted as the giver of sympathy and deep concern, throughout the various stages of Livy's last illness, for the two of them, both husband and wife.

Twain's own views, too, continued to develop in these years and the gap between his misanthropy, mechanistic philosophy, and increasingly antiestablishment views and Twichell's much more conventional frame of mind becomes more pronounced. Twain's opinions on public affairs, both national and international, appear repeatedly, if sporadically, in the letters of this period, still with a noticeable anti-imperialistic and anti-missionary thrust. So in Letters 181 and 183 he speaks both of "this Philippine privy," in relation to U.S. policy there, and of the "idiot Christian pirates," the missionaries practicing their trade in China. The bleakness of his view of the human race as an entirety, too, remains apparent. In Letter 200 he manages to express both his low opinion of human nature and his ironic view of Christian fundamentalism and anthropocentrism at one and the same time when he notes, "We don't know any more about morals than the Deity knew about astronomy when he wrote Genesis." Twichell continues to chide his friend for his "abominable heresies" (Letter 202) but in a largely gentle and humorous manner.

In Letter 211, Twichell makes a rare reflexive comment on the two men's correspondence. He refers particularly here to Twain's latest letters—the last reporting on the lies the family have told Livy, as she lies ill in bed, to save her anxiety or distress:

> Mark, I've been getting letters from you many years; *numbers* of them letters to keep. But these last do certainly lay over all the rest—which is saying a very great deal. The story flows off the end of your pen taken carelessly up to beguile the tedium of an anxious, slow-footed day; perfect *literature* from the word go; lights and shades all right; the complex plot continuously limpid in clearness; the style M.T.'s own at its best; diction, for ease, vigor and grace the choicest—the whole all ready for the printer as it is; *any* change must mar it——
>
> By George, it is not fair—that inequitable distribution of talents by which it is given to only one man to do without consciously trying what to all others is, granting it possible, prodigiously difficult. The only comfort is that it is in the family, so to speak.

His appreciation of Twain's letter-writing skills and the status of this particular letter as "perfect literature" may refer to particular recent examples. It does, though, remind us of the way Twain's talent reveals itself in this whole area: his letters are never boring and are testaments to his range of interests, imaginative facility, and wit. The fact that Twain could speak his mind freely to Joe, discuss anything that struck his fancy at any moment without fear of censure, speaks of the virtual "family" connection by this time long established.

What remains the dominant event, though, the very center of this bunch of letters, is Livy's illness and death. Together with the death of Susy eight years earlier, this was the most serious emotional body blow of Twain's life. He would recover in part but would never thenceforth be quite the same man.

180. Twain to Twichell

23 and 24 January 1901. New York, New York

14 W. 10th st., Jan. 23/01.[1]

Dear Joe:

Certainly. I used to take it in my coffee, but it settled to the bottom in the form of mud, & I had to eat it with a spoon; so I dropped the custom & took my 2 teaspoonfuls in cold milk after breakfast.[2] If we were out of milk I shoveled the dry powder into my mouth & washed it down with water. The only essential is to *get it into the stomach,*—the method is not important.

No, blame it I can't go to the Alumni dinner, Joe. It takes two days, & I can't spare the time. Moreover I preside at the Lincoln birthday celebration in Carnegie Hall Feb. 11, & I must not make two speeches so close together. Think of it—two old rebels functioning there—I as President, & Watterson as Orator of the Day! Things have changed somewhat in these 40 years, thank God.[3]

Look here—when you come down you must be our guest—we've got a roomy room for you, & Livy will make trouble if you go elsewhere. Come straight to 14 West 10th.

Jan. 24. Livy says Amen to that; also, can you give us a day or two's notice, so the room will be sure to be vacant?

I'm going to stick close to my desk for a month, now, hoping to write a small book, full of playful & good-natured contempt for the lousy McKinley.[4] Oh, think of that nickle-plated patriot, Joe Hawley![5]

Ys Ever

Mark.

P.S. I forgot to add my gratification at the prospect of having flogging for certain offences resumed in our State. I hope the bill will become a law. Flogging is the only thing that has ever put a serious check upon the crimes & trespasses contemplated by it.[6]

Mark.

1. The Clemens family was now back in New York City, residing at 14 West 10th Street. They would live there for a year.

2. Twain is clearly responding to something Joe has written, evidently about Plasmon, a powdered food and nutrition supplement Twain invested in (and proselytized for) at this time.

3. On 11 February 1901, Twain spoke at Carnegie Hall at a celebration of Abraham Lincoln's ninety-second birthday. Twain had briefly been part of an irregular pro-Confederate

militia unit at the start of the Civil War. Henry Watterson, journalist and politician, who had fought for the Confederacy during the Civil War, spoke too.

4. William McKinley, elected president in 1900, was associated with imperialist policies in the Philippines. Twain was probably referring here to "To the Person Sitting in Darkness"—an essay condemning imperialism in its various current forms (the Philippines, China and the Boxer Rebellion, the South African War) which would be published in the February 1901 *North American Review*. McKinley is one of those attacked in the piece.

5. Twain had broken with Hawley, now a senator and making conventionally patriotic speeches about the Philippines, over the 1884 Cleveland-Blaine election (see also Harriet Elinor Smith et al., eds., *Autobiography of Mark Twain*, vol. 1 [Berkeley: University of California Press, 2010], 316–317).

6. The *Courant* (6 February 1901) would report on a bill introduced by State Representative Harrison B. Freeman Jr. in the Connecticut House of Representatives that would have reintroduced whipping as a punishment for some crimes, notably the beating of women by men.

181. Twain to Twichell

29 January 1901. New York, New York (Two typed transcripts by Albert Bigelow Paine)

---

14 W. 10th, Jan. 29/01.

Dear Joe:

Livy & I are booked for dinner up town Feb. 5, but that is no matter; you come here & dine with the girls—& don't you go to bed before we return.

I'm not expecting anything but kicks for scoffing at the McKinley, that conscienceless thief & traitor, & *am* expecting a diminution of my bread & butter by it, but if Livy will let me I will have my say. This nation is like all the others that have been spewed upon the earth—ready to shout for any cause that will tickle its vanity or fill its pocket. What a hell of a heaven it will be, when they get all these sons of bitches assembled there! But I'm not going to pester Hawley. Privately, I have never much believed in him since he exposed Blaine to his virtuous scorn during 3 years & then fervently supported him! Hawley has never respected himself since—at least I hope not; it would show that there was still a man concealed in him somewhere.

I can't understand it! You are a public guide & teacher, Joe, & are under a heavy responsibility to men, young & old; if you teach your people—as you teach me—to hide their opinions when they believe their flag is being abused & dishonored, lest the utterance do them & a publisher a damage, how do you answer for it to your conscience? You are sorry for me; in the fair way of give & take, I am willing to be a little sorry for you.[1]

However, I seem to be going counter to my own Private Philosophy—which Livy won't allow me to publish—because it would destroy me.[2] But I hope to see it in print before I die. I planned it 15 years ago, & wrote it in '98. I've often tried to read it to Livy, but she won't have it; it drives her mad & makes her melancholy. The truth always has that effect on people. *Would* have, anyway, if they ever got hold of a rag of it—which they don't.

You are supposing that I am supposing I am moved by a Large Patriotism, & that I am distressed because our idiot President has blundered in up to his neck in this Phillipine [*sic*] privy; & that I am grieved because this great big ignorant nation, which doesn't know even the A B C facts of the Phillipine episode, is in disgrace before the sarcastic world— drop that idea! I care nothing for the rest—I am only distressed & troubled because *I* am befouled by these things. That is all. When I search myself away down deep, I find this out. Whatever a man feels or thinks or does, there is never any but one reason for it—& that is a selfish one.

At great inconvenience, & expense of precious time I went to the chief synagogue the other night & talked in the interest of a charity school of poor Jew girls.[3] I know—to the finest shades—the selfish ends that moved me; but no one else suspects. I could give you the details if I had time. You would perceive how true they were.

I've written another article; you better hurry down & help Livy squelch it.[4]

She's out pottering around somewhere, poor house-keeping slave; & Clara is in the hands of the osteopath, getting the bronchitis pulled & hauled out of her. It was a bad attack, & a little disquieting. It came day before yesterday, & she hasn't sat up till this afternoon. She is getting along satisfactorily, now.

Lots of love to you all.

Mark.

1. It seems Twain's politics had been countered by Twichell in a missing letter. Twichell, always the more conservative, had apparently advised Twain not to openly condemn U.S. government policy.

2. *What Is Man?* (published anonymously in 1906). In this book, written in the form of a Socratic dialogue and often described by Twain as his "private gospel," he represented man as a machine, his behavior absolutely controlled by self-interest, and larger forces (heredity, environment, training) over which he has no control.

3. Twain spoke in New York on 20 January 1901 on behalf of women's suffrage at the Hebrew Technical School for Girls.

4. Probably "To the Person Sitting in Darkness."

182. Twain to Twichell

24 April 1901. New York, New York (Typed transcript)

New York, April 24, 1901.

Dear Joe:

Yes it was a slander. I am sound & well, but the report may have arisen from the fact that I am in the habit of telling people that I am sick. I know of no reason for doing this except that it is habit with me to say what is not so, as a usual thing.[1] Livy is gouty but otherwise well & the report that she is regaining her youth, as to looks, is true.

I am afraid we have failed in our quest in the Adirondacks.[2] We did some heavy traveling & some brisk rushing around hunting for a satisfactory house but we have come home with doubts which we have not been able to settle in these twenty-four hours. I think we shall start for Vermont in a day or two & see what we can find there. It is too bad that Harmony's health is in such bad shape, & I give you my word of honor that I believe that if she had put herself in the hands of the most incapable osteopath in New England she would be well now. I say this knowing you will take no stock in it but it is a satisfaction to me to say it, anyway. It is curious that Hartford has not found out that we live in New York; you & three others have rung our doorbell in the last half year, but I call no others to mind.

Say, Joe, old Ned Wakeman's method of accounting for miracles was discovered by old Sir Thomas Browne, a thing I never knew before.[3] William Lyon Phelps of Yale has quoted the passage to me.[4] It is a pity old Wakeman could not have had the joy of knowing before he died, that he was in such distinguished company.

We all send lots of love to you all, & I add this reminder—ring our doorbell, & ring it soon!

Yours always,

Mark.

1. Twichell must have shown anxiety about Twain's health, due probably to some (unknown) newspaper report.

2. Twain and his family would spend the summer of 1901 in the Adirondacks. Here, he refers to some early house-hunting.

3. Captain Ned Wakeman remained a source of fascination to Twain, for his storytelling style. Twichell (see Letter 21) had heard Wakeman's explanation of a miracle in which the prophet Elijah set fire to water—that the "water" was in fact petroleum. Twain reproduced the tale in "Some Rambling Notes of an Idle Excursion." In his *Religio Medici* (1642), Sir Thomas Browne offers a similar explanation for a fire/water miracle, although replacing petroleum by bitumen.

4. Phelps, a Yale professor whose specialty was modern literature, had just written to Twain on this matter.

183. Twain to Twichell

4, 11, or 18 June 1901. New York, New York

June (Tuesday)

Dear Joe:

Well, it *is* funny. The country's political morals & ideals have sunk pretty nearly to zero in the past two years, but I had not suspected that anybody had dropped to the point of thinking the clergy bribable. Seriously, it is an astonisher. Could it have happened 20 years ago? No, it couldn't. I don't know but that this *is* zero.[1]

In your excellent speech I discover no reference to foreign missions, & I am glad.[2] Whenever you ask people to support them, Joe, *do* bar China. Their presence there is forbidden by the Bible, & by every sentiment of humanity & fair-dealing; & they have done vast mischief there. I would bar no other country, I believe, but they have no business in China. Besides, there is plenty for them to do at home. In the presence of the home-missionary even the worst of us stand uncovered; there are no limits to our reverence for him; but when it comes to idiot Christian pirates like Ament, & professional hypocrites & liars like Rev. Judson Smith of the American Board we are disrespectful & indecent.[3]

I am enjoying Ament. He is doing my work for me—damaging his nefarious cause. If ever he shows signs of quieting down I will stir him up again. He is doing good, & must be kept at it. I believe China can be saved yet, from Christianity of the American Board breed, & I think that that old mud-turtle, Smith, & the talky Ament will accomplish it if some traitor doesn't gag them.

I'll send the tribe's love to you all. They are out house-hunting for the fall.

By the way, your secret is safe. Two publishers made me the same offer, & I don't know which one applied to you.[4] I didn't accept. I wanted to watch the missionaries.

Ys Ever
Mark.

1. Twain was at this time engaged in numerous disputes with churchmen angry at his stance against missionaries in China. He had accused some of corruption.

2. Reference unknown.

3. The Rev. William Ament had devoted his life to missionary activity in China. He became a central figure in such activities at the time of the Boxer Rebellion, and was a particular target of Twain's sarcasm and anger. Rev. Judson Smith was corresponding secretary of the American Board of Commissioners for Foreign Missions, with particular responsibility for Chinese affairs.

4. Reference unknown.

184. Twain to Twichell

28 July 1901. Saranac Lake, New York

Ampersand, N.Y. July 28/01.[1]

Dear Joe:

As you say, it is impracticable—in my case, certainly. For *me* to assist in an appeal to that Congress of land-thieves & liars & to that fine "patriot" in the Presidential chair would be to bring derision upon it; & for me to assist in an appeal for cash to pass through the hands of those missionaries out there, of any denomination, Catholic or Protestant, wouldn't do at all.[2] They wouldn't handle money which I had soiled, & I wouldn't trust them with it, anyway. They would devote it to the relief of sufferers—I know that—but the sufferers selected would be converts. The missionary-utterances exhibit no humane feeling toward the others, but in place of it a spirit of hate & hostility. And it is natural; the Bible forbids their presence there, their trade is unlawful, & why shouldn't their characters be of a necessity in harmony with——but never mind, let it go, it irritates me.

Later. I have been reading Yung Wing's letter again. It may be that he is over wrought [*sic*] by his sympathies, but it may not be so. There may be other reasons why the missionaries are silent about the Shensi 2-year famine & cannibalism. It may be that there are so few Protestant converts there that the missionaries are able to take care of them. That they are not likely to largely concern themselves about Catholic converts & the others, is quite natural, I think, after the revelations of the Aments, the Reids, the Tewksburys & the rest of that Maffia—not to mention those of dear Dr. Judson Twaddler Smith, DD. & his pals of the American Board.[3]

That crude idea of appealing to this Government for help in a cause which has no money in it & no politics rises before me again in all its admirable innocence! Doesn't Yung Wing know us *yet*? However, he has been absent since '96 or '7. We have gone to hell since then. [Lajos]

Kossuth couldn't raise 30 cents in Congress, now, if he were back with his moving Magyar-tale.

I am on the front porch (lower one—main deck) of our little bijou of a dwelling-house. The lake-edge (Lower Saranac) is so nearly under me that I can't see the shore, but only the water, small-poxed with rain-splashes—for there is a heavy down-pour. It is charmingly like sitting snuggled up on a ship's deck with the stretching sea all around—but very much more satisfactory, for at sea a rain-storm is depressing, while here of course the effect engendered is just a deep sense of comfort & contentment. The heavy forest shuts us solidly in on three sides—there are no neighbors. There are beautiful little tan-colored impudent squirrels about. They take tea 5 p.m., (not uninvited) at the table in the woods where Jean does my type-writing, & one of them has been brave enough to sit up on Jean's knee on his hams with his tail curved over his back & munch his food. They come to dinner, 7 p.m., on the front porch (not invited) but Clara drives them away. It is an occupation which requires some industry, & attention to business. They all have the one name—Blennerhasset, from Burr's friend—& none of them answers to it except when hungry.[4]

We have been here since June 21st. For a little while we had some warm days—according to the family's estimate; I was hardly discommoded myself. Otherwise the weather has been of the sort you are familiar with in these regions: cool days & cold nights. We have heard of the hot wave every Wednesday, per the weekly paper—we allow no dailies to intrude. Last week through visitors also—the only ones we have had—D^r. Root & John Howells.[5]

We have the daily lake-swim; & all the tribe, servants included (but not I) do a good deal of boating; sometimes with the guide, sometimes without him—Jean & Clara are competent with the oars. If we live another year, I hope we shall spend its summer in this house.

We have taken the Appleton country seat, overlooking the Hudson, at Riverdale, 25 minutes from the Grand Central station, for a year, beginning Oct. 1, with option for another year.[6] We are obliged to be close to New York for a year or two.

Aug. 3d, I go yachting a fortnight up north in a 20-knot boat 225 feet long, with the owner, (Mr. Rogers,) Tom Reid [*sic*], D^r. Rice, a Mr. Paine & one other.[7] Judge Howland would go, but can't [in margin: OVER] get away from engagements; Professor Sloane would go but is in the grip of an illness.[8] Come—will *you* go? If you can manage it, drop a post-card to me, c/o H. H. Rogers, 26 Broadway. I shall be in New York a couple of days before we sail—July 31 or Aug. 1, perhaps the latter—& I think I shall stop at the Hotel Grosvenor, cor. 10th st & 5th ave.

We all send you & the Harmonies lots & gobs of love.

Mark.

1. The family was spending the summer at Saranac Lake.

2. Deletion of "who squats" before "in the Presidential chair." In the absence of Twichell's letter (which Twain is answering) it is difficult exactly to know the letter's context, but it relates, apparently, to some kind of appeal for financial help to Chinese victims of famine in Shensi—with Twichell involved because of his close friendship with Yung Wing, who has brought the matter to his attention. Shensi, a normally fertile province of China, was suffering severely, with the deaths of a quarter of the population. Reports of cannibalism were rife.

3. Gilbert Reid, Presbyterian minister and China missionary. Elwood Tewksbury, North China missionary and assistant to William Ament. What these "revelations" were is unknown. Maffia is an alternative spelling for Mafia.

4. Irish landowner and emigré to America, Harman Blennerhassett, was involved in a military conspiracy with Aaron Burr in 1806. They were accused by Thomas Jefferson, then president, of treason in their apparent aim of establishing an empire in what is now the U.S. Southwest.

5. Edward K. Root was a prominent Hartford doctor. John Howells was the architect son of William Dean Howells.

6. The family was moving from New York to Wave Hill House, owned by publisher William Appleton, in theory to cut living costs.

7. For more on this trip and on those involved, see Peter Messent, *Mark Twain and Male Friendship: The Twichell, Howells, and Rogers Friendships* (New York: Oxford University Press, 2009), 149. Thomas Brackett Reed was one of the most powerful Republican politicians of the era, and former speaker of the House of Representatives (1889–91). Clarence Rice was Twain's sometime doctor.

8. Judge Henry Howland. William M. Sloane was Professor of History at Columbia.

185. Twain to Twichell

28 August 1901. Saranac Lake, New York

Ampersand, N.Y., Aug. 28.

Dear Joe:

Just a word, to scoff at you, with your extravagant suggestion that I read the biography of Phillips Brooks—the very dullest book that has been printed for a century.[1] Joe, ten pages of Mrs. Cheney's masterly biography of her father—no, *five* pages of it.—contain more meat, more sense, more literature, more brilliancy, than that whole basketful of drowsy rubbish put together.[2] Why, in that dead atmosphere even Brooks himself is dull.—he wearied me; *oh* how he wearied me!

We had a noble good time in the yacht, & caught a China missionary & drowned him. Don't you give it away; we are letting on that it was General Funston, U.S.A.[3]

You would teach *me* fishing? Go to—you make me shudder. I haven't caught a fish—for "sport"—in 42 years. I'd rather lose a finger-joint, than see the poor devil struggle. Why, I don't get any real satisfaction—that is, any lasting satisfaction—out of seeing a *man* in pain. Except the missionary the other day.

Joe, it's just too lovely here! Love from us-all to you-all.

Mark.

1. *Life and Letters of Phillips Brooks* (2 vols.) by Alexander V. G. Allen was published in 1900. Brooks was an American Episcopal clergyman.

2. Twain is referring to Mary Bushnell Cheney's biography of her father, *Life and Letters of Horace Bushnell* (1880).

3. Frederick N. Funston was an American commander in the Philippines and another particular target for Twain's invective.

186. Twichell to Twain

5 September 1901. Minerva, New York

Hewitt Lake Minerva, N.Y. Sept. 5, 1901

Dear Mark,

Here I am at Dean Sage's lodge, about twenty five miles south by east of you; and if the aerial motor were out of embryo and full-born as I have no doubt it will be in the event, I would sail over and spend the forenoon with you instead of writing.[1]

Harmony who reached home a week ago—I left her en route at Albany to come up here—has sent me your last note about Phillips Brooks &c. I think what sours your milk on that memoir is the preposterous and irritating physique of the second volume. I confess it nearly took a like effect on me; but P.B. had long been one of my heroes and I stood the strain.

But the rest of your milk is also pretty sour it seems to me, old fellow. Really you are getting quite orthodox on the Doctrine of Total Human Depravity anyway. And as a Protestant (in the original, literal sense) you surely hold the belt. But I didn't set out to dose you with flatteries. I only want to say again that I appreciate painfully how unlucky beyond measure I was that I couldn't join you on the yachting trip. Nothing could have been so wholly inviting to me. However, I've had a fair sort of vacation such as it was. The wind-up in this wilderness paradise, though, is the cream of it. Dean's place is much like yours, your description of which—your luscious description—made my mouth water. *His* veranda hangs over the lake's edge too, and the primeval forest encloses him on three sides. My! What a contrast to Chicago—this freshness, fragrance, solitude! But Chicago had some charms—other, I mean, than the company of our dear nurse.[2] Our presence, though, made no holiday for her, poor girl. In the month of August she had 42 patients to whom she made an aggregate of 183 visits i.e. in her own district. There were several days when she took on the duty beside of another nurse's district, who was sick. Yet she was perfectly well all the time, and I never saw a young woman in more cheerful spirits. Her conditions, you will be glad to know, are not so dismal as her calling would seem to imply. She has all the social pleasures she can accommodate—and of a choice kind—including the attention of some mighty nice fellows, confound 'em, who have managed to unearth her. But I don't believe any of them can win her away from her sick clients—not, at least, for a good while yet.

The news that you had provided for another year—and probably two year—absence from Hartford was to the last degree unwelcome to us all. I don't think you or Livy begin to understand how much your return thither is longed for. I am fairly worn out with answering the question of when you are to re-appear. *Can* we wait two whole years more for you? For my part I deem nothing so needful for you as to resume attendance at the Asylum Hill Cong. Church. There, now, don't you go and kick at that. Are you staying away to avert or postpone that salutary medicine?

I found here when I came two sons of Vice. Pres. Roosevelt; Theodore, Junior, 13 years old and Kermit 11 years old, nice well-mannered lads both. The V.P. himself and his wife are expected next Sunday.[3] But I'm not going to stay to see them, though I would like to. I leave Saturday, stay with Will Sage at Albany over Sunday and hasten on to Hartford Monday. Dave is home and I'd rather see him than your admired McKinley even. From what Dean says I think that Wendell Garrison of "The Nation" is a man you would enjoy meeting.[4] Your view of the American and English nations is roseate and optimistic compared with his, by Dean's account. Spain alone has any worth or virtue in his eyes.

But good-bye for now, you blessed old misanthrope. I persist in loving you and shall to the end of the chapter, I guess. With kisses to Livy and the girls

Your well-affectioned

Joe.

1. "In the event"—synonymous for "eventually."

2. Harmony Twichell had taken up an appointment with the District Nursing Service of Chicago in January 1901.

3. The day after this letter was written, President McKinley was shot by an assassin in Buffalo, New York. Vice President Theodore Roosevelt indeed traveled to the Adirondacks when it appeared McKinley might recover (and to convey an air of calm about the situation), but on 14 September he received word that McKinley was near death and had to make a four-hundred-mile rush trip to an emergency inauguration as president. Sage had been a close friend of Roosevelt during the latter's term as governor of New York.

4. Wendell Phillips Garrison, literary editor of the *Nation* from 1865 to 1906 and son of abolitionist William Lloyd Garrison.

187. Twain to Twichell

8 September 1901. Saranac Lake, New York

Ampersand, N.Y., Sept 8/01.

Dear Joe:

Ah me, I reckon we've *got* to stick to New York until Jean's doctors give us leave to quit. The Hartford house, with repairs, taxes, &c., has cost us $16,000 in the past ten years—a burden which we've got to go on carrying yet awhile; how long, we can't guess.

Joe, little Harmony is a wonder. I hope, with you, that those young fellows will have to retire, & leave her to her gracious work.

This news of the President! We never got it until yesterday evening, when a N.Y. paper wandered into the camp. I doubt if it is serious. Otherwise they would not have moved him. Doctors (& politicians) always get all the advertising they can out of a case; making it desperate, & then fetching it out all right, after they've sucked the profit out of it. I was never able to feel alarmed about Mrs. McKinley when she was ostensibly so sick. Once when she was apparently dying, in San F., the President (as usual) wasn't able to make up his mind as to whether he would keep a junketing-engagement next morning! (He kept it.) Considering the unbulky size of his mind it is odd that he has such difficulty in making it up. (If he dies, I desire to withdraw these remarks.)

You'll be surprised to find me writing so soon. It is because I am taking a day off. [PRIVATE.[1] I've just ended a 6-day tour de force—25,000 words, (25 pages of Harper); upwards of two weeks' work in one.[2] It pays a third of our year's expenses & a little over—including those tiresome Hartford costs.

[How long it takes a literary seed to sprout, sometimes; sometimes sprouts only to wither—& that's the *rule*; sometimes springs right up & is satisfactory—as in the present case.[3] This seed was planted in your house, many years ago, when you sent me to bed with the book of a new author, not heard of by me until then—Sherlock Holmes. I planned to make fun of that pompous sentimental "extraordinary man" with his cheap & ineffectual ingenuities—but the plan wouldn't sprout; I have planned again, several times in past years, but each time the sprout withered on my hands. But this time I've pulled it off. Too late for the October number, & I'm sorry, for the subject is temporarily fresh, through the recent resurrection of the "extraordinary man."[4] I can't start it in November, because it takes two numbers to hold it, & I am already in the Xmas No. with a small story. And so it must stand over till January.

[I've done a grist of writing here this summer, but not for publication soon—if ever. I did write two satisfactory articles for early print, but I burnt one of them & have buried the other one in my large box of Posthumous Stuff. I've got stacks of Literary Remains piled up there.][5]

We leave here for Elmira, Sept. 19; leave there for New York, Sept. 26; leave the city for our home at Riverdale on the Hudson, Oct. 1.

Goodbye, & love to you-all from us-all.

Mark.

1. This word is an insertion. The bracket remains unclosed and it is unclear where the closure is supposed to come.

2. "Double-Barrelled Detective Story," published in *Harper's* in January and February 1902.

3. Again, bracket unclosed.

4. In 1901, Arthur Conan Doyle—the "author" referred to above—"resurrected" Holmes (after the Reichenbach Falls episode which had seemed to end the story series) in "The Hound of the Baskervilles." "A Double-Barrelled Detective Story" (1902) includes a spoof of Holmes.

5. Twain felt that much of what he was writing at that time would be too radical or shocking for his contemporary audience, but planned that it should be published after his death.

188. Twain to Twichell

10 September 1901. Saranac Lake, New York (Two typed transcripts by Albert Bigelow Paine)

Ampersand, Tuesday, Sept. 10, 1901.

Dear Joe:

It is another off day; but tomorrow I shall resume work to a *certainty*, & bid a long farewell to letter scribbling.

The news of the President looks decidedly hopeful, & we are all glad, & the household faces are much improved, as to cheerfulness. Oh, the *talk*—in the newspapers! Evidently the Human Race is the same old Human Race. And how unjust, & unreflectingly discriminating, the talkers are. Under the unsettling effects of powerful emotion the talkers are saying wild things, crazy things—they are out of themselves, & do not know it; they are temporarily insane, yet with one voice they declare the assassin *sane*—a man who has been entertaining fiery & reason-debauching maggots in his head for weeks & months.[1] Why, *no* one is sane, straight along, year in & year out, & we all know it. Our insanities are of varying sorts, & express themselves in various forms—fortunately harmless forms as a rule—but in whatever form they occur an immense upheaval of feeling can at any time topple us distinctly over the sanity-line for a little while; & then if our form happens to be of the murderous kind we must look out—& so must the spectator.

This ass with the unpronounceable name [Czolgosz] was probably more insane than usual this week or two back, & may get back upon his bearings by & by, but he was over the sanity-frontier when he shot the President. It is possible that it has taken him the whole interval since the murder of the King of Italy to get insane enough to attempt the President's life.[2] Without a doubt some thousands of men have been meditating the same act in the same interval, but new & strong interests have intervened & diverted their over-excited minds long enough to give them a chance to settle, & tranquilize, & get back upon a healthy level again. *Every* extraordinary occurrence unsettles the heads of hundreds of thousands of men for a few moments or hours or days. If there had been ten Kings around when Humbert fell they would all have been in great peril for a day or more—& from men in whose presence they would have been quite safe after the excess of their excitement had had an interval in which to cool down.[3] I bought a revolver once & traveled twelve hundred miles to kill a man.[4] He was away. He was gone a day. With nothing else to do, I *had* to stop & think—& did. Within an hour—within half of it—I was ashamed of myself, & felt unspeakably ridiculous. I do not know what to call it if I was not insane. During a whole week my head was in a turmoil night & day fierce enough & exhausting enough to upset a stronger reason than mine.

All over the world, every day, there are some millions of men in that condition temporarily. And in that time there is always a moment—perhaps only a single one—when they would do murder if their man was at hand. If the opportunity comes a shade too late, the chances are that it has come permanently too late. Opportunity *seldom* comes exactly at the supreme moment. This saves a million lives in a day in the world—for sure.

No Ruler is ever slain but the tremendous details of it are ravenously devoured by a hundred thousand men whose minds dwell, unaware, near the temporary-insanity frontier—& over they go, now! There is a day—two days—three—during which no Ruler would be safe from perhaps the half of them; & there is a single moment wherein he would not be safe from any of them, no doubt.

It will take this present shooting-case six months to breed another Ruler-tragedy, but it will breed it. There is at least one mind somewhere which will brood, & wear, & decay itself to the killing-point & produce that tragedy.

Every negro burned at the stake unsettles the excitable brain of another one—I mean the inflaming details of his crime, & the lurid theatricality of his exit do it—& the duplicate crime follows; & that begets a repetition, & that one another one—& so on. Every lynching-account unsettles the brains of another set of excitable white men, & lights another pyre—115 lynchings last year, 102 inside of 8 months this year; in ten years this will be *habit*, on these terms.[5]

Yes, the wild talk you see in the papers! And from men who are sane when not upset by overwhelming excitement. A U.S. Senator—Cullom—wants this Buffalo criminal lynched![6] It would breed other lynchings—of men who are not dreaming of committing murders, now, & will commit none if Collum [*sic*] will keep quiet & not provide the exciting cause.

And a District Attorney wants a law which shall punish with death *attempts* upon a President's life—this, mind you, as a *deterrent*. It would have no effect—or the opposite one. The lunatic's mind-space is *all* occupied—as mine was—with the matter in hand; there is no room in it for reflections upon what may happen to *him*. That comes *after* the crime.

It is the *noise* the attempt would make in the world that would breed the subsequent attempts, by unsettling the rickety minds of men who envy the criminal his vast notoriety—his obscure name tongued by stupendous Kings & Emperors—his picture printed everywhere, the trivialest details of his movements, what he eats, what he drinks, how he sleeps, what he says, cabled abroad over the whole globe at cost of fifty thousand dollars a day—& him only a lowly shoemaker yesterday!—like the assassin of the President of France—in debt three francs to his landlady &

insulted by her—& to-day she is proud to be able to say she knew him "as familiarly as you know your own brother," & glad to stand till she drops & pour out columns & pages of her grandeur & her happiness upon the eager interviewer.[7]

Nothing will check the lynchings & Ruler-murders but absolute silence—the absence of pow-pow about them. How are you going to manage that? By gagging every witness & jamming him into a dungeon for life; by abolishing all newspapers; by exterminating all newspaper men; & by extinguishing God's most elegant invention, the Human Race. It is quite simple, quite easy, & I hope you will take a day off & attend to it, Joe.

I blow a kiss to you, & am
Lovingly Yours,
Mark.

1. McKinley was shot by Leon Czolgosz, a twenty-eight-year-old anarchist.

2. On 29 July 1900, King Umberto I was assassinated by Gaetano Bresci, an Italian-born anarchist. Bresci lived in America before returning to Italy to shoot the king.

3. Humbert: an Anglicization of "Umberto."

4. See *Mark Twain and Orion Clemens: Brothers, Partners, Strangers* (Tuscaloosa: University of Alabama Press, 2003), where Philip Fanning puts forth the controversial theory that on one occasion, when Twain was a young man, he intended to kill his brother Orion.

5. The references to lynching were no doubt prompted by the fact that Twain had been working on his "United States of Lyncherdom" essay that summer.

6. Senator Shelby Cullom of Illinois.

7. Marie-François-Sadi Carnot, president of France, was stabbed on 24 June 1894 by Italian anarchist Sante Geronimo Caserio. A new paragraph ("The damned human race is—") starts after "interviewer." but Twain then deletes it.

189. Twichell to Twain

27 September 1901. Hartford, Connecticut

Hartford. Friday Sept. 27th

Dear Old Mark:

It is mighty kind and thoughtful of you to plan me such a pleasure, and I am going to take it in if it is a fashionable thing.[1] I'll watch the papers and see when the third race comes and run down the night before. If I put up at the Murray Hill Hotel it will be because I shall arrive late; also to have my hand-bag handy when I take the train home. But I will report to you at the Grosvenor betimes in the morning.

If you *hear* when [race] No. 3 will take place scratch me a line.

You were no end of a good fellow to write twice to me during your breathing-spell. The reason why I haven't answered is that I haven't had any breathing spell at-all since I got home.

Of course a funeral—and

[Unknown amount of text missing][2]

1. Twichell is writing of upcoming plans to watch the heats of the America's Cup yacht race (off Sandy Hook, New Jersey) from the deck of the *Kanawha.* He refers in his journal to going to New York on 2 and 3 October for the race between the *Columbia* (U.S.) and *Shamrock* (England): "Was guest, with Mark Twain, of Mr. H. H. Rogers on his elegant steam yacht 'Kanawha'."

2. On the letter's first page Twain has written in the margins, "*Sunday.* Dear Mr. Rogers: I shall try to get in, tomorrow or Tuesday, & telegraph Twichell what day to come, & what hour in the morning, & whether at West 35th St., or where. He can't report to us at this hotel, because we remove to Riverdale in the morning."

190. Twain to Twichell

29 September 1901. New York, New York

THE GROSVENOR.
FIFTH AVE. & TENTH ST.
NEW YORK
Sunday:

Dear Joe:

It looks now as if No. 3 would be next Thursday.

We leave this hotel for Riverdale a couple of days before that.

My instructions for last Friday were, to appear at foot of *West 35th st at 8 a.m.*, where the "Kanawha" (Mr. Rogers's yacht) would be lying at anchor & his launch waiting to tote me out.

I mean to drop a note to Mr. Rogers & can get instructions sent to the Murray Hill for you.

Goodbye for the present—hoping to see you on board the Kanawha.

Mark.

191. Twichell to Twain

15 October 1901. Hartford, Connecticut

Hartford. Oct. 15.

Dear Mark:

You are coming to the Yale Bicentennial next week.[1] Hurra! Hurra!! And now I think it best, and only fair, to tell you that from what I hear I have no doubt that on that high occasion you are going to be asked to accept the honorary degree of L.H.D. (Doctor of Human Letters)—our only *literary* decoration.[2] You will be one of a very small number of Americans on whom it will be conferred at that time. I want you to understand, old fellow, that it will be, in its intention, the highest possible compliment; and emphatically so *in your case*, for the reason that it will be tendered you by a Corporation of gentlemen the majority of whom do not at-all agree with the views on important questions which you have lately promulgated in speech and in writing, and with which you are identified in the public mind. They grant, of course, your right to hold and to express those views, though, for themselves, they don't like 'em. But in awarding you the proposed laurel, they will make no account of them whatsoever. Their action will appropriately signify simply and solely their estimate of your merit and rank as a *man of letters.* And so, as I say, the compliment of it will be of a pure, unadulterated quality. I hope that it will please you accordingly. It ought to, I am sure.

I should explain that the reason why I speak of the honor as *doubtless* to befall you is, that there is to be yet another meeting of the University Corporation at which it, and a lot of such matters, are to be formally settled. But everybody thinks you a certain winner. You will smile, but the ministers are for you almost to a man, and they are the lads who least approve your bad opinions. They know something about literature though.

By the way your friend Ament has been in Hartford the past week attending the meeting of the American Board. He made a most noble address—which I wish to goodness you had heard—in which he made no slightest reference to the adverse criticism of which he has been the target. He is a big, fine fellow, Mark, and you would have felt it before you had listened to him five minutes. You see how he impressed the Courant. *[Pasted-in clipping:]*

The Rev. Dr. Ament, in his address before the American Board in this city on Wednesday, placed himself next after but very near to Sir Robert Hart, as a man who knows China, and the Chinese.[3] It was one of the great addresses at this meeting of the board. It was a brilliant, forcible and immensely instructive review of a complicated and often confused situation. It was both philosophical and statesmanlike; and it was full of that broad and truly religious feeling that recognizes an ethical kinship even where the evangelical basis is lacking. We have no doubt that very many educated Chinamen will be thoroughly pleased with his view of their country and people; and no Chinaman can fail to acknowledge the fairness and sense of brotherhood with which he drew upon his copious stores of exact knowledge. It was in the highest sense instructive, too, for Americans, and it ought to be very widely read. If the Rev. Dr. Ament correctly represents the dominant note of American missionary labor in China, this country has every reason to be satisfied that we have missionaries there.

[End of clipping.]

Have you chanced to see what Sir Robert Hart says of him?[4] I would send you that too, only I don't want to strain your patience to the breaking point.

My day with you on the "Kanawha" was a solid delight. But did you ever hear such a yarn as "the Sun" built up on it?[5] I have been to the reunion to-day of Col. Cheney's old regiment; and found that the veterans—who are simple minded as a class—all believed the whole of it—the Sun's yarn, I mean.[6] But good-night, I will see you soon in New Haven. I should explain, again, that my object—or one object—in informing you of your impending honor, is to give you time—if you require it—to get ready the remarks with which I *suppose* you will be called on in the course of the picnic to acknowledge it; doing as I would be done by in such circumstances. With love to Livy and the girls,

Yours ever aff.

Joe.

1. Twichell, senior fellow of the Yale Corporation, would preach in the chapel service held during the bicentennial celebrations.

2. Twain was indeed made an Honorary Doctor of Humane Letters by Yale in 1901.

3. Sir Roger Hart was a long-serving British consular official in China, serving as inspector-general of the Chinese Maritime Customs Service from 1863 to 1911. He was often referred to by his contemporaries as "the best known foreigner in China" and his word carried much weight.

4. Hart had published an article called "The Missionary Question in China" in a weekly news review, *The Great Round World* (vol. 18, no. 252, 7 September 1901). In it, he singled out Ament, praising him for his bravery during the siege of the legations the previous year, noting his "plucky, timely and self-sacrificing intervention" in rescuing others.

5. On 4 October, the *New York Sun* had printed a comic story, "Mark Twain at the Race," about Twain and Twichell's attendance at the event.

6. Frank Cheney (see Letter 172, note 3) had served with the 16th Connecticut Volunteer Infantry during the Civil War.

192. Twichell to Twain

17 October 1901. Hartford, Connecticut

Hartford. Oct. 17.

Dear Mark:

Yes: Wednesday the 23rd inst. is Commemoration Day when the honors will be conferred. But you are not going to wait till then, I hope, before appearing on the scene. The show *begins* Sunday Oct. 20*th* with the sermon assigned to me because Dr. Munger hadn't the voice for it.[1] *That* you can get along without. But you will not do well to miss the torch-light procession Monday night, which, if the weather suits will be the finest,—any way the most interesting—ever seen in this country. Rev. Anson Phelps Stokes, Secretary of the University, told me that his mother had invited you to be her guest, along with Ambassador Choate and others during the Bi-Centennial.

So come early.

Yours in haste

Joe

1. Theodore Munger, author, preacher, and liberal theologian.

193. Twichell to Twain

29 November 1901. Hartford, Connecticut

[Note in Twain's hand at the top of the letter, with partial double-underlining in the word "telephone":]

Do, Joe, tele*phone* from Grand Central—150 Kingsbridge

Hartford. Nov. 29.

Dear Mark:

Imprimis: Your article in the new Harpers [*sic*] "The Death Disk," is a perfect gem.[1] Upon my word I believe, not only that no live man can do that sort of thing as well as you, but that there's nothing else *you* do so well—which is saying much.

This is [to] tell you that Harmony plan[s] to leave home next Wednesday Dec. 4th by the 11.07 o'clock express, which will be due in N.Y. at 1.58.

We have some things to do in New York, and shall probably not get away for Riverdale til 3.40. or 4.05. or 4.30— —but will telegraph you when. How good it seems to think we are going to see you all!

Yrs aff.

Joe

1. "Imprimis" means "In the first place." The story was published in the December 1901 *Harper's Magazine.* Twain's sentimental tale of how a young officer in Oliver Cromwell's army is saved from execution by the intervention of his young daughter is not generally considered one of his better short works.

194. Twichell to Twain

31 December 1901. Hartford, Connecticut

Hartford. Dec. 31.

Dear Mark:

The Hartford Yale Alumni Association will banquet at the Allyn House Friday evening, Jan 31st 1902. The Committee of arrangements—you know the rest. Well, for my part, I do very much wish you would come. We want as Hartford men to congratulate [you] as a Hartford man, and ourselves in your presence, on the Bi-Centennial honor with which you were laureled in October—which is our honor also. Do incline the sceptre to us if you can.

If you really would like to pass an evening with the Scroll & Key boys in New Haven, and can stand it to suffer two evenings in succession, I will meet you in New Haven Thursday Jan. 30*th* and we will sup and sing with them that night and come up to Hartford together the next day—to our house, of course.

I don't know how much you would care to inhale for two or three hours the atmosphere of youth diffused by a company of collegians;—I love to do it now and then; nothing more regales my spirit.—but you spoke at the Bi-Centennial of wanting to do it *some* time. But very likely another time will be better. There isn't another time, though, for a meeting of the Hartford Yale men with Dr. Clemens.

Young Harmony is with us, having unexpectedly and without solicitation, been given her vacation now instead of at the end of her year, in March. So that she and Dave have been home together through the holidays;—a great felicity. Harmony the Elder is, for aught I can see, about as well as ever. Our excursion to Riverdale proved the best sort of medicine. Livy was just the osteopath she was looking for; and she improved the state of *my* nerve centres too—those that set the affections a humming. Love to her, dear Heart, and all of you.

Yrs as ever

Joe

195. Twain to Twichell

4 January 1902. Riverdale, New York

Riverdale, Jan. 4/02.

Dear Joe:

It is a most embarrassing situation. I have declined 5 public functions & banquets & things in Yonkers—two miles from here—on the plea that I go to *no* function outside the city limits—a rule which I made when we came here, & it has served me for all-sufficient answer to every outside invitation since—dozens & dozens of them—a rule which I have never once broken.

I can't go to Hartford upon that invitation or upon *any* invitation to a function there. Now then, you must see to it *strictly*, that none is *sent* me, by *any*body. For I want to be there, but an invitation would prevent it, for I should decline it. If even a word should leak into the papers that I was expected or was coming, I should have to remain at home. For I live upon the public confidence, & must not lie to it openly.

I will not say to you that I am coming. I will only say that I have to spend part of a day, & a night, in Hartford some time or other between this & April 1st—the particular date is not material. We will let it stand at that. I came blessed near going four or five days ago.

Say—Aldrich became a grandfather in the closing days of December. What late crops we are having!—we boys that foregathered together in New York & Boston thirty & thirty-three-&-four years ago. Hay, Aldrich, Howells, Whitelaw Reid, Clemens—all sterile in the second generation but that little poet.[1]

[Unknown amount of text missing.]

1. Whitelaw Reid was a journalist, statesman, and editor-in-chief of the *New York Tribune*. The "little poet" is Thomas Bailey Aldrich.

196. Twichell to Twain

13 January 1902. Hartford, Connecticut

Hartford, Conn., January 13, 1902

[Printed enclosure:]

YALE ALUMNI ASSOCIATION

The Annual Dinner of the Yale Alumni Association will be held at the Allyn House, Hartford, on Friday evening, January thirty-first, at quarter past seven o'clock.

The list of speakers will include President Hadley, Bishop Chauncy B. Brewster, President Smith of Trinity, Rev. Rockwell Harmon Potter and Walter H. Clark, Esq.

Herbert Knox Smith, Secretary and Treasurer.
847 Main Street
Hartford, Conn.[1]

[Enclosure ends. Twichell has written at the foot of this:]

There's no exploitation of M.T. in this, you see.[2]

Joe

1. Twichell has crossed out information about purchasing tickets to the dinner for $3.00.

2. Twichell writes in his journal for 31 January, "Mark Twain passes the night with us, coming to town to participate in the annual dinner of the Hartford Yale Alumni Association. He had promised his presence on the occasion to me privately, but required it to be kept strictly secret from the public. His appearance on the scene was, therefore, a surprise to all but the two or three that had to know of it beforehand. He seemed in excellent health."

197. Twain to Twichell

18 January 1902. Riverdale, New York (Mourning border)

RIVERDALE
ON THE HUDSON

Saturday
Jan. 18/02.

Dear Joe:

Can't go to New Haven.

Shall go to Hartford per 4 p.m. train.

Shall transact my business next morning, & leave for Hartford during the day.[1]

We leave here for Elmira day after to-morrow, and return Jan. 27.
Love to all!
Mark.

1. The meaning is confusing here. Twain may be expanding in the third sentence on what he would be doing before the departure described in the second.

198. Twain to Twichell

2 February 1902. Riverdale, New York (Two typed transcripts by Albert Bigelow Paine)

RIVERDALE
ON THE HUDSON
Feb. 2/02.

Dear Joe:

(After compliments.* From Bridgeport to N.Y. thence to home; & continuously until near midnight I wallowed & reeled with Jonathan in his insane debauch; rose immensely refreshed & fine at 10 this morning, but with a strange & haunting sense of having been on a 3-days' tear with a drunken lunatic.[1] It is years since I have known these sensations. All through the book is the glare of a resplendent intellect gone mad—a marvelous spectacle. No, not *all* through the book—the drunk does not come on till the last third, where what I take to be Calvinism & its God begin to show up & shine red & hideous in the glow from the fires of hell, their only right & proper adornment. By God I was ashamed to be in such company.

Jonathan seems to hold (as against the Arminian position) that the Man (or his Soul or his Will) never *creates* an impulse itself, but is moved to action by an influence *back* of it. That's sound!

Also, that of two or more things offered it, it infallibly chooses the one which for the moment is most *pleasing* to *ITSELF. Perfectly* correct! An immense admission for a man not otherwise sane.

Up to that point he could have written chapters III & IV of my suppressed "Gospel." But there we seem to separate. He seems to concede the indisputable & unshakable dominion of Motive and Necessity (call them what you may, these are *exterior* forces & not under the man's authority, guidance or even suggestion)—then he suddenly flies the logical track & (to all seeming) makes the *man* & not those exterior forces responsible to God for the man's thoughts words & acts. It is frank insanity.

I think that when he concedes the autocratic dominion of Motive and Necessity he grants a *third* position of mine—that a man's mind is a mere machine—an *automatic* machine—which is handled entirely from the *outside*, the man himself furnishing it absolutely nothing; not an ounce of its fuel, & not so much as a bare *suggestion* to that exterior engineer as to what the machine shall do, nor *how* it shall do it nor *when*.

After that concession, it was time for him to get alarmed & *shirk*—for he was pointed straight for the only rational & possible next-station on *that* piece of road: the irresponsibility of man to God.

And so he shirked. Shirked, and arrived at this handsome result:

> Man is commanded to do so & so;
> It has been ordained from the beginning of time that some men *shan't*, & others *can't*:
> *These are to blame: let them be damned.*

I enjoy the Colonel very much, & shall read the rest of him with an obscene delight.[2]

Joe, the whole tribe shout love to you & yours!

Mark.

*Meaning, "What a good time you gave me; what a happiness it was to be under your roof again, &c. &c. &c." See opening sentence of all translations of letters passing between Lord Roberts & Indian princes & rulers.[3]

1. Open parenthesis but no closing one. Twain has probably been reading Jonathan Edwards's 1754 *Freedom of the Will.* Edwards was an eighteenth-century minister known for his association with the First Great Awakening in New England theology and for his fiery sermons, including "Sinners in the Hands of an Angry God."

2. Perhaps a reference to another loaned book.

3. In the original letter, this asterisked note appears after the page ending "exterior forces." Lord Frederick Roberts of Kandahar was the author of *Forty-One Years in India: From Subaltern to Commander in Chief* (1897), and was possibly the "Colonel" referred to above.

199. Twichell to Twain

2 September 1902. Essex County, New York

Blue Ridge,[1]
Essex County, N.Y.
Sept. 2, 1902

Dear Mark:

The letter of that estimable and amiable lady which you passed on to me has caught up with me here in the woods where I am five mile from a P.O. and get mail only once a week.[2] It is amusing indeed. Her intention is good. She says she has many years been meaning to write it—in the lapse of which years she seems to have forgotten some things. Apparently she thinks that the convicts letter was your composition. Apparently too it has escaped her that the whole business was a fraud. Or can it be that she didn't get hold of that in the first place? For *me* that discovery killed the letter dead i.e. for purposes of moral improvement. May be, though, it didn't for her. Her tale of its holy power I shall paste into its proper place in the book (which book is it?) when I get home, for the ticklement of my posterity.[3]

When I received it I was on the point of forwarding *you* a letter that had just reached me and asking you to express to me your judgment and wishes on the matter broached in it. I deemed it only proper to do that before making reply to it. Of course I could grind out five thousand words on the noble theme proposed if I had my freedom in it; and there's plenty of room in my shrunk purse for $250.[4] Still, somehow, I recoil from the idea of making merchandise of my happy memories, and of exposing the peculiar treasures of my heart to the public curiosity. Really I feel a delicacy about it. Besides; I have already sometime since been urgently desired by Mr. Gilder to write an article for "The Century" on "M.T. *as a Humorist.*" (I have written one for him on Charley Warner—very very unsatisfactory, but the best I could,—which hasn't appeared yet and I guess it isn't going to.)[5] To be sure I have consciously neither the critical or the literary qualification for the special task Mr. G. sets me; yet I suppose he would let me disport myself in the broad field of M.T. about any way I might choose. And both on your account and on my own I would prefer The Century to The Ladies [*sic*] Home Journal as the medium of the display of your charms to mankind—though fewer ducats come of it. I think it hardly probable that I shall fill either order: still I would like to know your views. If I do conclude to shed ink in your defense may I again have your leave to quote from your letters? I had reason to judge that my citations from them in the Harper's Magazine article were considered of more interest and value than all the rest of it.[6] One source of my embarassment in the premises is that *you are alive*—and long *may* you live, dear old fellow, and keep winning new and brighter laurels to the last act.

By the way, what have you lately been writing about life and the things that constitute the good of life? I met a man the other day—a doctor of divinity any way—who demanded of me *why* I hadn't taught you something better than you had recently been expounding in a production of that style, of which I knew nothing. I shall have to look into it.[7]

Your report of your impressions of Edwards on The Will was vastly entertaining. I read it to Dean Sage when I was with him at Cornell University in May—'twas the last time I ever saw him—and he pronounced it sound i.e. as a criticism. While, of course, I do not believe—as you do—that we live move and have our being as moral creatures in a profound immitigable all encompassing element of Inveracity, I do think there's a deal of truth in what you say of Edwards. As a matter of fact he has always by many been held to be a flat necessitarian in spite of his disclaimers, and his flop to break the meshes of his own argument.

Dean Sage—speaking of him *reminds* that he is in his grave.[8] Generally, so far, I cannot take any sense of it, though I saw him buried. His wife and one of his girls drove in here from their camp, or lodge, on Lake Hewitt—20 miles away, and passed a couple of days with us, and did nothing i.e. the wife, all the while she was with us but talk, or make us talk, of Dean, the loved and lost. She seemed not unhappy: but only for the time void of interest in all things save that one. It was most pathetic to note.

We have been here in this sweet seclusion for a month—eight of us—but are now getting away to Hartford in detatchments (or is it detachments?) Harmony and three of the boys heading the column. Harmony is, for aught I can see once more as well as ever. The good news of Livy's better health gladdened us. Dave, Sally, Louise and I go this week [By the way, Sally's meeting up with you at Nassau flutters her spirit with rapture still.[9] To her it was an event of real grandeur]. Next Sunday I shall, please God, be looking in the eyes of the dearest congregation on earth—and the patientest. When are we to see you all? Our love to every one.

Yours ever aff.

Joe

Please return Mr. Bok's letter—if you can remember to.[10]

1. The Twichells summered in their final years at Elk Lake, near this Adirondack Mountain town.

2. Letter missing.

3. Chapter 52 of *Life on the Mississippi* features a convict's letter circulated by a clergyman friend of the narrator, presumably Twichell. The letter expresses repentance, but turns out to be a fraud.

4. Apparently, this letter was from the *Ladies' Home Journal* requesting an essay on Twain.

5. Twichell's essay on Warner was published in the *Century*, but not until January 1903, as "Qualities of Warner's Humor." The *Century* essay on Twain was never written. For a list of Twichell's publications, see Steve Courtney, *Joseph Hopkins Twichell* (Athens: University of Georgia Press, 2008), 308–10.

6. See Letter 127.

7. Twain's "The Five Boons of Life," a brief fable pronouncing death the greatest of these boons, had been published in *Harper's Weekly* in July.

8. Dean Sage had died on 23 June 1902 at his summer camp on the Restigouche River in New Brunswick, Canada.

9. Twain met Sally on March 20 in Nassau on one of his *Kanawha* trips. He wrote to Livy the next day, "The first person I saw when we came ashore yesterday & entered this vast & airy hotel, was Sally Twichell, fine & buxome [*sic*], (She was here with the Browns)" (Mark Twain Papers).

10. Edward Bok, editor of *Ladies' Home Journal*.

200. Twain to Twichell

7 September 1902. York Harbor, Maine (Two typed transcripts by Albert Bigelow Paine)

York Harbor, Me., Sept. 7/02.

Dear Joe:

I don't remember which book that convict's letter is in. I think maybe it is in the back part of the Tramp Abroad; or might it be Old Times on the Mississippi?

Bang away about me as freely as you please. When you include things from my letters it will be safest to select the extracts first & submit them to Livy—it will save wasting comment on passages which might perish under her blue pencil. You needn't let her see the article itself until it is in print, for over that she hasn't any sort of authority. If I were you, I would write my articles *my* way & let the editors take or leave, as they like. They spoil many a good thing by trying to tell a writer how to do it. The Century people once arranged with me for 10 chapters of round-the-world travel for $12,000: & presently sent me a document to sign in which I engaged to do the chapters—how? According to my mood? No—I was to imitate the style & manner, &c., of Innocents Abroad: a contract to squelch the mood when it wasn't the right one, and write out of a mood that didn't exist. It was an ignorant bid for artificial work. I was in debt & wanted the money, but not bad(ly?) enough to sign *that*—which I sent back without any considerable amount of comment.

I don't know of anything I've been "lately writing." I think the last was about Funston—away back in March or April (magazine articles) or the other day (short newspaper letter.)[1] I was blackguarding that military louse. I hope to do it some more before I die. McKinley, Jay Gould, Funston—isn't that a precious gang? The Holy Trinity of American worship, begetters of present American political, commercial & military morals. There's one good thing: we've struck bottom, & can't sink any lower.

"Moral creatures!" Now discard that slang. We haven't any morals—& never had any that weren't brummagem.[2] We don't know any more about morals than the Deity knew about astronomy when he wrote Genesis. And don't you keep on intimating that we have intervals wherein we are not liars. There aren't any such. I wrote a story about it last week—a *Xmas* story—for Harper. Entitled "Was it Heaven? Or Hell?" You wait & see.

Livy is getting along slowly but steadily.[3] More than once, between Aug. 11 & 25th I thought she would not go out of this house alive. She thought it herself several times, but she only revealed it by speech once. As soon as she is strong enough to travel (say a fortnight hence, or possibly a day or two earlier) we shall put her on a stretcher & start for Riverdale or Elmira.

If the truth has been uttered once (to Livy) by any member or servant of this household since Aug. 11, it was by inadvertence & was repented of with all dispatch. Among the daily lies we say no letters come from the friends. Whereas they *do*; but if she knew it she would force us to show them to her, & *every*thing injuriously excites her. She doesn't know a letter has come from you. She asked, 3 days ago, & I told her you were still in the woods & not expected home soon. "Is *that* any reason for not writing?" She can't be satisfied with one lie, but always pumps for another one, & soon becomes embarrassing. Sometimes we get discouraged, & want to fall back on the truth & just take the chances. But it wouldn't do.

With lots of love to you all

Mark.

1. "A Defence of General Funston," *North American Review* 174 (1 May 1902).

2. "Brummagem" means cheap, shoddy or counterfeit. The term originates in the local name for the English city of Birmingham.

3. Livy probably had a heart attack (it seems on 12 August—Twain himself is often approximate on dates), with chest pains and difficulty in breathing.

201. Twain to Twichell

25 or 26? September 1902. York Harbor, Maine

[A newspaper clipping pasted to a sheet from a legal pad heads the letter. It is titled "Twain's' [sic] *Guide in Hard Luck"; its subtitle is "'Harris' of 'Tramps Abroad' Says Every Incident Was Pure Fiction." But it focuses on "J. W. Verey"* [sic]*— whose experiences it identifies as those of "Harris." Joseph N. Verey had worked as a courier for Twain, but it was Twichell who was "Harris."]*

Verey was not along on that trip at all. In reply to a cable from a London paper, I said *you* were Harris.

Livy was close to the grave Sunday night & Monday & Tuesday, but she has been soaring up like a weed since. Love to you all.

Mark.

202. Twichell to Twain

28 September 1902. Hartford, Connecticut

Hartford. Sept. 28.

Dear Mark:

It must be that you really *were* in courage about Livy or you wouldn't have thought or cared to send me that newspaper clipping [see above at Letter 201]. The reason why I didn't write at once when two weeks ago you told me how very sick she had been, was that I didn't want to make you lie *unnecessarily* in answer to her inquiry if we had been heard from. I waited till she should be able to hear the truth. But that was the first intimation or information we had of her illness. Your previous comment scratched on the margin of the letter about the convict's letter, to the effect that Livy was on the mend had no meaning in particular to us.[1] When we found out what the case had been we were scared—a good deal as a man is who wakes up to discover that he has been unwittingly in an awful danger while asleep. It has been so really twice over. For of her relapse we knew nothing till it was past. Well, Mark, old fellow, what a dreadful time you have had! She truly *is* off the breakers now, is she? My! but what precious heart-freight Harmony and I have in that dear Livy ship! I don't know whether we are glad or not that we were unconscious of the jeopardy it was in. I don't think we are. No, we are not. We should have chosen to share the suspense and solicitude—agony though it was—with which you, who love her best and whom she loves best, watched to see—but I can't bear to name the alternatives. Thank God that when the door opened Life stood in the threshold. But how unimaginably you must have suffered! Do Mark, send us another word right off to assure us that Hope is keeping Fear at bay. And when you can tell Livy that we love her more than ever for staying out of heaven awhile longer. There would be no one on earth to take her place with Harmony and me, were she to leave us.

Our news all pretty good. We are settled down—the remnant of us that is here—doing the same old things that for so many years have been our daily and weekly round.

Your abominable heresies, of which you are now sporting such a menagerie, I will not delay to execrate at this time, but will return to later. Have you seen the enclosed, which has been sent me?[2] Probably you have; but you need not send it back for I have another copy.

I havn't written that article yet. It is doubtful if I do. I can't get time for it. And I'm no writer anyhow.

Love to the girls; and if you go to Elmira, as Molly Dunham—I hear, I havn't seen her—says you will, our kindest regards to the friends there.

Ever affectionately Yours

Joe

What is to be your *address* the next few weeks?

1. This "comment" must be on a letter now lost, most probably on that enclosing the "letter of that estimable and amiable lady" to which Twichell refers on 2 September (Letter 199). This letter was probably sent around 25 August or a few days later.

2. Enclosure missing.

203. Twain to Twichell

30 September 1902. York Harbor, Maine

Private.[1]

York, Maine, Sept. 30/02

Dear Joe:

We *think* the above will be our address for only a week longer, but there's no certainty. It depends on Livy's picking up strength enough in that time to qualify her to sit up 30 minutes in a chair without harm. She sat up ten, yesterday. We have to wait & see.

We show her some of the letters, but not those that would stir her; she can't see yours yet, but I will tell her it is here.

Clara assumed control nine days ago, seeing that everything was going to destruction for want of a centralized power & authority. Her first act saved her mother's life. Since then, things have gone well & rationally. She seems to be as good a general as her mother, & with even more (perhaps) than her mother's bravery in doing the disagreeable thing. To a physician who had an appointment for a certain day she wrote a letter excusing him. Without calling a council of war, she contracted for a successor to the trained nurse by telegraph last Saturday; installed her yesterday morning (per enclosed letter to D^r. Hawkes)* & discharged the previous occupant of the post.[2] Yesterday at 10 a.m. she went alone to Boston in the deluge to consult the specialist & find out *why* such-&-such things were so-&-so & involved in disquieting mystery. It was a valuable journey for us. Meantime she conceived of an excellent way of conveying Livy to the RR station; (I believe I have improved on it this morning, & so does Clara—but we shall see.) She reached home (again in the deluge) a little after dark, & went to bed tired.

With a power of love to you all,

Mark.

---

*No, I'll destroy the letter—that's fairer to Clara.

1. This word is an insertion. "Private," most likely, because of the information about Livy's health.

2. Dr. Wilson Hawkes of York Harbor would be threatened by Twain with a lawsuit for his excessive fees ($3 per visit rather than his normal $1).

204. Twain to Twichell

11 October 1902. York Harbor, Maine

[In the top margin of a printed circular:]

We shall try to take Livy home in an invalid car next Wednesday, 15th, Joe. But she is *very* weak.

[The circular takes the form of a two-page printed pamphlet which had been sent to Twain. Written by British travel writer Robert Allbut, it relates to the 25 or 26 September letter above. The pamphlet is headed Travellers' Bureau, Savoy Hotel, The Strand, and addressed "to the Editor of Tramp Abroad"—the last two

words a handwritten insert on the printed document. The pamphlet concerns Joseph Verey, his present difficult financial circumstances, a public appeal made on his behalf, and Verey's subsequent denial of the facts on which the appeal had been based. Allbut writes, "[m]y object in now directing your attention as above is not to obtain any further publicity on my part, in the Daily Press, but to obviate, if possible, any further editorial reference which may be inadvertently made, without a complete knowledge of the real facts of the case." *Presumably he sent his pamphlet to the press and to those (like Twain) who had some kind of concern with Verey's predicament. Twain also writes above the pamphlet the words, "Remember Joseph, Joe?"]*

205. Twain to Twichell

31 October 1902. Riverdale, New York (Typed transcript by Albert Bigelow Paine)

Riverdale, N.Y. City, Oct. 31/02.[1]

Dear Joe:

It is ten days since Susy [Warner] wrote that you were laid up with a sprained shoulder, since which time we have had no news about it. I hope that no news is good news, according to the proverb; still, authoritative confirmation of it will be gladly received by this family, if some of you will furnish it. Moreover, I should like to know how & where it happened. In the pulpit, as like as not, otherwise you would not be taking so much pains to conceal it. This is not a malicious suggestion, & not a personally-invented one: you told me yourself, once, that you threw artificial power & impressiveness into places in your sermons where needed, by "banging the Bible"—(your own words.) You have reached a time of life when it is not wise to take these risks. You would better jump around. We all have to change our methods as the infirmities of age creep upon us. Jumping around will be impressive now, whereas before you were gray it would have excited remark.

Poor Livy drags along drearily. It must be hard times for that turbulent spirit. It will be a long time before she is on her feet again. It is a most pathetic case. I wish I could transfer it to myself. Between ripping & raging & smoking & reading, I could get a good deal of a holiday out of it.[2]

Clara runs the house smoothly & capably. She is discharging a trial-cook to-day & hiring another.

Jean is coming along miraculously (unberufen!) It is 92 days since we have been disturbed about her. The longest previous free interval in 5 years was 39 days. It is those 5 years that put Livy where she is.

Mildred Howells is engaged to be married.[3]

A power of love to you all!

Mark.

1. The family had returned to Riverdale on the 15th by an especially chartered train, with an invalid car. Livy's health would remain extremely poor from this point on.

2. This comic note no doubt a defense mechanism in the face of his deep anxieties.

3. Howells's daughter was engaged to celebrated botanist David G. Fairchild. She would break off the engagement later.

206. Twichell to Twain

3 November 1902. Hartford, Connecticut

Hartford Nov. 3. 1902

"It is absurd to speak of forgiveness," he said presently, and slowly, "as it is absurd to speak of restitution. These are mere words, having no real tally in fact. We appear to have volition, but actually and essentially we are as leaves driven by the wind. Where it blindly drives, there we blindly go. So it has been from the beginning. So it always will be. In the last twenty-four hours there are many things I have ceased to believe in, and among them, is human responsibility."[1]

Dear Mark;

I didn't believe it, but the above shows that, by George, there are *two* of you.

I forget now who your fellow is. I clipped his creed from some periodical—"The Bookman" I think—before I twisted my shoulder, on purpose to send you.

Don't approve or applaud him, for his judgment is a purely automatic matter, and not *his* in any proper sense, of course.

My said damaged shoulder is about half mended. I can write, as yet, only with difficulty. And so I will only say that we are glad the news from Livy is no worse, but wish it were better. What you tell of Jean reveals, we conjecture, the cause of Livy's break-down. She had long been under an awful strain and no wonder she gave out. May the brightening of her skies in the dark quarter prove lasting.

President Harry Hopkins of Williams College has told me of seeing you at the Princeton Inauguration, and of your good appearance there—hearty and healthy.[2]

Mrs Dean Sage was here last week visiting her daughter Betty (Mrs Walter Goodwin). A sad, sad woman she seemed. Her being alone made me *feel*, really for the first time, that Dean was gone from earth. She told Harmony that she and Dean used in late years often to say to one another that their most delightful social experience in life had been in those old times when they came to Hartford and met you and Livy and Charley Warner and Libbie Hamersley and some others at our house.[3] Well, they *were* dear old times Mark, and we had the heart of youth in us to taste their sweet fellowship to the full. They can never return; but, still, something is left; and I do want consumedly to see you—and Harmony does too—both of you. When shall it be?

Ever affectionately Yours

Joe

1. Typed extract at head of letter. The excerpt is from *The History of Sir Richard Calmady: A Romance* (1901) by Mary St. Leger Kingsley (the daughter of Charles Kingsley), writing as Lucas Malet. The book was presumably serialized in the periodical Twichell clipped it from.

2. This refers to the 25 October 1902 inauguration of Woodrow Wilson as the president of Princeton University. Henry (Harry) Hopkins attended the Union Theological Seminary in New York with Twichell. Both served as chaplains in the Civil War. He became president of Williams College in Williamstown, Massachusetts, in 1902.

3. Twichell refers to her as Libby and Libbie interchangeably.

207. Twichell to Twain

15 November 1902. Hartford, Connecticut

Hartford, Nov. 15

Dear old Mark:

Harmony says "Do drop Mark a line and tell him that we are thinking of him all the while!"

She means all of you, of course. And what she says is quite true. We don't know accurately what the situation is; but we gather that these are anxious days with you.[1] That makes them so with us.

How much we love you, especially how much we love Livy, we are finding out as never before.

You needn't write. We write only for the relief of saying that our hearts are yours—which we trust you already know.

My sprained shoulder—which, by the way, I *didn't* get in the pulpit, but by jumping off a street car in motion—is about well, though I can't yet use the pen with comfort.

I am promising Stedman a speech at the next New England dinner,——which means that I have a month of misery before me.[2] Good morning, old fellow. God bless you, and grant you brighter skies—if it may be.

Ever affectionately yours

Joe

1. No doubt referring to Livy's continuing poor health.

2. Edmund Clarence Stedman, Civil War journalist, poet, literary man, and stockbroker. Stedman was to preside at the ninety-seventh annual festival of the New England Society in the City of New York, held on 22 December.

208. Twichell to Twain

30 December 1902. Hartford, Connecticut

Hartford. Dec. 30. 1902

Dear Mark:

We can't go any longer without some more definite report of Livy than rumor affords. Harmony and I thought we might possibly see you in New York whither we went to the New England Dinner last week Monday (where by the way, I may tell you in confidence, I made a not very successful speech) but we only heard that you had *been seen* there by somebody that day;—which did us no good. We suppose—and are happy to—that Livy is mending right along. Please send us a word assuring us that it is so. And is Clara also recovered from *her* upset?[1] And how are the rest? *What* a night it was—that of Nov. 28th![2] And to think of the Shadow sitting there beside Tom Reed![3]

I asked Pres. Hadley the last time I was in New Haven what he had *intended* to say in decorating at the Yale Bi-Centennial.[4] "Just what I *did* say. (he answered) I knew what would happen when Mr. Clemens came forward, and made ready accordingly." A bright Boy, that!

If you are coming up here Jan. 21*st* you can make a speech at the Dinner—in the Foot Guard Armory—of the Sons of the Revolution; or if you prefer at the meeting of the Working Men's Club in the Lafayette St Public School Hall.[5] Or perhaps you might do *both* things. I have been requested to press both honors on your acceptance.

Your Christian Science article I am going to read as soon as I can get hold of it. The last time I was down town not a copy of the N.A. Review could be had—the demand having exhausted the supply in the wink of an eye almost.[6]

Is there to be no further report of your birth-day party printed than the press gave the next day after? I want Mr. Howells' sonnet and Dr. Van Dykes [*sic*] graceful verses, and have been looking for their appearance somewhere.[7] And parts of your speech—the Western part especially—were far too good to be lost.[8] You did play on the chords of memory with an exquisite touch that night, Mark. The felicity of your reference to Livy I never heard exceeded, and I want the very words to keep and show.

But do hurry up and send us a line of the best news you can about her. Heaven bless you all. Our love to every one.

Ever affectionately Yours

Joe.

1. He may possibly mean Jean, who came down with pneumonia on 22 December.
2. Mark Twain's sixty-seventh-birthday dinner, hosted by Colonel George Harvey (of *Harper's*) at the Metropolitan Club, New York.
3. Thomas Reed, who had attended the dinner, had died on 7 December.
4. Arthur Hadley, president of Yale University from 1899 to 1921. Hadley introduced Twain at the Bicentennial. By "in decorating" Twichell probably meant "in awarding you the decoration" (that is, the honorary degree).
5. The First Company Governor's Foot Guard, modelled on the British Army's Coldstream Guards, is the oldest continuously serving military body in the United States and dates back to 1771. The dinner Twichell refers to took place on 21 February, not January. The school where the Working Men's Club met was in "Frog Hollow," an industrial section of Hartford.
6. Three articles on Christian Science (parts of Twain's manuscript for his 1907 book) were published in the *North American Review* in December 1902, January 1903, and February 1903.
7. Henry Van Dyke was a popular and prolific author and Presbyterian clergyman.
8. In his speech, Twain spoke nostalgically of Hannibal, Missouri, and the Mississippi, which he had visited the previous June.

209. Twain to Twichell

31 December 1902 and 1 January 1903. Riverdale, New York

Riverdale-on-the-Hudson
The Last day of a—in some respects—
Tough Year, being A.D. 1902.

Dear Joe—

It is 10 a.m., & the post has just brought your good greeting of yesterday. Yesterday at mid-afternoon there was a memorable episode: I was in Livy's presence 3 minutes & 50 seconds! (the trained nurse holding the watch in her hand) for the first time in 3½ months.[1]

Livy was radiant! (And Joe, I didn't spoil it by saying, "you poor unsuspecting thing, Jean is lying low with pneumonia these 7 days."

End of Chapter I

[A good deal of the rest of the week can be found in my Xmas story (Harper's) entitled "Was it Heaven? Or Hell?" which is a true story & was written in York Harbor in August or September.]

In that story mother & daughter are ill, & the lying is attended to by a pair of aged aunts—assisted by the doctor, of course, though I suppress his share to make the story short. In this Riverdale home the liars are the doctor, Clara, & Miss [Margaret] Sherry (Livy's trained nurse). Those are the regulars. I am to see Livy again to-day for 3½ minutes & it is possible that she may say "Who was it you were talking with at breakfast?—I made out a man's voice." (And confuse me.) (The man was the doctor; he spends his nights here with Jean, & is not due to visit Livy until noon—he lives 2 or 3 miles away.) She sent Miss Sherry down to ask that question, during breakfast. We three consulted, & sent back word it was a stranger. It will be like Livy to ask me *what* stranger it was. Therefore I am to go prepared with a *stranger* calculated to fill the bill.

Yesterday morning the doctor left here at 9 & made his rounds in Yonkers, then came back & paid Livy his usual noon visit; but this morning he had a patient or so within half a mile of here, & to save travel he thought it would be a good idea to go straight up to Livy from the breakfast table; so he sent up to say he had called in passing, & couldn't he come up & see Livy *now*? Of course she said yes, & he went up. He ought to have kept his mouth shut; but some devil of injudacity [*sic*] moved him to say—

"Mr. Clemens says you are looking distinctly better than when he last saw you in York."

Livy was back at him instantly:

"Why—have you seen him? How did you come to see him since yesterday afternoon?"

Luckily the doctor did not exhibit the joggle she had given him, but said composedly—

"I ran across him in the hall a minute ago when I came in."

So then he had to get Miss Sherry outside & arrange with her to tell me that that was how he came to know my opinion of the patient's looks. To make doubly sure he hunted me up & told me himself; then called Clara & instructed *her*; for although her watch is not in the forenoon, she takes

Miss Sherry's place a little while every morning while Miss Sherry goes down & plans Livy's feed for the day with the cook.

I am to see Livy a moment every afternoon until she has another bad night, & I stand in dread; for with all my practice I realize that in a sudden emergency I am but a poor clumsy liar, whereas a fine alert & capable emergency-liar is the only sort that is worth anything in a sick-chamber.

Now, Joe, just see what reputation can do. All Clara's life she has told Livy the square truth & now the reward comes: Clara lies to her 3½ hours every day, & Livy tranquilly takes it all at par, whereas even when I tell her truth it isn't worth a penny without corroboration. Jean put it cleverly during the terrible days in York:

"Clara is the only person who can tell mamma an *improbable* lie & get it believed."

Clara makes many a slip, but covers it up instantly with a brilliant impromptu addition which saves the situation. Some of her feats in this kind are astonishing for swiftness & competency of invention.

Clara's talents are worked plenty hard enough without this new call upon them—Jean. Of course we do not want Jean to know that she is in danger & that the doctor is spending his nights 30 feet from her. Yesterday at sunrise Clara carried an order from him to Jean's nurse; & being worn & not at her brightest self, she delivered it in Jean's hearing. At once Jean spoke up:

"What is the doctor doing here—is mamma worse?"

It brought Clara to herself, & she said—

"No. He telephoned this order late last night, & said let it go into effect at 6 or 7 this morning."

This morning Clara forgot herself again. She was in a long hall that leads past Jean's room, & called out to Katy about something, "take it to the doctor's room!"

Then she flew to explain to Jean with an explanatory lie, & was happy to find that Jean was asleep & hadn't heard.

I wish Clara were not so hard driven—so that she could take a pen & put upon paper all the details of one of her afternoons in her mother's room. Day before yesterday (Monday), for instance. We were all desperately frightened & anxious about Jean (both lungs affected, temperature 104⅖, with high pulse & blazing fever) the whole household moving aimlessly about with absent & vacant faces—& Clara sitting miserable at heart but outwardly smiling, & telling her happy mother what good times Jean was having, coasting & carrying on out in the snow with the Dodges these splendid winter days![2]

Consider it. Jean was taken the evening of Dec. 22d. Ever since then Clara has had to give her mother a *detailed* account of Jean's day, every afternoon; & keep Jean out of doors the most of the time; & tell how fresh she is looking; & how she doesn't show fatigue; & dresses warmly; & is obediently careful & doesn't get overheated—& a lot more. And then Livy goes into bursts of wonder & admiration over Clara's faithful guardianship of Jean, & especially her marvelous tact in beguiling that wilful child to do the sane & right thing. "It is perfectly wonderful, Clara, how *do* you do it, you gifted little thing!" & goes on & deluges poor Clara with undeserved praises that boil her down & disintegrate her & wash her away till there is nothing left of her but a small wad of contrition & shame. And she's always trembling, on the inside, lest her mother flash out on her & say—

"Why, Clara, you told me it was Christmas she went to the dance, now you say it was Christmas-*Eve*."

Clara's invention is on the rack all the time, & in various ways. A day or two ago she had to give Mark Hamburg a headache which he hadn't had.[3] Her mother thought it so inhospitable not to ask him to play on the piano, & was distressed about it. [The piano is close to Jean's room.] On Sunday she inadvertently tallied only 3 at the lunch-table: herself, John Howells, & me.

"Where was Jean?"

"Well—strictly speaking, she doesn't count. She was in one of her thinking moods, & didn't say a word."

On Monday—without stirring from the house—Clara did these various things: she received from her mother a list of shoppings to do in New York; put on company dress (for a lunch party); carried loving messages to the hostess (Mrs. Hapgood); went to New York; took the car to her music lesson; took a cab thence to Mrs. Hapgood's because it was wetting & snowing; returned in a cab after the luncheon; was to be home in time for her watch (3.30); *was* home on time, & appeared in the sick-room with the shopping-purchases in her hands (she had sent Miss Lyon to New York for them); & sat down & told her mother all the conversation of the lunch-table; & when required to furnish the menu, did it (a thing Livy *always* requires)—& slipped up on one little detail: little-neck clams, or some other thing that was out of season—I think it was clams.[4] Livy inquired sharply into that, & Clara furnished a properer dish at the same price. I wish I was the father of a hundred liars like Clara.

Joe, Livy is the happiest person you ever saw. And she has had it all to herself for a whole week. What a week! So full of comedy & pathos & tragedy!

Jean had a good night last night, & she is doing as well as in the circumstances can be expected.

Joe, don't let those people invite me—I couldn't go. I have canceled all engagements, & shan't accept another for a year.

There'll be a full report of that dinner—issued by Col. Harvey as a remembrancer—& of course he will send it to all the guests. If he should overlook you—which he won't—let me know.

The episode detailed in my Xmas story ["Was it Heaven? Or Hell?"] happened in our York cottage 3 years ago; it was told me there by Howells, on our verandah; & I wrote it up while Livy lay prostrate in the room where that mother died—happy in the belief that her daughter was well, & not suspecting that she had been buried from the house a few days before.

With great love to all of you

Mark.

Soon my brief visit is due. I've just been up, listening at Livy's door. For the first time in months I heard her break into one of her girlish old-time laughs. With a word I could freeze the blood in her veins.

P.S.

Dec. 31, 4 p.m. A great disappointment. I was sitting outside Livy's door, waiting. Clara came out a minute ago & said Livy is not so well, & the nurse can't let me see her to-day. And Clara whispered other things. In the effort to find a new diversion for Jean, she sent her down to a matineè [*sic*] this afternoon. Livy was pleased, but at once wanted the name of the play. Clara was balled up. She was afraid to name one—in fact couldn't for the moment think of *any* name. Hesitances won't do; so she said Jean hadn't mentioned the name of it, but was only full of seeing Fay Davis again.[5]

That was satisfactory, & the incident was closed. Then—

"Your father is willing to go with you & Jean to-morrow night?" (To Carnegie Hall.)

"Oh, yes. He is reformed since you are sick; never grumbles about anything he thinks you would like him to do. He's all alacrity to do the most disagreeable things. You wouldn't recognize him, now. He's spoiling himself—getting so vain of himself he—"

And so-on & so-on—fighting for time—time to think up material. She had sent back the tickets a week ago, with a note explaining why we couldn't come; the thing had passed out of her mind, & to have it sprung upon her out of the hoary past in this sudden way was a perilous matter & called for wariness. (It is my little juvenile piece "The Death-Wafer," which Livy loves; & longs to hear about it from an eye-witness.[6])

"Who else is going?"

"Mary Foote and—& Miss Lyon and—& Elizabeth Dodge—and—I think that is all."[7]

"Why—has Jean invited Elizabeth & not her *sister*?"

(Clara had forgotten there was a sister, & was obliged to explain that she didn't really remember, but believed Jean *had* mentioned the sister.)

"Well, to make sure, speak to her about it. But is that all she has invited? It is a great big box, & the management have been very kind. It mustn't have a thin look."

And so Livy began to worry.

"Oh, don't you bother, Mousie. You can depend on Jean to have it full. She mentioned names but I had the cook on my hands & wasn't paying attention."

And at this point, sure enough, I fell heir to *my* share; for Clara said—

"Day after to-morrow she'll want to know *all* about it. *I* can't furnish details, they've gone out of my head. You must post me thoroughly, to-morrow."

She had to get back to Livy's room, then—& perhaps explain what kept her so long.

This is a perplexing place. Livy knows the story, & I don't. I wrote it 3 years ago, or more. I think I will suggest some such procedure as this—to Clara:

"*Generalize*—keep *generalizing*— about the scenery, & the costumes, & how bluff & fine the old Lord Protector was, & how pretty & innocently audacious the child was, & how pathetically bowed & broken the poor parents were, & all that, & how *perfectly* natural & accurate the Tower of London looked——work the Tower hard, Livy knows the Tower well—work it for all it's worth—keep whirling it in—every time you get stuck, say "Oh, but the Tower! ah, the Tower!" And keep your ears open—your *mother* will furnish the details, without knowing it. She'll mention the child's climbing up into Cromwell's lap uninvited—& you must break into the middle of her sentence & say "Oh, you should have *seen* it!" & she'll say, "When the child put the red wafer into her own father's hand—" you will break in & say, "Oh, mousie, it was too pitiful for anything—you could hear the whole house sob;" & she'll say, "Was the child equal to her part when she flew to Cromwell & dragged him out & stamped her foot and—" you must break in & say "It was great! & when he said '*Obey!* she spoke by my voice; the prisoner is pardoned—set him free!' you ought to have *been* there! it was just grand!"

Mark.

1903.

Jan. 1/03. The doctor did not stay last night. Just as I was beginning to dress for dinner Livy's nurse came for me, & I saw the patient 4 minutes. She was in great spirits—like 25 years ago.

She has sent me a New-Year greeting this morning, & has had a good night.

Jean has had a good night, & does not look to me so blasted & blighted as on the previous days. She sleeps all the time. Temperature down to within a shade of normal, this morning. Everything looking well here (unberufen!)

Mark.

1. Doctors would exclude Twain from his wife's sickroom for long periods of her final illness. K. Patrick Ober says, "I think the idea was that Livy needed rest, not commotion, and Twain could not be trusted to avoid commotion-bearing." Ober says of Livy that she "had typical features of congestive heart failure, and she probably suffered from hyperthyroid heart disease" (e-mail correspondence).

2. William Dodge Jr., mining company executive and friend of Theodore Roosevelt Sr., had built his family home in Riverdale in 1863.

3. Mark Hamburg was a prominent New York pianist of this era.

4. Mrs. Hapgood was probably Emilie B. Hapgood, wife of editor of *Collier's Weekly* Norman Hapgood. Isabel Lyon had been hired as a secretary to help Twain with his correspondence during Livy's illness. After Livy's death in 1904, she took on an increasingly dominating role in his household, but Twain broke with her acrimoniously in 1909.

5. Fay Davis was an American stage actress, particularly known for her performances in Shakespeare.

6. Twain's "The Death Disk" was dramatized by him in 1902 prior to its Carnegie Hall performance.

7. Mary Hubbard Foote, who would become an American artist of some significance. From the age of thirteen she had been brought up in Hartford by an aunt. Elizabeth Dodge was the eighteen-year-old granddaughter of William Dodge Jr.

210. Twain to Twichell

3 and 4 January 1903. Riverdale, New York

[Twain encloses a typewritten 2 January letter from Harper's *asking him to "read and correct,* if necessary, *the enclosed proof of your speech made at the dinner*

given by Colonel Harvey on your 67th birthday."[1] *The letter adds: "It is Colonel Harvey's intention to issue* [to guests only] *a little book of the speeches delivered that evening."]*

Joe, this is the very *worst* piece of reporting I have ever seen in my life. Be glad you made no speech there. A dead & damned stenographer could have done better.

Mark

[In margin:] *Sunday.* Jean & Livy doing finely. Jean no longer in danger.

1. The "if necessary," has been underscored by Twain, with two exclamation marks added in left margin. Twain also underscores "to guests only."

211. Twichell to Twain

5 January 1903. Hartford, Connecticut

Hartford. Jan 5. 1903

Dear Mark:

The marginal P.S. of yours just received, saying that Livy and Jean are better, and the latter out of danger—My! how good to read! I felt that your narratives of Holy Lying, Nos. 1 and 2, dated Dec. 31*st* were projected on a background of tragedy from which, by their means, you were averting your thoughts. They were, therefore, more than any thing else pathetic—though, indeed, they *were* everything else. I trust the day is not distant when—with your consent—I may read them to Livy and Jean; with you and Clara, of course, sitting by. But, my dear old fellow, the skies were pretty dark over while you were so deliciously spinning that yarn of Clara's heroic untruth. 'Twas surely a brilliant performance,—in strategy and in tactics both—and in the profoundest sense, I agree with you, a pious one, deserving the reward of success. There's nothing in the Bible against it that I know of.

Mark, I've been getting letters from you many years; *numbers* of them letters to keep. But these last do certainly lay over all the rest—which is saying a very great deal. The story flows off the end of your pen taken carelessly up to beguile the tedium of an anxious, slow-footed day; perfect *literature* from the word go; lights and shades all right; the complex plot continuously limpid in clearness; the style M.T.'s own at its best; diction, for ease, vigor and grace the choicest—the whole all ready for the printer as it is; *any* change must mar it——

By George, it is not fair—that inequitable distribution of talents by which it is given to only one man to do without consciously trying what to all others is, granting it possible, prodigiously difficult. The only comfort is that it is in the family, so to speak.

But do send us a health bulletin again pretty soon.

I have received from Gen. Hawley a big parcel of Eulogies of deceased members of Congress. He means well; but can you imagine anything one would have less use for? One of them, however,—John Arnot's—I'm going to send to Livy.[1]

Affectionately Yours

Joe

Can you give Livy our love the next time? *Do*, if it is permitted.

1. Elmira-born Arnot was U.S. congressman for New York's Twenty-Ninth District.

212. Twichell to Twain

26 January 1903. Hartford, Connecticut

Jan 26. 1903.

Dear Mark:

Do for mercy's sake, send us—or let somebody—a word telling us how things are with you and your house now. It *must be* that Jean is *way* out of the woods, but we want to hear it. Take a second or two of your next three minute call on Livy to give her the love of us all.

Judy, who is for the time being in Brooklyn, would, if she may, like to run up and see those of you who are *to be* seen, an hour or so, some day, pretty soon, so she says.

Affectionately Yours

Joe.

213. Twain to Twichell

28 January 1903. Riverdale, New York

Jan. 28.

P.S. Livy had a slight backset yesterday, so the doctor has just told me he is going to shut off my daily visit for a few days & then reduce it to 8 or 10 minutes a day. It will distress her, & may have an ill effect at first, but later results will show the wisdom of it no doubt.[1]

Katy's absence with Jean makes a new difficulty: Livy charges Clara with orders for Katy every day.[2] For months Katy has prepared special dishes for Livy, & now Livy wants her stirred up—she is growing careless in her cooking the past few days & isn't up to standard! By gracious *we* can't counterfeit Katy's cookery!

Ys Ever

Mark.

[In margin:] Jean is enjoying herself very well at Old Point Comfort. Clara has asked Judy to come up, & we are hoping she will say yes.

1. This postscript is all there is of this letter.

2. Jean and Katy Leary had traveled to Old Point Comfort (on the tip of the Virginia peninsula) to aid Jean's recuperation.

214. Twain to Twichell

4 April 1903. Riverdale, New York

Apl. 4/03.

Dear Joe:

Livy does really make a little progress these past 3 or 4 days, progress which is visible to even the untrained eye. The physicians are doing good work with her, but *my* notion is, that no act of healing is the best for *all* ills. I should distribute the ailments around: surgery cases to the surgeon; lupus to the actinic-ray specialist; nervous prostration to the Christian Scientist; most ills to the allopath & the homeopath; & (in my own particular case) rheumatism, gout & bronchial attacks to the osteopathist.[1]

Mr. Rogers was to sail southward this morning—& here is this weather! I am sorry. I think it's a question if he gets away tomorrow.

Ys Ever

Mark

1. Twain originally wrote "actinic-light" but deleted "light" and inserted "ray." He refers to a type of radiation treatment through violet or ultraviolet rays.

215. Twain to Twichell

21 July 1903. Elmira, New York

[Twain encloses a letter to "His Italian Majesty's Ambassador" in Manchester, Massachusetts. This is heavily revised by both Livy, in pencil, and also by Twain himself.]

QUARRY FARM
ELMIRA N.Y.
July 21/03.

Dear Joe:

That love-letter delighted Livy beyond any like utterance received by her these thirty years & more. I was going to answer it for her right away, & said so; but she reserved the privilege to herself. I judge she is accumulating Hot Stuff—as George Ade would say.[1]

That clipping is delicious.[2] The form of it, too: President's Message, Speech from the Throne, Survey of Our Relations with the Universe. Everything the old sow does, interests me.

By George it's fine about Dave! It's a handsome promotion; & he is in choice hands, too, for Trudeau is a good man, an able man, & a great physician.[3] And I am so glad young Harmony is out of those Chicago slums. I was always cordially glad to have her ease the pains of those unnecessary people, but it distressed me to have her trying to delay their dissolution.[4]

Livy is coming along; eats well, sleeps some, is mostly very gay, not very often depressed; spends all day on the porch, sleeps there a part of the night, makes excursions in carriage & in wheel-chair; &, in the matter of superintending everything & everybody, has resumed business at the old stand.

Did you ever go house-hunting 3,000 miles away? It costs three months of writing & telegraphing to pull off a success. We finished 3 or 4 days ago, & took the Villa Paniniano (dam the name, I have to look at it 2 minutes after writing it, & *then* am always in doubt) for a year by cable. Three miles outside of Florence, under Fiesole—a darling location, & apparently a choice house.[5] Near Fiske.

There's 7 in our gang; all women but me. It means trunks & things. But thanks be! To-day (this is private) comes a most handsome voluntary regal document with seals & escutcheons on it from the Italian Ambassador (who is a stranger to me) commanding the Customs people to keep their hands off the Clemens's [*sic*] things. Now wasn't it lovely of him? And wasn't it lovely of me to let Livy take a pencil & edit my answer & knock a good third of it out. I refer you to the rough draft, & ask for admiration.

And that's a nice ship, the Irene!—new—swift—13,000 tons—rooms up in the sky, open to sun & air——& all that. I was desperately troubled—for Livy—about the down-cellar cells of the ancient "Lahn."[6]

The cubs are in Riverdale, yet; they come to us the first week in August.

With lots & lots of love to all of you,

Mark.

1. George Ade, newspaperman and writer, best known for his humorous fables.

2. Missing but clearly referring to Mary Baker Eddy.

3. David Twichell had been appointed, as a just-qualified doctor, to Dr. Edward Livingston Trudeau's new Adirondack Cottage Sanitarium at Saranac Lake. Trudeau was a pioneer in the treatment of tuberculosis in the United States.

4. Harmony had left her Chicago nursing post.

5. The family were planning to go to Italy for Livy's health. This particular arrangement must have fallen through. In fact, they would stay at the Villa di Quarto (also near Florence).

6. The SS *Princess Irene* was built in 1900 and was thus much more up-to-date than the 1887-built *Lahn.*

216. Twichell to Twain

24 August 1903. Blue Ridge, Essex County, New York

Blue Ridge, Essex Co. N.Y, Aug. 24. 1903

Dear Mark:

We i.e. Harmony, I, Sue, Harmony Jr., Sally, Joe and Louise, are off here in the heart of the Adirondacks, far from the world, several miles from a post-office, where we receive mail regularly only once a week. We learn from the latest papers that have reached us that the big yacht race has come off.[1] Which has set me thinking. You told me the last time I saw you that I was booked for a place on Mr. Rodgers' [*sic*] yacht to spectate that contest.[2] It is at least my impression that you said something amounting to that. My notion was, however, that you so warned me that I was—not invited, but *going to be* invited. I am now wondering if *that* was not the invitation, understood as such by you and Mr. Rogers. Whether it was or not is of no consequence as regards my seeing the race, for I should have had to miss that pleasure any how. But if it was, I owe Mr. Rodgers an apology and explanation which I should lose no time in making—and I want his address, please, for the purpose. Quite likely, though, the case is not as I conjecture—but only conjecture—it may be, and I have no occasion to epistolize Mr. Rodgers.

The news—a month old now—your last letters gave us about Livy was so cheerful that we sang a "Te Deum" over it. Pray God she has continued getting better and better ever since, and that her grip on the sceptre of domestic dominion, of which you speak, may strengthen week by week till her ancient and dear tyranny is completely restored. B,'gosh, I'd like to have her crack *my* head with it, I love her so.

The prospect of your expatriation, except as it means benefit to her, is to us extremely dismal. I do wish I might have just a look at her before you go. We shall return to Hartford about the 25th of Sept. You did not say when you were going to sail. But if it is later than the end of Sept. why may not I—and Harmony perhaps—run down to New York and give her a good-bye kiss? Of course it may not be allowable, but 'twould do our souls good. We are all pretty well. En route hither we passed ten days at Lake Placid whence we paid Dave a couple of visits at Saranac Lake. He was in fine spirits and full of interest in his work. Dr. Trudeau is a prince in his eyes. With thousands of love and benediction to you, each one, Yours ever

Joe.

1. The America's Cup race between England and America. The series started on 20 August off the New Jersey coast. Twain saw several of the races from the *Kanawha* and wrote a humorous account of the contest for the *New York Herald*: "Mark Twain, Able Yachtsman, on Why Lipton Failed to Lift the Cup."

2. Twichell tends to spell Henry Rogers's name wrongly.

217. Twain to Twichell

1 September 1903. Elmira, New York

QUARRY FARM
ELMIRA N.Y.
Sept. 1/03.

Dear Joe:

Livy sends "bushels and bushels of love" to you people, & says she sometimes feels well & sometimes does not (I grieve to say that to-day she does not), but she hopes to be well enough in New York to be able to see you & Harmony & say good bye. We land there Oct. 5, Hotel Grosvenor, 5th ave & 10th street, & I do hope & expect that by then she will be in greatly improved health and strength. We sail Oct. 24.

[Ms. page 2 (according to the Mark Twain Papers, there are about 110 words missing here).]

I feel perfectly sure Livy can see you in New York—she could not go away happy without that good-bye kiss. She is dearer & dearer all the time—if such a thing can be possible, considering that she was always dear to the limit. Indeed that kiss must be arranged for—for all the sakes concerned.

I was on hand at all the races, barring to-day's. I was in New York the whole month under wearing & hateful compulsion of business, & the races were a blessed rest & diversion for me. I must go back soon & stay a few more days.

With lots of love to all of you,

Mark.

218. Twichell to Twain

30 September 1903. Hartford, Connecticut

[Commencing with a pasted-in item from the Courant*:]*

> Mr. Clemens used occasionally, in those days, when Mr. Twichell would be away from home, to come down to the South Church. He put me at ease, one Sunday morning, as we entered the church together, by saying, in a most artless and confidential tone and manner, "They have no choir up to Twichell's meetinghouse, and I like to come down here, now and then, to sit with Robinson and enjoy—the music!"[1]

Hartford. Sept. 30

Dear Mark,

Perhaps you take "The Courant" and perhaps you dont [*sic*]. If you do, perhaps you noticed the above, from a recent communication—historic and reminiscent of Parker's on the "Old South Church Choir," and perhaps you didn't.[2]

We are home again i.e. those of us who belong here, straining and grunting—i.e. I am—to get the tread-mill started for another year. We had the best sort of a vacation and are all improved in condition by it—especially Harmony. We hope for good news of Livy. When you get to New York let us know when we may come down—*if* we may—and——But, lo, at *this moment* Sue opens my door and tosses on to my table Livy's letter of the 28th inst. just brought by the postman!!! Livy's own letter, from her own dear hand! 'Tis the event of the season! Hurra! Hurra!!

Thank God. She says that we are to let *you* know when between Oct. 7th and 24th we will lunch with you at the Grosvenor. We *will*, we *will*—and now I must go out and have a tooth pulled. I feel so good. How can we wait? But good morning, old fellow. You must be happy and thankful with Livy *able* to write such a letter.

Ever affectionately Yours

Joe.

1. Henry C. Robinson, a close friend of Twain, was an active member of Hartford's South Congregational Church.

2. Edwin Pond Parker, the musically oriented minister of South Congregational Church. His church had a choir when Twichell's Asylum Hill still only featured less tuneful congregational singing. The clipping is an excerpt from a 25 September letter from Parker to the *Courant*.

219. Twain to Twichell

9 October 1903. New York, New York

VIRTUS NON STEMMA
THE GROSVENOR,
FIFTH AVE & TENTH ST.
NEW YORK
Oct. 9/03.

Dear Joe—

Yours of yesterday has just arrived, & I have told Livy & she joins us in saying Good! The 19th it is! So we shall expect you & Harmony. I don't suppose you can see Livy, but anyway it will do her heaps of good to know you are near by & under the same roof. You'll see Clara & Jean & me. Also Katy. Katy goes to Italy with us. We have got a villa at last—possession given Nov. 1. The news came by cable day before yesterday; & the price of the villa made Livy swear; but it is the first time in over 2 weeks, & is easily forgiven. I paid the steamer-fares at once.

[Unknown amount of text cut away.]

220. Twain to Twichell

25 November 1903. Florence, Italy (Two typed transcripts by Albert Bigelow Paine)

Villa Reale di Quarto
Castello
Florence, Nov. 25/03.

Dear Joe:

You are one of the Governors of Yale, aren't you—or Trustee, or something? Then tell me—what was the sum that Mr. Hand bequeathed to Yale, or to one of her colleges?[1] The courts sustained the will, didn't they?

Hand was a New Haven blacksmith, wasn't he? Went South before the war? had a business-partnership with a young Southerner? returned North when the war broke out? drifted hither & thither in search of a living? disappeared, & was lost sight of? at the close of the war was patiently hunted out by the partner, who had made a fortune in cotton out of the joint capital, & who surprised Hand with a check for his half of it? Are those the facts? What was the Southerner's name?

That is as I heard it twenty years ago, or along there.

I've made a short story of it, & now I should like to know all about it. Come, get me the facts! Wake up!

[Unknown amount of text missing.]

1. Daniel Hand (who died in 1891) of Madison, Connecticut, was a businessman and Christian philanthropist. In *Memories of Yale Life and Men* (New York: Dodd, Mead, 1903), Timothy Dwight writes, "The late Daniel Hand also, whose bequests to the American Missionary Association have proved of so great service in our Southern States, was a most helpful contributor to our work." (292).

221. Twichell to Twain

22 December 1903. Hartford, Connecticut

Hartford. Dec. 22. 1903

Dear Mark:

If you have received the little pamphlet I mailed you last week—I had to get it from New York, which took three days—you know that it was not to Yale that Daniel Hand bequeathed the pile his grand partner made for him, but to the emancipated slaves who had raised the cotton out of which it was made; which, to my mind, is a finer thing; in fact a thing approaching the sublime.[1] To what uses the income of his money goes year after year, and will go for all the future, you saw from the pages cut out of the last Annual Report of the American Miss[ionary]. Association which I enclosed with the pamphlet.

For your more particular information—if desired—respecting the Society Mr. Hand chose for the almoner of his bounty I send you the statements of its objects &c taken from our Cong[regational] Year Book.[2]

Here, too, is a note from Dr. Dave—to what purpose, you see. He bade me use my discretion about forwarding it, and though I don't see how you can comply with his request I send it along.[3] You might do this if you saw fit—write a presentation on a sheet (or page) of small note-paper and let me get the book and paste it on the fly leaf. Dave is a mighty good boy and is working away with immense enthusiasm under Dr. Trudeau who is his hero-in-chief at present. Did you know that Young Harmony is also at Saranac Lake as nurse? It is a huge comfort to us that she and Dave are together. She wrote the other day that she had just been assisting Dave in an operation which (she said) "he performed *beautifully.*" You can imagine her look of admiration bent on Dave as the blood squirted out. Both of them were lately invited to the Aldriches to tea—Aldrich the *son* I suppose, though I saw—as I think I told you—Aldrich père there last Summer who said that he and his wife took turns staying there.[4]

Your secretary's appendix to your letter gave us cheer as its account of Livy was more favorable than that which had lately been going the rounds of the papers. For that reason I let Charley Clark say in "The Courant" that to a friend in Hartford you had written so and so. For I knew that every body would be glad to hear it. There is no mistake about it, there is a great fondness for Livy in these parts. But of course there is. A dearer woman never lighted among us, and grief for her departure is an abiding pain.

I have just been to Scranton Pa. to bury my classmate "Billy" Boies, one of my most cherished college friends.[5] A few days since I was called to say the last words at the grave of our old neighbor H. Clay Trumbull. Our regiment in the marching column of life is fast melting away. Yes, indeed, Mark "It will soon be good-bye with us" as you said on my souvenir of your Birth-day party. Well, "the past, at least, is secure," and I hope the future too. Lately I went with a funeral to Bloomfield. En route we crossed the old road by which we used to travel to Talcott Mountain. And again I saw those two young fellows plodding merrily along, swapping stories, exchanging no end of lively talk, full of their manifold themes of common interest, feeling the years before them. My! My! *what* good times they had! And *now*—Can it be that the play is so nearly played out? Yet I am just setting out on my 39th year in Hartford, and my baby Louise is *nineteen* years old to-day! God bless us all and give us a meeting in a world that is not a dream. Never before did I feel so mortal as now. Yet I do hope to set eyes on you again—and all of you—before we quit this planet. Do let us hear from you once in awhile. Our remembrances to Prof. Fiske and our love without measure to Livy and the girls.

Ever affectionately Yours

Joe

1. The pamphlet referred to here is now missing.

2. An annual publication listing statistics and information for all the Congregationalist churches and seminaries in the United States.

3. Clearly, a request for a signing of one of Twain's books.

4. Charles Aldrich, who suffered from tuberculosis. His father had built him a house at Saranac Lake where he took treatment. He would die in 1904.

5. Twichell's Yale classmate, Henry M. ("Billy") Boies, banker, prison reformer, and investigator into the causes of crime.

222. Twain to Twichell

7 and 10 January 1904. Florence, Italy (Typed transcript by Albert Bigelow Paine)

Villa di Quarto
Castello
Florence, Jan. 7/04.

Dear Joe:

I got the pamphlet a week ago & used its figures concerning the Hand Fund in a footnote—many many thanks![1] As a rule a footnote after a story is a way of saying "it is true," & is a sneaking apology that bettern't be made, but this time it is all right, my wish being to *make Hand known*, not the story; & the footnote does that. The story—as a story—has no importance. Its like has been imagined, & improved upon, a thousand times.

I have had a handsome success, in one way, here. I left New York under a sort of half-promise to furnish to the Harper magazines 30,000 words this year. Magazining is difficult work because every third page represents 2 pages that you have put in the fire (because you are nearly sure to *start* wrong twice); & so when you have finished an article & are willing to let it go to print it represents only 10 cents a word instead of 30.

But this time I had the curious (& unprecedented) luck to start right in each case. I turned out 37,000 words in 25 working days; & the reason I think I started right every time is, that not only have I approved & accepted the several articles, but the court of last resort (Livy) has done the same.[2]

On many of the between-days I did some work, but only of an idle & not necessarily necessary sort, since it will not see print until I am dead. I shall continue this (an hour per day) but the rest of the year I expect to put in on a couple of long books (half-completed ones.) No more magazine-work hanging over my head.

This secluded & silent solitude, this clean soft air & this enchanting view of Florence, the great valley & the snow-mountains that frame it are the right conditions for work. They are a persistent inspiration. To-day is very lovely; when the afternoon arrives there will be a new picture every hour till dark, & each of them divine—or progressing from divine to diviner & divinest. On this (second) floor Clara's room commands the finest; she keeps a window ten feet high wide open all the time & frames it in that. I go in, from time to time, every day & trade sass for a look. The central detail is a distant & stately snow-hump that rises above & behind black-forested hills, & its sloping vast buttresses, velvety & sun-polished, with purple shadows between, make the sort of picture we knew what time we walked in Switzerland in the days of our youth.

I am so glad Dave & Harmony are so choicely situated, & that they have won the approval & regard of such a man as Dr. Trudeau. The book will go to Dave direct from Harpers [*sic*]; will you send him the enclosed autograph for it?—with our love to him & Harmony. I would answer his letter myself but for lack of time.

I wish I could show your letter to Livy—but she must wait a week or so for it. I think I told you she had a prostrating week of tonsilitis a month ago; she has remained very feeble ever since, & confined to the bed of course, but we allow ourselves to believe she will regain the lost ground in another month. Her physician is Professor Grocco—she could not have a better.[3] And she has a very good trained nurse.

This is our "day," & pretty soon the people will be arriving. I must knock off & dress. Love to all of you from all of us.

Mark.

And to all of our dear Hartford friends.

P.S., 3 days later. Livy is as remarkable as ever. The day I wrote you—that night, I mean—she had a bitter attack of gout or rheumatism occupying the whole left arm from shoulder to fingers, accompanied by fever. The pains racked her for 50 or 60 hours; they have departed, now—& already she is planning a trip to Egypt next fall, & a winter's sojourn there! There is life in her yet.

You will be surprised that I was willing to do so much magazine-writing—a thing I have always been chary about—but I had good reasons. Our expenses have been so prodigious for a year & a half, & are still so prodigious, that Livy was worrying altogether too much about them, & doing a very dangerous amount of lying awake on their account. It was necessary to stop that, & it is now stopped.

Yes, she *is* remarkable, Joe. Her rheumatic attack set me to cursing & swearing, without limit as to time or energy, but it merely concentrated her patience & her unconquerable fortitude. It is the difference between us. I can't count the different kinds of ailments which have assaulted her in this fiendish year & a half—& I forgive none of them—but here she comes up again as bright & fresh & enterprising as ever, & goes to planning about Egypt, with a hope & a confidence which are to me amazing.

Clara is calling for me—we have to go into town & pay calls.

Mark.

1. Twain used Hand's tale in the short story "You've Been a Dam Fool Mary. You Always Was," unpublished until 1972.

2. Twain was apparently working on various magazine articles and on *No. 44, The Mysterious Stranger.* It was in this month, too, that he started on his autobiographical dictations.

3. Professor Pietro Grocco, an (expensive) Florentine doctor. Twain would later fire him as he grew dissatisfied with his treatments.

223. Twichell to Twain

25 January 1904. Hartford, Connecticut

[Clipping enclosed:]

The arrangements for the funeral have been completed. It will be held from the home tomorrow afternoon at 2 o'clock. The services will be in charge of Rev. Joseph H. Odell, pastor of the Second Presbyterian church, assisted by Rev. James McLeod, D.D., Rev. S. C. Logan, D.D., and, in all probability, by Rev. Joseph Twitchell [*sic*], D.D., of Hartford, Conn., one of the most famous after-dinner speakers in America.[1]

Hartford. Jan. 25. 1904

Dear Mark:

How's that above for *booming* a funeral? For the unconscious violation of the proprieties the newspaper boys do beat all. In this case they intended well. They meant to get the deceased a good house. But imagine *my* sensations on reading the advertisement, and subsequently on appearing before the audience!—and seeing "*Now* we are going to *have* something!" written in their faces. It almost made me laugh in spite of myself. I fear my performance was extremely disappointing.

Your letter, with the P.S. following, afforded us both entertainment and comfort—the latter because it was new evidence of the splendid unconquerable tenacity of Livy's hold on life. I remember dear old [Rev. Nathaniel] Burton's once saying to a fellow who had suffered and survived the assault of no end of maladies, "You are like a *raft*. Much of the time you are half under water, and some of the time three quarters, but all the same you *float*: you never sink." That surely describes Livy. Somewhere in her there is lodged an inexpugnable vital principle that, Lord be praised, keeps her in a world that can't spare her. I shouldn't a bit wonder if she outlasted the whole of us yet. That will suit me for one. Tell her I say so. One of our undertakers here in Hartford lately told me of an old woman who having made arrangements with him for her funeral in every detail, bearers and every thing, was coming to him every little while with an air of annoyance, almost in a pet, to report the death of one of those bearers, and to name a candidate for the vacancy. The last time she came on that errand, she was (he said) quite out of temper and grumbled "If this sort of thing goes on, there will be *nobody* to attend my funeral!" as if all her anticipated enjoyment of the occasion was in danger of being destroyed. Human Nature! I don't think so ill of it as you do, Mark, but it is, indeed, a queer affair, in spots.

Your delicious, exquisite picture of the view from Clara's window made me sigh with longing to look on that country again. It recalled the vision celestial outspread before young Harmony and me from the Hill of Fiesole one bright November afternoon in 1900, the thrill of which abides with me as does that of one and another like ravishment of the senses I shared with you in our pilgrimage through Switzerland. Gracious, Mark, can't you and I *walk* any more? I feel as if *I* could. I believe we both could, with a little training at 10 miles per day.

What I had chiefly in mind in taking up my pen at this time (I *don't* want to impose the task of correspondence on you, i.e. by writing to put you in *debt* for a letter. With your power of transmuting ink into gold you can't *afford* to throw it away. I fully recognize that. I said to myself when I had finished reading your last "Here's at least A Hundred Dollars Worth wasted"—though to be sure *I* had that value in it.) *was* to thank you for your instant kind compliance with Dave's wish regarding your autograph. He'll thank you too, I guess. The "Prince and Pauper["] which you ordered for him was duly sent (addressed *Rev.* D.C.T. but he got it all right) and, as enriched with your delightful presentation, will be a life treasure to him. From what we hear we judge that Dave is greatly commending himself to Dr. Trudeau's approval. Anyway he is fascinated with his work—bacillus culture—rabbit and guinea pig inoculations and all that sort of thing—and is confident that tuberculosis is doomed. Harmony has always wanted him to be a family doctor—here in Hartford—but begins now to fear that the Tuberculosis War will claim his service. We mean to run up to Saranac Lake by and by, to pay him and Young Harmony a visit. Sally is up there now, not as a pulmonary patient, but taking a rest-cure for a nervous debility into which she had fallen. She is reported about well again.[2] The rest of us are hearty.

That you are so hard at work is good news for the human race. Blessed are those big bills that "prick the sides of your intent" with compulsion.[3]

But what the nation is that labor of yours the product of which is to be posthumous? I am hugely curious to know.[4] Your plan of withholding it makes it likely that I never *shall* know—to my deep discontent. Why not handle the money yourself? Or if you are going to shock humanity—which of course I suspect—why not see the fun?

Oh, Mark, what a pity you are just now so far off and inaccesible [*sic*] when there is so much to talk upon! I grieve over it every day. I long for the music of your malediction. My old college friend Bob Stiles has written a book "*Four Years under Mars[e] Robert*" being the tale of his experience and adventure as a rebel soldier, that would entertain you—it is *so* like him, so beautifully, unconsciously boastful. Here I stop. I am full of matter but will detain you no longer. Good morning! Love and worship to Livy and a hug to the girls.

Yours ever.

Joe

1. Though the subject is not identified, this is a press notice for the funeral of Henry M. (Billy) Boies (see Letter 221).

2. Daughter, Sarah Dunham Twichell—"Sally"—who suffered bouts of depression.

3. *Macbeth*, act 1, scene 7.

4. The autobiographical dictations, no doubt.

224. Twichell to Twain

26 April 1904, Hartford, Connecticut

Hartford. Apr. 26. 1904

[Newspaper clipping pasted in:]

> There is no more difficult task than to write for boys and girls of the age to which these books appeal. No longer children, nor yet grown-ups, the scorn of the school-boy and the school-girl for the juveniles written for them is equalled only by their indignation at the judgment which forbids Dumas and Hardy as being too old for them. A few writers for young people have solved the difficulty successfully. Louisa Alcott's *Little Women* is almost a classic, if classic means the best and most enduring of its kind. The creator of Tom Sawyer and Huckleberry Finn has a shrine in the hearts of boys, both old and young, that no one dares desecrate.

Dear Mark:

While at Cornell University on pulpit duty last Sunday I picked up at Pres. Schurman's a late copy of "The Catholic World"—a magazine, and in the Book Notices department came upon the above, which ought to please you, hardened as you are to that species of confection—no, *hardened* isn't the word but—what is it? I can't at this moment think.[1]

On the way home I found in The Sunday World which somebody had left in his seat in the train the enclosed illustrated article which I don't suppose Mr. Rogers will send you for all it is so interesting. I fancy that he is cussing mad over it, though I dont [*sic*] know.[2]

They have been enlarging and adorning Sage Chapel at Cornell (Will Sage paying the bill) and one of the new features is an elegant Caen Stone pulpit (*that,* I think, Sarah Sage gave) with *Dean's name* carved on its base, with the record of his benefaction 30 years or so ago of a Fund out of which the preaching of the place is paid for. What, think you, would Dean have said to that? It made me laugh right out in Church almost—the vision of him contemplating it. It is very proper it should be there though on all grounds except his intense antipathy to being celebrated in that fashion.

En route to Cornell I passed three days at Saranac Lake with Dave and young Harmony where, in spite of cold and snow, I had a charming time with them and in the society of the tuberculous circles in which they move. I was lunched and dined by people who have bacilli to dispose of and have seldom been in more cheerful company. At the Monday

Evening Club meeting last night (Arthur Shipman, host) Charley Clark read a paper on "Modern Conveniences"—the seamy side of them of course—which I wish you and Livy might have heard it was so bright and witty.[3]

Livy—that brings up the real object of my present writing. Isn't it time, dear old Boy, that we had a word from you concerning her? Please send us a bulletin on that subject which lies very near our hearts. Love to you each and all.

Ever affectionately

Joe

1. Jacob Gould Schurman, president of Cornell University, 1892–1920.

2. This would be the issue of Sunday, 24 April 1904.

3. Arthur L. Shipman, author of works on early Connecticut history and a leading Hartford businessman.

225. Twain to Twichell

11 May 1904. Florence, Italy (Typed transcript by Albert Bigelow Paine)

Villa di Quarto, May 11/04.

Dear Joe:

Yours has this moment arrived—just as I was finishing a note to poor Lady Stanley.[1] I believe the last country-house visit we paid in England was to Stanley's. Lord, how my friends & acquaintances fall about me now, in my gray-headed days! Vereschagin, Mommsen, Dvorak, Lenbach, Jokai—all so recently, & now Stanley. I had known Stanley 37 years.[2] Goodness, who is it I *haven't* known! As a rule the necrologies find me personally interested—when they treat of old stagers. Generally when a man dies who is worth cabling, it happens that I have run across him somewhere, some time or other.

Oh, *say!* Down by the Laurentian Library there's a marble image that has been sitting on its pedestal some 450 years, if my dates are right—Cosimo I.[3] I've seen the back of it many a time, but not the front; but yesterday I twisted my head around after we had driven by, & the profane exclamation burst from my mouth before I could think: "——there's Chauncey Depew!"

I mean to get a photo of it—& use it if it confirms yesterday's conviction.

That's a very nice word from the Catholic Magazine & I am glad you sent it. I mean to show it to my priest—we are very fond of him. He is a sterling man, & is also learnedly scientific. He invented the thing which records the seismatic disturbances for the peoples of the earth. And he's an astronomer & has an observatory of his own.[4]

Oh, no, Mr. Rogers doesn't mind—he sends me all the things about Miss Harrison; sent me, also, (cuss that fool word, it can seldom be placed where it means what you mean it to mean) the one you sent.[5] But I can't plague Miss Harrison into doing any commenting on her celebrity.

Ah, many's the cry I have, over reflecting that maybe we could have had young Harmony for Livy, & didn't have wit enough to think of it.

Speaking of Livy reminds me that your inquiry arrives at a good time (unberufen). It has been weeks (I don't know how many!) since we could have said a hopeful word, but this morning Katy came the minute the day-nurse came on watch & said words of a strange & long-forgotten sound: "Mr. Clemens, Mrs. Clemens is really & truly *better*!—anybody can see it; she sees it herself; & last night at 9 o'clock she *said* it."

There—it is heart-warming, it is splendid, it is sublime; let us enjoy it, let us make the most of it to-day—& bet not a farthing on to-morrow. The to-morrows have nothing for us. Too many times they have breathed the word of promise to our ear & broken it to our hope. We take no tomorrow's word any more.[6]

You've done a wonder, Joe: you've written a letter that can be sent in to Livy—that doesn't often happen, when either a friend or a stranger writes. You *did* whirl in a P.S. that wouldn't do, but you wrote it on a margin of a page in such a way that I was able to clip off the margin clear across both pages, & now Livy won't perceive that the sheet isn't the same size it used to was. It was about Aldrich's son—I came near forgetting to remove it. It should have been written on a loose strip & enclosed. That son died on the 5th of March & Aldrich wrote me on the night before that his minutes were numbered. On the 18th Livy asked after that patient, & I was prepared, & able to give her a grateful surprise by telling her "the Aldriches are no longer uneasy about him."

I do wish I could have been present & heard Charley Clark. When he can't light up a dark place nobody can.

With lots of love to you all

Mark.

1. Widow of explorer Henry M. Stanley who had died on 10 May, Lady Stanley was the neoclassicist painter and author, Dorothy Tennant. Stanley was a close friend of Twain.

2. Vasily Vereshchagen, Russian realist painter, died 13 April 1904; Theodor Mommsen, German classicist, historian, and politician, died 1 November 1903; Antonin Dvořák, Czech composer, died 1 May 1904; Franz von Lembach, German artist, died 6 May 1904; Mór Jókai, Hungarian novelist and playwright, died 5 May 1904.

3. In fact Cosimo I was a sixteenth-century Florentine politician.

4. Don Raffaello Stiattesi, director of the Seismographic Observatory of Quarto Castello, Florence, who became a close friend of the family.

5. Katherine Harrison, Rogers's secretary. A number of American newspapers had published an unsigned article about her importance to Standard Oil and the large salary ($10,000) she was paid for her discretion about corporate issues.

6. Twain's comment on not taking "tomorrow's word any more" was tragically apt, for, on 5 June 1904, Livy passed away.

226. Twichell to Twain

8 June 1904, Hartford, Connecticut[1]

June 8. Hartford

Dear, dear Mark:

There is nothing that we can say. What is there *to* say? But here we are—with you all every hour and every minute—filled with unutterable thoughts; unutterable affection; affection for the dead and for the living.

Harmony and Joe

1. This letter follows Livy's death in Italy on June 5.

227. Twain to Twichell

8 June 1904. Florence, Italy

Wednesday afternoon.
(Clara's Birthday)
Villa di Quarto, June 8/04.

Dear Joe: We were eager to serve her, all these piteous months. She couldn't devise a plan, however staggering, that we didn't applaud, & do our best to bring it to fruitage. Every day, for weeks & weeks, we went out armed with the enclosed paper, hunting for a villa—to rent for a year, but always with an option to *buy* at a specified figure within the year; & yet, deep down in our unrevealing hearts we believed she would never get out of her bed again.

Only last Sunday evening, with death flying toward her, & due in one hour & a quarter, she was full of interest in that matter, & asked me if I had heard of any more villas for sale. And many a time, these months, she said she wanted a *home*—a house of her own; that she was tired & wanted rest, & could not rest & be in comfort & peace while she was homeless. And now she is at rest, poor worn heart! Joe, she was so lovely, so patient—never a murmur at her hard fate; yet—but I *can't* put her sufferings on paper, it breaks my heart to think of them. She sat up in bed 6 months, night & day, & was always in bodily misery, & could get but little sleep, & then only by resting her forehead against a support—think of those lonely nights in the gloom of a taper, with Katy sleeping, & with no company but her fearsome thoughts & her pathetic longings; it makes my heart bleed, it makes me blaspheme, to think of the gratuitous devilishness of it.[1]

How sweet she was in death, how young, how beautiful, how like her dear girlish self of thirty years ago. Not a gray hair showing. This rejuvenescence was noticeable within 2 hours after death; that was at 11.30; when I went down again (2.30) it was complete; the same at 4, 5, 7, 8—& so remained the whole of the day till the embalmers came at 5; & then I saw her no more. In all that night & all that day she never noticed my caressing hand—it seemed strange.

She so dreaded death, poor timid little prisoner; for it promised to be by strangulation. Five times in 4 months she went through that choking horror for an hour & more, & came out of it white, haggard, exhausted, & quivering with fright. Then cursing failed me; there was no language bitter enough whereby to curse the cowardly invention of those wanton tortures. But when death came, she did not know it. Nor did we. She was chatting cheerfully only a moment before. We were all present, I was stooping over her; we saw no change—yet she was gone from us! Why am I required to linger here?

S L C

1. Livy's heart condition affected her ability to breathe. Though she received regular oxygen treatment, this condition, combined with the choking fits Twain then mentions, and Livy's own fears of dying through such choking, explains her inability to lie down. See K. Patrick Ober, *Mark Twain and Medicine: Any Mummery Will Cure* (Columbia: University of Missouri Press, 2003), 314–15.

PART 5

1904–1910

After Livy's Death; the Final Years

TWAIN WAS DESOLATED by Livy's death. So were his two surviving daughters, Clara and Jean. As Twichell wrote at the time concerning Twain, "All who knew [Twain and Livy], and the manner of their life together, are saying, 'How will he ever do without her?' With what pitiful dismay he is now saying it, poor fellow, to himself, can only be imagined."[1] Twichell's heart went out to Twain ("I love you inexpressibly"—Letter 229), offering him what comfort he could. While Twain saw Livy's death as one more piece of evidence of a meaninglessness world ("[T]here is no God"—Letter 230), Twichell continued to posit a "Hidden and Awful Wisdom" (Letter 231) behind such events.

Following Livy's death the family returned to New York to live at 21 Fifth Avenue. Isabel Lyon was with them, taking an ever-more-important role in the family until Twain fell out with her and her by-then husband, Twain's business advisor, Ralph Ashcroft, in the spring of 1909.[2] This falling-out features significantly in the letters of that time. During the New York years Twain relied heavily on Henry H. Rogers and his family for companionship and emotional support, at a time when his relationship with his daughters became—at different points and with each in turn—problematic. (Jean was still suffering from epilepsy.) Finally, in June 1908, Twain moved to Stormfield, the house W. D. Howells's architect son, John, had designed for him in Redding, Connecticut. Clara's wedding to Ossip Gabrilowitsch would be celebrated there, with Twichell conducting the service, on 6 October 1909.[3] Both Jean and Twain would die there: Jean, tragically, of what was apparently a heart attack following an epileptic fit, while in her bath, on Christmas Eve 1909. Twain himself died not long after, in April 1910, of heart failure.

In these last years the friendship with Twichell remained strong, though the years had had their effect. Twichell would visit him in the city relatively frequently, with Twain managing the odd Hartford visit despite the painful emotions associated with the place. The two men would reprise their holiday in Bermuda on 2–9 January 1907, this time with Isabel Lyon in attendance. This second visit took place almost thirty years after the two men's previous trip. Twichell's pleasure in the trip is evident in one of his journal notes: "The weather was perfect every day; the company altogether delightful, M.T. being in excellent spirits all the while. . . . We took several long drives, and a lovely sail in the waters about Hamilton, delighting ourselves on the soft, balmy air, and in viewing again the scenes that had enchanted us thirty years before." Twichell's remarks about Miss Lyon, however, were telling: "Miss Lyon did everything. M and I like two children in her charge." Lyon's own notes tell a different story, claiming, "Mr. Twichell tires him beyond words—so that the King [her name for Twain] almost loses patience." She refers, too, to the nervousness induced in Twain by Twichell's presence, and the lack of comfort he took in their companionship, "as Mr. T. is so deaf & can only hear when shouted at." After the trip Twichell wrote a confidential note in his journal that he repeats in slightly different form in his 14 January 1907 letter: "MT 1907[.] If you have enjoyed your fame I have enjoyed my obscurity." The note may indicate the different responses the two men met from the Bermudan public while on holiday, but it also provides an accurate mirror of the relative celebrity of the two.[4]

The correspondence with Twichell—who, at the start of this period, had helped conduct Livy's funeral service in Elmira—also continued unabated until the very final years. Even before this time, Twain had tended to use letters to his close male friends as a way of letting off steam, of expressing ideas that he would rein in in the public arena—as possibly affecting his popularity as a celebrity and (primarily) a humorist. Thus, in a 24 June 1905 letter to Joe (Letter 247), he refers to him as an "equilibrium-restorer," adding, "I *have* to work my bile off, whenever it gets to where I can't stand it." In a 17 April 1909 letter to Howells, too, he writes of a scheme of writing letters to friends and then not sending them. He plans this in the context of the drawbacks of dictating his autobiography and finding it difficult to express to his immediate audience—his stenographer—the profanities, indecencies, and (what a religiously-inclined person would see as) blasphemies he wished to utter, or indeed just the "sluice of intimate, personal, & particularly private things" he was "burning to pour out." Twain's solution was his plan of the unsent letter—to say these things to "a very close personal friend, like Howells, or Twichell, or Henry Rogers." Accordingly, he continues, "I will fire the profanities at Rogers, the indecencies at Howells, the theologies at Twichell. Oh to think—I am a free man at last!"[5]

Twain rehearses the pleasures of such frankness and immediacy, expressing his thoughts and feelings freely as the moment strikes. He imagines Twichell's response to his theological outbursts, as making him "writhe & squirm & break the furniture." If the unsent letter, for Twain, acted as a tactic for autobiographical writing, he did in fact allow many of his deepest and most risky thoughts—that is, risky from the point of view of the sustaining of his public persona—spill into the letters he *did send* to Twichell. For he knew that even where Twichell profoundly disagreed with his views, he would treat his friend's outbursts with good humor and equanimity, even as he gently chided him for being a "dog-goned pessimist" (Letter 242).

The extant letters from Twain to Twichell (though not vice versa) do tail off in the final few years of Twain's life. This may signal a loss of energy for such an activity on Twain's part, or perhaps a transfer of such energy primarily into his autobiographical dictations, which would, in some ways, cover similar ground and allow Twain an outlet for his more contentious views.[6] But in the years immediately following Livy's death (1904 and 1905) the letters between the two men take on, even more than previously, the quality of an ongoing debate and dialogue about the shape and philosophical meaning of life, its theological base, and political and public affairs. The sharp interest Twain took in current affairs is nowhere more evident than in his biting scrutiny of Roosevelt's presidency. In the important 4 November 1904 letter (Letter 236), he warns Twichell away from the latter's recent involvement in the political arena ("Oh, dear! get *out* of that sewer—party-politics—dear Joe")—when Joe attached his signature, along with other ex-soldiers, to a lengthy pro-Roosevelt statement appearing in the press. Here and elsewhere Twain shows his close knowledge of the intricacies of political issues of the time, commenting both on the current debate about the gold standard and on the matter of the Panama Canal and American interests in that region. In these letters, too, Twichell's optimistic attitude toward the human race and its "progress" increasingly sticks in Twain's craw, in contrast to his own much darker vision.

Despite the widening gap between the two men in such areas, the friendship remained firm. Twain was able, at the end of the day, to treat Twichell's conservatism with a wry humor. Twichell's continuing value in Twain's eyes is clear in the 15 March 1906 *Autobiography* entry: "Twichell, with his big heart, his wide sympathies, and his limitless benignities and charities and generosities, is the kind of person that people of all ages and both sexes fly to for consolation and help in time of trouble."[7] Joe, meanwhile, always tolerated Twain's various apostasies, never attempting to do more than gently chide him for his views, continuing in his attempt to "take your pessimist tricks with my optimist trumps" (Letter 242). In the last few years, the correspondence reverts mainly to day-to-day affairs, but still with the occasional outburst from Twain on larger matters (see Letter 279, for example, on religion). If the letters may at this stage be a touch one-sided, it is nonetheless clear that Twichell remained a very important figure in Twain's life. And when disasters struck, as they now did only too frequently, Twichell was always there with both sympathetic words and a generous heart. The intimate exchanges between the two men remain, then, right to the end, both fascinating and revealing.

1. A "Tribute" to Olivia Clemens in the *Hartford Courant,* pasted in Twichell's journal.

2. For more on the Isabel Lyon affair, see Karen Lystra, *Dangerous Intimacy: The Untold Story of Mark Twain's Final Years* (Berkeley: University of California Press, 2006); Laura Skandera Trombley, *Mark Twain's Other Woman: The Hidden Story of His Final Years* (New York: Alfred A. Knopf, 2010); and Michael Shelden, *Mark Twain: Man in White* (New York: Random House, 2010). Disputes remain, however, about the exact nature of Twain and Lyon's relationship. Twain's own version of the incident, the Ashcroft-Lyon Manuscript, has recently been published in Benjamin Griffin and Harriet Elinor Smith, eds., *Autobiography of Mark Twain,* vol. 3 (Berkeley: University of California Press, 2015), 321–440.

3. For more on Twain's relationship with Clara (and with Jean) and particularly on Clara's 1906–08 scandalous relationship with (the already-married) Charles Edwin Wark, the "extraordinary speed of events" surrounding her October 1909 marriage to Gabrilowitsch (127), and Twain's (possibly) manipulative hand in both these affairs, see Laura Skandera Trombley, "Mark Twain's *Annus Horribilis* of 1908–1909," *American Literary Realism* 40 (2) (Winter 2008): 114–36.

4. See Peter Messent, *Mark Twain and Male Friendship: The Twichell, Howells, and Rogers Friendships* (New York: Oxford University Press, 2009), 55, 58.

5. Henry Nash Smith and William M. Gibson, *Mark Twain–Howells Letters: The Correspondence of Samuel L. Clemens and William D. Howells, 1872–1910* (Cambridge, Mass.: Belknap Press, 1960), 844–45.

6. Twain saw his autobiography as remaining unpublished until long after his death.

7. Harriet Elinor Smith et al., eds., *Autobiography of Mark Twain,* vol. 1 (Berkeley: University of California Press, 2010), 414. In 1906, Twain would also call Twichell (along with Henry Rogers and Joseph H. Choate) one of the three "handsomest men in America." Benjamin Griffin and Harriet Elinor Smith, eds., *Autobiography of Mark Twain,* vol. 2 (Berkeley: University of California Press, 2013), 161.

228. Twain to Twichell

18 June 1904. Florence, Italy

Villa di Quarto
Florence June 18/04

Dear Joe—

It is 13 days. I am bewildered & must remain so for a time longer. It was so sudden, so unexpected. Imagine a man worth a hundred millions who finds himself suddenly penniless & fifty millions in debt in his old age.

I was richer than any other person in the world, & now I am that pauper without peer.

Some day I will tell you about it. Not now.

Mark.

229. Twichell to Twain

25 July 1904. Castine, Maine

"The Devereux" Castine. Me.
July 25.

Dear Mark, dear old Friend:[1]

It is but a week since I parted from you: yet somehow the time seems long—for the reason, I suppose, that I have had so many, many thoughts of you,—mostly guessing at *your* thoughts, trying to imagine them, though knowing that I could not. But I have wondered how the days were passing with you—how life and the world—the past and the future—were looking to you. Of course, as I say, it is consciously quite out of my power to imagine anything about it. I seem to be beholding you, as it were, from a great distance. Yet I cannot get you out of my mind. One thing I am sure of: that I love you inexpressibly. In fact, I never knew till now how deep and how large your room in my affection is.

The thought of Livy has a revealing effect upon me that way. You and she have been, and are, so bound up together in my heart's experience, have been so inseparable there, that all my feeling toward Livy carries over to you. And ought not the love—the kind of love—she inspired, now by her passing from us made to know itself, as, alas, it could not before, to quicken in its quickening the love all round that lived and grew in its surest light?—as yours and mine did.

Harmony and I reviewing in our talk the memorable years in which we were favored to taste so many pleasures within your doors now see, how clearly, that Livy was the centre of it all. Without her, without her atmosphere, everything would have been different. In her native modesty she was quite unaware of this; but it was so. Oh dear, Mark, I keep thinking of things I wish I had said to her. And there are *looks* of hers that come back to me—as, for instance the face with which she used to greet and welcome us when we rejoined her during our Switzerland journey.—I sharing the benediction of it because I was with you—a face shining like an angel's.

Harmony hardly ever speaks of her without saying, "How she did love Mark!"

We would like to hear from you: but still don't write if you don't feel like it. I will write to you now and then anyhow.

Harmony wants me to suggest to you that you come and stay with us a few days in Hartford by and by. She fancies it may be good for you. I trust you know how deeply she loves you—and always did.

Our most affectionate, tender remembrances to Clara and Jean, poor girls. And God bless you all,

Yours ever,

Joe

1. This is the first letter extant from Twichell after Livy's death—though he must have written earlier with his condolences. It is written after Twain's return to New York (he landed on 12 July). Twichell had met up with Twain since his return, and writes from his summer vacation home.

230. Twain to Twichell

28 July 1904. Lee, Massachusetts (Mourning border)

Lee, July 28/04.[1]

Dear Joe:

"How life & the world—the past & the future—are looking"—to me?

(A *part* of each day—or night) as they have been looking to me the past 7 years: as being NON-EXISTENT. That is, that there is *nothing*. That there is no God & no universe; that there is only empty space, & in it a lost & homeless & wandering & companionless & indestructible *thought*. And that I am that thought. And God, & the Universe, & Time, & Life, & Death, & Joy & Sorrow & Pain only a grotesque & brutal *dream*, evolved from the frantic imagination of that insane thought.

By this light, the absurdities that govern life & the universe lose their absurdity & become natural, & a thing to be expected. It reconciles everything, makes everything lucid & understandable: a God who has no morals, yet blandly sets Himself up as Head Sunday-school Superintendent of the Universe; Who has no idea of mercy, justice, or honesty, yet obtusely imagines Himself the inventor of those things: a human race that takes Him at His own valuation, without examining the statistics; thinks itself intelligent, yet hasn't any more evidence of it than had Jonathan Edwards in his wildest moments; a race which did not make itself nor its vicious nature, yet quaintly holds itself responsible for its acts.

But—taken as unrealities; taken as the drunken dream of an idiot Thought, drifting solitary & forlorn through the horizonless eternities of empty Space, these monstrous sillinesses become proper & acceptable, & lose their offensiveness.

I suppose this idea has become a part of me because I have been living in it so long—7 years—& in that time have written so long a story embodying it & developing it; a book which is not finished & is not intended for print.[2]

And so, a part of each day Livy is a dream, & has never existed. The rest of it she is real, & is gone. Then comes the ache, & continues. Then comes the long procession of remorses, & goes filing by—uncountable, & both ends dimming away & vanishing under the horizons.

How well she loved you & Harmony! as did I, & do I, also.

Mark.

1. The family were staying for the summer in seclusion, in a cottage owned by Richard W. Gilder (editor of the *Century*) in Tyringham, in Massachusetts's Berkshire Hills.

2. He refers to *The Mysterious Stranger* manuscripts, where the words he writes here are echoed directly.

231. Twichell to Twain

17 August 1904. Castine, Maine

Castine. Me. Aug. 17. 1904.

Dear Mark:

I can't wonder—and I don't—that with the light of your life gone out you sit dazed in the dark seeing no meaning or reason in anything, the Universe appearing to you only a confusion of unintelligible phantasmagoria. But it makes my heart ache for you, old fellow. I wish I was with you—why I hardly know—I have nothing to *say* to you; not now; but I would like to be where you are, and have you in sight, and wander about with you, silent or talking or what not. For I am not ignorant of the thoughts you are thinking. They have visited me too. I, indeed, *believe*, that behind the riddle there is a Hidden and Awful Wisdom; that for one tempest-tost on these wide weltering seas there is an Anchorage, that for the mortal spirit there is a practicable victory over the world with all its baffling mysteries.

Of course I do, or I wouldn't be a Christian minister. But I am not going to preach to you. I don't feel in the least like it. I would, though, as I say, like mightily to be at your side just now. Maybe, Mark, we would kneel together once in a while, as we have done in times past. Really, it seems to me, that is the posture for a man *to* take in the midst of these unfathomable realities. I do hope that you have some company to your taste. It is because I don't know that, probably, that I so wish I was with you. I fancy you more or less solitary.

We are ever so much obliged for the word of Jean's good prospect of recovery brought by Miss Lyon's letter to Sue.[1] And we shall be most thankful to learn that Clara has found benefit in her visit to New York.[2] What a year this last has been to those girls—and the past few years to all of you! I am conscious that I have small power to frame an imagination of it. i.e, the inside of it.

As for yourself, Mark, in some ways those same years have been how splendidly prosperous and successful! They have seen your *name* steadily grow—and it was illustrious already. In fact you have won—or earned—one of the magnificent prizes of your age. You must take huge satisfaction in it. You ought to. At all events I do. Harmony and I have a good deal talked over your career this vacation. How marvellous it has been! And other chapters are to be added to it yet, we expect. Do hold yourself to think on your more than royal fortune and lift up your head.

Yours ever aff.

Joe

1. In late July, Jean had been horse-riding late one evening with Rodman Gilder (the son of Richard W. Gilder) in Pittsfield, Massachusetts. During the outing, a trolley car struck and killed her Italian saddle horse after it bolted. Jean was thrown but suffered only a sprained ankle and bruised shoulder and side.

2. Prostrate with grief, Clara had gone to New York with Katy Leary.

232. Twain to Twichell

23 October 1904. New York, New York (Mourning border)

The Grosvenor,
Oct. 23/04.

After I got your telegram, dear Joe, I came upon Mrs. Boyce, & she read me a paragraph from Sue's letter.[1] But it was too new to furnish any real particulars, it only re-stated the telegram, substantially. I hope the boy is getting along well, & that the conceded seriousness has passed. I will talk no sadness—it is enough to have had it for hourly mind-company so many age-long months. I could not talk it to you & Harmony, anyway, to whom (blessedly) its deepest reaches are an unknown tongue as yet. . . . I will believe everything is going well with the boy.

To-day Clara goes into strict seclusion (a week ahead of the time set) to remain in bed & see no one for half a year.[2] Jean is in the Berkshire hills. I am by myself. I find myself poor company. To-morrow, a year ago, we took Livy on board the ship; & how bright she was, & beautiful!

I send my best love to you all.

Mark.

1. Twain is responding to a telegram from Twichell telling him of the latter's son Joseph's football injury at Yale (Joe Jr. was unconscious for several days). The letter was probably from Susan Twichell; Mrs. Boyce has not been identified.

2. Clara had suffered a nervous breakdown and would spend much of 1905 in Norfolk, a small community about thirty-five miles northwest of Hartford that contained many summer homes for the New York and New England elite.

233. Twichell to Twain

27 October 1904. Hartford, Connecticut

Hartford. Oct 27

Dear old Mark:

We all thank you for manifesting an uncle's feelings about Joe. He is coming along finely and will apparently be all right again in a few days.

Burt—who is in the Yale Law School—brought him home last Saturday, still suffering—though less than he had been—from the effects of the concussion and wrench he sustained the previous Tuesday on the field of battle. From that time the progress of his recovery has been rapid. He is now up and about the house and will probably be able to go back to College early next week. I doubt, however, if he plays any more foot-ball this season—with which outcome of his accident Harmony is much more content than he is.

It distresses us to think of poor Clara's long, long imprisonment, however advisable and necessary it is. 'Twill be dismal and forlorn as an Arctic night. Can't she have even letters to mitigate the loneliness of it? If that be not prohibited we will write to her.

As for yourself, old Fellow, what you say of your companionless state at present goes to our hearts. Isn't Jean to be with you soon? Of course you know lots of people and everybody is after you. But that you are separated from those of *your own* that are left—especially now—must be a sad solitude. Why won't you come up here and stay a few days with us? I shall be mighty glad to give up my time to you, for in-door fire-side talk, or roving the autumn woods, or anything you like. Harmony and the girls, who love you dearly and long to comfort you, beg you to come.

A Yale professor has sent me an extract from Moncure Conway's Autobiography just out, in which (Vol II p. 144) I am very pleasantly spoken of.[1] He must be telling, in the place, of his visit to you, which I remember, and what he says of me is no doubt connected with larger mention of you—and probably Livy. I'm going to look and see when I have the chance. Should you happen to encounter Gen. Sickles—he is your near neighbor, 23 Fifth Ave—give him my kind regards.[2] Another neighbor of yours (he is quartered at "The Berkeley") is Jack Johnson, who was stroke oar of the Yale crew the year I was a member of it (1859) when we beat Harvard for the first time. If he makes himself known to you, you will know why. He was Brayton Ives['] partner in Wall St. and has "made his pile", I suppose.[3]

Harry Hopkins—you will recall him, I guess,—now President of Williams College, was here yesterday attending the inauguration of the new President of Trinity College and spent the night with us. He spoke of you with warm regard and sympathy, as did others who participated in the function. Do drop me a line once in a while. By the way the next time you do it please enclose a "Yours truly, Mark Twain" (with date) for a Hartford gentleman who wants your autograph for his collection and don't dare ask you for it. His modesty merits reward. But tell me that you will come and see us.

Yours ever aff.

Joe

1. Moncure Daniel Conway was an expatriate American minister and writer and long-time friend of Twain's. The two men met in London in 1872, and Conway acted as Twain's literary agent there from 1876 until 1881. His *Autobiography* was first published in 1904. "In no country have I met a more delightful man in conversation than Twitchell [*sic*]," Conway wrote, "and his ministerial adventures if printed would add a rich volume to the library of American humour." Moncure Daniel Conway, *Autobiography*, vol. 2 (New York: Cambridge University Press, 2012), 131.

2. General Daniel Sickles was Twichell's commanding officer in the Civil War. Twichell would be a longtime defender of Sickles, whose actions at the battle of Gettysburg (he moved his troops without orders) were said by some to have compromised the Union position. On Twichell's deep feelings for Sickles, and Twain's own response to him, see *Autobiography of Mark Twain*, 1:287–90.

3. General Brayton Ives was a major figure in the banking business and past president of the New York Stock Exchange.

234. Twain to Twichell

28 October 1904. New York, New York (Mourning border)

The Grosvenor, Oct. 28/04

Dear Joe—

It is good & relieving news that you send me about Joe. Now, then, let him make a sacrifice for his mother's sake & call Jean's hand.*[1] Jean has given up horse-back riding, for my sake. I shall try to make it up to her some way.

No, Clara can't have letters, or books, or anything interesting.[2] [*Damn* those Or's & Nor's—they *never* fit.] I go out to Clara's regularly, but I don't ask to see her. This morning's news (by telephone) is good; she slept well & is not dreary but cheerful. [She is approaching the desired stage in the rest-cure business—the stage where all things cease from troubling & the wicked are at rest, & don't worry about anything, & are lazy & comfortable. And then she has that wonderful cat, you know—the best company I ever saw.]

[I wish to gosh you would page your letters, & not make me waste profanity which I can but ill spare, in helping me hunt my way through. I have reformed Jean & Susy Crane. Whenever a stranger sends me a letter made up of foolish and affected summersaults, I put it in the fire without looking to see what it is about.] *Damn* a stranger, anyway! Did you ever care for one? Understand:

[I am whetting up for King Leopold of Belgium. By January I shall have all the material (& venom) I want.[3]]

Oh, yes, indeed, Jean is coming as soon as I tip the word that the house is ready. That will end the lonesomeness. Doubtless Nov. 15 or 20. I couldn't go to Hartford, Joe—not for a long, long time yet, if ever. Oh, never, I am sure![4]

Wong came to see me, yesterday.[5] Ah in every way he is splendid, just splendid! How squalid the little nasty Roosevelt's [*sic*] are, beside such a man! I hadn't seen Wong since he was a boy.

Ever

Mark

* Ecclesiastical poker term.

1. In his footnote, Twain identifies this as a poker term. If there has been a bet in a round of poker play, a player may "call" the player to match the current bet made by an opponent. Twain is recommending that Joseph Hooker Twichell give up football, as Jean has given up riding after her accident. In fact, neither gave up their respective sport for long.

2. Twain originally wrote "nor books, nor" then twice deleted the *n*.

3. He would publish his *King Leopold's Soliloquy* pamphlet (a polemic against the brutal Congo policies of King Leopold II) in September 1905.

4. Hartford remained "the city of Heartbreak" for him.

5. Wong Kai Kah, a former student at the Hartford Chinese Educational Mission who had also attended Yale, was part of a Chinese delegation to the St. Louis Exposition.

235. Twichell to Twain

1 November 1904. Hartford, Connecticut

[Enclosures: A clipping from the Hartford Courant *of 20 October 1904 of a letter from Twichell inviting the public to a lecture by Dr. Kakichi Mitsukuri on "Ideals for the Future of Japan"; a clipping from the* Courant *of 29 October 1904; also a letter from Twichell wishing the newspaper well on its 140th birthday.]*

Hartford. Nov. 1. 1904

Dear Mark:

Your call from Wong Kai Kah—which I was mighty glad to hear of—I don't wonder that you were pleased by it, and him,—reminds me of a visit we have just now i.e. a few days since, had from Kakichi Mitsukuri, one of the Japanese boys [Edward H.] House brought over with him—as you will remember. And as I am not sure that you are taking "The Courant" at this time I enclose a communication about him I sent to that paper, which, may be, will be informing to you. And while I am about it, I will put in besides, a note of greeting and congratulations I wrote for the same paper on a certain recent occasion—as did a lot of other fellows. 'Twill interest you a little bit, perhaps.

Your grumble at my not paging my letters shows you to be in the same mood and temper of mind with the man who kicked down stairs the harmless wight who was "*always* tying his shoes."[1] I am lucky to have stirred you up anyhow. I wish I could think of something to say about Roosevelt that would "draw" you in like manner.

Yours

Joe

1. There is an anecdote in the playwright Richard Brinsley Sheridan's biography concerning his once tripping over a man in the street. The man said in his defense, "I am only tying up my shoe." Sheridan is said to have replied, "Damn it, sir, you are *always* tying up that shoe!"

236. Twain to Twichell

4 November 1904. New York, New York

The Grosvenor, Nov. 4/04.

Oh, dear! get *out* of that sewer—party-politics—dear Joe.[1] At least with your mouth. We had only two men who could make speeches for the two parties & preserve their honor & their dignity. One of them is dead.[2] Possibly there were four. I would have believed John Hay could do it. I am sorry for John Hay; sorry & ashamed. And yet I know he couldn't help it. He wears the collar, & he had to pay the penalty. Certainly he had no more desire to stand up before a mob of confiding human incapables & debauch them than you had. Certainly he took no more real pleasure in distorting history, concealing facts, propagating immoralities, & appealing to the sordid side of human nature than did you; but he was his party's property, & he had to climb away down & do it.[3]

It is interesting, wonderfully interesting—the miracles which party-politics can do with a man's mental & moral make-up. Look at McKinley, Roosevelt & yourself: in private life spotless in character; honorable, honest, just, humane, generous; scorning trickeries, treacheries, suppressions of the truth, mistranslations of the meanings of facts, the filching of credit earned by another, the condoning of crime, the glorifying of base acts: in public political life the *reverse* of all this.[4]

McKinley was a silverite—you concealed it. Roosevelt was a silverite—you concealed it. Parker was a silverite—you publish it.[5] Along with a shudder & a warning: "He was unsafe then. Is he any safer now?"

Joe, even *I* could be guilty of such a thing as that—if I were in party-politics; I really believe it.

Mr. Cleveland gave the country the gold standard; by implication you credit the matter to the Republican party.

By implication you approve the whole annual pension-scoop, concealing the fact that the bulk of the money goes to people who in no way deserve it.[6] You imply that all the batteners upon this bribery-fund are Republicans. An indiscreet confession, since about half of them must have been Democrats before they were bought.

You as good as praise Order 78. It is true you do not shout, & you do not linger, you only whisper & skip—still, what little you *do* in the matter is complimentary to the crime.

"It means, if it means anything," that our outlying properties will all be given up by the Democrats, & our flag hauled down.[7] *All* of them? Not only the properties stolen by Mr. McKinley & Mr. Roosevelt but the properties honestly acquired? Joe, did you believe that hardy statement when you made it? Yet you made it, & there it stands in permanent print. Now what moral law would suffer if we should give up the stolen ones? But—

"You know our standard-bearer. He will maintain all that we have gained"—by whatever process. Land, I believe you!

Shall we turn over "our" Canal to men who tried to defeat the treaty enabling us to build it? Oh, by no means! Let us leave it in the Presidential hands that made it ours—by methods which might even have wrung a shudder out of the seasoned McKinley.[8]

By George, Joe, you are as handy at the game as if you had been training for it all your life. Your campaign Address is built from the ground up upon the oldest & best models. There isn't a paragraph in it whose facts or morals will wash—not even a sentence, I believe.

But you will soon be out of this. You didn't *want* to do it—that is sufficiently apparent, thanks be!—but you couldn't well get out of it. In a few days you will be out of it, & then you can fumigate yourself & take up your legitimate work again & resume your clean & wholesome private character once more & be happy—& useful.

I know I ought to hand you some guff, now, as propitiation & apology for these reproaches, but on the whole I believe I won't.[9]

I have inquired, & find that Mitsikuri [*sic*] does not arrive here until tomorrow night. I shall watch out, & telephone again, for I greatly want to see him.

My, but his people & the Russians are making an astonishing fight![10] It is the human race at its very finest & highest. [Twain inserts the last full-stop and deletes "; that noble race which was made out of the excrement of the angels."] If God has any sense of humor, He—but no, He hasn't; He can *make* ridiculous things, up to the best of us, but *He* doesn't know they are ridiculous.

Always yours

Mark

P.S. Nov. 4. That erasure was an ungentle slur at the human race. Ungentle, & unfair. I retract it. I wish I could learn to remember that it is unjust & dishonorable to put blame upon the human race for any of its acts. For it did not make itself, it did not make its nature, it is merely a machine, it is moved wholly by outside influences, it has no hand in creating the outside influences nor in choosing which of them it will welcome or reject, its performance is wholly automatic, it has no more mastership nor authority over its mind than it has over its stomach, which receives material from the outside & does as it pleases with it, indifferent to its proprietor's suggestions, even, let alone his commands; wherefore, whatever the machine does—so-called crimes & infamies included,—is the personal act of its Maker, & He, solely, is responsible. I wish I could learn to pity the human race instead of censuring it & laughing at it; & I could, if the outside influence of old habit were not so strong upon my machine. It vexes me to catch myself praising the clean private citizen Roosevelt & blaming the soiled President Roosevelt, when I know that neither praise nor blame is due to him for any thought or word or deed of his, he being merely a helpless & irresponsible coffee-mill ground by the hand of God.

1. Insertion of "party-". The presidential election was four days away at the time of this letter. It is clear that Twain had read the pro-Roosevelt statement signed by old soldiers, including Sickles and Twichell, which was printed in the *New London (Connecticut) Day* on 17 October 1904—and no doubt elsewhere too.

2. It is not certain whom Twain is referring to, although he consistently admired former president Grover Cleveland for his honesty during this period.

3. Hay, tremendously prestigious because of his personal connection to Lincoln and long service to the Republican Party, had given a number of speeches in favor of Roosevelt.

4. For more on Twain and Roosevelt, see the various entries on the latter in *Autobiography of Mark Twain*, vol. 3.

5. Twain refers to the then-current intense debate over whether a gold or silver standard was preferable for the nation's economy. Democrat Alton B. Parker was standing for the presidency on a gold-standard plank. His party was looking to distance itself from William Jennings Bryan and his (by then) long-standing call for the free coinage of silver. But the appeal of Sickles and his fellow-signatories to ex-soldiers reads: "Judge Parker voted twice to [debase our money], in 1896 and 1900." The "He was unsafe then" sentence then follows.

6. In the run-up to the election, Republican president and candidate for re-election Theodore Roosevelt had issued an executive order (Pension Order 78) providing pensions for all Civil War veterans between the ages of sixty-two and sixty-seven.

7. The Sickles letter refers to the "hostility of the Democratic party toward . . . our outlying possessions, which are not independent." It then mentions not just the Philippines but also the Panama Isthmus, Porto Rico, Alaska, the Sandwich Islands, Guam, Samoa, and the Panama group of islands, claiming "all must be given up and our flag hauled down" if Democratic attitudes prevail. The quote marks should in fact end after "down."

8. The Sickles letter reads, "Shall we turn over the Panama canal to men who tried to defeat the treaty enabling us to build it?" While many Democrats had opposed the canal, the Democratic platform was specifically in favor of its construction. As to presidential methods, Twain apparently refers to the U.S. manipulation of political events in Colombia, of which Panama was then a part, to obtain control of the Canal Zone.

9. In Twichell's journal (a page that includes an entry for 12–14 December 1904) there's a pasted-in undated article headlined, "The Rev. Mr. Twichell Cautious." It runs in part: "The Rev. Joseph H. Twichell, the pastor of the Asylum Hill Congregational Church of this city, asked to be excused from making any statement in reference to the United States senatorship." This alluded to the choice of senators by the Connecticut General Assembly at that time. This may well reflect Twichell "getting out of the sewer"—perhaps in response to Twain's admonition.

10. He is referring to the 1904–5 Russo-Japanese War.

237. Twain to Twichell

16 February 1905. New York, New York

Feb. 16/05[1]

Dear Joe—

I knew I had in me somewhere a definite feeling about the President if I could only find the words to define it with. Here they are, to a hair—from Leonard Jerome [*sic*]: "For twenty years I have loved Roosevelt the man & hated Roosevelt the statesman & politician."[2]

It's mighty good. Every time, in 25 years, that I have met Roosevelt the man, a wave of welcome has streaked through me with the hand-grip; but whenever (as a rule) I meet Roosevelt the statesman & politician I find him destitute of morals & not respectworthy. It is plain that where his political self & his party self are concerned he has nothing resembling a conscience; that under those inspirations he is naievely [*sic*] indifferent to the restraints of duty & even unaware of them; ready to kick the Constitution into the back yard whenever it gets in the way; & whenever he smells a vote, not only willing but eager to buy it, give extravagant rates for it & pay the bill—not out of his own pocket or the party's, but out of the nation's, by cold pillage. As per Order 78 & the stealing of the Indian trust funds.[3] A man who will filch trust-money from a pauper Indian to buy votes with is pretty low down.

But Roosevelt is excusable—I recognize it & (ought to) concede it. We are all insane, each in his own way, & with insanity goes irresponsibility.

Theodore the man is sane; in fairness one ought to keep in mind that Theodore, as statesman & politician, is insane & not responsible.

[Unknown amount of text cut away.]

Do not throw these enlightenments aside, but study them, let them raise you to higher planes & make you better. You taught me in my callow days, let me pay back the debt now in my old age out of a thesaurus plethoric with wisdom smelted from the golden ores of experience.

Ever yours for sweetness & light,

Mark.

Love to Harmony, & don't forget us when you come down. I am still in bed, but having good times writing diligently.

Say, Joe—I am the first that noticed the parallel.

1. Though there is a break in the correspondence here, it does not seem caused by any offence given in Twain's letter. Indeed, Isabel Lyon speaks of a visit Twichell and Harmony made to Twain in New York in January 1905 and its beneficial effect. She writes (on 6 February), "Last month Mr. and Mrs. Twichell were here for a night, and it did Mr. Clemens a great deal of good for he had been depressed. He lives much in the past, speaking constantly of those who are gone" (Mark Twain Papers).

2. Twain means William Travers Jerome, New York district attorney, who made the comment at a Hungarian Republican Club dinner on 15 February 1905 (after Roosevelt, who was also there, had left the event), as reported in the *New York Times* the next day.

3. The government had recently diverted money from Indian trust funds for the support of Catholic mission schools.

238. Twichell to Twain

27 February 1905. Hartford, Connecticut

Hartford. Feb 27. 1905

Dear Mark:

It is highly probable that I (and may be Harmony) shall go to New York next Monday (March 6th) for a day and possibly two days. In which case, of all the hotels public and private there to make choice of we prefer yours—for sentimental reasons chiefly.

Of course there may be, and are not unlikely to be, circumstances of one sort or another, to bar you from letting us in at that time. If it be so, it will not in the least embarrass you—we trust—to tell us of it. The hour of our arrival will be the latter part of the afternoon. Should we stay over Tuesday, we shall be off your hands from morning till evening. With love to Jean.

Affectionately yours

Joe

239. Twichell to Twain

6 March 1905. Hartford, Connecticut[1]

Hartford. March 6.

Dear Mark

You will remember, I guess, that while I was at your home, we were called upon by that absurd inventor who is going to end war by anaesthesia, whom we denied audience.

A few days since I came across a long letter I had from him months ago, thanking and blessing me in a strain not unlike that of Mr Rogers['] correspondent for having previously given him an introduction to Gen. Hawley; and somehow it struck me with a sort of pity for the poor old duffer, — — so much so that I dropped him a line explaining why you and I couldn't see him; —— that you were sick in bed and I just seated at the dinner-table with a company of ladies; that I was leaving early the next morning and so couldn't ask him to come again; but that, all the same, I wished him luck. And here's his answer, which you needn't return.[2]

I am rather glad I wrote to him, for at my time of life, I don't want to hurt anybody's feelings. I imagine, though, that it will land him on me again sometime, — — not on you I hope. I haven't the least idea how he knew I was at No. 21.

We are enjoying Dave's visit hugely, but wish it hadn't so fallen as to upset our plan of going to New York.

With love to the girls,

Ever affectionately yours,

Joe

1. The events of this letter mesh with the events of January–March 1905 as recorded in Twichell's journal and Twain's letters, hence the dating of 1905.

2. Enclosure missing.

240. Twain to Twichell

7 March 1905. New York, New York (Typed transcript by Albert Bigelow Paine)

21—5th ave., Mch 7/05

Dear Joe—

By George! but Mr. Wheaton does shovel the sackcloth & ashes onto your head in a most gentle & blistering & competent way![1] I have not seen it better done in my life-days, as the Germans say. I think I divine how you feel, & about how much boot you would give to change places with almost anybody who has been caught in a disreputable performance—for instance, with that young friend of yours, courting his girl in her log home, & excused himself to go outside & "look after his horse."[2]

You must bring Mr. Wheaton here, some time when you are down, so that we can find out *why* he wants to stop war, which, to my mind, is one of the very best methods known to us of diminishing the human race. (What a life it is?? this one! Everything we try to do, somebody intrudes & obstructs it. After years of thought & labor, I have arrived within one little bit of a step of perfecting my invention for exhausting the oxygen in the globe's air during a stretch of 22 minutes, & of *course* along comes an obstructor who is inventing something to *protect* human life. Damn such a world, anyway.)

Send Dave back!—that breeder of disappointments.

Lovingly
Mark

1. Mr. Wheaton is unknown. This no doubt refers to the letter from the "absurd inventor" referred to in Letter 239.

2. The expression "I've got to see a man about a horse" is an excuse to leave the room to urinate.

241. Twain to Twichell

10 March 1905. New York, New York (Typed transcript by Albert Bigelow Paine)

21 5th ave., Mch 10/05.

Joe dear, read it![1] *Isn't* it a pathetic human race? And can there be anything *more* pathetic than the New England vote-peddling citizen's guileless admiration of his Puritan forefathers & Revolution-ancestors, & his conviction that they averaged higher, in virtue, than *he* does? Well—I believed as he does until Charley Clark & John Fiske debauched me with the truth.[2] About '85 Charley Clark astounded me by saying that the farmer-vote of Connecticut was as purchasable as his potatoes, & at about the same price. I was an innocent person (then) & I was horrified. I had my opinion of the man who would buy a vote, or sell one, or would *contribute money* to be used in so degraded a commerce. Why, dang it, Joe, my own white soul surrendered, with hardly a pang, at the very first temptation! Yes sir, in our library one morning Charley Warner asked me for *$25 to buy votes with, in Hawley's interest,* & I fell, there & then, never to rise again.

Do you notice the last sentence of the printed slip? Isn't it good & sarcastic? They are going to lay Bulkeley's matter (no doubt without a smile) before the U.S. Senate, a body which has been helping to buy the Grand Army & bounty-jumper & Revolution-great-grandchild vote every year for a generation![3]

Love from

Mark.

1. Enclosure missing.

2. Author of copious New England histories that gave a view of the region as a paragon of political progress, Fiske's mention here may well be ironic.

3. Morgan Bulkeley, former governor of Connecticut, had just been elected to fill the U.S. Senate seat for Connecticut to replace Joseph Hawley, who had died. Bulkeley needed senatorial approval to overcome War Department objections to plans for a new Connecticut River bridge. Twain may have been referring to this issue.

242. Twichell to Twain

13 March 1905. Hartford, Connecticut (typescript)

Hartford. March 13.

Dear Mark;

Here is the same thing done in slang.[1]

Still I am so happy as not to be convinced. What Charley Clark told you twenty years ago of the Coo-farmers may have been, I fear was, true of the *bulk* of them, or is true now.[2] Nor do I believe that a majority of the votes that elected Bulkeley were purchased, or a half, or a quarter, or a tenth of that majority. Nor, again, for all you and Charley Warner *were* drawn into the league of corruption in Hawley's interest, do I believe that the General himself was a party to it.[3] Nor, once more, do I believe that more than a small fraction in numbers of the U.S. Senate is venal, but that, on the contrary, as a body, it is honest. Hence I do not despair of the Republic, or of the Human Race, for that matter. Dig down in history anywhere you like five hundred years, and take a look around you there, and then go down on your knees and ask forgiveness for being such a dog-goned pessimist at the opening of the twentieth Century. At the same time felicitate me on its being given me to see, in spite of the selling of votes in Connecticut and Washington, that the coming in this world in a steady progress from age to age is the kingdom of God—of righteousness. Yes, sir; the signs preponderantly of a brief millenium point that way; they surely do.

Oh! there's an eddy now and then, here and there, but the *stream* flows in that direction. Climb out of your hole, Mark; get up where you can see a distance; drop your cussing and shout Glory—not, of course, without stopping once in a while to cry over the bloody fight the beaten and retreating Kuropatkin keeps up against the victor Oyama.[4] The *war* isn't ended yet, nor will be for more milleniums. But the parsons are winners, I tell you.

To return to our muttons—we had a delightful visit with Dave—a real feast of bacilli and anti-toxins, and serums etc—but didn't forget that it cost us a parliament with you. We hope, though, to indemnify ourselves for that loss ere long.

We are all pretty well but sick of work i.e. I am. I'd give two days of life for a day with you, in Switzerland say, in which to take your pessimist tricks with my optimist trumps. Young Harmony is spending a month with Sarah Sage in Albany (Hillside) most enjoyably as we judge from her reports.[5]

We are going to-night to the meeting of the Monday evening club at Will Hamersley's, where Parker is to read a paper on the "Mission of the Beautiful," or something of the sort. You can fancy Charley Perkins' poetic observations to follow.[6]

With love to the girls,

Yours ever affect.

Joe

1. This letter, unlike almost all the others, is a typescript. After the word "slang" someone (the hand looks very much like Twain's) has written "(Newspaper clipping)." Twain may possibly have had the letter typed to include in his autobiographical dictations. The clipping is missing.

2. "Coo-farmers" looks like a mistake in transcription—probably "Conn. farmers."

3. General Hawley served in the U.S. Senate from 1881 to his death (18 March 1905). Until 1884, Twain, Warner, and Twichell were Republican supporters and may well have donated money that was used to buy votes. Twichell, though, appears to refer to a "league of corruption" in an ironical way.

4. A reference to the decisive battle of Mukden (Manchuria) in the Russo-Japanese war which ended on 18 March 1905 with a Japanese victory (under Marshal Oyama Iwao) over the Russians (under General Alexei Nikolajevich Kuropatkin).

5. Widow of Dean Sage. Hillside was the name of the Sage family home.

6. See *Autobiography of Mark Twain*, 1:272, to appreciate Twain's low opinion of Perkins's ramblings at club meetings. He calls him "the dullest white man in Connecticut."

243. Twain to Twichell

14 and 19 March 1905. New York, New York (Typed transcript [carbon copy] by Albert Bigelow Paine)

P.S. March 19.
Delayed by my laziness[1]

March 14/05.

Dear Joe:

I have a Puddn'head maxim:

"When a man is a pessimist before 48 he knows too much; if he is an optimist after it, he knows too little."

It is with contentment, therefore, that I reflect that I am better & wiser than you. Joe, you seem to be dealing in "bulks," now: the "bulk" of the farmers & U.S. Senators are "honest." As regards purchase & sale with *money*? Who doubts it? Is that the only measure of honesty? Aren't there a dozen kinds of honesty which can't be measured by the money-standard? Treason is treason—& there's more than one form [of] it; the money-form is but one of them. When a person is disloyal to any confessed duty, he is plainly & simply dishonest, & knows it; knows it, & is privately troubled about it & not proud of himself. Judged by this standard—& who will challenge the validity of it?—there isn't an honest man in Connecticut, nor in the Senate, nor anywhere else. I do not even except myself, this time. There isn't a clergyman in your state who is dishonest as regards money-obligations, but there is only one who is honest when it comes to a political duty.[2] Why, Joe, treason to citizenship is immensely worse than treason to a money-obligation; don't you know it is? Don't you know it is the highest of treasons? In time of war the penalty is death. Yet all Connecticut is committing it every day—& sleeping quite serenely every night. Your place was by the side of that solitary & splendid ecclesiastical paladin: you know it perfectly well—now don't make it worse by trying to lie out of it, for I shouldn't take any stock in your statements. Your conscience has given you several private bites about it—you are not to try to lie out of *that*, either, Joe.

Am I finding fault with you & the rest of the populace? *No*—I assure you I am not. For I know the human race's limitations, & this makes it my duty—my pleasant duty—to be fair to it. Each person in it is honest in one or several ways, but no member of it is honest in all the ways required by—by what? *By his own standard.* Outside of that, as I look at it, there is no obligation upon him.

You purge Hawley of knowledge of that transaction. I agree. But you shout, Joe. We must not venture to shout for any man. There was a time when for two years Hawley & the Courant had been painting Blaine daily with deserved mud. Blaine was nominated one afternoon.[3] The question was, should the Courant bolt? should it stand true to its convictions, or should it sacrifice good clean patriotism to party expediency? should it choose treason to the country, or treason to the party? Hawley was in Washington. The telegrams went to & fro—lots of them. What stand must the paper take in the morning? That Hawley was reluctant to go back on the country we do know. It took him till midnight & after to make up his mind. Warner withdrew to privacy & non-political writing, and relinquished his salary. On election day he voted against Blaine by keeping his ballot in his pocket.

Am I blaming Hawley? *No,* sir. He is a member of the human race, & he *has* to be traitor to a duty now & then in times of storm & stress; he cannot help it.

Am I honest? I give you my word of honor (privately) I am not. For seven years I have suppressed a book which my conscience tells me I ought to publish.[4] I hold it a duty to publish it. There are other difficult duties which I am equal to, but I am not equal to that one. Yes, even I am dishonest. Not in many ways, but in some. Forty-one, I think it is. We are certainly *all* honest in one or several ways—every man in the world—though I have reason to think I am the only one whose black-list runs so light. Sometimes I feel lonely enough in this lofty solitude.

* * * * * *

Yes, oh, yes, I am not overlooking the "steady progress from age to age of the oncoming of the kingdom of God & righteousness." "From age to age"—yes, it describes that giddy gait. I (& the rocks) will not live to see it arrive, but that is all right—it will arrive, it surely will. But you ought not to be *always* ironically apologizing for the Deity. If that thing is going to arrive, it is inferable that He wants it to arrive; & so it is not quite kind of you, & it hurts me, to see you flinging sarcasms at the gait of it. And yet it would not be fair in me not to admit that the sarcasms are deserved. When the Deity wants a thing, & after working at it for "ages & ages" can't show even a shade of progress toward its accomplishment, we—well, we don't laugh, but it is only because we dasn't. The source of "righteousness" is—in the heart? Yes. And engineered & directed by the brain? Yes. Well, history & tradition testify that the heart is just about what it was in the beginning; it has undergone no shade of change. Its good & evil impulses & their consequences are the same to-day that they were in

Old Bible times, in Egyptian times, in Greek times, in Middle Age times, in Twentieth Century times. There has been no change.

Meantime, the brain has undergone no change. It is what it always was. There are a few good brains & a multitude of poor ones. It was so in Old Bible times & in all other times—Greek, Roman, Middle Ages & Twentieth Century. Among the savages—*all* the savages—the average brain is as competent as the average brain here or elsewhere. I will prove it to you, some time, if you like. And there are great brains among them, too. I will prove that also, if you like.

Well, the 19th century made progress—the first progress after "ages & ages"—colossal progress. In what? Materialities. Prodigious acquisitions were made in things which add to the comfort of many & make life harder for as many more. But the addition to righteousness? Is that discoverable? I think not. The materialities were not invented in the interest of righteousness; that there is more righteousness in the world because of them than there was before, is hardly demonstrable, I think. In Europe & America there is a vast change (due to them) in ideals—do you admire it? All Europe & all America are feverishly scrambling for money. Money is the supreme ideal—all others take tenth place with the great bulk of the nations named. Money-lust has always existed, but not in the history of the world was it ever a craze, a madness, until your time & mine. This lust has rotted these nations; it has made them hard, sordid, ungentle, dishonest, oppressive.

Did England rise against the infamy of the Boer war? No—rose in favor of it. Did America rise against the infamy of the Phillipine [*sic*] war? No—rose in favor of it. Did Russia rise against the infamy of the present war? No—sat still & said nothing. Has the Kingdom of God advanced in Russia since the beginning of time?

Or in Europe & America, considering the vast backward step of the money-lust? Or anywhere else? If there has been any progress toward righteousness since the early days of Creation—which, in my ineradicable honesty, I am obliged to doubt—I think we must confine it to ten per cent of the populations of Christendom, (but leaving Russia, Spain & South America entirely out.) This gives us 320,000,000 to draw the ten per cent from. That is to say, 32,000,000 have advanced toward righteousness & the Kingdom of God since the "ages & ages" have been flying along, the Deity sitting up there admiring. Well, you see it leaves 1,200,000,000 out of the race. They stand just where they have always stood; there has been no change.

N.B. No charge for these informations. Do come down soon, Joe.
With love,
Mark.

Oh, I *would* like to hear Charley Perkins uncork his tar-keg.

1. This P.S. is an insertion.

2. Possibly the Rev. Francis Goodwin, an Episcopalian minister and civic activist who stood with Twain and Twichell in defying the Republican establishment in 1884.

3. James G. Blaine's corruption, and the opposition of Twain and Twichell to his candidacy, is described in a note to Letter 87.

4. *What is Man?* See Letter 181, note 2.

244. Twain to Twichell

23 April 1905. New York, New York (Mourning border)

21 FIFTH AVENUE
Midnight, Apl. 23/05

Dear Joe—

I have just finished reading the history of Joe Hawley—a noble man, truly. I see that he was not the man to allow votes to be bought for him, & I do not believe he ever knew it. I thank you for sending me that paper.

I suppose the "Henry E. Burton" is the one who married Alice Day's sister.[1] I did not know he was dead.

With love
Mark.

1. Hartford attorney Henry Eugene Burton (brother of Nathaniel J. Burton, pastor of Park Congregational Church, Hartford) was married to Mary Beecher Hooker, sister of Alice Hooker Day. He died in 1904.

245. Twain to Twichell

1 and 2 June 1905. Dublin, New Hampshire (Two typed transcripts)

Dublin, N.H. June 1/05.[1]

Dear Old Joe:

Certainly, give Osborn a letter.[2] It will compromise me, but that is nothing, I don't write any other kind except to strangers. I had a long talk with [Charles Erskine Scott] Wood when I was in Portland in '95. He was lawyer for a railroad—salary, $35,000 a year. He has written some poetry, & it is good & on a high plane.[3]

I have read a little of his article which you sent. If I have not misunderstood him, he stands for morals without any qualifying adjective in front of the word. Just *morals*, I like it. It makes me cuss to see people talking about "public" morals & "private" morals & "legal" ones. There *aren't* any. There's merely just morals.

The legalizing of an immorality doesn't purify it, it only whitewashes it. I could mention a few existing samples—but never mind. Joe, I don't know how I would vote on the Rockefeller donation as a Congregational minister but speaking for my own unsanctified self I should say like this, if it is tainted money *take* it, by all means & ship it to China—no other kind can legitimately be used in the missionary business there, when the Aments are sent to dance on the Golden Rule & bully better men into adopting a civilization which is inferior to our own.[4] We do enjoy having Patrick with us again—the best man that ever wore clothes. And our old Katy is his match. Livy raised that pair.[5]

Good bye & love to you all.

Mark.

Togo forever![6] I wish somebody would assassinate the Russian Family. So does every sane person in the world—but who has the grit to say so? Nobody.

Try for Clara when you get to Norfolk. Jean & I are to see her before—before—well, we haven't any idea when, yet.

P.S.

June 2/05

Joe, although you are a Congregational minister, you know there are proprieties that must be observed. You know quite well that if the chair of Applied Chastity at Vassar should accept a donation from a *reputed* whore house, just that mere notorious *repute*, unconfirmed by any court, would settle it. Don't you know that? Withdraw your mind from the wordy confusion & hair splitting "reasonings" of the day, & rest it & tranquillize it with contemplation of a simple & easy object-lesson, like this.

Let us imagine that the American Board is the trustee of Vassar, & responsible: that Granny Judson occupies the chair of Applied Chastity, a chair supported wholly by the donations of kindly people who, having been brought to practice a little chastity now & then & enjoy it, desire to extend its sweet restraints to the gentle Vasserlings sitting in innocent darkness & unaware.[7] Now then let Granny *take that money*: those contributions are not *public*: for all Granny knows, they are pure: So far as she knows, their money is clean. Let her take it, & boom chastity with it: she is justified. But when America's boss whore—by rumor mind you, mere *universal* & unchallenged *rumor*, & nothing more—sends a contribution wherewith to stimulate the spread of practical chastity in the college right at that point Granny *must call a halt.* Common propriety, elementary propriety requires it, Joe.

Mark.

To Rev. Joseph Twichell

1. Twain spent the summer of 1905 (and the next) in Dublin, New Hampshire, renting a house (on this occasion) from artist Henry Copley Green. He enjoyed the company of a group of congenial neighbors from the literary, scientific, and political worlds.

2. During his Riverdale residency, Twain had come to know the prominent paleontologist and eugenicist Henry Fairfield Osborn. It is unclear whether this is a reference to him.

3. The title and publication details of the pieces referred to here are unknown, but Twain may be referring to one or more of Wood's many "Impressions" pieces published in the *Pacific Monthly*.

4. Standard Oil tycoon John D. Rockefeller had gifted a hundred thousand dollars to the American Board of Foreign Missions (Twichell was about to attend the annual meeting of the Board). A number of Congregationalist ministers had criticized the Board for accepting money from such a source. "Our own" seems an error for "their own."

5. Twain had just reemployed coachman Patrick McAleer after a considerable time away from the family. Katy Leary was also there in Dublin with him.

6. Admiral Togo Heihachiro was in command of the Japanese naval forces which destroyed two-thirds of the Russian fleet in the battle of Tsushima on 27–28 May 1905.

7. Granny Judson, that is, the Rev. Judson Smith, secretary to the American Board of Foreign Missions.

246. Twichell to Twain

13 June 1905. Hartford, Connecticut

Hartford. June 13. 1905

Dear old Mark:

What a Mark you are! I am going out to Seattle in September to preach the sermon at the Anniversary meeting there of the American Board. It is not my intention in the said discourse to touch on the matter of the Rockefeller gift; but if I do, I shall scarcely venture to cite your views of it, particularly as clothed in the lively figure of your "unexpurgated" P.S. though it is so luminous a statement of a point I should want to make, did I discuss the subject.

A sad mischance has recently befallen me. I was giving a Memorial Day address at Middletown. Right in the middle of it, just as I was swinging into its most impressive passage, my voice sunk to the proper pitch of pathos, a huge dog came up the church aisle, ascended the platform and began nosing my legs. Whereat the environing swarm of boys and girls on hand to sing patriotic songs burst into universal titter, in which, after a brief struggle of resistance the veterans of the Grand Army joined: and my eloquence went utterly to pot. I had to stop and laugh too.

Next week Thursday (June 22) I am going out to Norfolk to a wedding. *Can* I call on Clara, and where? I much desire to see the girl, if I may.

If you chance on a history of the town of Dublin published a few years since, it will show you that among the early settlers of the town were those of the name of Twichell (or Twitchell) and that they were people of consequence in their day.[1] If any of their descendents [*sic*] are now there I do not know.

We have had a scare over Col. [Frank] Cheney, who being on a trip to California, had, a few days since, in San Francisco, I think, to undergo a severe surgical operation, by which at first he was in great danger. The latest word relieves the fears felt for him, thank God.—yet not wholly. Our old friends are leaving us fast. So it must needs be. "One generation goeth and another cometh." Let us love one another, then,—we who for awhile remain—till the whole Round Table is dissolved.

I love you, old fellow, in spite of all your bad behavior, very, very dearly.

Ever affectionately Yours

Joe

1. A Joseph Twichell was born in Dublin, New Hampshire, on 16 September 1786. But the family history in the United States extends further back than this.

247. Twain to Twichell

24 June 1905. Dublin, New Hampshire

St. John's Day, 1905.
Dublin, N.H.

Dear Joe:

When I was a boy, two or three centuries ago, there was an anecdote:

The orator was just going it! His stump was in the centre of a mass of citizenship a hundred yards across. The applause was thunderous, irruptive, earthquaky—quite comprehensively volcanic; & so the speaker was delirious with admiration of his performance. He was doing the "scathing" act. He was exposing the defects of the opposition, with that sweeping confidence which—well, you know that style: the style that forgets that there can be some home-defects, too, & in the very nature of human concerns, *must* be.

Then he overheard one citizen behind him say to another, "Reckon he don' know 't the bottom of his pants has fell out."

It modified him.

Our Theodore is at it again, you notice. You've considered his irruption of day before yesterday which emptied his crater of that most unvolcanic of material—whitewash.[1] Whitewash & slumgullion. (See "Roughing It.")[2]

Wasn't it just like him to jump at this chance to do some more "fearlessness" before the audience, & add another Claudian triumph to his showy score of that sort?[3] Just like him, you see, to fetch out his Big Stick & mash poor little insignificant Bowen into the earth, then reach for his whitewash, & plaster coat No. 9 onto his shabby big railroad pet & pal. *He* isn't afraid of any little Bowen that ever lived—not he! & he isn't afraid of any little helpless Columbia [*sic*], neither; nor any little feeble Nicaraguan President—until he shows fight; nor any bloated big Beef Trust—until he has to face its men, instead of a corporate shadow.[4] Joe, he is all bluster, all pow-wow, all gas. He hasn't any real courage, he has no staying power, he backs down every time. Curious! he is like Grovener [*sic*] Cleveland in one way: when he starts in, you can always tell to a dead certainty where he is going to come out. When Cleveland starts in, we know—& the shabbiest republican in the land never dreams of doubting it—that he is going to come out right, & with dignity; & when Theodore starts in, we know with the same serene certainty, that he is going to come out the other way. There is something most remarkable about the unwavering stability of these two characters. Each in its way is perfect. I believe you may canvass all the public men of the day, both here & abroad, & not be able to say of any other two of them, "Furnish me an exigency & its circumstances, & I *know* what they'll do."

How this nation stood speechless with adoring admiration of our Theodore's matchless daring when he lifted up that shout audible at the two poles, "My duty is to my country & to my oath, & I here & now proclaim that the Canal supplies shall be bought in the cheapest market, let that market be where it may!" and how the exulting nation did let go & clamor out its said admiration of that matchless daring (the "daring" to do one's simple duty!) when it got back its voice a moment later! And one brief moment later, still, when the paladin's masters, the Trusts, tweaked his nose & ordered him to translate, how promptly he slumped to his knees & took it all back![5] Joe, even the jelly McKinley was a man, compared with this kitten that masquerades in a lion's skin.

You mustn't imagine I think I would be something better in Theodore's place. I don't. I wouldn't climb up there, with the bottom of my pants the way it is, to *save* the country, let alone amuse it. I do not claim any credit for this sagacity, neither do I put blame upon Theodore for lacking it. I had nothing to do with constructing my character, he has had nothing to do with constructing his'n; praise & blame are unwarrantable terms when applied to coffee-mills, & we *know* it; it may be that I am the only person who knows that a man has no more command over his acts than a coffee-mill has, but I *do* know it. Therefore I wish you to understand—& I say it seriously, not jestingly—that I am not laughing at Theodore, but only at the funny *results* of his make. I keep it clearly in mind all the time—try to, anyway—that he had nothing to do with building any part of himself & is not in any way to blame for the resulting conduct.

It is *handiest* to name the *man*—& it is habit, too, old lifelong silly habit, & now ineradicable—but understand me I always *mean* the coffee-mill.

Oh, think of him standing up before the whole world, with a Presidential brush reaching to the stars, & whitewashing that microscopic microbe Loomis! Now there's a spectacle for you! Why, there isn't enough *of* Loomis to whitewash. There's no room; even a camel's hair pencil would sqush [*sic*] over on both sides. He & Taft—great big President of the United States & great big Secretary of War—shutting an eye to speer [*sic*] for the object, & then splashing away, turn about! They find a spot—a little diplomatic ulcer, oozing fetid pus—*dab,* & that's covered; they find another just like it—some more pus, some more stench—*dab,* & that's covered; they find another, then another—*dab-dab,* & *they're* gone. No more surface on that side—turn him over, paint his belly. The job is done. Verdict, he hain't done nothing, only some "indiscretions," that's all; only a hatful of indiscretions; he isn't a virgin, true—they admit it, with a tear or two trickling down their noses—but he wasn't on the street *all* the time! Joe, that is the actual verdict—examine its terms & you will see.

Bowen was indiscreet, but not dishonest, Theodore & Taft were *both.*

Even as the coffee-mill is made, so must it grind when circumstances turn the crank. It can't help it. Theodore's mill *had* to refuse to listen to the Loomis scandal,—that was its build; it *had* to suppress & conceal the scandal; it *had* to stick to that little strumpet as long as it could; & when it couldn't any longer, it *had* to let her down with a nickel-plated health-certificate "diseased, but good enough for *this* diplomatic service." And very true, too: witness Whitelaw Reid's father-in-law's money sent Ambassador to England![6] In the room of Choate, Hay, Phelps, Lowell, & those others.[7] Again my native sagacity would protect me. Not to *save* my country, let alone amuse it, would I put on Whitelaw Reid's breeches & climb away up *there*. Neither would he, if he had wit enough to examine their southern exposure. Well, we sent all those fine giants to exhibit America's brains, perhaps it was time to send a dwarf to display her—her cash.

Oh, look at the Morton case!—that frantic certificate of character from his last place![8] The papers think Theodore whitewashed him merely because he was a friend. Yes, that is what they *say*, but the papers are not so innocent as all that—privately. We know that that *would* have been sufficient, for we know he has no more notion of official duty than an untrained child has; but we also know that our notorious Trust-Buster found himself caught at last where he had to either make his blustering good & actually prosecute a big law-breaker or turn tail & run. Well, we always know what Mr. Cleveland will do when there is a formidable public duty to be encountered, & we always know what Theodore will do in the like case. And sure enough, Theodore did it.

I began a new book here in this enchanting solitude 35 days ago. I have done 33 full days' work on it.[9] To-day I have not worked. There was another day in this present month wherein I did not work—you will know that date without my telling you.[10]

I have written you to-day, not to do you a service, but to do myself one. There was bile in me. I had to empty it, or lose my day tomorrow. If I tried to empty it into the North American Review—oh, well, I couldn't afford the risk. No, the certainty! The certainty that I wouldn't be satisfied with the result; so I would burn it, & try again to-morrow; burn that, & try again next day. It happens so, nearly every time. I have a family to support, & I can't afford this kind of dissipation. Last winter when I was sick I wrote a magazine article three times before I got it to suit me. I put $500 worth of work on it every day for ten days; & at last, when I got it to suit me it contained but 3,000 words—$900. I burned it, & said I would reform.

And I have reformed. I *have* to work my bile off, whenever it gets to where I can't stand it, but I can work it off on you economically, because I don't have to make it suit me. It may not suit you, but that isn't any matter, I'm not writing it for *that*. I have used you as an equilibrium-restorer more than once in my time, & shall continue, I guess. I would like to use Mr. Rogers, & he is plenty good-natured enough, but it wouldn't be fair to keep him busy rescuing me from my leather-headed business-snarls & make him read interminable bile-irruptions besides; I can't use Howells, he is busy & old & lazy, & won't stand it; I dasn't use Clara, there's things I have to say which she wouldn't put up with—a very dear little ashcat, but has claws.

And so—you're It.

I suppose you saw Clara day before yesterday. She wrote that she was going to ask you to stay over night in her house. I judge by that that D$^{r.}$ Quintard is beginning to be less exacting with her, less strenuous.[11] It's a happy sign. Jean is in fine strength, & does a deal of wholesome driving & horsebacking. There is nothing like the open air; I often look out of the window myself. Love to you all.

Mark.

1. The papers at the time reported on Roosevelt's scathing censure of Herbert W. Bowen, whom he dismissed as U.S. minister at Caracas, Venezuela, due to his accepting money from the Bermudez Asphalt Company to promote its interests. Twain had this in mind. Roosevelt exonerated Assistant Secretary of State Francis B. Loomis of charges brought against him by Bowen. Loomis was (rightly) accused by Bowen of also being involved in Venezuelan schemes (loans and a mining venture) for his own personal profit. Loomis was, among other things, a promoter of railroad interests.

2. In chapter 4 of *Roughing It*, Twain describes the menu at an overland stagecoach station as including "Slum gullion": "It really pretended to be tea, but there was too much dish-rag, and sand, and old bacon-rind in it to deceive the intelligent traveler."

3. The Julio-Claudian dynasty, from Augustus through Nero and including Claudius, celebrated a series of showy "triumphs."

4. Both Colombia and Nicaragua had been victims of Roosevelt's "speak softly, and carry a big stick" approach (peaceful negotiation while at the same time displaying U.S. military capability) in the Panama Canal negotiations. The reference to the Beef Trust probably alludes to the fact that, although the Supreme Court ruled in the government's favor, sustaining Roosevelt's injunctions against the meat packers for alleged price-fixing, a subsequent administration report generally exonerated the packers. The report was criticized loudly in the press and embarrassed Roosevelt.

5. In May, Roosevelt had supported the Panama Canal Commission's decision to buy supplies for construction through the open market. This enraged American manufacturers who had previously held a monopoly on this business. Several days later he decided that Congress should make the decision about the issue, effectively delaying, if not killing, the measure.

6. Wealthy banker and railroad man Darius Mills was Whitelaw Reid's father-in-law. Reid was appointed ambassador to England in 1905.

7. All of these, too, had served as ambassador to the Court of St. James. Edward John Phelps was a lawyer and politician from Vermont. James Russell Lowell was the poet, editor, and diplomat.

8. Paul Morton, secretary of the Navy, "flagrant, persistent and self-confessed railway rebater" (*Boston Evening Transcript*). Exculpated by Roosevelt in July 1905 of his crimes, despite legal advice to the contrary. The "certificate of character" is Twain's dismissive way of describing Roosevelt's whitewashing Morton—as an employer "from his last place" might provide such a certificate to a servant (Morton's "last place" in this case being the Navy Department).

9. He worked that summer on *A Horse's Tale*, "Eve's Diary," and *Three Thousand Years among the Microbes*.

10. The anniversary of Livy's death, 5 June.

11. Dr. Edward Quintard, the family physician who would attend Twain at his death, was monitoring Clara's condition in her cottage in Norfolk.

248. Twichell to Twain

3 July 1905. Hartford, Connecticut

Hartford. July 3. 1905

Dear Mark:

While young Harmony was taking her course in the Nurses Training School in the Hartford Hospital, I went down one day on invitation to see a woman operated on for an abdominal tumor. An huge, big tumor it was, distending her abdomen into a semi-globular shape.—and was hard as a pumpkin. The first thing the surgeons did after chloroforming her and laying her on the table, was to make an incision and insert a syphon, and let out the fluid contents of the tumor—a full gallon in quantity. Of the bouquet of that product the less said the better. But the distention was completely relieved—to the pleasure of the spectator.

Such a pleasure I had in the reading of your letter received a few days since,—just as I was leaving to attend a wedding in Pittsburg [*sic*], Pa, or I should have acknowledged it sooner,—in which obviously, (and as you yourself said), *your* distention sought relief, and, I trust, obtained it.

All right, Mark; go ahead. I give you free leave to syphon out to me all such secretions whenever they accumulate to the pitch of discomfort. And I think it better, on various accounts, that I should catch them in my pail than that you should (are these '*shoulds*' correct?) empty them into the N. A. Review [*North American Review*], or Mr Rodgers [*sic*] or Mr Howells, who might not as you suggest be able, for one reason and another, to accommodate as conveniently as I can. 'Tis an old saying that "some mens oaths are more worshipful than some mens prayers." The *motive* of your automatic curses is, I allow, pure, though the *object* of them might, in my opinion, be more judiciously selected. But I will not argue that point with you.

Regarding, however, the object (or subject) of your benedictions—Mr Cleveland—I am happy to say that I am quite of your mind. He surely is a man to tie up to.

As to Theodore—he has yet three years left in which to get a smile on your face, and I guess he will do it.

Yes, I did see Clara last week in Norfolk—to my great satisfaction—she was looking and feeling so well. She wrote asking me to be her guest over-night, but I thought it, on the whole, advisable to make her a brief call only, not knowing for sure that her doctor would approve anything more. But I told her that I would come again, and I will,—unless she can get leave to come down and pass a day with us—which she thought she could. She seemed to me perfectly well. Young Harmony is just back from a six weeks excursion to Holland and England with Mrs Dean Sage—with whom she will probably live the coming winter. Burt has just graduated at the Yale Law School with "magna cum laude" honor—if you know what that means. We had a fine Commencement at Yale this year. Lots of people I met there asked for you. Mark, you have a world full of friends; and you ought to rejoice in the rich fortune of it.

But nobody under the canopy loves you any more than does

Your ever aff

Joe.

I am sending you the copy of a review from "The Nation."[1] I am rather disposed to take its view of Mr. Rockefeller. It seems to me *just.*

1. Ida Tarbell published her "John D. Rockefeller: A Character Study" in *McClure's Magazine* in July 1905. This may possibly refer to a review of that work.

249. Twichell to Twain

4 July 1905. Hartford, Connecticut

Hartford. July 4. 1905

Dear Mark:

In hastily closing my letter yesterday, I forgot to tell you that while in Pittsburg [*sic*] I lunched at the Duquesne Club with a party of gentlemen, among whom was ex-Judge Shiras of the U.S. Supreme Court.[1] At table he suddenly asked me if I had ever been told that I *looked like you.* I answered, with modest confusion, that No, I hadn't. Upon which, he said that he was impressed with the resemblance the moment he saw me, and that the principal feature of likeness was the *profile.*

Now put that in your pipe and smoke it.

In the course of talk a discussion arose, in which Judge Shiras bore leading part, on the question of the proper term by which to express the converse of "white washing."

"*Black washing*" was disallowed because it wasn't in the dictionary. All the same it struck me as a good word of description to add to the language. And remembering your last letter, I thought that when I wrote to you—but I forgot that too—I would apply it to your discourse on Theodore—as felicitously characterizing the general gait of it. Yes, truly, a masterly black washer you are, when Theodore is your theme—the official Theodore, of course, I mean. Theodore bears a feeble hand with his pigment compared with you with yours. Another thing I meant to tell you is that I have been trying Plasmon lately—a des[s]ert spoon-ful in my morning dish of oat-meal.[2] Is that a fact of any interest to you *now*?

Yours aff.

Joe

1. The Duquesne Club on Sixth Avenue, Pittsburgh, founded in 1873, at that time composed mainly of prominent industrialists. Pittsburgh-born Judge George Shiras Jr. served on the Supreme Court from 1892 to 1903.

2. Regarding Plasmon, see Letter 180.

250. Twain to Twichell

13 July 1905. Dublin, New Hampshire (Mourning border)

Dublin, N.H., July 13/05

Dear Joe—

I want you to accept this $1500 conscience-money if you will, as it marks the turning of a reform-corner for me: I've been into Wall street again in a small way & am out again with a profit of $4,700 & am not going in any more. This profit is tainted money; & lies heavy on my conscience; but I remember with a spiritual uplift that other new convert who found that her jewelry was dragging her down to hell, so she gave it to her sister Mary.[1]

With love

Mark

1. The Twichells were always hard up and Twain had (in a number of ways) given financial help to them over the years. Now Henry H. Rogers stepped in to help, on condition Twain took the credit for the gift. Twain accordingly disguised it as Wall Street profits.

See Lewis Leary, ed., *Mark Twain's Correspondence with Henry Huttleston Rogers, 1893–1909* (Berkeley: University of California Press, 1969), 590.

251. Twichell to Twain

15 July 1905. Hartford, Connecticut

Hartford
July 15. 1905

Dear old Mark:

I would give anything if I had your command of the English language, just for now. Never before did I so much feel my need and lack of it. After the avalanche slid down on us yesterday morning we lay pretty still for an hour or two; dazed like, wondering what had struck us. Harmony came to and got to her feet, first. When, presently she found her tongue—well, I wish you could have heard her! The cantata of our wood thrush is not so melodious as was the song that broke from her glad heart. For, you understand, Mark, that our financial pressures are more afflictive to her than to me.

I crawled away up into my study, and by force of habit began fumbling at my table, but couldn't for the life of me get my mind off that check, the reality and import of which I seemed somehow not quite able to grasp. Then Harmony all the forenoon kept rushing in on me at frequent intervals, and each time with some new suggestion or proposal respecting the use to be made of our sudden fortune as, e.g. "Joe; we can pay for our furnace"—"We can pay our tax without asking the Collector to hold our check till Fall."—"We can pay our bill for next winter's coal right off instead of by instalments for the next six months" "We can, and we will, lift part of the mortgage on our house! Hurra!" &c. &c. &c. That was one line. But thoughts of another kind impelled some of her irruptions. Once she came in to say impetuously "Joe; it is your duty *now,* while you are alive to do it, to write a full and careful description of Mark from the stand point of our experience of him. If you don't, the world will never know what he really is,—will never know his best side." Again, she opened the door and flung in this remark, "Joe, I'm inclined to think there is considerable truth in what Mark says about Roosevelt!!"—breaking ground, you see, in the process of your canonization,—removing certain rubbish in the way of it.

Again she entered softly and stood a minute silent; then said with tears in her voice "Joe; who ever had such friends as we have had? There's — — and —— and — — (naming beloved benefactors; more than my dashes indicate, —dear Dean Sage among them) and here's Mark—crowning generosities past with this—this." —the rest of the speech was fluid.

What sort of a time Harmony is having over it, you may gather from the foregoing data. I'm having the same; except that I let her do the crying.

It comes to this old fellow:—you have taken a good lump off our mortgage; which is not large, indeed, but still an incumbrance; making part of your gift an investment with the "tick of interest" for us instead of against us:—You have paid every earthly cent we owe, leaving us with a handsome, big balance on which to begin a new celestial life of *forehandedness.*[1] Yes, Mark, you have put us financially where we never were before, and where we are going to be able to stay. The comfort of it—the sweet peace; deep, inward—is past all telling. We feel ourselves permanently better off, and in a vital respect happier than we were two days ago. How we feel about it all I will further unfold when I write again, saying only now that we bless you for a dear old gambling coffee mill, and are glad that you reformed just when you did—and not earlier. The fact is, Mark, the thoughts of our hearts toward you and upon you are quite unspeakable.

Your ever

Joe

1. The Twichells had presumably re-mortgaged their house since 1888, when members of the Asylum Hill congregation and other friends—including Twain—had paid it off.

252. Twichell to Twain

14 August 1905. Hartford, Connecticut

Aug. 14.

Dear Mark;

A school-boy in writing a composition on the subject of the Western Hemisphere began by saying "The Western Hemisphere is one of the biggest hemispheres there is in the world."

You have commanded Harmony and me to spare you any further expression of our feelings about the great thing you did for us last month—it is just a month to-day since the convoy arrived—but really old fellow, we can't quite make up our minds to let you off so easily. That check was a fact of more than hemispherical bigness,—the biggest that has struck us for a long time—and as we may not *tell* of it (for fear of the papers) you positively must hear a few more words upon it from us—for our sakes anyhow. We keep discovering what it meant—and means—to us. The first of August—more accurately the second—Harmony brought the morning mail into the study, and stood by while I inspected it.

"Do you see?" she exclaimed.

"Do you notice?"

"See *what*?" I said "Notice *what*?"

"Why, no *bills*!!!" It hadn't occurred to me till that moment; but, by George, it was so! A new experience: almost unimaginable up to then: it seemed too good to be true. But, yes, we had our little August salary whole, and a lot beside that—and no account outstanding anywhere! And 'tis not a dream, but a blissful reality.

Had the fortune come to us at an earlier period—say twenty years ago, or even ten—we might have been demoralized by it to the extent of feeling that we had money to spend—on peanuts and candy e.g. and other luxuries. At our age, however, we have outgrown that weakness. We have, indeed, dispensed a modest percentage of our wealth to a few local charities. We *had* to do that to preserve our self-respect. But otherwise our scale of expenditure is unaltered. The *change* you have wrought for us is an invisible one—that viz: of the *inner consciousness* of being out of debt. How sweet a luxury that is you know yourself, and in it we do luxuriate, I assure you—Harmony more than I even. The increase of her cheerfulness thereby is very perceptible. She says she thinks of it when she wakes up in the night, and resolves that it shall be lasting and permanent—which, as she is our domestic treasurer, it will be, I am confident.

There, Mark, you may go now. I won't trouble you any more about this business for the present. In disobeying your orders I have reckoned on your indulgence in view of your appreciative consideration of the pressure I am naturally under in the case.

I have been writing to Clara asking her leave to pay her a short visit at Norfolk. If she says "yes" I shall run up there some day this week. 'Twill have to be—and, I suppose, would better be—a call of a couple of hours only, but I greatly want to see the child. When, oh, when, are we going to see you? With love to Jean.

Yours ever affectionately

Joe.

253. Twain to Twichell

17 and 19 August 1905. Norfolk, Connecticut
(Typed transcript by Albert Bigelow Paine)

Private.

Norfolk, Conn., Aug. 17/05

Dear Joe:

Mrs Isabella Beecher Hooker is fully as remarkable to-day as ever she was in her life.[1] She dragged her 83 years up those steep stairs this morning—with a mission, need I say?—& sat by my bed an hour, & talked with all her old brightness, & deep earnestness, & passion for easing the sorrows & enlarging the happiness of the children of men. Her mission was to put me in the way of learning what spiritualism really is, in the hope that I might come to believe in it & then use my reputation in its service. Joe, (this is the privacy) she has for 15 years had spiritual communication with a *miscarriage* in heaven! (I have never come nearer to smiling in my life & escaped.) This miscarriage has a name—the name its parents had intended to call it by if it had not miscarried. In heaven it has borne that name for 30 years. It knows English & talks it fluently, & takes as much interest in Nook Farm affairs as any miscarriage that ever lived. I wish I could see it with its halo on.

Do you remember the astonishing remark she made to you in 1873 in possible extenuation & abridgement & modification of Henry Ward's alleged commerce with Mrs. Tilton?[2] Well, this new outbreak is a close second to that one, it seems to me.

I am not a spiritualist yet. Still, she isn't done with me—other evidences are to follow.

P.S. 19th. Your letter arrived from Dublin yesterday evening. It gave me great pleasure, although it was a breach of the prohibition.[3]

I am still in bed—it is the sixth day, but seems the 40th—& there is no immediate prospect of my getting on my feet. However, "prospects" go for nothing in gout, I may be on my feet in three days.

Clara brought in various reverberations of your thunders at that luncheon—no, I mean cordial compliments evoked *by* those thunders. I am dreadfully obliged to you for filling that breach so compactly & effectively; it leaves me barren of any sense of guilt or shame—& I should certainly have felt both guilt & shame, otherwise, as knowing that those people would blame me. Other things are forgiven, but the failure of [a] chief guest is never forgiven, except he be dead. With lots of love to both,

Mark.

1. Twain was presumably on a visit to Norfolk to see Clara. Hooker, a fervent spiritualist, had a summer cottage there.

2. The specific remark is unknown. John and Isabella Hooker had both used Twichell as a go-between to carry their sometimes confusing views on Henry Ward Beecher's alleged adultery to other members of the Nook Farm community. (For more on this episode, see the introduction to part 2, note 3 to Letter 19, and Letter 97.) In a letter to Beecher (her half-brother) in November 1872, Isabella had urged him to admit his adulterous relationship with Elizabeth Tilton and defend himself as one who was a reformer of the love and marriage relationships. It may be that she made some such suggestion to Twichell too.

3. Presumably the 14 August letter, sent to Dublin and forwarded to Norfolk. Its continuing expression of gratitude for the monetary gift breached Twain's prohibition against any more such letters. Twichell had spoken at a 16 August Norfolk luncheon in place of Twain, who was suffering from gout.

254. Twichell to Twain

19 January 1906. Hartford, Connecticut

Hartford. Jan 19.

Dear Mark:

I declare that the *deeps* penetrated and explored in such researches as this of radium more affect me with the sense of *sublimity* than those disclosed by the telescope.[1] Really this would be an admirable sort of an universe if it wasn't for the Human Race. Yet it's the Human Race that has captured the knowledge both of the Light Year and of Radio-activity. Perhaps it will amount to something eventually.

Yrs aff.

Joe

1. After the Curies' discovery of radium in 1898, there was great excitement in the press, especially over its potential application in medicine.

255. Twichell to Twain

27 January 1906. Hartford, Connecticut

[Clipping attached:]

Mark Twain's Coachman Ill.

Patrick McAleer, who was coachman for Samuel L. Clemens during Mr. Clemens's residence in this city and who has worked much for Mr. Clemens and members of his family since, is very ill at St. Francis's Hospital. Mr. McAleer, who is married, lives at No. 80 Flower street. He is reported to have cancer of the liver and his friends have little hope for his recovery. He is about 65 years old.

Jan 27.

Dear Mark:

The above is from yesterday's Courant. I am going to see Patrick this afternoon without fail. I met him on the street not long since and had a word with him—as usual. I marked nothing in his look then to indicate ill health and he told me nothing.

I had a call last night from the President of the Hartford Yale Alumni Association whose errand was to extend to you, through me, an urgent invitation and request to come up to the Annual Banquet of said Association *Feb 9th* and offer a few remarks. What you will say to it I don't know but I can guess. By your acceptance, however, you would kill several birds with one stone, as you can understand. You would meet and greet a crowd of old friends with little expenditure of time, and you could give Patrick a sight of your face to his great comfort.

You will stay at our house of course.

Yrs aff.

Joe

256. Twichell to Twain

31 January 1906. Hartford, Connecticut

Hartford. Jan 31.

Dear Mark:

I am sorry to say that the news about Patrick is very bad. I saw him Monday. He *looked* pretty well and was in cheerful spirits. He told me that he was fast recovering from an operation performed on him last week Wednesday, and would soon be out again. But a nurse who followed me from the room when I left told me that the poor fellow was deceived. The operation had simply disclosed the fact that nothing could be done for him.

Yesterday I asked the Surgeon ([Dr. Marcus Morton] Johnson, living opposite us) if that were so, He said "Yes"; that the trouble was cancer of the liver, and that there was no help for it in surgery; the case was quite hopeless; the end was not many weeks off. A pitiful case indeed! Poor Patrick! His face brightened when he saw me. He told me, the first thing, that he had just heard from Jean. His wife and son were with him.

Whether they suspect the truth I don't know. I doubt if the wife does: but the son looked very sober. May be he only has been told.

Yrs aff.

Joe

257. Twain to Twichell

26 February 1906. New York, New York (Per Isabel V. Lyon; draft telegram)

Rev. J. H. Twichell

Hfd, Ct.

Shall reach Hartford about two thirty today to attend Patrick's funeral Wednesday I desire to be a pall bearer.[1]

Mark

Feb. 26

1. Patrick McAleer died on 25 February. Twain evidently planned to use the occasion of the funeral for a catch-up with some old friends. On 26 February he wrote to one of them, Charles H. Clark, then president of the Hartford Courant Corporation, "Will you assemble some Cheneys & Twichells & other friends at Hartford Club Thursday & lunch them & me at my expense" (letter transcript by Isabel Lyon, Mark Twain Project).

258. Twichell to Twain

4 March 1906. Hartford, Connecticut[1]

Sunday P.M.

Dear Mark;

I dropped Charley Clark a line telling him what you said to me on the way to the station Thursday about the bill for the lunch at the Club. I enclose his reply received yesterday.—with his permission. i.e. I met him after he had mailed the note but before it was delivered, and asked him if I might send it to you, to which he answered, "yes, if you want to, when you have read it." You see what he says. I thought your feelings about the matter entirely natural and reasonable. But I really think you would do him a kindness by letting it stand as it does now.

However, you are plainly entitled to pay that bill if you claim your right to. Unless you see fit to oblige him by waiving that right. I will get the figure of it from him and tell you what it is.

The glow of our pleasure in your little visit is upon our spirits still. 'Twas a refreshment to have you within our doors once more. Oh, do come again! All Hartford delighted in your coming.

I enclose that piece about me of which I spoke to you.[2] With love to the girls and their dear dad from us all.

Yours aff

Joe

1. Twain lunched with Twichell, Clark, and others on Thursday, 1 March 1906, after Patrick McAleer's funeral the day before. He took a late-afternoon train back to New York. See *Autobiography of Mark Twain*, 2:322–23, 412–13.

2. Two recent items had appeared in the *Hartford Courant* about Twichell: one a humorous story, the second a 4 January 1906 short letter of praise from Gen. Horatio C. King, Civil War hero and Democratic politician, for "everybody's friend, Joseph H. Twichell." One of these was likely Twichell's enclosure—most probably the King letter.

259. Twichell to Twain

30 March 1906. Hartford, Connecticut

March 30th 1906

Dear Mark:

I am ordered on duty—as reader of a Scripture Lesson only—at the service named on the enclosed card, which will be in commemoration of the close of the Civil War.[1]

Harmony proposes to attend it with me. It will require us to be in New York from Saturday night to Monday morning. There are plenty of places where we could stay while there, but our choice of all is 21 Fifth Avenue; and there shall be our quarters if you say so.

Of course there may be reasons why not,—in which case you will not hesitate to avert us.

I called on Patrick's people the other day. Their comfort in your coming up to the funeral is deep, and their gratitude for it unbounded. The terms in which they spoke of it were really pathetic.

Yours affectionately

Joe.

P.S. It is possible that we shall want to be in New York *Friday* night too.

1. Card missing. Twichell traveled to New York on 7 April for observances of the anniversary of the surrender of Lee to Grant at Appomattox, Virginia, on 9 April 1865. He read the lesson at a Sunday service at Trinity Church on Wall Street on 8 April.

260. Twichell to Twain

12 April 1906. Hartford, Connecticut

Hartford. Thursday Apr. 12th

Dear Mark,

This is to advise you that Harmony and I expect to arrive at your door at a little after 4 oclock [*sic*] Saturday P.M.—on our part a joyful expectation.

Yrs aff

Joe

261. Twichell to Twain

18 April 1906. Hartford, Connecticut

[Enclosure: A typed letter is enclosed from the Periodical Publishers' Association of America, dated 16 April, inviting Twichell to speak at a 4 May dinner in Atlantic City, New Jersey. Twichell has marked a passage that reads, "The Board of Directors thought that you might be willing to come and add a zest to the entertainment of the evening by giving our guests some of those stories which you know so well how to tell."]

Hartford. Apr. 18.

Dear Mark:

See what you've brought me to! What stories *could* I tell such an audience? Were I to undertake it, I should have to ask you to give me a lesson or two in the art. But I can't go, fortunately. May 4th I shall be in Lexington. Ky. Attending Mr. Ogden's Southern Education Conference.[1] Harmony is going with me. We leave New York May 1st and shall be away till May 9th. We are, of course, to be Mr. Ogden's guests for the whole trip.

My, how we wish you were going, too!

The taste of our last visit with you is sweet in our mouths still.

Love to the girls

Yrs aff

Joe

Thanks for your just comment on Gorky's bad mistake.[2] Poor fellow; he didn't understand our bigotry. Too bad!

1. Robert C. Ogden, businessman and philanthropist, led conferences on rural education in the South from 1900 to 1914.

2. Twain had helped organize the U.S. tour of Maxim Gorky, the Russian author and revolutionist, but withdrew his support after press reports that Gorky was traveling with a woman who was not his wife. This was not necessarily because Twain disapproved, but because he felt this rendered Gorky ineffective as a fund-raiser.

262. Twichell to Twain

10 July 1906. Hartford, Connecticut

Hartford. July 10. 1906

Dear Mark;

I can give no justifying reason for sending you this photograph.[1] It is a purely impulsive act. I simply thought I would.

But I was going any way to write to you just to say that your discourse on Howells in the last "Harpers" [*sic*] is certainly one of the most delicious things you ever did.[2] I would like to see what Howells himself said to it.

Your loving obituary of dear old Schurz was of like merit.[3] The pilot figure was happy in the extreme.

How are you these days—all of you? We are getting ready to take to the woods ourselves. It happens that just now—for two or three days—Harmony and I are holding the fort here alone. Sue is in Keene Valley with Sally Dunham. Burt is on his vacation. The young girls are away on a visit. Joe, who has just graduated, is in mid-Atlantic en route for Europe on a tour of three months as guest of a classmate of his i.e. the classmate's father pays the bills. So he inherits the Twichell luck.

When our play-time comes we are going into an Adirondack camp—of the log shanty species—forty miles from a rail-road, where the human race will be quite rid of us for two months—with the exception of [a] small group of those we have added to it. I am glad the day is near, for I am tired. I have had to keep a pace of late much too rapid for an old man, and I'm getting "bellust" as Uncle Remus says.[4]

Our dear love to the girls and kind regards to Miss Lyon.

Yours ever aff.

Joe

I have just been writing a note of sympathy (a proper one) to Chauncey Depew—he is an old friend of mine, and I am sorry for him. Think of *me* being sorry for *Chauncey Depew*!!![5]

1. One of Twichell himself, apparently. See Letter 264.
2. Twain's "William Dean Howells," in *Harper's Monthly*, July 1906, 221–24.

3. Mark Twain, "Carl Schurz, Pilot," *Harper's Weekly*, 26 May 1906. Newspaperman and politician, the German-American Schurz was in 1884 a leader of the Independent Republicans, the group Clemens and Twichell joined in opposition to the Hartford Republican establishment. Twain writes of his confidence in Schurz as a "political channel-finder," thus his title.

4. In one of the Uncle Remus stories, "Mr. Rabbit Finds His Match at Last," Joel Chandler Harris writes, "Brer Rabbit, he lit out. . . . Den he had one mo' mile fer ter run, en he feel like he gittin' bellust."

5. It is not clear to what Twichell is referring, but during 1906 Depew was under attack by the muckraking journalist David Graham Phillips.

263. Twain to Twichell

5 August 1906. Dublin, New Hampshire (Transcript by Isabel V. Lyon)

Aug 5, 1906.

Dear Joe:

Certainly archaeology comes to the very front, now! This triumph places it at the head of the sciences. You have heard of it?—how Professor Hübner has established beyond shadow of doubt that the Virgin was 47 years old?[1]

I think it is wonderful, perfectly wonderful. He did not need to also prove that she was black, for all Nazarenes were colored people, & are to this day.

Think of it. *Black & 47*. Do you believe there is any temptation He *could* resist? Do you?

Are you going to preach about it? When?[2]

Yours Ever
Mark

1. Perhaps Emil Hübner, philologist and archaeologist of the University of Berlin, though Hübner had died in 1901.

2. Twain had made a passing reference to a black Moses in *Innocents Abroad* (1869). Here, he ups the ante. In fact, this letter to Twichell was not sent directly to his clergyman friend but instead to H. H. Rogers as an enclosure in a letter of the same date where he writes, "Upon second thought it will be better for this to come from you. In theological matters Twichell attaches much more value to your commendations than he does to mine. Just copy it in your own hand & sign it & send it to him. It will be all right." Rogers's secretary in fact mistakenly sent the letter directly to Twichell. See *Mark Twain's Correspondence with Henry Huttleston Rogers*, 614.

264. Twain to Twichell

14 September 1906. Dublin, New Hampshire

DUBLIN
NEW HAMPSHIRE
Sept. 14/06.

Dear Joe:

It's all right about the Westminster, I am hoping to get converted, & I don't wish to leave any promising bait unswallowed.[1]

I see that you wish me to help you deceive the guide into believing that you enjoy the distinction of being acquainted with me, & so, out of the weakness of inherent good-nature I consent, though I'm damned if I think it is good morals.

When Miss Lyon arrives at 8 p.m. from New York she will hunt up one of my books & I will autograph it & forward it, with pleasure.

I did get the photograph, Joe, & am glad to have it, though in my opinion it slanders you. This is a common fault of photographs.

I leave for Fairhaven in the morning to go down in the yacht, to speak at the Associated Press banquet Wednesday night.[2] This does not mean that I am going to talk myself to death *this* season, like last. I shall keep pretty still next winter.

I shall return here, & Jean & I will remain until toward November, but Clara is already home in New York & will not go back to Norfolk. She found the weather too cold there.

With love to you both
Mark.

1. Twichell may have apologized for sending Twain a religious book or pamphlet. He had apparently also requested that Twain supply an autographed book for a friend.

2. Fairhaven, Massachusetts, Henry Rogers's home. Twain spent a good deal of time there as a guest, indeed as an honorary family member, in these years.

265. Twichell to Twain

14 September 1906. Blue Ridge, New York

Elk Lake. Blue Ridge. N.Y. Sept. 14. 1906

Dear Mark:

In writing to you day before yesterday, I forgot something —

This viz: Shortly before I came away from Hartford I had a call from a gentleman residing in St. Paul Minn.—a leading lawyer of that city—name of White—father of a classmate of Joe's at Yale—whose errand, it transpired, was to invite *you and me* to the Annual Dinner of the Minnesota "Society of Colonial Wars" to be held at St. Paul, any day of October we may choose, expenses of the trip to be paid by said society.[1] We are, of course, desired to contribute eloquence to the occasion. I told him to take the business directly to you. He said he hadn't the courage. He was such a nice man that I couldn't refuse to promise my service as go-between in the case. That promise I am now keeping. Will you go? I guess I will if you will. Anyhow, I would think seriously of it—which I do not feel the need of doing at present, I confess.

But "*Colonial Wars*"! doesn't the subject fire your blood?[2]

At your convenience please tell me what to say to Mr. White. Really, an answer is due him i.e. from me.

Yr aff.

Joe

[On 15 or 16 September 1906, Twain gave instructions to Isabel V. Lyon, writing on Twichell's 14 September letter:]

Miss Lyon, tell him NO—I wouldn't make such a journey to see the Resurrection.

Love to Jean

S L C[3]

1. "A classmate of Joe's": that is, a classmate of Joseph Hooker Twichell.

2. Twichell's deep interest in America's colonial history is evident here. This society was composed of others like him, who, in their case, would see their New England roots as a way of distinguishing themselves from other German or Swedish immigrants. Twain clearly failed to share Joe's enthusiasm.

3. Twain's uses of Lyon as an intermediary probably speaks of a reluctance to bother with correspondence (with any friend) where requests are being made which he had no intention of meeting.

266. Twichell to Twain

26 November 1906. Hartford, Connecticut

Hartford. Nov. 26.

Dear Mark;

I am to be in New York next Monday evening Dec. 3rd to attend a dinner to Mr. Robert Ogden at the Waldorf-Astoria and, if I may, I will lodge at your house. I am sure you love me well enough, if anything is in the way of it to tell me so without discomfort. We are grieved to hear that Jean has had to leave home for her health's sake.[1] May it not be for long.

Affectionately Yours

Joe

PS I also am a man of international reputation. A sermon of mine has been printed *in England*![2]

1. After severe epileptic seizures, Jean had entered a sanitarium in Katonah, New York.

2. The sermon was "A Modern Knight of the Cross," on the English missionary John Coleridge Patteson.

267. Twichell to Twain

24 December 1906. Hartford, Connecticut

Hartford. Dec. 24. 1906

Dear old Mark:

Yes, indeed, I will go to Bermuda with you, and be overjoyed to.[1] Hurra! Hurra!!

Only let me know, as soon as you know, if we are really going, and the date of departure, that I may make necessary arrangements.

Yours aff.

Joe

1. Twain and Twichell would go to Bermuda from 2 to 9 January 1907. Isabel Lyon accompanied them. See Twain's entry for 6 January 1907, *Autobiography of Mark Twain,* 2:359–60.

268. Twichell to Twain

27 December 1906. Hartford, Connecticut

Thursday Evening

Dear Mark;

I didn't doubt there was a letter on the way (it is here) but there was a reason why I wanted to know this afternoon if we were to sail Jan 2. Hence young Harmony's assault on you by telephone.

I shall come down Tuesday so as to be there by mid-afternoon. To think of another lark with you makes me feel like a boy. Everybody here is happy with me in the prospect.

How the nation I came to leave all those things behind that some one of you—on whom my benediction—took the trouble to make a parcel of and mail to me, I can't conjecture. I knew the pyjamas were missing, but I supposed they were out of sight—under the pillow maybe—when I packed my grip. Probably because there seemed to be no room for anything more I judged that everything was in. But Harmony had packed it before, and as you have lately pointed out, there is a difference between a man's packing and a woman's. I distinctly recall that I took pride in the fact that I *didn't* forget my tooth-brush.

But good night. We can talk next week.

Yrs ever aff.

Joe

269. Twichell to Twain

14 January 1907. Hartford, Connecticut

Jan. 14.

Dear Mark:

Sunday is over, and I am free again to let my thoughts return to the happy week long dream out of which I awoke when I opened my study door last Thursday afternoon. A dream, indeed, it was and is. Looking off over the wide expanses of snow in view from my window, I say to myself every hour "Can it be that it is *real*, or is it a *seeming* memory only?" Either way it is delicious and an unalloyed felicity, and you are the good providence behind it—you and Miss Lyon.

Miss Lyon! A daisy—a bouquet of daisies—a bushel of'em, is she!

Setting out for Judy's Wednesday noon, I felt lost without her—alone in the dark, as it were. A month of her care and I shouldn't have dared leave 21 Fifth Ave, till she could go with me and see me safe on board the train for Hartford.

But, dear old Mark, wasn't it a lovely time, all through! I think I enjoyed it more than you did. You were encumbered by your fame. I had the freedom of my obscurity—an advantage that has always been mine when traveling in your company. Moreover it [is] morally salutary. It takes the conceit out me. It is good for a man to be made once in a while to feel that he is nobody. This time I had unusual pleasure in it; it left me to myself to taste the honey of each passing moment undisturbed.

How I do like to be with you, my Boy! What fortune has long been mine in that respect! Yes, truly, I have there been fortunate "to a degree."

But I didn't set out to write you a letter. I simply wanted to thank and bless you for the latest of a series of kindnesses dating in their beginning back to our youth—some of them haloed by sacred associations, all of them enduring treasures of memory.

Ever affectionately Yours

Joe

[Over the page, Twichell adds a note:]

I have a letter from a former college acquaintence begging me to dissuade you from writing against Christian Science.—in the interest of your far future reputation. I will send it to you if you care to see it—which I don't suppose you do.

270. Twain to Twichell

26 January 1907. New York, New York

---

21 Fifth Avenue
Jan. 26/07

Dear Joe:

All the periodicals have refused this poem—ever since election day. Get Charley Clark to put it in the Courant.

With love

Mark.

[Enclosure:]

The Battle of Ivry
Man For His Own Hand.[1]

Being a Campaign Anthem.

Air—Jerusalem the Golden.

Ho, burghers of Dutch Albany,
Ho, buggers of New York,
Ho, sons of bitches from the slums
And painted whores from Cork,*
Ho, gallows-birds from Hell's Delight
And convicts prison-nursed,
O, gather, gather to the polls
And 'lect the bloody Hurst![2]

* A poetically-licensed divergence from fact. They don't come from there.

1. A loose parody of "The Battle of Ivry" by Thomas Babington Macaulay.

2. Twain probably means newspaper baron William Randolph Hearst, who ran unsuccessfully for the governorship of New York in 1906. Hearst had been elected to the House of Representatives as a New York Democrat in 1902 and 1904. The large bankroll that financed his political activity and his very poor attendance record once elected were sources of considerable criticism.

271. Twichell to Twain

1 April 1907. Hartford, Connecticut

Hartford, Monday A.M.

Mark Mavourneen,[1]

A week from next Sunday (Apr. 14) I am ordered on duty—as last year—at a Loyal Legion memorial service in your city. Harmony is also expected. You, of course, are our first choice as host for the two nights and intervening day we shall be there. But we don't insist on you—such being our modesty.

In fact, we give you full leave to consult your convenience in the case. If you can take us in, say so. If, to your sorrow, you cannot, say so.

But, really, I am quite eager to hear all about your latest trip to Bermuda.[2]

With love to the girls and to Miss Lyon,
Yours aff
Joe

1. From the Irish *mo mhuirin* ("my darling"), a term of endearment used in sentimental songs of the era. Twain had also named the dog in his 1903 story, "A Dog's Tale," Aileen Mavourneen from a ballad by Mrs. S. C. Hall.

2. Twain had returned to Bermuda briefly (18–19 March) with Lyon and Paddy Madden, a nineteen-year-old girl he had befriended on the January trip.

272. Twichell to Twain

14 July 1907. Hartford, Connecticut

Hartford. July 14. 1907

Dear old Mark:

You will soon be getting ashore and I want to be on hand to hug you welcome.[1] I should almost think you would rather see an enemy though:—*for a change.* What is there that could give you a new sensation but a *hostile frown*?

I am sure I never wanted to see you so much as now—which is saying a very, very, great deal. You have such a lot of unprecedented things to tell! This is to let you know that I am to be on pulpit duty at Plymouth Church next Sunday (July 21) and that I can pay you a call either Saturday or Monday if you are anywhere accessible.[2] I shall not be surprised however to hear that you are submerged in engagements, and that I'd best wait till another time. Harmony and I, you bet, have had our telescope on you sitting up there on the top of the world these last weeks—as you and I followed the lads going up Mong Blong when we were in Chamouni.[3]

Its queer—but some how your conquering Hero Progress through England has revived our memories of the early days of your and our acquaintance—when we lived in Willard St, and we were all young.—and Harmony used to [feel] sort of sorry for you because you had no home.

Love to the girls and to Miss Lyon.

Yours ever aff.
Joe

1. In the summer of 1907 (18 June to 13 July) Twain was in England, on his final visit there, to collect an honorary degree from Oxford University.

2. Plymouth Church was Henry Ward Beecher's former church in Brooklyn.

3. Twichell spells Mont Blanc this way, no doubt a private play of his (and perhaps Twain's) on the French pronunciation. The telescope story is in chapter 64 of *A Tramp Abroad.* "Chamouni" is an archaic spelling for Chamonix, used by Shelley in his poem "Mont Blanc."

273. Twichell to Twain

6 December 1907. Hartford, Connecticut

Hartford. Dec. 6.

Dear Mark;

I am just setting out with Charley Clark for Buffalo, where we are to be on duty at a Yale Alumni Dinner tomorrow night.

My present intention is to leave Buffalo Sunday evening and to arrive in New York Monday morning—in which case you may look out for a call from me rather early Monday forenoon—say 9 o'clock or so. *But,* if at that hour you are busy with your stenographer you will not let me interrupt you.[1] Who am I that I should deprive the Human Race &c &c? I can put in the little time I stay agreeably with Miss Lyon.

Yrs aff

Joe

1. Twain was dictating his autobiographical reminiscences during this period.

274. Twichell to Twain

11 December 1907. Hartford, Connecticut

Hartford. Dec. 11

Dear Mark,

Congratulate us. By what other peoples wealth has brought us all long, we have certainly been the richest poor folk I ever heard of.

Harmony wants me to tell you that she has just received a letter from a lady—an Englishwoman, Miss Riddell—a nurse—founder of a leper hospital in Japan—friend of Mitsukuri from whom she brought a most hearty introduction to us (she was here six months or so ago) saying that she (Harmony) promised her that if and when she (Miss R) should ask for it, she (Harmony) would give her a note to you;—and will she please do so now.[1] Harmony says that probably she made the promise, but wishes she hadn't. However, she is going to keep it to the extent of sending Miss R. her card with your name and Miss Riddell's on it.

So be on the lookout for her. She is a fine woman though. We liked her ever so much.

Yours aff.

Joe

[Enclosure: A clipping on the bequest by Ellen M. Case of a hundred thousand dollars to individuals and charitable institutions, including ten thousand for Twichell. Her father was Newton M. Case of printing company Case, Lockwood & Brainard—the incontinent parishioner with whom Twichell had traveled to Europe in 1882 (see Letter 77). Newton Case died in 1890. Ellen Case died on 5 December and the clipping is from the Hartford Courant *of 11 December. Twain has written on it (he often made notations on items he received in the mail), "No one could be more gratified than I am for part of that money was mine. Old Case stole it from me." Case had been a director of the American Publishing Company, Twain's Hartford publisher, and Twain considered Case a party in efforts to swindle him out of his royalties (see Letter 279).[2]]*

1. Hannah Riddell founded the Kaishun Hospital in Kumamoto, Japan, and devoted her life to the cause of treating and eradicating leprosy.

2. Twain discusses Case's role in *Autobiography of Mark Twain,* 2:52 and following.

275. Twichell to Twain

16 December 1907. Hartford, Connecticut

[Enclosure: A photograph of the house described, labeled on the back "Robert Louis Stevenson's House / Samoa."]

Hartford Dec. 16

Dear Mark:

Here is a photo of R. L. Stevenson's house at Samoa, given me by the man who took it—Mr Werry, a Canadian, a traveler, at present a tuberculosis patient at Saranac Lake and lodging in the house next to Dave's.[1] As you well knew Stevenson it has seemed to me that the picture will be, not only interesting to you, but better placed in your hands than in mine.[2] I am glad to give it to you.

Yrs aff.

Joe

1. F. W. O. Werry, who had previously worked as Dominion land surveyor in Ottawa, would be resident at Saranac for sixteen years and was a valued member of its community.

2. Twain and Stevenson admired each other's writing. They met in September 1887, when Twain came in by train from Hartford to rendezvous with Stevenson in Greenwich

Village. They evidently spent about five hours in conversation. Stevenson, who suffered from tuberculosis, was on his way to treatment in Saranac Lake. He died in 1894.

276. Twichell to Twain

6 January 1908. Hartford, Connecticut

Hartford. Jan 6. 1908

Dear old Mark:

I have received an invitation to the dinner to be given you by the Lotos Club next Saturday evening.[1] For so great a favor I am duly thankful, but to my sorrow I am forced to decline it. Saturday night would be pretty nearly impossible for me anyway. Yet in ordinary circumstance I might manage to spend the evening in New York and by taking a late train home be on hand for duty Sunday morning. But by long-standing appointment I am preacher at Williams College—of which Harry Hopkins is President—next Sunday. And that puts it quite out of my power to be present at the dinner.

It is heart-breaking to miss so huge a treat, the chance of which may never recur. But I've got to. I shall always count it a big misfortune. But I hope you will have a splendid time among your worshipers. You will, of course. How I *would* have liked to contribute my puff of incense to it! They asked me to *speak*, you know. That was the crowning honor, by George. I am glad to judge that [you] are pretty well, or you wouldn't venture on a night orgy. We are so here, except for a grippe or two.

God bless you, dear old fellow. With love to all the house.

Yours affectionately

Joe

1. Lotos Club dinner in honor of Mark Twain, New York, 11 January 1908.

277. Twain to Twichell

21 February 1908. New York, New York

[One of three similar letters, one addressed to "Dear Joe," the other two addressed "To any friend or acquaintance of mine." *The first letter was reproduced in the sales catalog of American Art Association–Anderson Galleries, 11–12 November 1937, no. 4346, item 88, and reads as follows:]*

By the note of general introduction I desire to recommend to your fullest trust & confidence the bearer Albert Bigelow Paine, my biographer & particular friend, who is seeking information concerning me for use in his book.[1]

1. Twain had met Paine in 1906. He was to be his official biographer and was virtually a member of the household during Twain's final years.

278. Twichell to Twain

15 April 1908. Hartford, Connecticut

Hartford. Apr. 15. 1908

Dear Mark:

You were doubtless grieved to learn—if you did learn—on your arrival home that you had missed the honor and privilege of my "keep" over last Sunday.[1]

But dry your tears. It is wonderful how Providence does favor some people. I am called to New York again:—this time to attend a meeting in Carnegie Hall next Monday evening (Apr. 20) and I will lodge with you then— if you say so.

But there's no *compulsion* about it, you understand.

Yours aff

Joe

1. Twichell had been in New York, taking part in a Military Order of the Loyal Legion service commemorating the end of the Civil War. He was to attend a meeting of the Laymen's Missionary Movement on 20 April. See *Autobiography of Mark Twain,* 3:557–58.

279. Twain to Twichell

17 April 1908. New York, New York

[This letter exists in draft form only, with the following written at its head: "Reverend Twichell is coming down from Hartford, & I will send him a word of welcome right now." The body of the letter then follows.][1]

I am glad, Joe—uncommonly glad—for you will tell me about the "new movement" up your way which your clergy have been importing from Boston.[2] Something of it has reached me, & has filled me to the eyelids with irreverent laughter. You will tell me if my understanding of the New Movement is correct: to wit, that it is just Christian Science, with some of the earmarks painted over & the others removed, after the fashion of the unanointed cattle-thieves of the wild, wild West. My word, how ecclesiastical history do repeat herself! The Jews steal a God & a Creation & a Flood & a Moral Code from Babylon; Egypt steals the like from a forgotten Antiquity; Greece steals the swag from Egypt; Rome steals it from Greece; Christianity comes belated along & steals morals & miracles & one thing & another from Budh & Confucius; Christian Science arrives & steals the Christian outfit & gives it a new name; & now at last comes the Boston puritan—hater of Christian Science—& steals the plunder anew, & re-baptises it, & shouts tearful & grateful glory to God for winking at the mulct & not letting on—according to His shady custom these thirty million years.[3]

Oh yes, I am aware that the Science was emptying New England's churches, & that the wise recognized that something had got to be done or the Church must go out of business & put up its pulpits at auction; I am aware that the peril was forestalled, & *how*; I am aware that Christian Science, disguised & new-named, has arrived in Hartford & is being preached & thankfully welcomed——where? In the most fitting of all places: The Theological Factory, which was largely built out of stolen money. Money stolen from me by that precious Christian, Newton Case, & his pals of the American Publishing Company.[4]

Oh, dear Joe, why doesn't somebody write a tract on "How to Be a Christian & yet keep Your Hands off of Other People's Things."

1. The word "solid" in brackets appears in a square box below this introductory remark. The same word, again in brackets, is written along the left margin on page 1 of the letter. See *Autobiography of Mark Twain*, 3:21–22.

2. The Emmanuel Movement of mental healing, a psychotherapeutic method of healing that was seen as an alternative to Christian Science. The motive force behind the movement was Dr. Elwood Worcester, an Episcopal priest based at the Emmanuel Church in Boston's Back Bay.

3. Twain writes "Budh" here—an abbreviation, one presumes, for "Buddha."

4. See Twichell's letter of 11 December 1907. Twain refers here to the Hartford Theological Seminary, of which Case was a major benefactor. His portrait hangs in the seminary library today.

280. Twichell to Twain

11 May 1908. Hartford, Connecticut

Hartford. May 11.

Dear Mark:

For several years past I have been receiving at intervals from an anonymous source, communications of which you have been the principal theme. They have come from various places, Bristol Conn. Washington D.C. Brooklyn. but all in the same handwriting. We have judged that the writer was a person to some extent insane and have dubbed him accordingly "The Crazy Man." I have not the least idea who he is.[1]

I enclose a copy of his latest effusion, the original going to one of the boys.

I was in New York last week Tuesday to attend a meeting of "The Third Corps Union"—my old Army society, but I hadn't time to call on you—for which I was sorry as I had Joe with me and I would have liked you to see him. Gen. Sickles who, though in a rather feeble condition, sat out the evening with us, inquired for you in a very friendly manner.

We are pretty well here now, Harmony having nearly recovered from the Grippe.

Yours aff.

Joe

[Attached to the letter after the closing signature is a short clipping from the Hartford Courant *of 11 May:]*

WILL GO TO EUROPE.

Rev. J.H. Twichell and Mrs. Twichell to Sail on June 20.

Rev. J.H. Twichell of the Asylum Hill Congregational Church and Mrs. Twichell will sail June 20 on the steamship Mesaba for London, and thence they will proceed to Edinburgh, where Mr. Twichell, in response to an invitation from the International Congregational Council, will preach on Sunday, July 5, in Bristo Place Church. This will be the third annual meeting of the council and its proceedings will be participated in by representative ministers and laymen from various parts of the world. Such oversea appreciation of Mr. Twichell, as a man and a preacher, should be a matter of congratulation, to both himself and his church.

[Under the clipping Twichell has written:]

This is probably due to you[2]

[Enclosure: In Twichell's hand, his transcription of the "Crazy Man's" poem:]

Here lies Mark Twain, skin and bones,
All covered o'er with cobble stones.
To keep the cuss from stinking.
He uttered many a willful lie,
And caused his parents many a sigh,
He smoked in bed, I'm thinking.

Yet he paid dollar, one for one,
As honest as the New York Sun
Or as the N.Y. Clipper—
He does not swear for practice now,
Some of his drink is from the cow,
And some is from the dipper.

1. The correspondent may have been Wallace W. Muzzy, a Bristol, Connecticut, grocer and later employee in a clock works, who sent at least five bizarre letters to Twain during his lifetime. See R. Kent Rasmussen, ed., *Dear Mark Twain: Letters from his Readers* (Berkeley: University of California Press, 2013), 78–81, 95. The surviving letters to Twain date, however, from an earlier period.

2. In his journal, Twichell notes that his parishioners had raised a purse of $1,050 for the trip. This note seems to imply that Twain had helped, too.

281. Twichell to Twain

18 June 1908. Hartford, Connecticut

[Two notes at the top and bottom of a printed wedding invitation:]
[In Twichell's hand:]

June 18

Dear Mark,

Harmony—old lady Harmony, and I sail for England Saturday. Good bye. We have just received a quite long and very nice letter from Jean at Gloucester. Yrs Joe

[Printed:]

Reverend and Mrs. Joseph Hopkins Twichell
Announce the marriage of their daughter
Harmony
to
Mr. Charles Edward Ives
on Tuesday, the ninth of June
nineteen hundred and eight
Hartford, Connecticut[1]

[In Twichell's hand:]
Harmony Jr. is to be domiciled in N.Y. at 70 West 11th St. so that she will be your rather near neighbor

1. Harmony Jr. had married Charles Ives, the composer, a Yale classmate of David Twichell's. Ives was an insurance executive and actuary whose now-iconic music was ignored for many years. Harmony was able to turn her nursing skills to caring for him: the composer was ill for much of his life.

282. Twichell to Twain

13 July 1908. Chester, England

Chester. July 13. 1908

Dear Mark:

While we were in Edinburgh—whence we departed three days syne completely "bellust" with hearing eloquent and able addresses morning, afternoon and evening for nine days hard-running—a certain man—I am obliged to confess that like myself he was a "divine"—did me a great favor entitling him to my fervent gratitude.[1] What it was, I will not stop to tell you now. When, in parting from him I thanked and blessed him for the same and expressed the wish that I might make him some return for it, he answered "Well, there is something I suppose you can do for me that will make us square, and a good deal more. Send me a photograph of Mark Twain with his autograph written under." I really couldn't help promising him that I would do my best endeavor to fulfill his desire. So, Mark, my dear Boy, if you love me, do instruct Miss Lyon to mail me forthwith a photo, duly subscribed, addressed care of Lloyd's Bank, Ltd. 72 Lombard St. London. E.C.

So much do I want it that I am almost of a mind to use in the case the argument of the poor fellow who prayed, "O, Lord, grant me this request, and *I'll never ask you for any thing again, as long as I live.*" I have a sort of special claim on you in the present instance, for I have been suffering for your sake. How that benefactor of mine found out that you and I were pals I don't know. I didn't tell him, or anybody. But the fact is I had not been a day in Edinborough [*sic*] before I began to be spoken to, and spoken of, as "M.T.'s pastor." As such I was introduced when called up to make a table speech. In various ways it was indicated to me that therein was my main—my *only*—significance in the general esteem. I was tempted to wish you had never been born. But I trust my proud and vain spirit was chastened by it. I was the prey of reporters. Happening to say to my host—Sir Alexander Simpson—that I had met "Uncle Remus" whose death had just been announced, I was presently interviewed by a representative of the press about him, with what result the paper I sent you showed.[2] Then a representative of "The London Graphic" asked for, and obtained, an interview on the subject of M.T., the outcome of which I am awaiting with curiosity and some anxiety.[3] He wanted a picture of *me*!! to go with his report. I didn't have one but told him where perhaps one could be procured. I will send you a copy of "The Graphic"—if I dare. We'll see. Harmony and I are enjoying our vacation hugely *now.* i.e. now that my sermon at Edinburgh is off my mind. Harmony thought that I did pretty well *for me.* I was thankful that the minister whose pulpit I occupied did not announce to the congregation that I was "M.T.'s pastor," but allowed me the benefit of my obscurity. We are going up and down here in England for the coming month, taking things easy, doing nothing but what we like. We sail from London by the Atlantic Transport S.S. Minnehaha Aug. 8th. We are on the look-out for Clara, though we are not sure that she is still in the country.[4] We mean to appear to her if she passes our way, or we her's.

Love to you, dear old Fellow. Kind regards to Miss Lyon & Mr Paine.

Yours ever aff.

Joe

I am sad to think that I shall see "Uncle Remus" no more. I liked him well; and he was your very warm admirer.

1. Twichell was attending the International Congregational Council, held in Edinburgh that July. "Syne" is Scottish dialect for "ago." For "bellust," or "tired out," see Letter 262, note 4).

2. Sir Alexander Simpson was professor of midwifery at the University of Edinburgh. "Uncle Remus" was Joel Chandler Harris, who died on 3 July 1908.

3. The interview could not be located.

4. Clara was on a European concert singing tour. She had made her London debut at Queen's Hall in the first week of June (the *New York Times* reported the event on 7 June) and gave another recital at Bechstein Hall on 16 June.

283. Twichell to Twain

13 July 1908. Chester, England

Chester, England

Dear Mark:

In writing to you in some haste this morning, I forgot to tell you that a man—an English "divine" again—in Edinboro' brought me [a] copy of "A Tramp Abroad," and saying that he was informed that I was the "Harris" of that book, asked me to enrich the volume with my distinguished autograph!! Which, of course, I did. He must have got his information from some one of the American contingent of the 400 delegates assembled in the big Council. I have no doubt that they—the Americans—were responsible for my being clothed—as I related—with the glittering distinction of "M.T.'s pastor." But it shows how you stand in both Gt. Britain and the U.S. It shows too what manner of behavior is required of you as a man advertised to the whole world as a *parishioner*—with all the term implies.

A poor-white Virginia woman whose children I baptized during the Civil War, said to the kids after the benediction, speaking with much severity of tone, "You've always got to be mighty good now!!" You are under like compulsion to righteousness; or what becomes of *me*? I have received a note from Mr. J. Y. W. McAlister [*sic*] of London, who says that you are his dear friend, begging me to let him see something of me when I am in town.[1] If I have time I think I will give him a call, anyhow to thank him for his courtesy. I much need a treatise of the Rules of Proper Manners for a Satellite—or is it Sattelite as I wrote it first?[2] Harmony and I can't agree on the point, but I am about sure I am right.

Yrs

Joe

1. Sir John Young Walker MacAlister was a notable librarian, editor of the *Library Journal*, and indeed a good friend of Twain.

2. An initial "Sattelite" is deleted before Twichell's "Satellite."

284. Twichell to Twain

24 August 1908. Hartford, Connecticut

Hartford. Aug. 24.

Dear old Mark:

So here we are again—since last Tuesday. Our homecoming is glad and sad, both—sad because it meets us with the news of the death abroad of our long-time beloved friend Harry Hopkins, President of Williams College, one of the noblest, gentlest most generous spirits life has made us acquainted with. You will remember him, I think. The first paper I took up on my arrival—a copy of Colliers Weekly—told me that Sam Moffett was gone.[1] So you are in sorrow too, and by a bereavement that comes closer to you than ours to us, and is intrinsically more afflictive.

For Harry had done a full day's work, but Sam is "dead ere his prime," cut off in the bloom of his promise.[2] As we speak of him the face and voice of his sweet mother come back to us. We have never forgotten her.[3]

Our vacation has been full of interest and pleasure throughout. I can't stop to tell you about it now, but will say that few things coming into it are so delightfully memorable as two evenings we passed with Mr MacAlister in London, who showed us great favor for your sake. It is scarcely necessary to remark that you were the principal theme of our converse with him—as you were with everybody everywhere who knew that we knew you. By the way, did you send me the autographed picture I begged for? It was to be addressed 72 Lombard St—or was it 52? Any how, whichever it was, I called for it when in London, just before we sailed, and didn't find it.

I trust that this is one of your amiable days; so that if I ask you—as I do—to autograph another, and send it to me here, you will take it patiently. For I want it the worst way.

All are well here but Sally. She is having a distemper of the nerves of some sort.[4]

Love to the girls and to Miss Lyon,
Yours ever aff.
Joe.

1. Henry Hopkins died 18 August 1908. Samuel E. Moffett, Twain's nephew, died of a stroke while swimming in heavy surf at Normandie, New Jersey, on 1 August 1908.
2. The quote is from Milton's "Lycidas."
3. Twain's sister, Pamela Moffett, had died in 1904.
4. This nervous debility was a repeated problem.

285. Twichell to Twain

1 September 1908. Hartford, Connecticut

Hartford. Sept. 1.

Dear Mark:

It is very highly probable that you have received the enclosed. But if you have not it will interest you. However otherwise it will affect you I can't judge. But I confess that it impresses me unpleasantly. It seems to me a melancholy come down for a man of even fair rank in literature—and such I suppose J. H. to be—to renounce the service of the Muses and turn himself into the exploiter of [a] mining scheme.[1] Especially a man of his royal descent. However I do not know his circumstances. He may be poor and have a family that he cannot feed with the earnings of his pen, and have no friends, (like a certain poor minister I am thinking of) to succor his necessities. In that case I trust that his mine may prove a bonanza.

Harmony and I spent the first night after our landing week before last with the newly-wedded Harmony Jr. in New York. She lives at 70 West 11th St. in the near neighborhood of your late residence.[2] Taking an afternoon walk with her, I passed 21 Fifth Ave, and inferred from the look of things that your tenancy there is ended, and was sorry for it fearing that the principal pleasure of my occasional visits to the city was to be lacking henceforth. I rang Gen Sickles' door bell, and to my surprise found him at home. He was glad to see me, but seemed sadly old and feeble.[3]

But why don't I hear from you? Are you mad? I begin to be afraid so.[4] I wish to goodness you would come over and stay two or three days with us. We both want consumedly to see you. We are much at leisure for the present—the parish being mostly out of town—and could give you our whole time sitting out under the trees smoking and talking.

Love to you each and all.

Yours ever aff.

Joe

1. A Mark Twain Papers note identifies this as Julian Hawthorne, author, journalist, and son of Nathaniel Hawthorne, this based on a letter from Julian Hawthorne to Twain of 8 August 1908. Hawthorne had joined an effort to promote what turned out to be a bogus silver mining scheme in Ontario, using his writing and his family name to boost the sale of stock. Hawthorne and his partner in the deal, William Morton, were convicted of mail fraud in 1913 and spent time in jail.

2. Twain had moved to Redding, Connecticut, on 18 June 1908.

3. Twichell's wartime commander was eighty-eight; he would die in 1914 at the age of ninety-four.

4. Twichell indicates here that Twain has been a silent partner in the correspondence for some time.

286. Twichell to Twain

16 December 1908. Hartford, Connecticut

Hartford Dec. 16.

Dear Mark:

Harmony and I were delighted to receive your invitation to pay you a day's visit, and accepted it instantly and unconditionally. We want much to see the house, but more a great deal to see you. We wish we might come right off. We can't, however, till after the holidays. Then, we will name a date and shall hope to hear that it suits your convenience. There are lots of things I am eager to know your views upon—Roosevelt for one—as he is figuring now-a-days, I like him better than ever.[1]

With love to the girls and warm fraternal regards to Miss Lyon.

Yours aff.

Joe

Can we call on Clara when we are in New York? Is she in day times? God grant the word from Jean is favorable.[2]

1. Roosevelt was in the final months of his presidency, having hand-picked William Howard Taft as his successor in the 1908 election. Twichell was proud of his association with Taft in the Yale Corporation, the college's governing body. Roosevelt was to split with Taft and run on his own Bull Moose Party ticket in 1912.

2. Jean Clemens had been in Berlin under the care of a specialist since September, but Twain ordered her home on 17 December after Frederick Peterson, Jean's American doctor, disapproved of the German's methods.

287. Twichell to Twain

5 January 1909. Hartford, Connecticut

Hartford. Jan 5.

Dear Mark:

I am to be on pulpit duty at Yale University next Sunday. As that will take me part way to Redding I plan to proceed thither on Monday—if there is no reason why not with you—arriving, via South Norwalk, at 2.08 P.M. Harmony hopes and expects to come with me, and we both are glad to think of seeing you once more.

If another time will be more convenient for you don't hesitate to say so. All are pretty well here except for a severe domestic jolt occasioned by Louise's engagement to marry a youngster of the name of Hall, from New York—who is a nice enough fellow, but takes us rather unprepared.[1]

Dick Burton gave a lecture here last night—the first of a course of three—on Dickens, which was delightful.[2]

But we will tell you about that, and everything, Monday.

Yours ever aff.

Joe.

1. New York attorney John Raymond Hall.

2. Richard Burton's lecture, delivered in the parish house of Hartford's Church of the Redeemer, was on "Charles Dickens: The Man and His Time."

288. Twain to Twichell

19 April 1909. Redding, Connecticut

[This letter was presumably unsent, as its contents explain. Only two days previously Twain had written Howells with his "splendid scheme" to "write letters to friends & not send them.*" This was a way of writing material for his* Autobiography *unhindered by the presence of a stenographer. One of his aims, accordingly, was "to fire . . . the theologies at Twichell." That this (preparing* Autobiography *material) was exactly what he was doing here is confirmed by his note at the letter's end concerning the last pasted newspaper clipping: "These paragraphs to be in small type, solid." The fact that Twain had Twichell in mind as he wrote this letter and its importance in terms of Twain's late thought and opinions justify its inclusion here. Twain, however, seems not to have continued with this new project, for there are no further letters of this type.]*

Stormfield, Apl. 19/09.

To Rev. Joseph H. Twichell,
of Hartford.

Joe dear, I think I will write you a letter—but you'll never see it. The reason why you have plunged into my mind all of a sudden is, that among some old letters of mine that Clara has been collecting from friends, I find one to you which reads as follows:

[The letter, about two pages, is missing][1]

I had just finished reading that old Adirondack letter & was arranging to write you some malicious things about missionaries—just in a general way, to feed my long-time grudge against that criminal industry—when the morning paper arrived from New York, & these scare-heads caught my eye.

[Twain here pastes in a clipping relating to the March–April Adana massacre in Turkey, in which twenty to thirty thousand Armenian Christians were slaughtered by Muslims against the background of the struggle between secular and Ottoman forces. It reads:]

> Maurer of Hadjin and Daniel Miner Rogers of Tarsus near Adana confirmed the belief that at least fifteen of the American board's missionaries were in Adana when the outburst began last week.
>
> The annual conference of the Central Turkey Mission was to have been held in that city, and the reported murder of Mr. Rogers has lessened the

hopes of the officers of the organization that the outside workers had not reached the city before the outbreak began. It is thought quite probable that missionaries of other denominations were also in Adana. This is indicated from the reported death of Mr. Maurer of Hadjin, who is not under the control of the American board.

Dr. Barton said to-night there were thirty musicians connected with the Central Turkey missions distributed at various stations in that section. He thought that fully half of this number would have been in Adana to attend the conference. It is thought likely that the following were included among the delegates to the convention: Miss Alice C. Brewer of Washington, D.C., a niece of Chief Justice Brewer of the United States Supreme Court; Miss Isabelle M. Blake of Vermont, Cornelia P. Chambers of Philadelphia, Dr. Lucius Ole of Owaso, Mich.; Mrs. Margaret R. Trowbridge of Brooklyn, Miss Ellen M. Blakely of Winchendon, Mass.; Miss Kate E. Ainslee of Ohio, Dr. Thomas D. Christie and wife of Hartford, William N. Chambers of Canada, Fred F. Goodsell and wife and Lulu K. S. Goodsell of San Francisco, Dr. Frederick W. McCullum and Mrs. McCullum of Toronto and Miss Clara L. Peck of Chicago.

Daniel Miner Rogers was about 28 years old and was married. His home was in Connecticut and he began work in the field

[End of clipping.]

When I wrote the above old letter the horrors of the Boxer revolt in China were making Christendom gasp & shudder—a revolt largely—mainly?—caused by the Chinaman's quite justifiable hatred of the foreign missionary; & I had recently been venting my opinions of two of those missionaries (Reed [*sic*] & Ament) in the North American Review. That pair of looters have never yet been whitewashed clean, Joe, & they never will be. Every attempt at it has failed; although the American Board did its best.

Joe, where is the fairness in the missionary's trade? His prey is the children: he cannot convert adults. He beguiles the little children to forsake their parents' religion & break their hearts. Would you be willing to have a Mohammedan missionary do that with your children or grandchildren? Would you be able to keep your temper if your own government *forced* you to let that Mohammedan work his will with those little chaps? You can't answer anything but No to those questions. Very well, it closes your mouth. You haven't a shadow of right to uphold & bid Godspeed to the Christian missionary who intrudes his depraved trade upon foreign peoples who do not want him. "Do unto others, etc.," is a Christian sarcasm, as long as Christian missionaries exist.

Joe, it is a trade that does not pay—according to my ciphering. This morning's news figures out 1,000 murders; The Boxer revolt is charged with 5,000. Six thousand murders due largely to native hatred of foreign missionaries. Six thousand homes made desolate, ten thousand hearts broken, six thousand murderers manufactured, & provoked to do deeds of blood. All inside of ten years. To my mind the Christian missionary is easily the most criminal criminal that exists on the planet, & the lowest down in the scale of malefactors.

Here—read the morning's news, Joe, & repent, reform, & call that dear & sweet daughter of yours home from the Turkish missions; & meantime be thankful that her name is not in the list of the slaughtered:[2]
[A further clipping is pasted in:]

Special Cable Despatches to THE SUN.

CONSTANTINOPLE, April 18.—The American missionaries murdered at Adana were named Maurer and Rogers. The other members of the mission are safe, as is also Mr. Christie, who is at Tarsus.

Telegraphic communication with Adana has been restored, but in consequence of five of the operators being killed there is much delay in the transmission of messages and few details of the trouble there can be obtained.

The American Vice-Consul at Mersina has been trying to reach Adana, but so far has been unable to get transportation.

Mersina itself is now reported to be in desperate straits. It is threatened by a host of Mussulmans [Muslims] from the north. Foreigners and many Christians are taking refuge at the consulates there.

French warships are expected at Mersina but have not yet been sighted. A British warship has been ordered to Alexandretta, where a Mussulman attack is expected.

Many Armenian farms in the neighborhood have been sacked. Kharput is also threatened. The local commanders, it is stated, are doing everything possible to stop the outrages.

The Sheik-ul-Islam has sent a message to the priests at Adana warning them that massacres are contrary to the religious law.

Late to-night it is reported that more than a thousand persons have been massacred at Alexandretta and Tarsus. The burning and killing are still going on.

The mission staff at Adana are practically besieged on the mission premises. They dare not venture out and are suffering from want of food and medicines.

They have appealed to the military commander for protection.

The mission's school at Tarsus, which escaped Saturday, is now threatened. Three thousand persons are homeless at Tarsus.

Despatches from Adana say to-night: More than 1,000 people have been killed and a big portion of the city has been burned during the last three days. Rioting and shooting have been going on all that time.

Several thousand refugees are at the American mission, but only two Americans, Maurer of Hadjin and D. H. Rogers of Tarsus, were killed.

[End of clipping.]

[Twain then writes, "These 4 paragraphs to be in small type, solid." (Twain appears to miscount: there are five paragraphs. He is referring to the text running from "The mission staff at Adana" onwards, which he has pasted on a separate page.) A roughly horizontal line, with a much shorter, not-quite vertical line descending at its left end, is placed below. Sideways, in the left margin, are the words "My comments upon the above were these:"]

1. Probably Letter 185, 28 July 1901, when Twain was in the thick of his squabble with the missionary Ament and his colleagues.

2. Twichell's half-sister Olive was a missionary in Turkey. Presumably, Twain means to refer to her.

289. Twain to Twichell

23 June 1909. Redding, Connecticut

[Twain writes this letter in the period following the huge upset that had occurred in his household: his disillusion and anger with Isabel Lyon. He had come to believe that Lyon had been looking to extend her influence over him, his affairs, and his money, in conspiratorial partnership with her recently married husband and his business advisor, Ralph Ashcroft. In part, she had done this (or so he judged) by deliberately removing Jean from his presence—for Jean had been in and out of various sanatoriums between 1904 and 1909 and Twain had seen little of her during this time. In April 1909, Twain consequently fired Lyon, drove her from the cottage on the Stormfield estate he had deeded to her, and turned her secretarial duties over to Jean.][1]

STORMFIELD
REDDING
CONNECTICUT
June 23/09.

Dear Joe:

I have escaped the interviewer thus far. It has been difficult, still I have escaped.

The public probably think the Ashcroft incident a very trifling matter, & the newspapers doubtless think the same. That is my protection.

Last August, at Sam Moffett's funeral, the heat broke me (with the help of fatigue,) & I was forbidden to stir from Stormfield until frosty weather should come. Two weeks ago I had to go to Baltimore, & this time *cold* & rain & fatigue knocked me out. Dr. Quintard came up today & examined me, & gave very positive orders that I am not to stir from here upon any account before autumn. However, I would not have ventured anyway.

With lots of love to yous

Mark.

[In margins:]

It's fine to have Jean at home again!

Damn that reptile Miss Lyon for keeping her out of her natural home so long.

1. See note 2 in the introduction to part 5 of this book for bibliographical information on this subject.

290. Twain to Twichell

19 and 27 September 1909. Redding, Connecticut

STORMFIELD
REDDING
CONNECTICUT
Sunday, Sept. 19/09.

Dear Joe—

Nine days ago it was all arranged, & the writings drawn & signed, & yesterday the last little details were accomplished which wiped the slate clean of *all* connection with that criminal couple & dismisses them out of our lives. And by George! *yesterday* was an *anniversary*—the date that the two burglars broke into this house![1]

Now consider the unfairness of everything in this life: it was *her* testimony that sent those two hungry & hard-up poor devils to 4 & 9-year terms in prison—*her's*! *They* got not a penny here, whereas she was stealing money from me every day of her life, & had been diligently at it—& liberally—for more than a year. She was stealing money without the excuse of need—& because of my low-quality citizenship she escapes jail; whereas *they* were in dire need, & all they got was jail.[2]

And yet she is awfully punished:

1. She has lost her house & home;
2. She has married *him*! (& he *her*!)

3. She has to live in Brooklyn;

4. She adores Society—& is out of it for good;

5. And he? He's a stevedore, now. Much too respectable a calling for that sandhog.[3]

[New page:]

Sept. 27. Yesterday the lawyers settled *every*thing that was in dispute

[No signature.]

[On 17 October 1909, Jean Clemens would write to Twichell from Stormfield, on her father's behalf, "As Father didn't sleep well last night and is very tired, I stopped his writing to you tonight, saying I could convey the message for him." Part of her letter runs:]

> Since Father gave you a copy of his letter to Mr. Ochs, he has been troubled for fear it might possibly be quoted by some unthinking person, which quotation, reaching the ears of certain charming friends of his, might give them an excuse for starting an action.[4] Because of this feeling, Father begs you to return the copy you now have to him. He was very much relieved to judge by your letter of the 12th that you didn't leave the letter with Mr. Clarke, but merely read him the contents of it. I am sure you won't feel hurt at this request of Father's. It isn't that he is afraid of your allowing it to fall into undesirable hands, merely that if it should be quoted largely, it might make trouble.

1. Stormfield had been burgled just after midnight on 18 September 1908 by thieves Charles Hoffman and Henry Williams, who entered via an unfastened kitchen window. The two men stole furniture (an English serving table) and silverware. They were disturbed by Isabel Lyon (who had woken), Twain's butler, and a houseguest, and were apprehended at a local railway station.

2. Perhaps Twain is saying that he is not a good enough citizen to pursue the case?

3. In fact, Ashcroft pursued a career in advertising after the rupture with Twain. He divorced Lyon in 1926.

4. The *New York Times* had published a story saying that Twain had settled his differences with Ashcroft and Lyon in the litigation he had instigated against them. Twain had consequently written a long letter to Adolph S. Ochs, publisher of the *Times*, challenging the report and accusing the paper of publishing untruths. The "them" here refers to the Ashcrofts.

291. Twichell to Twain

25 December 1909. Hartford, Connecticut

Dec. 25

Dear Mark, dear old friend;

We do not know what to say.[1] What *is* there to say? We do not know what to think, nor yet, in our bewilderment, what to do. Our impulse is to go to you—for nothing but to be with you—in silence—And we should set out at once—or Harmony would—if we were sure that you would not rather be alone.

We know perfectly that it is quite beyond our power to imagine your desolation. It breaks our hearts to imagine you wandering through your empty house.

We never knew till now how we love you—or how we loved Jean. But we did know that the child had grown very, very dear to us. We are thankful that we have told her so.

What are you going to do? Had you not best come out and stay awhile with us? We wish you would. You can have a room to yourself and a fire. You will need to see no one but ourselves. No one else shall know that you are here, if you desire it to be so. We feel that you are [the] lonesomest man in the world. Can't we somehow help you a little, poor fellow?

We cannot bear to think of you sitting there solitary amid your ruins. [Harmony, at this moment, has brought in crying the photograph of Jean, just received, addressed by her own dear hand, sent us for a Christmas gift. How beautiful it is: how lovely:! [*sic*] Is it possible that we shall never see that sweet face, or hear that sweet voice again in this world?] God pity us all.

Yours with unutterable affection
Joe and Harmony

1. Jean had died the day before, on Christmas Eve, at just twenty-nine years old (see the introduction to this section). Twichell would write in his journal of his own family's response: "we were all oppressed in spirit by the thought of desolate M.T. in his lonely house." Twain would write "The Death of Jean," his last substantial prose piece, immediately following the event.

292. Twain to the Twichells

27 December 1909. Redding, Connecticut

REDDING
CONNECTICUT
Dec. 27/09.

Dear, dear Joe & Harmony:

Do not come—until by & bye. I am not suffering. My darling Jean is set free! That is the blessed music that rings in my heart all the time. For sixteen years she suffered—exile, pain, humiliation, despair—& now that dear sweet spirit is at rest. Jean was so fine, so admirable, so noble,—just her incomparable mother over again! Think what I have lost in her. But think what *she* has gained.

We had two splendid days together—Wednesday & Thursday. Then at 7.30 the next morning Katy appeared at my bedside & said—without preliminary—

"Miss Jean is dead!"

When Clara got married & would have to go to Europe, my thought was, "My God, what is to become of Jean if I die!"

That terror cost me much sleep since.

Joe, Jean had a fine mind, a most competent brain. That shit said she was insane![1] She & her confederate told that to everybody around here. Jean's last act, Thursday night, was to defend her when I burst out upon her! It makes me proud to remember that. . . O blessed Jean, and precious!

I saw Livy buried. I will never consent to see another dear friend put under the ground.

How sweet, & peaceful, & beautiful Jean was, in her coffin, with that classic face!

With lots & lots of love—
Mark.

1. Isabel Lyon.

A Brief Afterword

Twain, true to his word, did not attend Jean's funeral. It is not known what contact or correspondence the two men had thereafter but Twain's health was fading fast. He went to Bermuda again in January to return to New York on 14 April. He died a week later, on 21 April 1910, of heart failure at his Redding home. Clara and Ossip returned to Redding in that same month, four days before Twain's death.

For Twichell, his close friend's death was something of a knockout blow. This was doubled and redoubled when, three days later, his wife Harmony suddenly died. Harmony fell ill after Twichell had left Hartford for Twain's funeral at Brick Presbyterian Church on New York's Fifth Avenue, and her death followed swiftly, following an operation for ulceration of the bowels. Twichell's journal entry explains what happened:

> After the funeral service . . . I was to have accompanied the family to Elmira where at a furthur [*sic*] service I had been asked to make an address. But I had to change my plan. The summons home—it was by *telephone* from Joe [Twichell's son] to the Schoonmakers—reached me immediately *before* the service—which was at three oclock [*sic*].[1] I took the 4 o'clock train for Hartford. She died that night—soon after midnight at the Hartford Hospital. I had gone to New York with not the least apprehension of her peril.

The newspaper report about the New York service, pasted at this point into Twichell's journal, takes on added resonance with this knowledge:

> [I]t was no wonder that when [Twichell] came to deliver a prayer at the death of his friend his voice should fail him. Throughout the short service he had sat with bowed head to conceal the fact that tears had found their way to the surface. Now he made a determined effort to control himself, and finally was able to say what he had to say.

Twichell's grief was clearly intense. His journal entry of the time reads, "Apr 21. Our beloved friend Mark Twain dies at Redding. The sorrow caused was soon to be followed by one nearer still. Little can be said of either in this diary."[2] The blow, indeed, was such that even Joe's confidence in his religion seems to have briefly wavered. The note in his son David's memoranda about the time following the death is suggestive here: "In bed with Dad,—He said that once Uncle Mark said to him, 'Now, Joe, if it had been left to you and seriously, would you have started the human race.'" Twichell also took to reading over and over the 18 June 1904 letter Twain had sent him when Olivia died.[3] But even in this desolation he was finally able to keep faith. David again reported on "Dad getting out of bed Wednesday morning,—'I may as well get up, Dave, and face life, with God's help. We have many, many blessings to be thankful for.'"[4]

These letters, when taken as a whole, show the huge importance of the friendship in the lives of the two men. On Twain's side, Joe's easygoing companionship and generally undemanding nature buoyed him, while his reliability and affirmative spirit helped to sustain him in some of his darkest hours. Twichell, meanwhile, delighted in his friend's celebrity and the minor fame it helped bring his way. More than this, though, he delighted in the warm companionship and good talk they shared, and the Hartford family lives that came to bind both men so intimately together. When Twichell died in 1918, Howells would comment on the depth of Twain's affection for his clergyman friend: "[W]hen [Twain] spoke of 'Joe' Twichell, the famous author's face assumed a wonderfully affectionate aspect, and he showed in every word that he loved the simple, manly, unassuming clergyman who had been his friend for so many years."[5] This love was undoubtedly a two-way street.

1. The Schoonmakers were David Twichell's in-laws.

2. Twichell Journal, Beinecke.

3. David C. Twichell, "Memoranda on His Mother's Death," 1910 (Mark Twain Papers). Twichell's response here may be seen as unusual. It perhaps suggests a telling additional dimension to the two men's relationship—that Twichell appreciated (but knew he could not match) Twain's considerable verbal skills and ability to articulate emotion in a moving and heartfelt way.

4. David C. Twichell, "Memoranda on His Mother's Death."

5. In Twichell Family Scrapbooks, Beinecke.

Appendix 1

Undated or Fragmentary Correspondence

[Some undated letters and letters which cannot be accurately dated complete the available set. Twain's are given first.]

293. Twain to Twichell

Unknown date. Unknown place (fragment)

In a Gentleman's Magazine of something over a century ago I lately came across a pathetic account of the funeral of a venerated scholar & devotee of Homer—out back in England, in a country town. It told how he had himself left directions for this funeral; & how, in accordance with them, the Greek scholars came from London, Oxford, &c., & dressed themselves in Greek costumes & buried him with Greek hymns & speeches. The account finished thus: "His Sister sat weeping by his Coffin above four & twenty Hours, it being open & green-painted, she taking no Nourishment in the meantime; He lying within, at peace: in his right Hand a small Homer, in his Left a small Homer, & another one under his Arse."

I read it four times, Joe, & yet not in any case without emotion.

I shall now try to smuggle this into the mail when Livy is not watching. Good-bye, with love to you all.

Mark.

294. Twain to Twichell

Unknown date. Unknown place

[Text embedded in Twichell's address at the Carnegie Hall, New York, memorial for Twain held on 30 November 1910.]

. . . He once broke out in a letter I had from him: "Oh, this infernal Human Race! I wish I had it in the Ark again—with an auger!"

295. Twichell to Twain

Undated. Hartford, Connecticut

Friday Morning[1]

Dear old Fellow:

Welcome Home!! I am in my feelings, on this glad occasion of your return to us a triumphal arch and a brass band and a shouting populace; *but* I have a scarlet fever funeral to attend this afternoon; and so I must not come over to see you tonight as I had intended, nor yet tomorrow night, I suppose. And when I do come I will not have on a single garment that I wear today—be sure of that, and tell Livy so.

It is a great privation to be a leper at this precise moment, when I am so immensely hungry for a sight of you. I shall have to stand it though.

But Welcome Home: and may it be long before you leave us again.

Yours affectionately,

Joe.

1. The greeting and somewhat stilted phrasing of this letter suggests the very early Hartford years—perhaps the early 1870s after a Twain return from Elmira (Livy seems to be part of the reunion). The *Courant* shows that scarlet fever was certainly prevalent in that period. But Twichell himself refers to scarlet fever in his letters to Twain of 1881.

296. Twichell to Twain

Unknown date. Hartford, Connecticut[1]

6 ½ oclock [*sic*]

Dear Mark

You will have to go without me.

I am asked by a family in great trouble to do them the service of going down to the 7.40 train to meet a young fellow called home from a business trip west by a telegram announcing his wifes sudden illness and tell him that she's dead—which is quite another affair than the Yale Glee Club Concert. How long I shall be detained I do not know. But I hope to join you by half past eight oclock. I may, however, be kept from coming at all.

Joe

1. According to the *Hartford Courant*, the Yale Glee Club performed in Hartford (if we can assume this to be the concert venue) three times during the 1870s (which the orthography of this letter seems to indicate is the decade involved): 3 April 1873, 15 Dec 1874,

and 9 May 1877. Twain and Twichell attended the 1874 concert, so it could have been this (if Twichell made it back in time) or—more likely perhaps—either of the others. There is no other evidence available for the dating of the letter.

297. Twichell to Twain

Undated. Hartford, Connecticut[1]

Friday Morning

Dear Mark

I speak on a hint I received yesterday from a respectable source, to the effect that since you are going to ask a few folks in to hear the music this evening, Burton's choir would much enjoy seeing him among them. For aught I know you have invited him, or may be you don't choose to. I only report the suggestion made to me, and that because the pleasure of the Choir was the reason of its being made.

Yrs aff

Joe

1. Possibly October or November 1877. On 9 November 1877, in a letter to E. S. Sykes, Twain mentions his involvement with the Rev. Nathaniel Burton's choir in an event to raise money for the poor of Hartford and complains eloquently, and at length, about Burton's blaming him for the failure of the event. That fits with Twichell's implication that all was not well between the two men. Sykes was a prominent member of Park Congregational Church, at one point its Sunday school superintendent.

298. Twichell to Twain

Undated. Hartford, Connecticut

Wednesday A.M.[1]

Dear Mark,

What will the *subject* be Monday night?

I intend to go down to Charley Howard's observatory and look at the stars tonight, if it is clear.[2] Shall I call for you? There are certain planets to be seen at specially good advantage just now.

Yrs aff

Joe

1. Quite probably between 1883 and 1887. Twichell's question likely refers to a meeting of the Monday Evening Club (Twain read a total of thirteen papers at club meetings between 1873 and 1887).

2. Manufacturer and amateur astronomer Charles P. Howard, of 116 Farmington Avenue, had acquired a 9.4-inch telescope built by a well-known maker, Alvan Clark, in 1880, and set it up in his home. Howard also built his own telescopes.

299. Twichell to Twain

Undated. Hartford, Connecticut

Tuesday a.m.[1]

Dear Mark,

Stevens *was* an ass, and no mistake—for calling your attention to that confounded thing, which otherwise you wouldn't have known anything about. I never should have told you, you'd better believe.

As for Stevens' not thinking to resort to you by telephone, I acquit him there. *That* don't make an ass of him—at least in my sight.

But the Post's notice was not very bad. It gave your performance just a pleasant word or two, after speaking of the gatherings of the season on like occasions and naming the whole list of those who had contributed entertainments before you. It was as inoffensive as possible; still I was mad that there was anything of the sort, after what had been done to prevent it.

But to think that Stevens should give us away so stupidly by thrusting his inopportune information upon you—that's what gravels me.

Yrs. Aff

J.H.T.

[On facing blank page:]

The Club, last night, was altogether delightful. I felt like staying till day break.

But the *next* one—Why, Oh! why, should I have been so inconveniently enlightened!

1. The letter seems to express displeasure over a Twain charitable performance that was not supposed to be publicized. Details of Mr. Stevens's infraction are not explained, and neither are the comments on the previous night's Monday Evening Club talk, though the admiring tone implies it may have been one at which Twain himself read a "paper." If so, this (again) would be in the 1873–87 period. The *Hartford Evening Post* ceased publication in 1890.

300. Twichell to Twain

Undated (postmark: October). Hartford, Connecticut

[A clipping, attached to letter paper, headed "How Bicycling Makes Health and Muscle—A Novel Prescription," describes the medical benefits of bicycling. It is followed by Twichell's words:]
Tomorrow (Tuesday) at about 2 ½ p.m.?[1]

1. Twain's attempts to learn to ride a bicycle, coached by Twichell, took place in May 1884.

301. Twichell to Twain

Undated. Hartford, Connecticut

Tuesday Eve.[1]

Dear Mark, They are to have some "doings" in their particular line, at the deaf and dumb Asylum *Friday* evening.

Principal Williams has desired me to ask you, in his name, to come and see the same.[2] He offers, as a bribe, the spectacle of one of your stories told in signs by one of the young women pupils. If you are disposed to comply with Mr. Williams' wish, and can manage the billiard difficulty; say the word and I'll come round and go with you.

Yrs aff
Joe

1. The letter's postmark is June 13, 11:30 a.m. (Hartford). The "Tuesday eve" heading may be assumed to be on 12 June. This is possibly written in 1888. Job Williams took the role of principal in 1879 (see next note), which would place the letter (given the day and date) in either 1883 or 1888. There is no mention of this Asylum event in the *Courant* or in Twichell's journal or Twain's letters. In 1883 Twain left for Elmira on 14 June (the day before this Friday, 15 June event), but Twichell may not have known about this. He seems, though, to know of a Friday billiard gathering as a possible conflict. This nudges the date toward 1888.

2. Job Williams was principal of the Asylum for the Deaf and Dumb, a pioneer institution in deaf education dating from 1817. It has survived as the American School for the Deaf and is in West Hartford, Connecticut.

302. Twichell to Twain

Summer 1888 or 1889?[1] *Hartford, Connecticut*

Saturday

Dear Mark

The check for Judy came all right—with modest mien and step like all its predecessors. There's no bounty crossing our threshold that makes so little fuss as this does. It drops its shy courtesy, gives us a smile, and skips off to Northampton leaving us with the consciousness of a warm spot under our own jacket—that stays warm too. In fact it is like Livy.

Yrs ever

Joe.

1. Probably summer 1888 or 1889. There is a clear reference to Twain and Livy paying for Julia Twichell to attend Smith College in Northampton, Massachusetts. Twichell's journal for 25 May 1887 speaks of going to Northampton with Julie and Susie to visit Smith College: "Our dear friends M.T. and wife have generously offered to bear the expense of Julie's going there to complete her education. . . . How kindly does Providence care for us!" Julie started college in the autumn of 1888. The Smith College alumnae directory (1906) has her attending "88–90."

303. Twichell to Twain

Undated. Hartford, Connecticut

Friday Morning.[1]

Dear Mark,

Here is our fine young Tramp, whose name, as you are already informed, is Joseph May. He tells me that his father, *James May*, was a Mississippi steamboat Captain. Upon my saying to him as he knocked off work last night that a friend of mine had promised to find him something to do for a day or two, he remarked that he wished he knew if Mark Twain didn't want somebody to work for him, "for if he did," he added "I think I'd stand a chance, for he is a steamboat man himself."

"He is the very man I am going to send you to," I answered.

Really, Mark, this is quite touching, isn't it? May be it's a deep and cunning device, but I don't believe he has heard you spoken of on these premises. The fellow has worked like a beaver for us three days, for which I have paid him $1.50 per diem and his keep (except lodging) and he has fully earned his wages.

He is a sailor, sure, for Harmony sent him up a tree after some red leaves, and he climbed it with surprising agility.

I commend him to your good graces. How is your cold? Are you going to the Tower Saturday?

Yours

Joe

1. At an indefinite point during Twain's Hartford residency. Probably autumn ("red leaves").

304. Twichell to Twain

16 January. Hartford, Connecticut[1]

Jan. 16

Dear Mark:

I am mailing you a couple of pamphlets which will show you the kind—or *one* kind—of work Dave is doing.

The subjects are occult and the language is obscure. But may be, as in the case of the Higher Astronomy, you spoke of, that will not render them *meaningless* to you.

Yrs. Aff.

Joe

1. After graduating from Columbia's College of Physicians and Surgeons in 1903, David Twichell worked with Dr. Edward Livingston Trudeau at his laboratory at Saranac Lake, New York, spending two years there, then practicing in the same town for ten years. If Twichell is writing of the Trudeau period, as seems a real possibility, the dating could be 1904—by January 1905 this would seem to be old news—but the information given is too indefinite to allow a firm dating.

305. Twichell to Twain

March 28. Hartford, Connecticut[1]

March 28.

Dear Mark:

The reason why I didn't write is that I have the grippe, and am too weak to "haul a shad off a gridiron"[2]

Yrs aff

Joe

1. Possibly 1905 on the basis of orthography (post-1890), plus Twichell's report of a bad case of the grippe preceding his journal entry for 1–11 April 1905. But this is conjecture.
2. The phrase is from chapter 31 of Richard Henry Dana's *Two Years before the Mast.*

306. Twichell to Twain

21 November. Hartford, Connecticut[1]

Hartford. Nov. 21

Dear Mark;

In view of Clara's approaching visit to our town, we write to say that while we suppose there's no use in it, still we cannot deny ourselves the pleasure of sending her word that the best room in our house—and I might add, in our hearts—will be open to her the 29th inst, and before and after, and always henceforth to the crack of doom.

And if her Dad will come with her, he can have the next choice of quarters.

Yours aff.

Joe

1. Most probably 1907, as Clara gave a recital at Unity Hall, Hartford, on 29 November of that year.

Appendix 2

Four Further Letters

[In the course of publication, the editors learned of four more very short letters written between the two men. They are as follows:]

307. Twichell to Twain

Per *Telegraph Operator 28–31 January 1870. Hartford, Conn.*

You haven't invited the Blisses.[1]

1. To Twain and Livy's wedding.

308. Twain to Twichell

Per *Telegraph Operator 28–31 January 1870. Elmira, N.Y.*

I *have* invited the Blisses.[1]

1. The details of this exchange, dated according to the Mark Twain Papers, are taken from Samuel C. Webster, Mark Twain's business manager and nephew, recalling a reminiscence by his mother, Annie Moffett (daughter of Twain's sister, Pamela). See Samuel C. Webster, ed., *Mark Twain, Business Man* (Boston: Little, Brown, 1946), 108. The Blisses did not attend the wedding. The two exchanges above follow Letter 8 in the main body of the text.

309. Twain to Twichell

29 January 1876. Hartford, Conn.

[Written on the envelope of a letter from W. D. Howells. In this letter, of the same date, Howells reports on the "immense success" of Twain's "A Literary Nightmare" (also published as "Punch, Brothers, Punch!").[1] *"In my own family," Howells writes, "it is simply a nuisance. [Son] John clacks it off at mealtimes till boxed*

into silence, and then [daughter] Pilla starts up with, 'Punch, brullers, punch with care!'[2] *I heard of its raging similarly in families all along this street, and of course Harvard is full of it." Howells also says: "I shall not be able to come down to Hartford this Saturday, but . . . you may depend upon seeing me very soon."]*
You may return this, Joe.[3]

1. Twichell, along with his walks with Twain to Talcott Mountain Tower, is referenced in this sketch.

2. Pilla was Mildred Howells's nickname.

3. This letter follows Letter 30 in the main text. Twichell refers to the Howells visit in Letter 31.

310. Twain to Twichell and George P. Bissell and Co.

23 May 1878. Heidelberg, Germany

Schloss-Hotel,
Heidelberg, May 23/78

[Enclosure: a bank order for $300 dated 23 May, Heidelberg]
Messrs. Geo P Bissell & Co
Hartford.

Gentlemen:

Please pay to the order of Rev. Joseph H. Twichell Three Hundred Dollars, & charge to ac/ of

Ys Truly
Saml. Clemens[1]

1. This follows the present Letter 40. The Twichell Journal entry quoted in note 1 of that letter shows that the money took some two weeks to arrive.

Index